Practice-Based Standards for the Preparation of Special Educators

Complete Update to the Earlier "Red Book,"
*What Every Special Educator Must Know:
Professional Ethics & Standards, 7th Edition*

Council for
Exceptional
Children

EDITORS:
Dee Berlinghoff
Virginia L. McLaughlin

© 2022 by Council for Exceptional Children

Council for Exceptional Children
3100 Clarendon Blvd., Suite 600
Arlington, VA 22201
www.exceptionalchildren.org

Library of Congress Cataloging-in-Publication data

Council for Exceptional Children

Practice-Based Standards for the Preparation of Special Educators
    Editors: Dee Berlinghoff and Virginia L. McLaughlin

p. cm.
Includes biographical references.

ISBN 978-0-86586-553-2 (soft cover)
ISBN 978-0-86586-552-5 (eBook)

CEC Product No. P6352

Last published in the United States of America by the Council for Exceptional Children, 2015, as the
7th Edition of the book, *What Every Special Educator Must Know: Professional Ethics & Standards*.

Permission is granted to reproduce and adapt any portion of this publication with acknowledgment.
Reference:
    Berlinghoff, D. & McLaughlin, V.L. (Eds.) (2022). *Practice-Based Standards for the Preparation of Special Educators*.
    Council for Exceptional Children.

Cover and layout by Tom Karabatakis, Tompromo Marketing

Printed in the United States of America

First edition

10 9 8 7 6 5 4 3 2 1

Table of Contents

About the Editors

Dee Berlinghoff, Ph.D., is Professor Emerita in the Division of Education at Mount Saint Mary College in Newburgh, NY, where she taught for 17 years. She has been working in public education and higher education for over 30 years, serving as a classroom teacher, professor, and embedded coach for teachers. She spent the 2014-2015 school year on sabbatical working in a high-needs school identified by the New York State Education Department as "in need of improvement." Her responsibilities included modeling effective instructional strategies in classrooms, providing professional development, and embedded coaching. Dr. Berlinghoff has served as President of the New York State Council for Exceptional Children, New York State Division for Learning Disabilities, and the Small Special Education Programs Caucus of the Teacher Education Division of CEC. She served on the presidential line of the Teacher Education Division of CEC and co-chaired the CEC Standards Development Workgroup. Dr. Berlinghoff has presented at local, state, and national conferences and conducts professional development workshops for teachers. She is editor of the Evidence-Based Instruction in Special Education series, published by Slack, Inc.

Dr. Berlinghoff holds a baccalaureate degree in Elementary & Kindergarten Education, with a minor in Early Childhood Education, from Penn State. She earned a master's in special education from Lehigh University, and a doctorate in special education from Penn State. Prior to her work at Mount Saint Mary College, Dr. Berlinghoff was a special educator in the Winooski and Essex Town School Districts in Vermont. She was an Assistant Professor at Belmont Abbey College in Belmont, NC and director of the program for students with learning disabilities at Limestone College in Gaffney, SC. In recognition of her leadership and service contributions, Dr. Berlinghoff has received several awards, including the Mid-Hudson School Study Council Leadership Award (2012), Small Special Education Programs Caucus Nasim Dil Service Award (2016), and Teacher Education Division Distinguished Service Award (2021).

Virginia (Ginnie) McLaughlin, Ed.D., is Chancellor Professor Emerita of the School of Education at William & Mary (W&M). From 1995-2013, she served as Dean of the School of Education. Dr. McLaughlin was a gubernatorially appointed member of the Virginia Board of Education from 2009-2013. She served on numerous boards for professional organizations including AACTE and NCATE, and she was President of the Council of Academic Deans from Research Education Institutions (CADREI). Dr. McLaughlin co-chaired the CEC Standards Framing Paper Workgroup and Standards Development Workgroup.

Dr. McLaughlin has taught courses in special education, inclusive practices, and collaborative partnerships at baccalaureate through doctoral levels.. Her scholarship focuses on educational policy and teacher preparation issues. She has co-authored and served as co-principal investigator on more than $10 million of externally funded projects.

Dr. McLaughlin holds a baccalaureate degree in psychology from W&M, a master's in special education from Peabody College at Vanderbilt, and a doctorate in special education from University of Memphis. Prior to her appointment as Dean, Dr. McLaughlin was Chief of Staff for W&M President Tim Sullivan, Associate Dean for Academic Programs in the School of Education, and a faculty member at W&M, Old Dominion, and Clemson Universities. In recognition of her leadership and service contributions, Dr. McLaughlin has received many awards, including W&M's Alumni Medallion (2015) and the Jefferson Award (2021).

Introduction

In 1995, The Council for Exceptional Children (CEC) adopted Knowledge and Skills Standards for initial areas of specialization and published the first edition of *What Every Special Educator Must Know: International Standards for Preparation and Certification of Special Education Teachers*. As standards were updated regularly over the years, CEC published subsequent editions, the most recent being the seventh edition released in 2015.

The present publication represents more than a straightforward update of the last edition. The majority of the publication is devoted to comprehensive introduction of the first two sets of CEC standards developed to meet requirements of the Council for Accreditation of Educator Preparation (CAEP), the new accrediting body fully implemented in 2016 with the merger of the National Council for Accreditation of Teacher Education (NCATE) and the Teacher Education Accreditation Council (TEAC).

Additionally, the two sets of CEC 2020 Standards emphasize *practice-based preparation* of both K-12 special educators and early interventionist/early childhood special educators (EI/ECSE). The standards do not prescribe program models or curriculum; those decisions are left up to the educator preparation providers (EPPs). Practice-based standards take the emphasis off program inputs, processes, and products to focus instead on documented proficiencies that candidates demonstrate through program completion. This publication also includes expanded resources to guide the design, assessment, and review of preparation programs.

In light of the substantial changes from previous editions, this new publication has a different title, *Practice-Based Standards for the Preparation of Special Educators*, as well as a new cover design to distinguish it from the "Red Book," the nickname given to prior editions of *What Every Special Educator Must Know* by many users in the field. The current publication does build upon content included in the previous publications and incorporates existing CEC preparation standards still in effect:

both the Initial and Advanced Gifted Education Professional Preparation Standards and the Standards for the Preparation of Advanced Special Education Professionals. Future editions of *Practice-Based Standards for the Preparation of Special Educators* will introduce new standards as they are developed or revised.

CEC's Commitment to Educator Quality

From its earliest days, CEC recognized the crucial role of standards in defining special education as a profession. At its inaugural meeting in 1922, the founders of CEC specified the establishment of professional standards as one of the primary aims of the organization. In 1965, CEC held a conference to highlight professional standards, and in 1981, the CEC Delegate Assembly charged CEC to develop, promote and implement preparation and credentialing standards along with a professional code of ethics for special educators.

CEC has embraced this responsibility and has been a leader among educational associations in the development of preparation standards for special educators at all levels. CEC professional preparation standards are built on the premise that well-prepared special educators are the cornerstone of delivery of quality, evidence-based services to individuals with exceptionalities. CEC standards define the specialized expertise special educators must master for safe and effective practice of special education at initial and advanced levels.

To promote the application of high quality standards for special educators, CEC staff and members have worked at local, state, and national levels to ensure that CEC standards are embedded in state licensure and program approval frameworks and used in national accreditation processes. CEC has played important roles in the development of other national standards such as the Interstate Teacher Assessment and Support Consortium (InTASC) standards and the National Board for Professional

Teaching Standards (NBPTS) that affect special educators. CEC has also contributed to national and state assessment initiatives, such as PRAXIS II and edTPA, to make sure that these align to the extent possible with CEC preparation standards.

The CEC preparation standards have been revised several times. Originally the standards were entitled "Knowledge and Skill Specialty Sets" and were used for design and evaluation of preparation program curriculum. In 2001, CEC used the specialty sets as the foundations for developing a single set of initial and of advanced preparation standards. For each level, CEC's 10 standards explicitly aligned with the InTASC standards. (Council of Chief State School Officers, 1992). In 2012, CEC again revised its standards, organizing them around NCATE requirements for Specialized Professional Association (SPA) standards.

As explained above, the 2020 Initial Practice-Based Professional Preparation Standards for K-12 and EI/ECSE introduced in this publication were developed to meet CAEP guidelines. Additionally, the 2020 standards were designed to comply with recommendations of the CEC Standards Framing Paper Workgroup (Blanton et al, 2017), approved by the CEC Board of Directors, that emphasized a shift to practice-based standards for professional preparation.

Stakeholder Audiences

The CEC standards included in this publication were designed to represent the best thinking of the profession regarding performance expectations of candidates for initial or advanced roles as special educators. As such, the standards are intended for use by multiple audiences, and they are particularly relevant to the work of the following groups: (a) policymakers and agencies that accredit, approve, or recognize special educator preparation programs; (b) faculty and administrators who design, deliver, and evaluate educator preparation programs (EPPs); (c) agencies and organizations that promulgate and implement regulations governing licensing/credentialing of special educators; (d) EPP applicants and students who are reviewing program and candidate requirements; and (e) school administrators who hire and support special educators.

As noted above, CEC has developed its standards to meet requirements of national accrediting agencies for SPA review and recognition of special educator preparation programs. States have the responsibility for review and approval of teacher education programs, typically accomplished through a professional standards board, department of education, or board of regents. A number of states require their EPPs to be nationally accredited through individual partnership agreements with CAEP. In some states, CEC SPA program review is mandated; in other states, it is optional for preparation programs.

The faculty of special educator preparation programs are key stakeholders. Although the CEC standards are directly embedded in processes for SPA Program Review with National Recognition, they also should be used more broadly by EPPs to guide program development and assessment. When designing new programs or revising existing ones, faculty work to align curriculum with the most current and relevant professional standards and research. They collaborate with one another and their administrative support teams to create assessment systems that provide useful information for internal and external program reviews and for ongoing program improvement standards.

While some states and higher education institutions require special education preparation programs to complete the CEC SPA review process, other programs voluntarily seek this national recognition. The standards, resources, and tools provided in this publication should prove useful to faculty and administrators whether or not they pursue CAEP Accreditation and CEC SPA National Recognition.

Professional standards prepared by organizations such as CEC serve as important resources to agencies engaged in professional credentialing. Historically, the licensing of individuals to practice in special education has been the responsibility of states or provinces, typically implemented through departments of education or separate professional licensing and standards boards. Although state approaches to licensure have been variable and sometimes idiosyncratic, the majority of states use CEC standards in developing licensure frameworks for special educators by either adopting CEC standards or ensuring that their state standards are closely aligned with CEC standards. Beyond state licensure, NBPTS offers National Board Certification as a voluntary system to recognize accomplished teaching. NBPTS has collaborated with CEC staff and members to assure that NBTPS Standards for National Board Certification as an "Exceptional Needs Specialist – Early Childhood through

Young Adulthood" were complementary with CEC standards.

EPPs often cite their standards alignment and CEC SPA National Recognition when marketing their programs to applicants. Referencing the CEC standards gives prospective and enrolled candidates an excellent overview of performance expectations for program completers. As candidates progress through their programs, they are able to track the standards linked to specific course objectives, activities, and assessments. Often candidates develop portfolios, complete self-assessments, or document their proficiencies in other ways as culminating requirements for program completion. Mastery of the practices delineated in CEC standards can help candidates perceive themselves—and present themselves to employers—as career-ready.

By clearly articulating the expectations for a well-prepared special educator, the CEC standards also will be useful to school administrators who have responsibilities for hiring, supporting, and evaluating them. Many of these school leaders have limited backgrounds in special education and may not understand the complexities of special educator roles. The CEC initial and advanced standards provide comprehensive descriptions of what is required for safe and effective practice of the profession. The standards may be helpful in guiding the search and selection processes and in providing professional development and support to individuals who are employed.

Applicability of the Standards

Given the variability of licensure systems and preparation program designs, it is sometimes difficult for users to decide which set of CEC standards apply to their needs. Figure 1.1 on the following page may be helpful to guide appropriate selection of initial or advanced preparation standards. CEC's initial special education preparation program standards are designed for candidates in their first special educator preparation program. Whether offered at the baccalaureate, post-baccalaureate, or master's degree level, a program is considered initial if it leads to the first credential to practice special education. The advanced standards are designed for candidates who are already credentialed special educators and are seeking further preparation for a new role, such as educational diagnostician or transition specialist. Advanced programs may be at the master's, specialist, or doctoral level.

Additional decisions may be driven by the age or grade levels addressed by initial preparation programs. The following criteria should be used to determine which set of CEC standards are applicable:

- If the program prepares educators for K-12 or K-12+, or separate elementary or secondary levels within this grade range, use the Initial K-12 Special Educator Standards.
- If the program prepares educators for children birth (B) through 5 years of age or kindergarten, use the EI/ECSE Standards.
- If the program prepares educators for children B through 8 years of age or primary grades, use the EI/ECSE Standards.
- If the program prepares educators for age 3 through higher grade levels, use EI/ECSE Standards for the portion of the program for 3-8 year olds (grade 3) and the K-12 Standards for the remaining grade levels. For this very broad age span, it is not sufficient to submit just one report, since the EI/ECSE and K-12 Standards are based upon different sets of essential practices (DEC Recommended Practices and High Leverage Practices) tailored to the specific developmental needs and service delivery models of early childhood or K-12 special education.

Role of the Specialty Sets

There has also been confusion between the preparation standards and the CEC knowledge and skill specialty sets. The specialty sets, often called the "knowledge and skill sets," were the first sets of standards developed by CEC, beginning in 1984, to delineate the essential knowledge and skills that beginning special education professionals must possess to be ready to begin their practice. Since then, CEC has developed 10 Initial Specialty Sets and 12 Advanced Specialty Sets that reflect different disability areas, state licensure structures, and roles of special educators. Until 2004, the specialty sets were used as the "standards" for the review of special education preparation programs seeking national recognition through NCATE (now CAEP) and CEC.

Special education teacher preparation programs were required to demonstrate, primarily through syllabi, that their curriculum addressed all of the appropriate knowledge and skills. When the NCATE program review process changed in 2004 to be more

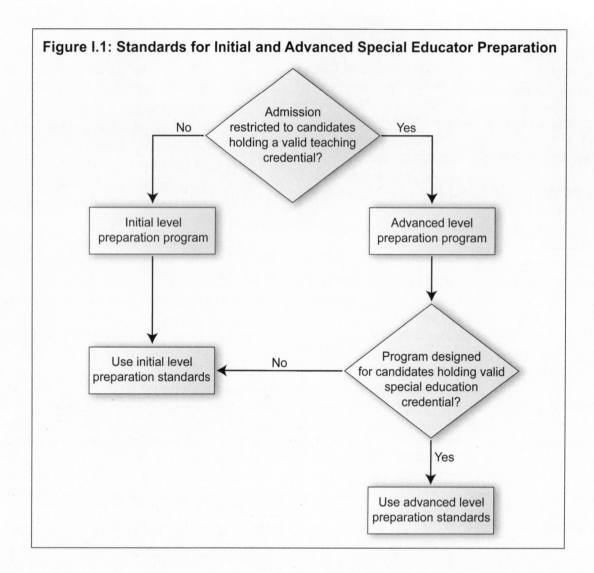

Figure I.1: Standards for Initial and Advanced Special Educator Preparation

Admission restricted to candidates holding a valid teaching credential?

No → Initial level preparation program

Yes → Advanced level preparation program

Initial level preparation program → Use initial level preparation standards

Advanced level preparation program → Program designed for candidates holding valid special education credential?

Program designed for candidates holding valid special education credential? — No → Use initial level preparation standards

Program designed for candidates holding valid special education credential? — Yes → Use advanced level preparation standards

performance based, CEC developed a single set of initial preparation standards that were more effective in evaluating performance-based evidence. Since that time, preparation programs have been directed to use the initial CEC preparation standards as *informed by the appropriate specialty set* as they design their curricula and performance assessments to demonstrate that candidates have met the standards.

The CEC Standards Framing Paper Workgroup (FPWG) described above considered the multiple sets of standards that EPPs have been expected to address and the differing interpretations of "being informed by the specialty sets" applied by teacher educators and SPA reviewers. The Framing Document (Blanton et al, 2017) approved by the CEC Board

of Directors, includes the recommendations that (a) the 2020 Practice-Based Professional Preparation Standards be used as the basis for CEC approval of initial preparation programs and (b) the knowledge and skill sets no longer be used to inform program reviews. The FPWG acknowledged that the specialty sets have served as a resource for preparation programs and left it up to the divisions and other groups to determine if they will continue to produce specialty sets in current or different form after the 2020 Practice-Based Professional Preparation Standards are fully implemented. The CEC website at www.exceptionalchildren.org continues to provide access to the most up-to-date specialty sets that have been developed.

Section 1

Overview of the 2020 Initial Practice-Based Professional Preparation Standards for Special Educators (K-12)

Focusing in on the 2020 Kindergarten-Grade 12 (K-12) Standards, this section describes the standards development process and recent influences that shaped the framing of these standards. It then highlights some of the current features, including alignment with InTASC standards and the CEC high-leverage practices (HLPs). Sections 1-4 of this book are devoted to comprehensive presentation of the seven standard sets, complete with supporting explanations and knowledge bases for the 23 components. The Field Experience and Clinical Practice Standard for K-12 is also presented. Additional resources for candidate and program assessment are also provided.

Process of Development

Development of the CEC standards was a consistently collaborative, iterative, and open process (CEC, 2020). A Standards Development Work Group (SDWG), comprised of 13 members representing the various stakeholders and constituencies involved in special education, led the three-year effort of reviewing relevant resources, achieving consensus on key concepts, drafting the standards and related content, and completing continuous rounds of revisions based on internal and external feedback. Names and institutional affiliations of SDWG members are presented in Appendix 1.

Early on, the SDWG hosted listening sessions at the CEC Teacher Education Division (TED) Conference and CEC Convention to gather constituent input on standards revision. At these conferences in 2018 and 2019, the SDWG shared drafts and received feedback on the standard sets. The SDWG also hosted webinars in 2018 and 2019 and solicited public feedback through online surveys. Throughout the process, the CEC Professional Standards and Practices Committee (PSPC) and the CEC Board of Directors received updates, and both groups formally approved the 2020 Initial Practice-Based Professional Preparation Standards for Special Educators (K-12 Standards) in July 2020. In October 2020, the Council for the Accreditation of Educator Preparation (CAEP) accepted these standards for inclusion in the Specialized Professional Association (SPA) review process for education program providers (EPPs) to achieve national recognition.

Influences from the Field

CEC began work on conceptualizing the 2020 Standards in 2013, immediately after the National Council for Accreditation of Teacher Education (NCATE) approved the 2012 CEC Standards. The CEC Board of Directors established a Professional Standards Workgroup (PSWG) to consider and make recommendations for CEC's ongoing work around professional standards for the next seven years. An outgrowth of the PSWG was the creation of the CEC Standards Framing Paper Workgroup (FPWG), which was charged with developing recommendations and guidelines for the process of updating CEC standards according to the parameters and timelines prescribed by CAEP. Their recommendations were published in *Shaping the Future of Special Education: Framing CEC's Professional Preparation Standards* (Blanton et al, 2017). The Framing Paper recommendations have served as the roadmap for the development of the draft K-12 and Early Interventionists/Early Childhood Special Educators (EI/ECSE) standards.

CEC standards established a vision for what professionals do in practice to deliver effective instruction that improves the learning of children and youth with disabilities. Given the less-than-desirable outcomes for students with disabilities related to achievement and post-school outcomes, as well as a range of factors that compromise the ability of special educators to deliver effective instruction, it was important to consider how high standards expected of all providers may contribute to better preparation of special educators, early childhood special educators, and early interventionists that will equip them to serve the complex needs of students with disabilities.

Ongoing trends in education—including the increasing complexity of students' needs and contexts, expanding roles of special educators, and demands for accountability at all levels—continue to have critical implications for teacher preparation. Such changes in the landscape contributed to the development of the 2020 CEC professional preparation standards.

Both the Initial K-12 and EI/ECSE Standards used the following principles from the Framing Document (Blanton et al., 2017) to develop standards that:

- are practice-based;
- form the foundation for future professional development;
- address diverse populations along with individual differences and needs;
- promote continuous improvement of professional preparation programs; and
- clearly articulate the expectations for a well-prepared special educator with stakeholders (e.g., EPPs, candidates, employers, families).

Additionally, the development of both sets of standards was guided by one overarching principle: Clinical preparation must be integrated throughout every facet of preparation in a dynamic way to prepare special educators who are career ready. The core experience in educator preparation must be clinical practice. Content and pedagogy are then woven around clinical experiences throughout preparation, in coursework, laboratory-based experiences, and school and other community-embedded practice (NCATE, 2010).

Given the availability of research related to effective practice, as well as research and the wisdom of practice that have been used to reimagine a more effective, practice-based approach to teacher preparation (e.g., NCATE, 2010), the time is right to use this knowledge base to reconsider standards for special educators and early interventionists. In particular,

the work of major funded centers has consolidated this information and provides a knowledge base for reconceptualizing standards and the organization and function of EPPs.

During the past decade, research from several fields has supported the use of a practice-based approach to educating beginning teachers. Drawing from professions as diverse as medicine, aviation, and plumbing, this research has shown that preparation is substantially enhanced by defining critical practices and systematically providing candidates opportunities to learn to use these practices with feedback in natural or simulated settings (Ericsson & Pool, 2016; McLeskey & Brownell, 2015).

Teacher educators have begun to employ this research in preparation programs, with the goal of producing teachers who are classroom-ready upon program completion (Maheady, Patti, Rafferty, & del Prado Hill, 2019; McDonald, Kazemi, & Kavanaugh, 2013). This research has also been incorporated into standards for teacher preparation programs (NCATE, 2010; CAEP, 2013) which have shifted from "a norm which emphasizes academic preparation and coursework loosely linked to school-based experiences [to] programs that are fully grounded in clinical practice and interwoven with academic content and professional courses" (NCATE, 2010, p. ii).

The foundation of practice-based teacher preparation programs is a core curriculum that consists of frequently used practices that have been shown to improve academic or behavioral outcomes for students (McLeskey, Billingsley, Brownell, Maheady, & Lewis, 2019). Research in general and special education, and more generally in the learning sciences, has begun to identify many of these practices (APA, 2015; Deans for Impact, 2015; Harn, Fritz, & Berg, 2014; McLeskey et al., 2017; Sugai, Simonsen, Bradshaw, Horner, & Lewis, 2014; Windschitl, Thompson, Braaten, & Stroupe, 2019).

Further, national centers (e.g., CEEDAR Center, SWIFT Center) have developed resources to disseminate this information and provide support to those engaged in teacher preparation and professional development as they learn to use these practices (e.g., Benedict et al, 2016; Sailor, 2016). These research and development activities have provided teacher educators with clear direction regarding approaches that may be used to improve teacher preparation and ensure that beginning educators are well prepared to meet the academic and social/behavioral needs of students with disabilities.

Standards and Components At-a-Glance

The following chart is a summary list of the seven standards and 23 components, along with a Field Experience and Clinical Practice Standard. Careful review of the component-level supporting explanations and knowledge bases is important for an understanding of the meaning and relevance of each standard set. These expanded elements are presented in the sections that follow.

Table 1: 2020 Initial Practice-Based Professional Preparation Standards for Special Educators (K-12)	
Standards	**Components**
Standard 1: Engaging in Professional Learning and Practice within Ethical Guidelines Candidates practice within ethical and legal guidelines; engage in ongoing self-reflection to design and implement professional learning activities; and advocate for improved outcomes for individuals with exceptionalities and their families while considering their social, cultural, and linguistic diversity.	**Component 1.1** Candidates practice within ethical guidelines and legal policies and procedures. **Component 1.2** Candidates advocate for improved outcomes for individuals with exceptionalities and their families while addressing the unique needs of those with diverse social, cultural, and linguistic backgrounds. **Component 1.3** Candidates design and implement professional learning activities based on ongoing analysis of student learning; self-reflection; professional standards, research, and contemporary practices.
Standard 2: Understanding and Addressing Each Individual's Developmental and Learning Needs Candidates use their understanding of human growth and development; multiple influences on development; individual differences; diversity, including exceptionalities; and families and communities to plan and implement inclusive learning environments and experiences that provide individuals with exceptionalities high-quality learning experiences reflective of each individual's strengths and needs.	**Component 2.1** Candidates apply understanding of human growth and development to create developmentally appropriate and meaningful learning experiences that address individualized strengths and needs of students with exceptionalities. **Component 2.2** Candidates use their knowledge and understanding of diverse factors that influence development and learning including differences related to families, languages, cultures, and communities, and to individual differences, including exceptionalities, to plan and implement learning experiences and environments.
Standard 3: Demonstrating Subject Matter Content and Specialized Curricular Knowledge Candidates apply their understanding of the academic subject matter content of the general curriculum and specialized curricula to inform their programmatic and instructional decisions for learners with exceptionalities.	**Component 3.1** Candidates apply their understanding of academic subject matter content of the general curriculum to inform their programmatic and instructional decisions for individuals with exceptionalities. **Component 3.2** Candidates augment the general education curriculum to address skills and strategies that students with disabilities need to access the core curriculum and function successfully within a variety of contexts and the continuum of placement options to assure specially designed instruction is developed and implemented to achieve mastery of curricular standards and individualized goals and objectives.

Table 1: 2020 Initial Practice-Based Professional Preparation Standards for Special Educators (K-12)...(continued)	
Standards	**Components**
Standard 4: Using Assessment to Understand the Learner and the Learning Environment for Data-Based Decision Making Candidates assess students' learning, behavior, and the classroom environment in order to evaluate and support classroom and school-based problem-solving systems of intervention and instruction. Candidates evaluate students to determine their strengths and needs, contribute to students' eligibility determination, communicate students' progress, inform short and long-term instructional planning, and make ongoing adjustments to instruction using technology as appropriate.	**Component 4.1** Candidates collaboratively develop, select, administer, analyze, and interpret multiple measures of student learning, behavior, and the classroom environment to evaluate and support classroom and school-based systems of intervention for students with and without exceptionalities. **Component 4.2** Candidates develop, select, and administer multiple, formal and informal, culturally and linguistically appropriate measures and procedures that are valid and reliable, to contribute to eligibility determination for special education services. **Component 4.3** Candidates assess, collaboratively analyze, interpret, and communicate students' progress toward measurable outcomes using technology as appropriate, to inform both short- and long-term planning, and make ongoing adjustments to instruction.
Standard 5: Using Effective Instruction to Support Learning Candidates use knowledge of individuals' development, learning needs and assessment data to inform decisions about effective instruction. Candidates use explicit instructional strategies; employ strategies to promote active engagement and increased motivation to individualize instruction to support each individual. Candidates use whole group instruction, flexible grouping, small group instruction, and individual instruction. Candidates teach individuals to use meta-/cognitive strategies to support and self-regulate learning.	**Component 5.2** Candidates use effective strategies to promote active student engagement, increase student motivation, increase opportunities to respond, and enhance self-regulation of student learning. **Component 5.3** Candidates use explicit, systematic instruction to teach content, strategies, and skills to make clear what a learner needs to do or think about while learning. **Component 5.4** Candidates use flexible grouping to support the use of instruction that is adapted to meet the needs of each individual and group. **Component 5.5** Candidates organize and manage focused, intensive small group instruction to meet the learning needs of each individual. **Component 5.6** Candidates plan and deliver specialized, individualized instruction that is used to meet the learning needs of each individual.

Table 1: 2020 Initial Practice-Based Professional Preparation Standards for Special Educators (K-12)...(continued)	
Standards	**Components**
Standard 6: Supporting Social, Emotional, and Behavioral Growth Candidates create and contribute to safe, respectful, and productive learning environments for individuals with exceptionalities through the use of effective routines and procedures and use a range of preventive and responsive practices to support social, emotional and educational wellbeing. They follow ethical and legal guidelines and work collaboratively with families and other professionals to conduct behavioral assessments for intervention and program development.	**Component 6.1** Candidates use effective routines and procedures to create safe, caring, respectful, and productive learning environments for individuals with exceptionalities. **Component 6.2** Candidates use a range of preventive and responsive practices documented as effective to support individuals' social, emotional, and educational well-being. **Component 6.3** Candidates systematically use data from a variety of sources to identify the purpose or function served by problem behavior to plan, implement, and evaluate behavioral interventions and social skills programs, including generalization to other environments.
Standard 7: Collaborating with Team Members Candidates apply team processes and communication strategies to collaborate in a culturally responsive manner with families, paraprofessionals, and other professionals within the school, other educational settings, and the community to lead meetings, plan programs, and access services for individuals with exceptionalities and their families.	**Component 7.1** Candidates utilize communication, group facilitation, and problem-solving strategies in a culturally responsive manner to lead effective meetings and share expertise and knowledge to build team capacity and jointly address students' instructional and behavioral needs. **Component 7.2** Candidates communicate, coordinate, and collaborate with families and other professionals within the educational setting to assess, plan, and implement effective programs and services that promote progress toward measurable outcomes for individuals with and without exceptionalities and their families. **Component 7.3** Candidates communicate, coordinate, and collaborate with professionals and agencies within the community to identify and access services, resources, and supports to meet the identified needs of individuals with exceptionalities and their families. **Component 7.4** Candidates understand their role of working with paraprofessionals to implement efficiently and effectively necessary components of the IEP.
Field Experience and Clinical Practice Standard for K-12 Special education candidates progress through a series of developmentally sequenced field and clinical experiences for the full range of ages, types and levels of abilities, and collaborative opportunities that are appropriate to the license or roles for which they are preparing. These field and clinical experiences are supervised by qualified professionals.	

Alignment with InTASC Standards

The Model Core Teaching Standards published by the Council of Chief State School Officers (CCSSO), through its Interstate Teacher Assessment and Support Consortium (InTASC), are widely used to guide licensure and program approval efforts by state education agencies, as well as program design and improvement efforts by education preparation programs.

Additionally, evidence of alignment with InTASC standards is required for CAEP Accreditation. Originally developed in 1992 and most recently updated in 2021, these InTASC standards "outline what teachers should know and be able to do to ensure every K-12 student reaches the goal of being ready to enter college or the workforce in today's world" (CCSSO, 2013, p. 3). Throughout its work, the CEC Standards Development Workgroup was attentive to InTASC standards, and the following crosswalk illustrates the alignment of these two sets of standards.

Table 2: CEC K-12 Initial Preparation Standards' Alignment with InTASC Categories	
InTASC Model Core Teaching Standards	**2020 Initial Practice-Based Professional Preparation Standards for Special Educators**
The Learner and Learning #1: Learner Development. The teacher understands how learners grow and develop, recognizing that patterns of learning and development vary individually within and across the cognitive, linguistic, social, emotional, and physical areas, and designs and implements developmentally appropriate and challenging learning experiences. #2: Learning Differences. The teacher uses understanding of individual differences and diverse cultures and communities to ensure inclusive learning environments that enable each learner to meet high standards. #3: Learning Environments. The teacher works with others to create environments that support individual and collaborative learning, and that encourage positive social interaction, active engagement in learning, and self- motivation.	**Standard 2: Understanding and Addressing Each Individual's Developmental and Learning Needs** Candidates use their understanding of human growth and development; multiple influences on development; individual differences; diversity, including exceptionalities; and families and communities to plan and implement inclusive learning environments and experiences that provide individuals with exceptionalities high-quality learning experiences reflective of each individual's strengths and needs. **Standard 6: Supporting Social, Emotional, and Behavioral Growth** Candidates create and contribute to safe, respectful, and productive learning environments for individuals with exceptionalities through the use of effective routines and procedures and use a range of preventive and responsive practices to support social, emotional, and educational wellbeing. They follow ethical and legal guidelines and work collaboratively with families and other professionals to conduct behavioral assessments for intervention and program development.

Table 2: CEC K-12 Initial Preparation Standards' Alignment with InTASC Categories...(continued)

InTASC Model Core Teaching Standards	2020 Initial Practice-Based Professional Preparation Standards for Special Educators
Content #4: Content Knowledge. The teacher understands the central concepts, tools of inquiry, and structures of the discipline(s) he or she teaches and creates learning experiences that make the discipline accessible and meaningful for learners to assure mastery of the content. #5: Application of Content. The teacher understands how to connect concepts and use differing perspectives to engage learners in critical thinking, creativity, and collaborative problem solving related to authentic local and global issues.	**Standard 3: Demonstrating Subject Matter Content and Specialized Curricular Knowledge** Candidates apply their understanding of the academic subject matter content of the general curriculum and specialized curricula to inform their programmatic and instructional decisions for learners with exceptionalities.
Instructional Practice #6: Assessment. The teacher understands and uses multiple methods of assessment to engage learners in their own growth, to monitor learner progress, and to guide the teacher's and learner's decision making. #7: Planning for Instruction. The teacher plans instruction that supports every student in meeting rigorous learning goals by drawing upon knowledge of content areas, curriculum, cross-disciplinary skills, and pedagogy, as well as knowledge of learners and the community context. #8: Instructional Strategies. The teacher understands and uses a variety of instructional strategies to encourage learners to develop deep understanding of content areas and their connections, and to build skills to apply knowledge in meaningful ways.	**Standard 4: Using Assessment to Understand the Learner and the Learning Environment for Data-Based Decision Making** Candidates assess students' learning, behavior, and the classroom environment in order to evaluate and support classroom and school-based problem-solving systems of intervention and instruction. Candidates evaluate students to determine their strengths and needs, contribute to students' eligibility determination, communicate students' progress, inform short and long-term instructional planning, and make ongoing adjustments to instruction using technology as appropriate. **Standard 5: Using Effective Instruction to Support Learning** Candidates use knowledge of individuals' development, learning needs and assessment data to inform decisions about effective instruction. Candidates use explicit instructional strategies; employ strategies to promote active engagement and increased motivation to individualize instruction to support each individual. Candidates use whole group instruction, flexible grouping, small group instruction, and individual instruction. Candidates teach individuals to use meta-/cognitive strategies to support and self-regulate learning.

Table 2: CEC K-12 Initial Preparation Standards' Alignment with InTASC Categories...(continued)	
InTASC Model Core Teaching Standards	**2020 Initial Practice-Based Professional Preparation Standards for Special Educators**
Professional Responsibility #9: Professional Learning and Ethical Practice. The teacher engages in ongoing professional learning and uses evidence to continually evaluate his/her practice, particularly the effects of his/her choices and actions on others (learners, families, other professionals, and the community), and adapts practice to meet the needs of each learner. #10: Leadership and Collaboration. The teacher seeks appropriate leadership roles and opportunities to take responsibility for student learning, to collaborate with learners, families, colleagues, other school professionals, and community members to ensure learner growth, and to advance the profession.	**Standard 1: Engaging in Professional Learning and Practice within Ethical Guidelines** Candidates practice within ethical and legal guidelines; engage in ongoing self-reflections to design and implement professional learning activities; and advocate for improved outcomes for individuals with exceptionalities and their families while considering their social, cultural, and linguistic diversity. **Standard 7: Collaborating with Team Members** Candidates apply team processes and communication strategies to collaborate in a culturally responsive manner with families, paraprofessionals, and other professionals within the school, other educational settings, and the community to lead meetings, plan programs, and access services for individuals with exceptionalities and their families.

Alignment with CEC High-Leverage Practices

The following crosswalk has been prepared to demonstrate the strong influence of the HLPs (McLeskey et al., 2017) in writing the CEC Standards.

Throughout the development process, the SDWG referenced the HLPs and ensured that these were embedded in the standards. In addition, HLPs are cited in the knowledge bases that were prepared by the SDWG for each of the standard components.

Table 3: Crosswalk of CEC Standards with HLPs	
Standard 1: Engaging in Professional Learning and Practice within Ethical Guidelines	
Candidates practice within ethical and legal guidelines; advocate for improved outcomes for individuals with exceptionalities and their families while considering their social, cultural, and linguistic diversity; and engage in ongoing self-reflection to design and implement professional learning activities.	
CEC Standard Component	**High-Leverage Practice**
1.1: Candidates practice within ethical guidelines and legal policies and procedures. 1.2: Candidates advocate for improved outcomes for individuals with exceptionalities and their families while addressing the unique needs of those with diverse social, cultural, and linguistic backgrounds. 1.3: Candidates design and implement professional learning activities based on ongoing analysis of student learning; self-reflection; professional standards, research and contemporary practices.	HLP 3: Collaborate with families to support student learning and secure needed services.

Table 3: Crosswalk of CEC Standards with HLPs...(continued)

Standard 2: Understanding and Addressing Each Individual's Developmental and Learning Needs

Candidates use their understanding of human growth and development; the multiple influences on development, individual differences, diversity, including exceptionalities, and families and communities to plan and implement inclusive learning environments and experiences that provide individuals with exceptionalities high quality learning experiences reflective of each individual's strengths and needs.

CEC Standard Component	High-Leverage Practice
2.1: Candidates apply understanding of human growth and development to create developmentally appropriate and meaningful learning experiences that address individualized strengths and needs of students with exceptionalities.	HLP 4: Use multiple sources of information to develop a comprehensive understanding of a student's strengths and needs.
2.2: Candidates use their knowledge and understanding of diverse factors that influence development and learning, including differences related to families, languages, cultures, and communities, and individual differences, including exceptionalities, to plan and implement learning experiences and environments.	HLP 11: Identify and prioritize long- and short-term learning goals. HLP 12: Systematically design instruction toward a specific learning goal.

Standard 3: Demonstrating Subject Matter Content and Specialized Curricular Knowledge

Candidates apply their understanding of the academic subject matter content of the general curriculum and specialized curricula to inform their programmatic and instructional decisions for learners with exceptionalities.

CEC Standard Component	High-Leverage Practice
3.1: Candidates apply their understanding of academic subject matter content of the general curriculum to inform their programmatic and instructional decisions for individuals with exceptionalities.	HLP 11: Identify and prioritize long- and short-term learning goals. HLP 13: Adapt curriculum tasks and materials for specific learning goals.
3.2: Candidates augment the general education curriculum to address skills and strategies that students with disabilities need to access the core curriculum and function successfully within a variety of contexts as well as the continuum of placement options to assure specially designed instruction is developed and implemented to achieve mastery of curricular standards and individualized goals and objectives.	HLP 12: Systematically design instruction toward a specific learning goal. HLP 13: Adapt curriculum tasks and materials for specific learning goals. HLP 14: Teach cognitive and metacognitive strategies to support learning and independence. HLP 15: Provide scaffolded supports. HLP 21: Teach students to maintain and generalize new learning across time and settings.

Table 3: Crosswalk of CEC Standards with HLPs...(continued)

Standard 4: Using Assessment to Understand the Learner and the Learning Environment for Data-Based Decision Making

Candidates assess students' learning, behavior, and the classroom environment in order to evaluate and support classroom and school-based problem-solving systems of intervention and instruction. Candidates evaluate students to determine their strengths and needs, contribute to students' eligibility determination, communicate students' progress, inform short and long-term instructional planning, and make ongoing adjustments to instruction using technology as appropriate.

CEC Standard Component	High-Leverage Practice
4.1: Candidates collaboratively develop, select, administer, analyze, and interpret multiple measures of student learning, behavior, and the classroom environment to evaluate and support classroom and school-based systems of intervention for students with and without exceptionalities.	HLP 4: Use multiple sources of information to develop a comprehensive understanding of a student's strengths and needs. HLP 5: Interpret and communicate assessment information with stakeholders to collaboratively design and implement educational programs.
4.2: Candidates develop, select, administer, and interpret multiple, formal and informal, culturally and linguistically appropriate measures and procedures that are valid and reliable, to contribute to eligibility determination for special education services.	HLP 4: Use multiple sources of information to develop a comprehensive understanding of a student's strengths and needs.
4.3: Candidates assess, collaboratively analyze, interpret, and communicate students' progress toward measurable outcomes using technology as appropriate, to inform both short- and long-term planning, and make ongoing adjustments to instruction.	HLP 4: Use multiple sources of information to develop a comprehensive understanding of a student's strengths and needs. HLP 5; Interpret and communicate assessment information with stakeholders to collaboratively design and implement educational programs. HLP 6: Use student assessment data, analyze instructional practices, and make necessary adjustments that improve student outcomes. HLP 19: Use assistive and instructional technologies.

Table 3: Crosswalk of CEC Standards with HLPs...(continued)

Standard 5: Using Effective Instruction to Support Learning

Candidates use knowledge of individuals' development, learning needs and assessment data to inform decisions about effective instruction. Candidates use explicit instructional strategies and employ strategies to promote active engagement and increased motivation to individualize instruction to support each individual. Candidates use whole group instruction, flexible grouping, small group instruction, and individual instruction. Candidates teach individuals to use meta-/cognitive strategies to support and self-regulate learning.

CEC Standard Component	High-Leverage Practice
5.1: Candidates use findings from multiple assessments, including student self-assessment, that are responsive to cultural and linguistic diversity and specialized as needed, to identify what students know and are able to do. They then interpret the assessment data to appropriately plan and guide instruction to meet rigorous academic and non-academic content and goals for each individual.	HLP 6: Use student assessment data, analyze instructional practices, and make necessary adjustments that improve student outcomes. HLP 11: Identify and prioritize long- and short-term learning goals. HLP 19: Use assistive and instructional technologies.
5.2: Candidates use effective strategies to promote active student engagement, increase student motivation, increase opportunities to respond, and enhance self-regulation of student learning.	HLP 8: Provide positive and constructive feedback to guide students' learning and behavior. HLP 9: Teach social behaviors. HLP 18: Use strategies to promote active student engagement. HLP 19: Use assistive and instructional technologies. HLP 22: Provide positive and constructive feedback to guide students' learning and behavior.
5.3: Candidates use explicit, systematic instruction to teach content, strategies, and skills to make clear what a learner needs to do or think about while learning.	HLP 12: Systematically design instruction toward a specific learning goal. HLP 14: Teach cognitive and metacognitive strategies to support learning and independence. HLP 16: Use explicit instruction.
5.4: Candidates use flexible grouping to support the use of instruction that is adapted to meet the needs of each individual and group.	HLP 17: Use flexible grouping.
5.5: Candidates organize and manage focused, intensive small group instruction to meet the learning needs of each individual.	HLP 17: Use flexible grouping. HLP 20: Provide intensive instruction.
5.6: Candidates plan and deliver specialized, individualized instruction that is used to meet the learning needs of each individual.	HLP 13: Adapt curriculum tasks and materials for specific learning goals. HLP 14: Teach cognitive and metacognitive strategies to support learning and independence. HLP 15: Provide scaffolded supports. HLP 19: Use assistive and instructional technologies. HLP 20: Provide intensive instruction.

Table 3: Crosswalk of CEC Standards with HLPs...(continued)

Standard 6: Supporting Social, Emotional, and Behavioral Growth

Candidates create and contribute to safe, respectful, and productive learning environments for individuals with exceptionalities through the use of effective routines and procedures and use a range of preventive and responsive practices to support social, emotional and educational wellbeing. They follow ethical and legal guidelines and work collaboratively with families and other professionals to conduct behavioral assessments for intervention and program development.

CEC Standard Component	High-Leverage Practice
6.1: Candidates use effective routines and procedures to create safe, caring, respectful, and productive learning environments for individuals with exceptionalities.	HLP 7: Establish a consistent, organized, and respectful learning environment.
6.2: Candidates use a range of preventive and responsive practices documented as effective to support individuals' social, emotional, and educational well-being.	HLP 7: Establish a consistent, organized, and respectful learning environment. HLP 8: Provide positive and constructive feedback to guide students' learning and behavior. HLP 9: Teach social behaviors. HLP 22: Provide positive and constructive feedback to guide students' learning and behavior.
6.3: Candidates systematically use data from a variety of sources to identify the purpose or function served by problem behavior to plan, implement, and evaluate behavioral interventions and social skills programs, including generalization to other environments.	HLP 4: Use multiple sources of information to develop a comprehensive understanding of a student's strengths and needs. HLP 9: Teach social behaviors. HLP 10: Conduct functional behavioral assessments to develop individual student behavior support plans. HLP 15: Provide scaffolded supports. HLP 16: Use explicit instruction. HLP 21: Teach students to maintain and generalize new learning across time and settings.

Table 3: Crosswalk of CEC Standards with HLPs...(continued)

Standard 7: Collaborating with Team Members

Candidates apply team processes and communication strategies to collaborate in a culturally responsive manner with families, paraprofessionals, and other professionals within the school, other educational settings, and the community to plan programs and access services for individuals with exceptionalities and their families.

CEC Standard Component	High-Leverage Practice
7.1: Candidates utilize communication, group facilitation, and problem–solving strategies in a culturally responsive manner to lead effective meetings and share expertise and knowledge to build team capacity and jointly address students' instructional and behavior needs.	HLP 2: Organize and facilitate effective meetings with professionals and families.
7.2: Candidates communicate, coordinate, and collaborate with families, paraprofessionals, and other professionals within the educational setting to assess, plan, and implement effective programs and services that promote progress toward measurable outcomes for individuals with and without exceptionalities and their families.	HLP 1: Collaborate with professionals to increase student success. HLP 3: Collaborate with families to support student learning and secure needed services.
7.3: Candidates communicate, coordinate and collaborate with professionals and agencies within the community to identify and access services, resources, and supports to meet the identified needs of individuals with exceptionalities and their families.	HLP 1: Collaborate with professionals to increase student success.
7.4: Candidates work with and mentor paraprofessionals in the paraprofessionals' role of supporting the education of individuals with exceptionalities and their families.	HLP 1: Collaborate with professionals to increase student success.

Key Elements of Standards Sets

The 2020 Initial Practice-Based Professional Preparation Standards for Special Educators (Initial K-12 Standards) are comprised of multiple elements beyond the seven standards themselves. The package includes 23 components underlying the standards, along with their supporting explanations, knowledge bases, sample performance indicators and assessments.

Each standard outlines specific proficiencies candidates are expected to demonstrate upon completion of their initial K-12 special educator preparation programs. For easy referencing, working titles are given for each of the standards but should never substitute for the more complete and substantive

standards themselves. Several components accompany each standard to "unpack" important practices embedded in the standard. Components do not introduce additional practices but elaborate on those already incorporated into the overarching standard. Table 1 on page 7 presents the seven standards and 23 components of the 2020 Initial K-12 Standards. Note that CEC has retained a separate Field and Clinical Experience Standard.

If each standard represents what candidates are expected to do, then its supporting explanation describes how each component of the standard looks in practice. Specific skills and desired behaviors of candidates are fleshed out more fully in the supporting explanations. The knowledge base for each component explains *why* the target proficiencies are important by referencing foundational sources within the profession.

The knowledge bases note alignment with HLPs, InTASC standards, and other SPA standards as appropriate. They also cite relevant laws, policies and position statements, along with research that supports the specific practices. The knowledge bases are not intended to be comprehensive reviews of literature. In many instances, the work of major national projects is cited, since centers such as IRIS (www.iris.peabody. vanderbilt.edu/), CEEDAR (https://ceedar.education. ufl.edu), and PBIS (www.pbis.org/) have already reviewed and synthesized major research undergirding recommended practices.

Along with the standards, additional resources are provided to guide candidate and program assessment. Examples of performance indicators (specific tasks that might be used to assess candidate proficiency) are offered for each component. Matrices also are available to show how programs can provide evidence that standards are met by citing data from six to eight typical assessment sources.

Cross-Cutting Themes

Throughout the 2020 Initial Practice-Based Professional Preparation Standards for Special Educators (Initial K-12 Standards), two major themes are prominent: one focuses on diversity and another on technology. These themes are addressed when appropriate in the components, supporting explanations, and knowledge bases, as well as in the standards themselves.

The entire set of Initial K-12 Standards is devoted to one important dimension of diversity–disability. CEC also acknowledges how race, culture, language, gender, and other factors intersect with disability and must be considered when creating equitable opportunities for diverse learners. Standards 1 and 2 illustrate the prominence of the diversity theme. As explained elsewhere in this document, one of the changes made from the CEC 2012 standards involved moving the standard focused on professional and ethical practice from number seven to number one in the 2020 revision to emphasize its overarching importance.

Notably, Component 1.2 states that "candidates advocate for improved outcomes for individuals with exceptionalities and their families while addressing the unique needs of those with diverse social, cultural, and linguistic backgrounds." This sets the stage for attention to diversity issues throughout the set of CEC standards. Next, Standard 2: Understanding and Addressing Each Individual's Developmental and Learning Needs, targets diversity explicitly. For example, Component 2.2 specifies that "candidates use their knowledge and understanding of diverse factors that influence development and learning including differences related to families, languages, cultures, and communities, and to individual differences, including exceptionalities, to plan and implement learning experiences and environments."

Themes of diversity also are infused throughout the remaining standards that deal with curricular content, assessment, instruction, behavior management, and collaboration. The following examples illustrate some of the varied ways that diversity issues are addressed:

- Component 4.2 stresses use of culturally and linguistically appropriate assessment measures and procedures for eligibility determination and program development.

- Component 5.1 specifies use of multiple assessments responsive to cultural and linguistic diversity for planning and guiding instruction.

- The supporting explanation for Component 5.3 notes use of students' cultural and linguistic diversity as an asset integrated into explicit instruction to support student learning.

- The supporting explanation for Component 6.1 emphasizes respect for the varied aspects of diversity and how intersectionality of gender, racial, cultural, disability, and other identities may make individuals and or groups more vulnerable to discriminatory disciplinary practices.

- Standard 7 focuses on application of team processes and communication strategies to collaborate in a culturally responsive manner with families, paraprofessionals, and other professionals.

The Initial K-12 Standards are attentive to development of candidate skills for appropriate and effective integration of technology and digital literacy to support student learning. For example, Standard 4: Using Assessment to Understand the Learner and the Learning Environment for Data-Based Decision Making, includes the following statement:

"Candidates evaluate students to determine their strengths and needs, contribute to students' eligibility determination, communicate students' progress, inform short and long-term instructional planning, and make ongoing adjustments to instruction using technology as appropriate.

The supporting explanations that accompany all of the component statements elaborate on the specific practices that candidates are expected to demonstrate. Many describe appropriate applications of technology, including distance learning. The following examples from supporting explanations illustrate some of the different ways that the cross-cutting theme of technology is addressed across standards:

- **Supporting Explanation 1.3** draws attention to digital resources for ongoing professional learning, describing how candidates keep current with research and contemporary practices in multiple ways, including participation in professional associations and online professional learning networks, and by accessing digital resources.

- **Supporting Explanation 3.1** emphasizes use of instructional and assistive technology in face-to-face, virtual, or hybrid settings to meet the learning goals and curricular standards for students with exceptional learning needs in academic subject matter content of the general curricula.

- **Supporting Explanation 3.2** further describes implementation of appropriate instructional and assistive technology such as augmentative and alternative communication devices and other technologies to meet the learning goals of students with exceptionalities using specialized curricula.

- **Supporting Explanation 4.3** notes that ongoing assessment and progress monitoring requires candidates to use technology/assistive technology for specific purposes including test administration, testing accommodations, data storage, creating digital documents and logs, and charting and graphing results to identify patterns in learning and/or behavior. Candidates may use screening software programs in face-to-face or virtual formats, as appropriate, considering ongoing advancements in technology.

- **Supporting Explanation 5.2** stresses infusion of digital technology in instruction (e.g., use of interactive white boards, web-based documents,

assistive and augmentative communication) and assessment (e.g., real-time response systems) to assist in and enhance learning and engagement based on individual student need and interest. Candidates use appropriate platforms and applications when supporting students in blended or virtual learning environments.

- **Supporting Explanation 6.3** focuses on appropriate utilization of technology to assist in measurement, tracking, and instructional decision making related to student behavior.

- **Supporting Explanation 7.3** notes that communications with families should occur in a variety of ways, (e.g., email, e-messages, school/class websites, phone calls, as well as parent-teacher conferences, virtual meetings, home visits, annual reviews).

Differences from the 2012 Standards

The 2020 Initial K-12 Standards address the many changes in the field of special education since the current set of CAEP-approved standards (approved by NCATE in 2012). The role of special educators is ever evolving. While the many of the key concepts described in the current standards, such as effective instruction and the importance of supportive learning environments, remain critically important to special educator practice, the specific concepts and relevant practices have evolved.

The primary difference between the 2012 Standards and the 2020 Initial K-12 Standards is the change to performance-based standards. As explained in the earlier item in this section on Influences from the Field, the profession of teacher education has shifted the emphases in program design, delivery, and assessment to proficient application of knowledge and skills. Candidate understanding of theory and research is not sufficient; candidates must now be able to demonstrate mastery of essential content through the effective use of practices directly relevant to performance of their future roles as special educators.

In addition, the order of the 2020 standards is intentionally different from the 2012 CEC Initial Preparation Standards. The 2020 Initial K-12 Standards begin with two essential foundational standards: Standard 1: Engaging in Professional Learning and Practice with Ethical Guidelines and

Standard 2: Understanding and Addressing Each Individual's Developmental and Learning Needs.

These two standards undergird the remaining five standards: Standard 3: Demonstrating Subject Matter Content and Specialized Curricular Knowledge; Standard 4: Using Assessment to Understand the Learner and the Learning Environment for Data-Based Decision Making; Standard 5: Using Effective Instruction to Support Learning; Standard 6: Supporting Social, Emotional, and Behavioral Growth; and Standard 7: Collaborating with Team Members. Embedded throughout the standards—rather than in isolation—is continuous attention to culturally responsive instruction and assessment practices, working with and supporting families, and an emphasis on technology use, and universal design for learning planning and implementation.

Section 2

Initial Practice-Based Professional Preparation Standards for Special Educators (K-12)

The seven Initial Practice-Based Professional Standards (K-12) and 23 components, and the Field Experience and Clinical Practice Standard for K-12 are detailed in this section. A careful review of the component-level supporting explanations and knowledge bases is important for an understanding of the meaning and relevance of each standard set.

Standard 1: Engaging in Professional Learning and Practice Within Ethical Guidelines

Candidates practice within ethical and legal guidelines; advocate for improved outcomes for individuals with exceptionalities and their families while considering their social, cultural, and linguistic diversity; and engage in ongoing self-reflection to design and implement professional learning activities.

Component 1.1. Candidates practice within ethical guidelines and legal policies and procedures.

Supporting Explanation. Candidates have a strong knowledge of and work within all applicable federal (e.g., the Individuals with Disabilities in Education Improvement Act [IDEA] and Section 504 of the Rehabilitation Act of 1973) and state/provincial/local laws, regulations, and policies pertaining to individuals with exceptionalities and how these laws affect the delivery of services and supports.

For example, candidates should understand that present levels of educational achievement and functional performance drive goals and lead to a plan for services. Candidates maintain a high level of professional competence and integrity, exercise informed professional judgment, and practice within the codes of ethics in the profession. Candidates practice with a commitment to understanding that individuals with exceptionalities deserve to be challenged with high expectations and provided with meaningful and inclusive participation opportunities to develop the highest possible learning outcomes.

Knowledge Base. Among the essential knowledge associated with InTASC Standard 9 is the belief that teachers must understand "laws related to learners' rights and teacher responsibilities" (CCSSO, 2011, p. 18). Key among the laws for learners for special education practitioners are the Individuals with Disabilities Education Act (IDEA) of 2004 and Section 504 of the Rehabilitation Act of 1973. Balch, Memory, and Hofmeister (2008) acknowledged that "teachers who are knowledgeable about the law are more likely to articulate the individualized services needed for children with disabilities" (p. 6). Practitioners believe that beginning special education professionals must have a base knowledge of the laws that protect students with disabilities and that frame the backbone of the field of special education.

Additionally, the CEC has set forth a Code of Ethics for professional educators which grounds the profession in several beliefs to guide the work of educators in the field. Key among these beliefs is the idea that special educators should be "practicing within the professional ethics, standards, and policies of CEC; upholding laws, regulations, and policies that influence professional practice; and advocating improvements in the laws, regulations, and policies" (CEC, 2015, p. 1). Further, the Code of Ethics acknowledges that all special educators should be "maintaining challenging expectations for individuals with exceptionalities to develop the highest possible learning outcomes and quality of life potential in ways that respect their dignity, culture, language, and background" (CEC, 2015, p. 1).

Barret, Casey, Visser, and Headley (2012) acknowledged that the profession of education should approach professional ethics in ways similar to other licensed professions such as psychology, medicine, and law. Further, based on the results of their study comparing preservice and in-service teachers' attitudes about professional ethics, Barret and his colleagues concluded that preservice teacher education programs should include an emphasis on ethics that is integrated throughout the curriculum. In the field of special education, teaching ethics is especially important, given the fact that all professionals will be working with students with disabilities. Through the use of high-leverage practices, the current legal framework, and the Code of Ethics, and through direct instruction around ethical issues, candidates practice within ethical guidelines and legal policies and procedures.

Component 1.2. Candidates advocate for improved outcomes for individuals with exceptionalities and their families while addressing the unique needs of those with diverse social, cultural, and linguistic backgrounds.

Supporting Explanation. Candidates advocate for resources and the professional learning conditions to help individuals with exceptionalities meet instructional, behavioral, social, and transition goals and outcomes. For example, they work with colleagues, families, and others to adapt curricular materials, ensure service provisions, implement principles of universal design, and speak on behalf of children with exceptionalities in situations where their voice has been absent. They evaluate new technology options given student needs and advocate for administrative support in technology implementation.

Candidates seek a greater understanding of families' diverse knowledge and expertise (e.g., funds of knowledge) about their children's strengths and needs. Through their partnerships, they support families by acting in ways that build on family strengths and capacities in working with their students at risk for or with disabilities. For example, for adolescents, candidates jointly identify and implement transition planning and supports around the family's priorities to promote the child's engagement, learning, development, and well-being (e.g., accessing natural environments and inclusive settings within the community).

Together with families, candidates may identify strategies to facilitate the child's development of peer relationships, self-regulation, independence, and safety within the home, classroom, and/or community. Candidates understand barriers that exist for students with exceptionalities within educational settings and work with decision makers to design environments and select curriculum resources that include supports that address a range of student needs.

Knowledge Base. InTASC Standard 10 focuses on the development of advocacy skills in collaborating with parents and families to meet the unique needs of all learners. Specifically, it is noted that "the teacher advocates to meet the needs of learners, to strengthen the learning environment, and to enact system change" (CCSSO, 2011, p. 47). Here, it is important to note the importance of collaboration with others is an ongoing process and one that should not be unique to the field of special education. While special education professionals are tasked with meeting the needs of diverse learners, they are not the only ones who are inherently responsible for their learning, and through the use of universally designed curriculum and specially designed instruction, teachers and other professionals should work together toward meeting the needs of all learners in a school building.

In their definition of universal design for learning, Rappolt-Schlictman, Boucher, and Evans (2018) posited that "barriers to learning occur in the interaction with curriculum that are not inherent solely in the capacities of the learner" (p. 867). With this in mind, the understanding of a "disabling condition" is changing over time and, with that change, comes a responsibility for special education professionals to collaborate with others on the education of students. Hattie (2012) commented "for differentiation to be effective, teachers need to know for each student where that student begins and where he or she is in his or her journey toward meeting the success criteria of the lesson" (p. 98). Inherent in this understanding about differentiated instruction is the belief that every learner is unique and that each learner comes to the lesson with their own unique knowledge set. Indeed, every learner in a classroom comes with their own unique learning experiences, and it is the teacher's commitment to effective teaching and learning practices that will allow them to grow and learn.

Whitby, Marx, McIntyre, and Weinke (2013) suggest guidelines in supporting advocacy for students with disabilities at the school level. These apply to the preparation of candidates in special education and include: "(a) more information on the CEC Code of Ethics and Standards for Professional Practice (Fiedler & Van Haren, 2009; Hanhimaki & Tirri, 2009); (b) information on how to build and support teachers' beliefs that they are critically important agents of change in the lives of their students (Peters & Reid, 2009); (c) real-life examples of ethical and moral dilemmas faced in practice to support the development of preservice teachers' understanding of professional ethics (Husu & Tirri, 2001); and (d) information on how to advocate for the rights of disadvantaged populations, including individuals with disabilities (Peters & Reid, 2009)" (p.33).

Finally, and most importantly, the first set of CEC high-leverage practices (McLeskey et al., 2017) focuses by design on collaboration between professionals. The authors specifically describe the importance of collaboration and note that "collaboration is a means to an end, that is a way professionals work together to design and deliver directly and indirectly a wide range of services for students with disabilities" (McLeskey et al., 2017, p. 31). Without collaboration between and among professionals, the modern-day practices associated with special education are not likely to exist and students would not experience the levels of learning and support necessary to move forward in their daily lives.

Component 1.3. Candidates design and implement professional learning activities based on ongoing analysis of student learning; self-reflection; and professional standards, research, and contemporary practices.

Supporting Explanation. Candidates engage in professional learning activities and participate actively in peer and professional learning communities that benefit individuals with exceptionalities and their families, colleagues, and their own professional growth. They keep current with research and contemporary practices in multiple ways. For example, they participate in professional associations, conferences, and online professional learning networks, and they access resources from libraries and internet sites.

Drawing on that knowledge, they design and implement professional learning experiences to improve their skills that include areas for growth, goals, and strategies to accomplish those goals. Candidates regularly reflect on their professional performance, why they used specific practices and the impact on students, families, and other professionals. They adjust their practices based on this reflection and assessment of student performance. Candidates recognize their own skill limitations and know when to turn to others for guidance and support to meet the needs of students with exceptionalities and their families.

Knowledge Base. The need for professional development based on analysis of student learning has been well documented. For example, InTASC indicates that there is fairly strong research support for its Standard 9: The teacher engages in ongoing professional learning and uses evidence to continually evaluate his/her practice, particularly the effects of his/her choices and actions on others (learners, families, other professionals, and the community), and adapts practice to meet the needs of each learner (CCSSO, 2011). Evidence is primarily cited from the National Board for Professional Teaching Standards (NBPTS).

Multiple studies cited by NBPTS, such as Cavalluzzo, Barron, and Henderson (2014), and Vandervoort, Amrein-Beardsley, & Berliner (2004), indicate that teachers who have completed the NBPTS certification process have a more positive impact on student achievement. The NBPTS Exceptional Needs Standard XII Reflective Practice indicates that "exceptional needs teachers participate in a wide range of reflective practices to foster professional growth that leads to improvements in educating students with exceptional needs. They engage in continual self-evaluation activities regarding what they know and are able to do. They examine their own strengths and weaknesses and employ that knowledge in the analysis and planning of instruction" (NBPTS, 2010, p.73). Turnbull et al. (2015) also indicate that reflections on interactions with families and other professionals provide opportunities for teachers to assess their skills and determine needs for further development.

As indicated in the CAEP K-6 Elementary Teacher Preparation Program Standards (CAEP, 2018), self-study has developed into a powerful way for teacher educators to understand their own practices and the process of learning to teach (Loughran, 2005). The concept of self-study grew out of the teacher educator's desire to critically investigate and analyze their practice in teaching and mentoring students through collaborative reflections, applying reflective questions rather than adopting traditional strategies of guiding and advising (Loughran, 2005). Self-study stimulates teacher educators to continuously pay attention to their teaching and their students' learning, which are high primacies, intrinsically interrelated and constantly interacting with one another (Mukeredzi, 2014). It focuses on how teaching and learning experiences encourage teacher educators to see their practice in a different way (Bullock, 2012).

Polly et al. (2015) stated that learner-centered professional development calls for educators to: a) focus on student learning data to identify the focus of activities, b) provide active learning experiences that give educators some ownership of their activities, c) simultaneously develop knowledge of content and pedagogy, d) provide ongoing support that includes collaboration with colleagues and more knowledgeable professionals, and e) support teachers' efforts to implement new pedagogies in their classroom and support reflective activities that allow teachers to process their learning.

In order to access professional development, NBPTS indicates that teachers pursue both independent and organized professional development opportunities through videoconferencing, professional libraries, observing others, engaging in interacting with other professionals, and paying attention to what they learn from them (NBPTS, 2010).

The CEC Professional and Ethical Practice Standards (2010) which guide practice in the field provide support for this standard. They include "maintaining a high level of professional competence" (p. 1); "using evidence, instructional data, research, and professional knowledge to inform practice" (p. 1); "engaging in the improvement of the professional through active participation in professional organizations" (p. 1); and "participation in the growth and dissemination of professional knowledge and skills" (p. 1)

Standard 2: Understanding and Addressing Each Individual's Developmental and Learning Needs

Candidates use their understanding of human growth and development, the multiple influences on develop-ment, individual differences, diversity including exceptionalities, and families and communities to plan and implement inclusive learning environments and experiences that provide individuals with exceptionalities high-quality learning experiences reflective of each individual's strengths and needs.

Component 2.1. Candidates apply understanding of human growth and development to create developmentally appropriate and meaningful learning experiences that address individualized strengths and needs of students with exceptionalities.

Supporting Explanation. Candidates know how all individuals grow and develop, and they understand developmental milestones from birth through 21 years. They recognize that patterns of learning and development vary individually within and across the cognitive, linguistic, social, emotional, ethical, and physical domains. Candidates further understand that development in different domains occurs at different times for individuals in different contexts. Candidates use this knowledge and understanding to plan, implement, and assess developmentally appropriate and challenging learning experiences and environments. Candidates know and understand how learning occurs, how individuals construct knowledge, acquire skills, and develop disciplined thinking processes. Candidates further understand that each individual's cognitive, linguistic, social, emotional, ethical, and physical development influences learning. They also understand how development in any one domain may affect performance in others and how all together they influence learning. Candidates use this knowledge and understanding to make instructional decisions that build on individuals' strengths and needs and to select and use instructional strategies that promote learning.

From a framework of typical growth, development, and learning, candidates understand how different exceptionalities can interact with development and learning. They create developmentally appropriate learning experiences relevant to the learners' strengths and needs to provide meaningful and individualized learning experiences for children and youth with exceptionalities. Candidates understand that exceptionalities can interact with multiple domains of human development to influence an individual's learning in school, community, and throughout life. Candidates use this understanding to effectively apply strategies based on developmental principles so that individuals will be increasingly engaged, thus improving their learning outcomes.

Knowledge Base. Individuals have different experiences, capacities, needs, interests, and backgrounds. Candidates facilitate learning by recognizing these differences and using instructional approaches, methods, and strategies that are appropriate for each individual. Instruction that uses developmentally, culturally, and linguistically appropriate and effective teaching approaches to enhance each child's learning and development is emphasized in standards from the National Association for the Education of Young Children (NAEYC, 2010; Standards 1 and 3) and Standard 1 from the National Board of Professional Teaching Standards (NBPTS, 2010). These standards highlight building on learners' knowledge and skills related to developmental benchmarks and milestones, while addressing individual needs that influence learning. Candidates promote learning and improve learning outcomes by identifying and prioritizing appropriate learning goals that guide thinking and learning through the use of various instructional methods, processes, and practices. The CEC HLP 11 (McLeskey et al., 2017) emphasizes the importance of setting appropriate instructional goals to student success. These standards and high-leverage practices have emerged as effective frameworks for the provision of developmentally appropriate tasks for developing learners (e.g., Barnett et al., 2008; NAEYC Standard 4; NBPTS Early Childhood Standard 7).

An awareness of individual variability is essential for the provision of adaptive and effective learning environments to assure academic success for all students. The CEC Division for Early Childhood Recommended Practices A3, A4, and INS1 (DEC, 2014) emphasize the use of assessment and instructional approaches that are appropriate for the child's age and level of development; accommodate the child's sensory, physical, communication, cultural, linguistic, social, and emotional characteristics; and address each child's strengths, needs, and interests.

It is now widely acknowledged that cognitive development does not proceed in a predictable linear fashion for all children. Children's cognitive abilities (e.g., memory, utilization of effective self-regulatory strategies, etc.) vary and develop on differing trajectories that do not follow age-related progressions.

Whereas the cognitive developmental milestones identified by Piaget (1936) and others are acknowledged, current research on cognitive development in children identifies much variation across individuals, as well as across groups and cultures (Feldman, 2013). Moreover, it is now widely acknowledged that cognitive development in children is influenced by a number of contextual variables, including each individual's linguistic, social, emotional, and physical development (Kyllonen, 2016).

InTASC Standard 2 (Learner Differences) notes in particular that candidates should consider the needs of individual students for various aspects of language development (CCSSO, 2011). Thus, children in any given class may vary widely in their cognitive, linguistic, social, emotional, and physical development and abilities. Therefore, it is critical for candidates to be aware of the developmental milestones for typical development, as well as the specific needs for individual children, to match curriculum and instruction appropriately to the developmental readiness of the child.

Component 2.2 Candidates use their knowledge and understanding of multiple influences on individual development and learning to plan and implement learning experiences and environments.

Supporting Explanation. Candidates understand the multiple social, cultural, biological, physical, and psychological influences that affect learning and development when working with individuals with exceptionalities. They know that diversity includes individual differences such as personality, ability, interests, health, and life experiences, as well as group differences, including race, ethnicity, gender identity, gender expression, sexual orientation, nationality, language, religion, political affiliation, and socioeconomic background. Individual learning differences are manifested in areas such as differing rates of learning, motivation, attention, complexity of reasoning, persistence, foundational knowledge and skills, and preferred learning and response modes. Furthermore, candidates understand that individuals bring assets for learning based on their unique experiences, abilities, talents, prior learning, and peer and social group interactions, as well as home language, family, culture, and community values. Candidates know that development and learning occur within the contexts of specific families, languages, cultures, and communities as well as within a larger societal context.

Candidates use their knowledge and understanding of diverse factors that influence individual learning and development to plan and implement individualized instruction, which includes attention to an individual's personal, family, and community experiences as well as cultural norms. Candidates know and understand how home language, family, and culture interact with exceptionalities to influence the individual's academic and social abilities, attitudes, values, interests, and career and postsecondary options. Candidates not only understand these influences, but they structure and implement instruction that reflects the diversity of the learner and make informed decisions about content, which includes attention to the learner's personal, family, and community experiences as well as cultural norms. Furthermore, candidates reflect on and understand how their own experiences, family, race, gender, and culture biases may influence their instructional decisions and their relationships and interactions with learners and their families.

Candidates understand that the beliefs, traditions, and values across and within cultures can influence relationships among and between individuals, their families, and the school community. By understanding these influences, candidates structure and implement instruction that reflects the diversity of the learner with exceptionalities and make informed decisions about content, which includes attention to the learner's personal, family, and community experiences. Candidates use understanding of the interaction of an individual's areas of exceptionality, home language, family, culture, and other significant contextual factors to plan and implement instruction and learning environments that address the learner's strengths and needs. Candidates also use knowledge of families, culture, and community when involving paraprofessionals, general educators, specialists, resources, and supports to create and incorporate strategies for making content and instruction accessible and challenging for individuals with exceptionalities

Additionally, candidates ensure inclusive learning environments that enable individuals with exceptionalities and diverse backgrounds to meet high standards. Candidates design environments, curriculum, and instruction in ways that are accessible to all learners and that use each learner's strengths to promote growth.

Knowledge Base. The standards of several professional associations emphasize knowing and understanding the individual and combined contributions of students' diverse backgrounds, abilities, development, and experiences; the importance of family, culture, language, community, context, and opportunities to learn; and collaborating with essential partners when planning instruction and designing appropriate and supportive learning experiences for students. Specifically, InTASC Standard 1 (Learner Development) and Standard 2 (Learning Differences) identify essential information about the learner, including having knowledge regarding patterns of development within and across critical areas of cognitive, linguistic, social, emotional, and physical areas, in addition to understanding individual, cultural, and community-based differences (CCSSO, 2011). Similarly, teachers use their knowledge and understanding of the essential contribution of students' diverse backgrounds and experiences to their overall learning and development when designing appropriate, supportive, flexible, and inclusive learning environments. InTASC Standard 7 (Planning for Instruction) emphasizes that in order to plan effectively, teachers must purposefully access their knowledge of individual learners (CCSSO, 2011).

The CEC Initial Preparation Standards (CEC, 2015) further support the knowledge and skills reflected in this component. Specifically, Standard 1 (Learner Development and Individual Learning Differences) identifies the need for understanding the interaction of exceptionalities, individual differences, language, cultural, and family background on learning. CEC high-leverage practices in special education (McLeskey et al., 2017)—specifically HLP 11 (Identify and Prioritize Long- and Short-Term Learning Goals), HLP 12 (Systematically Design Instruction toward a Specific Learning Goal), and HLP 13 (Adapt Curriculum Tasks and Materials for Specific Learning Goals)—recognize the need for teachers to incorporate knowledge about students' backgrounds, language, and culture into their instructional decisions.

Other national organizations that address similar competencies for beginning educators include the National Association for the Education of Young Children (NAEYC, 2019) and the National Board for Professional "Exceptional Needs" Standards (NBPTS, 2010). The NAEYC Standard 1 (Child

Development and Learning in Context) and Standard 2 (Family Partnerships) as well as the NBPTS Standard 1 (Knowledge of Students), Standard 3 (Diversity), and Standard 4 (Family Partnerships) require candidates to have a foundational understanding of the multiple factors that influence development and learning. They understand students' individual needs and differences, diversity, and the importance of effective collaboration with families in order to achieve students' educational goals while creating quality and supportive learning environments and opportunities.

According to the National Center for Education Statistics, a significant growing number of students since 2004 have come from diverse backgrounds with increases specifically in Hispanic students and those identified as English language learners (McFarland et al., 2017). In addition to language and culture, research supports the need for an expanded conceptualization of diversity while understanding the importance of the simultaneous interaction of students' individual differences as well as responses to those differences (García & Ortiz, 2013). Educators must consider the diversity students bring with them to the classroom when designing appropriate instructional supports (Baker et al., 2014; Esparza-Brown & Sanford, 2011; Francis et al., 2006; García & Ortiz, 2013; Goldenberg, Rueda, & August, 2006; Ortiz & Robertson, 2018).

Moreover, research supports the need for teachers to reflect on their own understanding, experiences, and perspectives with diversity and how these can influence and positively inform their practice (Kozleski & Waitoller, 2010; Oritz & Robertson, 2018). Educators anticipate and plan for learner variability as part of their instructional planning and delivery systems. Specifically, by employing universal design for learning (Israel, Ribuffo, & Smith, 2014) and culturally responsive frameworks (Esparza-Brown & Doolittle, 2008; García & Ortiz, 2008; Ortiz & Robertson, 2018), educators consider students' diversity, individual needs, and experiences in advance in order to increase access while reducing barriers to learning.

Standard 3: Demonstrating Subject Matter Content and Specialized Curricular Knowledge

Candidates apply their understanding of the academic subject matter content of the general curriculum and specialized curricula to inform their programmatic and instructional decisions for learners with exceptionalities

Component 3.1. Candidates apply their understanding of academic subject matter content of the general curriculum to inform their programmatic and instructional decisions for individuals with exceptionalities.

Supporting Explanation. The phrase *academic subject matter* means the content of the general curriculum, including mathematics, reading, English/language arts, science, social studies, and the arts. It does not necessarily include the additional specialized knowledge and skills that special educators must possess in areas such as reading, writing, and mathematics (CEC Policy Paper on Academic Subject Matter Content for the General Curriculum and Special Educators, n.d.). Candidates have foundational understanding of the generalized content standards appropriate to the developmental and instructional levels of the students served. Candidates demonstrate an understanding of the applicable national and state/regional academic content standards and assessments, especially those focused on literacy and mathematics.

With an understanding of individual strengths, needs, and future goals derived from comprehensive assessments, candidates identify academic content standards necessary for students with exceptionalities to progress in their individualized programs towards appropriate completion requirements. Candidates develop individualized goals and objectives aligned as appropriate with general education curriculum and standards to meet the needs of each learner with exceptional needs. Candidates also provide modified access to subject-specific instructional materials to address individual learner needs in different contexts, including specialized and general classrooms.

Candidates possess solid foundational understanding of the general content area curricula (i.e., mathematics, reading, English/language arts, science, social studies, and the arts), sufficient to collaborate with general educators in teaching or co-teaching academic subject matter content of the general curriculum to students with exceptional learning needs across a wide range of performance levels. They design appropriate learning and performance accommodations and modifications for students with exceptional learning needs in academic subject matter content of the general curriculum. When a candidate assumes sole responsibility for teaching an academic subject matter class at the secondary level, the candidate should have sufficient foundational subject matter content knowledge to assure the students can meet state curriculum standards.

Candidates design appropriate learning and performance accommodations and modifications for individuals with exceptional learning needs in academic subject matter content of the general curriculum to address the specific goals and objectives of the individual's learning plan. In addition, candidates are knowledgeable of and have the skills to employ appropriate instructional and assistive technologies in face-to-face, virtual, or hybrid settings to meet the learning goals and curricular standards for students with exceptional learning needs in academic subject matter content of the general curricula.

Knowledge Base. InTASC Standards 4 (Content Knowledge) and 5 (Application of Content) delineate how teachers must have a deep understanding of their subject matter content, including central concepts, structure of the disciplines, and tools of inquiry, as well as be able to apply the content knowledge in a variety of contexts (CCSSO, 2013). This further aligns with CAEP Elementary Standard 2 (Understanding and Applying Content and Curricular Knowledge for Teaching), which provides guidance for candidates to demonstrate understanding of major concepts in core curricular areas such as literacy, mathematics, science, and social studies (CAEP, 2018). The CEC Policy on Academic Subject Matter Content highlights the need for special educators to "have a solid subject matter content knowledge base sufficient to assure the students can meet state curriculum standards" (n.d.). Several of the CEC high-leverage practices relate to academic subject matter content of the general education curriculum: HLP 11 (Identify and Prioritize Long- and Short-term Goals), HLP 13 (Adapt Curriculum Tasks for Specific Learning Goals), and HLP 16 (Use Explicit Instruction) (McLeskey et al., 2017).

U.S. federal legislation—the Individuals with Disabilities Education Act (IDEA) of 2004—guarantees individualized accommodations and specially designed instruction as part of the individualized education program and assures each student with a disability has the necessary instruction and support to have access to the general education curriculum as appropriate within the least restrictive environment. Further clarifying the intent of IDEA, in 2017 the U.S. Supreme Court issued a unanimous ruling in Endrew F. v. Douglas County School District (Opinion #15-827) emphasizing that full inclusion is the primary standard with the "child progressing smoothly through the regular curriculum." Alignment of individualized instruction with applicable national, state or provincial, and local curriculum standards is essential in order for students with disabilities to make demonstrable progress toward degree completion (Slanda & Little, 2018).

Special educators teach in settings as diverse as the students they serve. They may serve as a core subject teacher, a co-teacher, or an itinerant teacher in a self-contained or general education elementary, middle, or secondary school setting. A qualitative study to investigate skill domains considered essential for special educator effectiveness found consensus among special education teachers, administrators, and teacher educators on the importance of mastery of the general education curriculum (Woolf, 2019). Special educators must be knowledgeable in the core curriculum and secondary curriculum as dictated for the students they serve (NBPTS, 2010).

Beyond knowledge of applicable curriculum standards, special educators must also understand the critical components, key themes or big ideas, and learning progressions within the major subject matter content areas of general education (i.e., reading, writing, math, science, and social studies) in order to prioritize goals for individualized programs and to ensure that students with disabilities master critical prerequisite and foundational skills (Alber-Morgan et al., 2019). Therefore, knowledge of the general education curriculum, standards, and evidence-based practices are paramount to teacher preparation in special education (Little & Slanda, 2017).

Based on reviews of many studies of the impact of curriculum on student learning, Hattie (2009) noted the importance of balancing surface and deep understanding within subject areas to achieve "conceptual clarity" (p. 35). Hughes, Riccomini, and Morris (2019) emphasize clarity as an important aspect of explicit instruction and describe content knowledge as a key element of explicit instruction as follows:

> Content involves selecting academic skills that are important, that is, that are used frequently, now and in the future. It also includes

arranging content in ways that are logical (e.g., in sequence, separating similar skills and concepts initially to avoid confusion), as well as segmenting or "chunking" complex or multi-step skills and strategies for instruction in order to reduce cognitive load by teaching smaller amounts at a time (p. 216).

Component 3.2. Candidates augment the general education curriculum to address skills and strategies that students with disabilities need to access the core curriculum and function successfully within a variety of contexts as well as the continuum of placement options to assure specially designed instruction is developed and implemented to achieve mastery of curricular standards and individualized goals and objectives.

Supporting Explanation. Candidates apply their knowledge of individual learner characteristics and specialized curricula to make accommodations, modify, and/or adapt the curricula across contexts, including the community, home, and school. Candidates know that individual learners may require more specialized curricula than is appropriate for typically developing peers. Candidates are familiar with specialized curricula which may include curriculum for social skills, life skills, transition, orientation and mobility, social-emotional learning, independence, and self-advocacy.

With an understanding of individual strengths, needs, and future goals derived from comprehensive assessments, candidates identify appropriate specialized curricula and develop individualized goals and objectives aligned as appropriate with those curricula to meet the needs of each learner. Candidates also provide modified access to instructional materials to address individual learner needs in different contexts, while considering the continuum of placement options. Candidates design appropriate learning and performance accommodations and modifications for individuals with exceptional learning needs using specialized curricula. They use this knowledge to design effective and universally accessible environments and learning experiences.

Candidates recognize barriers to accessibility and acceptance of individuals with exceptionalities and plan for ways to address those barriers through the implementation of specialized curricula. Candidates design learning environments that adhere to universal design principles and that facilitate active participation, self-advocacy, and independence of individuals with exceptionalities in a variety of group and individual learning activities. In addition, candidates are knowledgeable of and implement appropriate instructional, adaptive, and assistive technologies, including augmentative and alternative communication devices as well as technologies to meet the learning goals of students with exceptionalities using specialized curricula.

Knowledge Base. InTASC Standard 4 (Content Knowledge 4) supports the need for specialized curricula, stating that "[t]he teacher realizes that content knowledge is not a fixed body of facts but is complex, culturally situated, and ever evolving" (CCSSO, 2013, p. 13). CEC's Initial Common Specialty Items (2015) include adapted curriculum across specialty sets, including Blind and Visual Impairments, Deaf and Hard of Hearing, and Early Childhood/Early Intervention, and include an item stipulating that candidates should be prepared to "select, adapt, and use instructional strategies and materials according to characteristics of the individual with exceptionalities" (ICSI.5.515, p. 6).

IDEA requires the use of specialized curricula, as appropriate, for individuals with exceptionalities, as indicated in the following:

> "Special education means specially designed instruction, at no cost to parents, to meet the unique needs of a child with a disability... Specially designed instruction means adapting as appropriate to the needs of an eligible child under this part, the content, methodology, or delivery of instruction" (34 CFR.300.39).

Individualizing content to meet the unique needs of a child with a disability may involve targeting knowledge and skills that go beyond what is provided in the ongoing general education program to include "access skills" that are not directly linked to specific subject matter standards but are critical to enable a student to engage with the content (Alber-Morgan et al., 2019). These efforts to expand the general education curriculum are "curriculum augmentations" which provide additional skills or strategies necessary to support student success (Lee et al., 2009; Lee et al., 2010). Examples of access or augmentation skills often targeted as instructional goals to be taught explicitly to students with disabilities include learning-to-learn, self-management, attention, social skills, functional communication, learning strategies, and foundational academic skills (Alber-Morgan et al., 2019; Deshler et al., 2004; Lee et al., 2009; Lee et al., 2010).

CEC included the teaching of cognitive and metacognitive strategies to support learning and independence as one of its high-leverage practices (HLP 14; McLeskey et al. 2017). To assist teachers with the selection of appropriate strategies for specific student needs, Budin, Patti, and Rafferty (2019) emphasized the importance of teaching cognitive and metacognitive strategies explicitly using evidence-based practices and routines, and they provided a list of online resources that offer a range of research-validated strategies to address typical academic, social, and/or behavioral challenges.

Additional curricular priorities emerge when planning for adolescents and their approaching transitions to postsecondary environments. Beyond the general education requirements for course and degree completion, individualized transition programs must address education, training, employment, and independent living skills needed to assist students with disabilities in reaching their personalized postsecondary goals (U.S. Department of Education, 2017).

Relevant domains for the planning of instruction and learning experiences include education, training, and employment options, as well as skill development for independent living, leisure pursuits, community involvement, and physical and emotional health (IRIS Center, 2016). Research has identified evidence-based instructional strategies (Curda, 2018; Kamil, 2008; Landmark, Ju, & Zhang, 2010, among others), taxonomies (Kohler, 1996), and policy frameworks (Kohler et al., 2016; Newman et al., 2011) to guide transition program development. Candidates must be able to teach curriculum standards while providing unique, specially designed instruction to each individual student with a disability (Leko et al., 2015).

Standard 4: Using Assessment to Understand the Learner and the Learning Environment for Data-Based Decision Making

Candidates assess students' learning, behavior, and the classroom environment to evaluate and support classroom and school-based problem-solving systems of intervention and instruction. Candidates evaluate students to determine their strengths and needs, contribute to students' eligibility determination, communicate students' progress, inform short and long-term instructional planning, and make ongoing adjustments to instruction using technology as appropriate.

Component 4.1. Candidates collaboratively develop, select, administer, analyze, and interpret multiple measures of student learning, behavior, and the classroom environment to evaluate and support classroom and school-based systems of intervention for students with and without exceptionalities.

Supporting Explanation. Candidates' skill in progress monitoring, explicit and targeted instruction, data-based decision making, and supporting students with varying needs allows them to provide, monitor, evaluate, and improve evidence-based instruction and interventions for all students. To this end, candidates actively and collaboratively engage with educational professionals and families in ongoing, data-based decision making to evaluate and improve school and classroom environments, instruction, and intervention across varying levels of support, as, for example, in multi-tiered systems of support (MTSS).

Candidates may participate as members of a school's site-based support team—collaborating with administrators, school psychologists, school counselors, classroom teachers, teacher leaders, school social workers, and others—to ensure the academic and social emotional learning needs are met in a holistic manner. As members of these teams, candidates individually and collaboratively, as appropriate, develop, select, and administer multiple measures. They may also be members of student problem-solving teams using evaluation data for the purpose of supporting individual and/or groups of students with and without exceptionalities. Candidates may collaboratively contribute as members of school-based teams in the selection, analysis, and use of data from a variety of sources (e.g., universal screening, healthy school surveys, family surveys, office referrals, state language and achievement reports, community resources) to inform building-level decisions around tiered behavioral and instructional practices such as whole class accommodations, small group intervention, and individualized support.

As part of this process, candidates participate in evaluating the effectiveness of existing school resources, programs, supports, and initiatives to improve school climate, professional development opportunities, academic, social/emotional, linguistic, and behavioral supports for all students. As members of a school's problem-solving team, candidates support individual students without exceptionalities, who may experience difficulty in the classroom and at school by collaborating with educational professionals and families through the problem-solving process (problem identification, problem analysis, plan development, plan implementation, and plan evaluation). To this end, candidates jointly analyze multiple measures to document and critically examine school, classroom, curricular, instructional, home, student, and other factors that may contribute to a student's learning and behavioral strengths and needs. Candidates use these data to make collaborative decisions to improve outcomes for students placed at risk for learning and behavior difficulties.

Knowledge Base. Candidate activities related to the assessment of student learning, behavior, and the classroom environment to support classroom and school-based systems of intervention for students with and without exceptionalities are addressed in InTASC Standards 2, 6 and 7. These standards consider learner differences, using formative and summative assessment to support and guide students' learning, collecting information to minimize sources of bias, collaborating with others to analyze student progress while using results to guide instructional planning, and using multiple measures of student performance to target students' learning needs (CCSSO, 2011).

Candidates' assessment practices included in this component can also be found in the CEC 2012 Standard 4 and HLP 4 and HLP 5, where candidates use multiple sources of data that are appropriate and technically sound, in collaboration with colleagues and families, to make educational decisions regarding students (McLeskey et al., 2017). Furthermore, this component relates to National Association of School Psychologists (NASP) Domains 1 and 9 and HLP 6, specifically, data-based decision making and accountability (McLeskey et al., 2017; NASP, 2010). This involves candidates' use of assessment methods and data collection to identify students' strengths and needs for the purpose of developing services and programs and measuring students' ongoing progress

and outcomes. In sum, candidates use assessment methods and processes to construct, implement, and evaluate interventions, services, programs, and systems designed to improve academic, social, and behavioral outcomes for individuals and groups of students.

National committees and work groups, such as the President's Commission on Excellence in Special Education (2002), have called for improved methods of teaching and supporting students in need of additional academic, social, and behavioral instruction. The Every Student Succeeds Act (2015), the primary education law in K-12 public schools in the United States, calls out MTSS specifically as a framework for supporting *all* students through a comprehensive coordination of services and supports for academic, social skills, and behavior.

Such efforts are meant to avoid "wait-to-fail" models for identifying students with more significant learning and behavioral needs. MTSS requires educators to implement periodic screening, ongoing progress monitoring, and data-based decision making as part of a targeted and intensive multilevel prevention and intervention for learners in need of additional support, including students with disabilities, to improve students' academic achievement, behavior, and social-emotional functioning (Esparza-Brown & Doolittle, 2008; Fuchs, Fuchs, & Compton, 2012; IRIS Center, 2015; Jung et al., 2018; National Center on Response to Intervention, 2010).

Within a multi-tiered framework, the special educator's role and responsibilities related to assessment may vary. However, it is likely to include assisting with (a) selecting tools and procedures, (b) implementing screening and progress monitoring with students, and/or (c) training, supporting, and coordinating other educators and staff to collect this data. The special educator may also collaborate with other appropriate personnel to interpret data for the purpose of making educational decisions to improve student outcomes (McLeskey et al., 2019). Recommendation 9 from the Committee on the Foundations of Assessment from the National Research Council notes that "instruction in how students learn and how learning can be assessed should be a major component of teacher preservice and professional development programs" (National Research Council, 2001).

The research clearly supports the use of initial and ongoing documentation or monitoring of student performance to identify and monitor diverse students in need of additional targeted instruction within a tiered model of service delivery (Richards-Tutor, Aceves, & Reese, 2016). For students exhibiting more intensive learning needs, research on data-based individualization (Jung et al., 2018; Kearns, Pollack, & Whaley, 2019; National Center on Intensive Intervention, 2013) provides a foundation for conducting such assessment for the purpose of intensifying instruction for students with exceptionalities.

To support individual and groups of students, special educators engage in collaborative problem-solving and data-based decision making. This is considered an essential skill set for beginning special educators (Lembke et al., 2019) and specifically within the context of providing early intervention and prevention efforts within an MTSS structure. Collaborative problem-solving involves analyzing the need for and the appropriateness of a problem-solving process; analyzing a problem; generating, evaluating, and selecting potential solutions; implementing those solutions; evaluating the effectiveness of selected solutions; and choosing to continue, adjust, or discontinue selected solutions as appropriate given the data (Lembke et al., 2019; McLeskey et al., 2019). Special education teachers ensure these components are culturally responsive (Esparza-Brown & Doolittle, 2008).

Component 4.2. Candidates develop, select, administer, and interpret multiple, formal and informal, culturally and linguistically appropriate measures and procedures that are valid and reliable to contribute to eligibility determination for special education services.

Supporting Explanation. Candidates serve as part of larger, multidisciplinary teams when evaluating students for special education services. Candidates contribute to eligibility determination by developing, selecting, and administering multiple assessments to evaluate students' academic and behavioral strengths and needs. Candidates develop informal assessments such as observation tools or family interviews to determine how students access and demonstrate knowledge in the core curriculum and other contextually relevant curricula such as adaptive behavior skills. Candidates select and administer culturally and linguistically appropriate formal assessments that systematically measure how well a student has mastered

learning outcomes. They understand constructs of validity and reliability and their impact on assessment selection and interpretation of results. Candidates use this knowledge as they work collaboratively with teams to administer assessments and interpret results in contributing to eligibility determination.

Throughout this process, candidates understand how students' cultural and linguistic diversity and family backgrounds impact the selection, administration, and interpretation of assessment results. Candidates understand how these results contribute to eligibility determination, understand the limitations of formal and informal assessments such as biases and test constructs, and consider contextual factors such as socioeconomic status, family structure, and previous instruction that may influence accurate interpretation based on individual student characteristics, including race, gender, gender identity, and cultural identity. Candidates collaborate with professionals with additional expertise as needed, for example, school psychologists, physical therapists, occupational therapists, speech-language pathologists, vision specialists, hearing specialists, assistive technology specialists, English as a second language specialists, bilingual specialists, social workers, or translators, to ensure an appropriate and valid assessment process.

Knowledge Base. The use of multiple methods of assessment to engage learners and to guide the candidate's decision making is emphasized in InTASC Standard 6 (CCSSO, 2011). Specifically, 6(a) indicates the teacher balances the use of formative and summative assessment as appropriate to support, verify, and document learning; 6(b) calls for designing assessments that match learning objectives with assessment methods and minimizes sources of bias that can distort assessment results; and 6(g) indicates the teacher effectively uses multiple and appropriate types of assessment data to identify each student's learning needs and to develop differentiated learning experiences. Administration of formative and summative assessments to determine students' competencies and learning needs is also included in the CAEP Elementary Standards in Standard 3, Key Element 3a (CAEP, 2018). This standard highlights the use of multiple, unbiased assessments to determine student needs.

Furthermore, using multiple methods of assessment and data sources in making educational decisions is emphasized in CEC Standard 4 (2015), as candidates select and use technically sound formal and informal assessments that minimize bias, use knowledge of measurement principles and practices to interpret assessment results, and use multiple types of assessment information in making decisions about individuals with exceptionalities. CEC also includes the use of multiple sources of information to develop a comprehensive understanding of a student's strengths and needs in its high-leverage practices (HLPs) (McLeskey et al., 2017). Specifically, HLP 4 refers to the use of multiple sources of information that are sensitive to language and culture to create profiles of student's strengths and needs, a first step in eligibility determinations. The CEC Division for Early Childhood Recommended Practices also emphasize the use of a variety of methods to gather assessment information from multiple sources, the use of assessment results to identify a child's current levels of functioning, and to determine the child's eligibility, and the use of culturally and linguistically appropriate assessment tools with sufficient sensitivity to detect child progress (see A3, A6, A8, A10; DEC, 2014, p. 8).

The National Board for Professional Teaching Standards emphasizes the need for candidates to design, select, and use a variety of assessments to obtain accurate, useful, and timely information about student learning and development (NBPTS, 2010). Finally, this component relates to National Association of School Psychologists Domain 1 (Data-Based Decision Making and Accountability) (NASP, 2010). This involves candidates systematically collecting data from multiple sources and using ecological factors as the context for all assessment and intervention decisions.

The Individuals with Disabilities Education Act (IDEA, 2004) requires that comprehensive evaluations of students with exceptionalities use a variety of assessment tools and strategies to develop an adequate picture of a student's strengths and needs (IDEA regulations, 2012, 34 CFR.300.304[b]; Center for Parent Information and Resources, 2014). As the special education teacher, the candidate plays a major role in the development of this "picture" as part of the eligibility determination team. Therefore, it is crucial that the candidate also understand the challenges of accurately assessing students from culturally and linguistically diverse backgrounds, as this population of students is disproportionately represented in special education due to inadequate evaluations (see Abedi, 2006; Chu & Flores, 2011; Linn & Hemmer, 2011; U.S. Department of Education, 2016; Zhang et al., 2014).

As with the previously mentioned standards and federal mandates, CEC HLP 4 recommends that special educators contribute to the development of individual learner profiles. These profiles should be created from a collection of information from a variety of sources. These could include comprehensive, multidisciplinary assessments; discussions with students' family members; curriculum-based measurement data; student interviews and surveys; inventories, classroom checklists, and student work samples; and direct observation of classroom performance and behavior. The information should be synthesized in order to develop a comprehensive understanding of each student. The synthesis of information can be used to develop a comprehensive profile of an individual student's strengths, needs, interests, and motivation in different areas, both academic and nonacademic. Understandings gained from these individual profiles can be used to communicate with professionals and parents in order to develop a team-based approach to the education of students with disabilities (McLeskey et al., 2017).

Finally, effective special educators are able to describe their students' academic, behavioral, and motivational needs in great detail (Bishop et al., 2010; Seo et al., 2008). Although a multidisciplinary team works together to determine eligibility, it may often be the special educator who has more in-depth knowledge of the student and family, therefore making the understanding of assessment tools and the appropriate use of assessment results critical for candidates (McLeskey et al., 2017).

Component 4.3. Candidates assess, collaboratively analyze, interpret, and communicate students' progress toward measurable outcomes, using technology as appropriate, to inform both short- and long-term planning, and make ongoing adjustments to instruction.

Supporting Explanation. Candidates engage in ongoing data-based decision making to inform immediate classroom practices, short-term goal development, and long-term planning using data regarding students' performance. These multi-sourced formative assessments should delineate individual student's strengths and academic and/or behavioral needs related to curricular standards and goals, and be used to develop, implement, evaluate, and revise instruction and interventions as needed. Candidates collect formative assessment data by regularly monitoring students' performance to ensure appropriate progress towards goal attainment.

Candidates work with educational professionals (e.g., general educators, speech-language pathologists, assistive technology specialists, full individualized education program teams) to conduct ongoing formal and informal assessments that are individualized to meet the needs of each student. They work collaboratively with teams to analyze and interpret results of multiple assessments across settings for each student. Candidates use results to determine if students are making adequate progress toward measurable outcomes.

Candidates are responsible for regularly monitoring students' ongoing progress as a critical component of the instruction and assessment cycle, including planning, teaching, assessing, and analyzing. Conducting short-term assessment may involve daily, weekly, monthly, and/or other periodic evaluation of students' immediate learning needs and goals. Candidates use brief, formal or informal, curriculum-based (e.g., oral reading fluency), performance-based, criterion-referenced measures, and/or observational tools or methods (e.g., progress logs, interval recording, frequency counts) appropriate for the student. They use these data regularly to observe, document, synthesize, and analyze a student's performance to identify consistencies and/or inconsistencies. They also use these to purposefully guide immediate instructional changes (e.g., increase, adjust, decrease targeted instruction) and supportive practices as needed.

Candidates support students in understanding their own assessment data and using those results to self-monitor and self-regulate. Candidates document students' performance outcomes and corresponding adjustments to instruction, for example, graphing instructional changes, and they use this documentation to provide detailed, task-specific feedback to learners about their achievement and engagement. Candidates regularly communicate progress and adjustments to instruction with family members and other educational professionals to support individual student's progress towards short-term and long-term outcomes.

Candidates collaboratively use assessment results to inform students' long-term planning (e.g., individualized education program development). As a member of a multidisciplinary team, candidates' evaluation of students' ongoing and annual academic, behavioral, social/emotional, and/or linguistic strengths and needs directly informs annual goal development and the type, frequency, location, and duration of students' special education services. Evaluation for long-term planning requires candidates to select formal and informal measures and methods that are culturally and linguistically appropriate and technically sound. Candidates consider sufficient opportunities for student learning and recognize the need for joint interpretation of data across settings and evaluations in collaboration with the multidisciplinary team.

Conducting ongoing assessment and progress monitoring requires candidates to use technology/assistive technology for specific purposes, including test administration, testing accommodations, data storage, creating digital documents and logs, and charting and graphing results to identify patterns in learning and/or behavior. Candidates may use screening software programs in face-to-face or virtual formats as appropriate, considering ongoing advancements in technology.

Knowledge Base. The assessment, analysis, interpretation, and communication of students' progress toward measurable outcomes for the purpose of contributing to short- and long-term planning and instruction are addressed in several professional organization standards. For example, InTASC Standard 6 (Model Core Teaching) indicates that teachers understand and use "...multiple methods of assessment to engage learners in their own growth, to monitor learner progress, and to guide the teacher's and learner's decision making" (CCSSO, 2013, p. 9). This includes using technology to support assessment practices and more fully involve learners in the process. The elements of this component are reflected in CEC HLPs 4, 5, 6, and 10 (McLeskey et al., 2017). These practices identify the importance of using multiple sources of data to better understand students' strengths and needs, interpreting and communicating evaluation results with important stakeholders, and collaboratively using data to design and implement instructional programming to improve students' academic and behavioral outcomes. DEC Recommended Practices also emphasize systematic, ongoing assessment (A9), the use of assessment tools sufficiently sensitive to detect progress, especially for children with significant support needs (A10), and the reporting of assessment results in ways that are understandable and useful to families (A11) (DEC, 2014).

The CAEP Elementary Teacher Standard 3 (CAEP, 2018), the National Board for Professional Teaching "Exceptional Needs" Standards 5 and 7 (NBPTS, 2010), and the Early Childhood Generalist (NBPTS, 2012a) and Middle Childhood Generalist Standard 5 (NBPTS, 2012b) each use assessment results to understand the learner, monitor student progress, and inform curriculum development, instructional planning, and practices. The National Association for Gifted Children Standards 4 and 5 (NAGC, 2013) also emphasize using data to make educational decisions, inform student learning and goal development, and employ technology to support instructional assessment. The knowledge base related to the present component is extensive.

The Every Student Succeeds Act (2015) mandates that states have measures in place to determine student progress in the general curriculum, and all students, including those with disabilities, are to participate in statewide assessments. Further, IDEA (2004) stipulates assessment as part of the annual Individualized Education Program (IEP) review.

Data collection and analysis should be a collaborative effort that includes parents, as parental involvement usually leads to better outcomes for students (Shonkoff, 2010). Although families have insight to develop relevant goals, families often report they are not a valuable part of the decision-making process. Special educators who plan carefully to communicate with families can facilitate better understanding of assessment results and more collaborative participation in educational programming (Weaver & Ouye, 2015).

When teachers use data to make instructional decisions, student achievement improves. Further, when teachers use data prior to instructional decision making, they make more frequent and appropriate decisions than when they do not use data (Stecker, Fuchs, & Fuchs, 2005). Although not nationally mandated, several states have policies or guidance related to the use of formative assessment to improve instructional outcomes (Gallagher & Worth, 2008). Also, the U.S. Department of Education encourages schools to use data for continuous improvement (Mandinach & Gummer, 2013). Formative assessment requires data collection from a range of sources

and the use of those data to "inform a cycle of continuous improvement." (What Works Clearinghouse [WWC], 2009b, p. 10).

Data-based instruction (DBI) is a cyclical approach the candidate can use to determine if instruction is effective for a student. The steps of DBI include: (a) establish a present level of performance, (b) set an ambitious long-term goal, (c) generate a hypothesis to select interventions and implement high quality instruction with fidelity, (d) monitor progress toward the long-term goal, (e) use decision rules to determine effectiveness of the instruction, (f) generate a new hypothesis regarding student progress as needed, and (g) implement instructional changes as needed and continue steps c-g (Lembke et al., 2019). Researchers have supported the use of formative assessment as a logical approach to continuous improvement that leads to more effective instructional practices (Mandinach & Gummer, 2013).

Technology-enabled assessments can help reduce the time, resources, and disruption to learning required for the administration of paper assessments (Gohl, Gohl, & Wolf, 2009). Assessments delivered using technology also can provide a more complete and individualized picture of student needs, interests, and abilities than traditional assessments, allowing educators to personalize learning and universally design assessment measures. Tools such as AIMSweb, Tally, Student/ Classroom Observation and Analysis, BehaviorSnap, and Microsoft Excel [MVK3] can be used to collect student level data, which in turn can be easily shared with the team using the DBI process to support effective instruction for students.

Standard 5: Supporting Learning Using Effective Instruction

Candidates use knowledge of individuals' development, learning needs, and assessment data to inform decisions about effective instruction. Candidates use explicit instructional strategies and employ strategies to promote active engagement and increased motivation to individualize instruction to support each individual. Candidates use whole group instruction, flexible grouping, small group instruction, and individual instruction. Candidates teach individuals to use meta-/cognitive strategies to support and self-regulate learning.

Component 5.1. Candidates use findings from multiple assessments, including student self-assessment, that are responsive to cultural and linguistic diversity and specialized as needed, to identify what students know and are able to do. They then interpret the assessment data to appropriately plan and guide instruction to meet rigorous academic and non-academic content and goals for each individual.

Supporting Explanation. Candidates effectively utilize an assessment-instruction cycle to examine, adjust, guide, and improve instruction by (a) interpreting formative assessments, (b) confirming the interpretation, (c) generating and selecting alternative instructional approaches, (d) considering and implementing instructional adaptations, (e) evaluating learning and engagement, and (f) providing feedback to students by communicating levels of proficiency and accomplishment.

Candidates specially design instruction for individual students based on a variety of formative and summative assessments (e.g., screening, identification, progress monitoring, curriculum based) and technologies. Standard 4 specifically addresses appropriate selection, administration, and interpretation of assessments to inform instruction. Candidates also identify learning goals and plan instruction aligned to academic, social, and behavioral standards as well as other appropriate academic and non-academic content to meet the needs of individual learners based on assessment data.

Knowledge Base. Using assessment data to inform and improve instruction is routinely included in a wide range of teacher preparation standards, including InTASC Standard 6 (CCSSO, 2011), CAEP Elementary Standards Component 3b (CAEP, 2018), National Board for Professional Teaching Standards Standard 3 (NBPTS, 2010), and CEC Initial Standards Key Element 4.2 (CEC, 2012). Furthermore, the CEC high-leverage practices include formative assessment such as HLP 6 (McLeskey et al., 2017). Each of these documents emphasizes the importance of assessment to inform instruction as central to effective teaching. For example, the InTASC standards emphasize the need to improve data literacy among all teachers, as this information is used to "understand each learner's progress, adjust instruction as needed, provide feedback to learners, and document learner progress against standards" (CCSSO, 2011, p. 4). Formative assessment is also emphasized as a critical high-leverage practice for special education teachers, who "...must be flexible problem solvers who not only have expertise in using highly effective practices, but also are proficient in monitoring the effectiveness of these practices with individual students and making decisions regarding changes in practice as needed" (McLeskey et al., 2017, p. 8).

Research support for formative assessment has varied from minimal to substantial (Hamilton et al., 2009; Hattie, 2009; Mandinach & Gummer, 2013). This variability has likely occurred primarily because formative assessment is not a direct intervention, may be used in any content area, and is effective only when used with effective instructional approaches and sound instructional decision making (McLeskey et al., 2017). The makeup of formative assessment varies substantially depending on variables such as the content area addressed, intervention or instructional approach employed, assessments used, intensity level of instruction, and student characteristics. Substantial research evidence has also shown that simply having assessment data is not sufficient to guide instruction, rather teachers must receive focused, systematic preparation to use formative assessment data to make informed decisions that effectively guide instruction (Coburn & Turner, 2012; Hamilton et al., 2009; Waldron, Parker, & McLeskey, 2014).

Research has shown that formative assessment is a critical component of effective instruction for students with disabilities, as no practice will be effective for every student, resulting in the need for special education teachers to "...make instructional decisions based on data related to student progress toward well-defined goals" (McLeskey et al., 2017, p. 48). The use of formative assessment to support instruction is a critical component of multi-tiered systems of support models that are widely used for students with disabilities and others who struggle to learn academic content (Gersten et al., 2008; Lane, Oakes, & Menzies, 2019). When used with students with disabilities, formative assessment has been shown to be most effective when high-quality instruction is used (e.g., explicit instruction) and instruction is appropriately adjusted in response to assessment data (e.g., increase intensity) (Grigorenko et al., 2020).

Component 5.2. Candidates use effective strategies to promote active student engagement, increase student motivation, increase opportunities to respond, and enhance self-regulation of student learning.

Supporting Explanation. Candidates use effective strategies that promote active student engagement, nurture intrinsic motivation for learning, offer frequent, equitable opportunities to respond, and guide self-regulation. Active student engagement strategies, including effective questioning and guided discussion, are purposefully selected and incorporated into instruction to reflect students' learning profiles and activate prior knowledge. Candidates use various strategies to maintain engagement and instructional focus across different group configurations (see component 5.4). Candidates explicitly teach, model, and reinforce self-regulation behaviors (e.g., turn-taking, assignment completion) for students in a variety of ways and settings. Digital technology is infused in instruction (e.g., use of interactive white boards, web-based documents, assistive and augmentative communication) and assessment (e.g., real-time response systems) to assist in and enhance learning and engagement based on individual student need and interest. Candidates use appropriate platforms and applications when supporting students in blended or virtual learning environments

Knowledge Base. Students' sense of belonging, active engagement, and subsequent academic achievement are predicated on their teachers' ability to structure learning environments and opportunities to ensure students have equitable opportunities to achieve. Students enter schools with an array of backgrounds and characteristics that require teachers to have knowledge, skills, and dispositions to know each student's needs, plan developmentally appropriate lessons, and consistently engage students through effective instruction and intervention. The National Board for Professional Teaching Standards acknowledges that "equitable learning opportunities often require the development of unique accommodations to allow for the full engagement of every learner" (NBPTS, 2012a, p. 41).

CAEP Elementary Standard 3 (CAEP, 2018) and InTASC Standard 3 (CCSSO, 2011) emphasize the connection between relationships and social and emotional development. Positive relationships between and among students and teachers increase engagement and motivation, which influence achievement. Effective teachers build classroom community based on high expectations for all with structures to support learning for all. InTASC Standard 3 describes teacher collaboration with learners, families, and colleagues to set norms that allow rigorous individual and collective learning to take place. Further, "improving the quality and consistency of student participation in school improves academic performance and increases student engagement in the classroom and the world at large" (NBPTS, 2012b, p. 29). The need to stimulate learning through culturally and linguistically responsive instruction and assessment are also evident in the CEC professional practice standards (CEC, 2015) and the high-leverage practices, specifically HLP 18 (McLeskey et al., 2017).

Roorda and colleagues (2011) conducted a meta-analysis to examine teacher-student relationships and student engagement and achievement. Their analyses included 99 studies across P-12 populations. They found significant associations between teacher-student relationships (TSR) and students' engagement and achievement. Similar to Hattie's (2012) research, relationships were more strongly related to engagement than achievement. Negative relationships seemed to impact students in the primary grades more than those at the secondary level; conversely, the role of positive TSR increased with age. The researchers suggested that the differences in the role the teacher plays (assistive vs. instructional) and direct contact time could influence student perceptions of support; these discrepancies are worth noting as teachers support the learning of students with disabilities and other needs across settings.

As students move more flexibly within and across settings, their ability to self-regulate and maintain motivation becomes increasingly important. Researchers have documented the need to explicitly teach self-regulation strategies for students with disabilities to support success across content areas, including literacy (Graham & Harris, 2000; Schunk & Zimmerman, 2007) and math (Fuchs et al., 2003; Montague, 2008). The findings in these studies are consistent with several principles outlined in American Psychological Association guidance (e.g., Principle 7: Student's Self-regulation Assists Learning and Self-regulatory Skills Can Be Taught; APA, 2015) and the CEC book, "High-Leverage Practices in Special Education" (e.g., HLP 18: Use Strategies to Promote

Active Student Engagement; McLeskey et al., 2017). Teaching students to self-regulate for independent and collaborative learning is critical. Collaborative learning groups have variable success in meeting intended outcomes. This is due in part to the need to engage in self-regulation and shared regulation among the group, which is improved through intentional instruction and grouping of students (Panadero et al., 2015).

Technology can be used as a means for student engagement within and beyond the classroom. As students come to school increasingly savvy in their use of web-based applications, teachers can tap into their use of technology to meet individual and standards-based learning objectives. For some students, technology is essential for accessing the curriculum (Edyburn, 2006; McLeskey et al., 2017) and for others it simply makes "learning more fun" (Spires et al., 2008, p. 511). According to InTASC Standard 8(g), an effective teacher "engages learners in using a range of learning skills and technology tools to access, interpret, evaluate, and apply information" (CCSSO, 2013, p. 38). Using assistive and instructional technologies is an identified high-leverage practice (HLP 19) for special education (McLeskey et al., 2017). Herburger, Holdheide, & Sacco (2020) describe specific applications of the HLPs to mitigate common barriers to student learning in virtual or hybrid arrangements.

Component 5.3. Candidates use explicit, systematic instruction to teach content, strategies, and skills to make clear what a learner needs to do or think about while learning.

Supporting Explanation. Candidates use explicit, systematic instruction to focus on individualized and important academic and non-academic content and make clear what each student needs to do or think about when learning. They make content explicit by providing a clear statement regarding the purpose for learning the content, strategy, or skill, and making explicit connections to existing knowledge and skills. Candidates also provide a clear explanation of the content, strategy, or skill to be learned, focus instruction on the steps that lead to learning, and use scaffolds and feedback to guide the learner. The candidate is able to demonstrate, think aloud, and describe relationships among content and related concepts while using clear and precise language. This includes providing step-by-step demonstrations that model the content, skill, or strategy, and providing a range of examples and non-examples to establish boundaries regarding when and how a learner should apply the content, strategy, or skill.

When using explicit instruction, candidates should logically sequence information within lessons, beginning with a statement of purpose and advance organizer. Candidates should then provide clear models and explanations of content, using a method such as "I do, we do, you do." Using this method in math, for example, the candidate would initially provide a model for solving a math problem while 'thinking aloud' to describe steps used to solve the problem. The candidate then guides students through solving the problem with scaffolding and feedback. Students are then provided opportunities for independent practice with feedback from the candidate. Explicit instruction is used to increase content coverage and enhance engagement and opportunities to learn content. Explicit instruction facilitates learning to think and act in ways that accelerate student learning and enable greater academic success. Candidates use students' cultural and linguistic diversity as an asset integrated into learning for all students. Candidates create opportunities to demonstrate knowledge and skill using different modalities and are provided with feedback (e.g., immediate discussion, written notes). Candidates are able to use distance learning technologies when delivering explicit instruction in virtual or hybrid arrangements.

Knowledge Base. Explicit, systematic instruction is emphasized in InTASC Standards 2, 4, 6, and 8 (CCSSO, 2013) as well as in CAEP Elementary Standard 4, Key Element 4c (CAEP, 2018). These standards highlight building on learners' prior knowledge and skills, addressing misconceptions that interfere with learning, providing models and processes that guide learners in examining their thinking and learning, and providing multiple models and representations of concepts and skills for learners. Furthermore, explicit, systematic instruction is emphasized in CEC Standard 5 (CEC, 2015), as candidates use explicit instruction with modeling and guided practice to assure acquisition and fluency related to disciplinary content.

CEC also includes both explicit instruction and systematic instruction in a set of high-leverage practices (McLeskey et al., 2017), which are described in the "Framing the Future of Special Education: Framing CEC's Professional Preparation Standards" document as "essential specialized practices for special educators" (Blanton et al., 2017, p. 9) that should influence the new practice-based standards for special education teachers. The CEC Division for Early Childhood (DEC) also emphasizes the use of systematic instruction as a critical component of instructional practice (see INS6; DEC, 2014, p. 12). In addition, the National Mathematics Advisory Panel (2008) supports using explicit instruction to teach computation and problem-solving skills. Finally, the National Board of Professional Teaching Standards emphasizes components of explicit systematic instruction, as candidates develop multiple pathways to knowledge, understand common student misconceptions related to disciplinary content, model acquisition of effective learning strategies, and build on previous student learning (NBPTS, 2010).

Students with disabilities require more systematically designed explicit instruction than typically developing peers (Archer & Hughes, 2011). Researchers have identified several critical elements of systematically designed instruction. Hattie (2009) summarized findings from 11 meta-analyses on learning goals and concluded that achievement increases when teachers set specific challenging goals rather than "do your best" goals and structure learning activities so students can reach them. Furthermore, Fuchs and Fuchs (1986) noted that challenging goals were more effective for students with disabilities and reported significant effect sizes for both long- and short-terms goals. Research also supports the use of well-sequenced lessons and unit design (Archer & Hughes, 2011; Marchand et al., 2004) as components of systematic instruction. Finally, Hattie (2009; 2012) reviewed findings from 16 meta-analyses and found significant effect sizes for the use of visual content displays, including advance organizers and the use of graphic organizers and concept maps. Effect sizes were largest among students least likely to understand relationships between lower- and higher-order constructs (Horton et al., 1993; Kim et al., 2004; Nesbit & Adesope, 2006; Vasquez & Caraballo, 1993).

Research has revealed that explicit instruction is particularly effective for students who are struggling to learn disciplinary content, including those with disabilities. For example, students who are struggling to learn to read, including English Language Learners and students with disabilities, benefit from explicit instruction (Baker et al., 2014; Connor et al., 2009; Gersten et al., 2009a; Swanson & Hoskyn, 2001). Similarly, syntheses of research on teaching mathematics to low-achieving students (Baker, Gersten, & Lee, 2002) and to students with disabilities (Gersten et al., 2009b) have revealed that the use of explicit instruction significantly improved math achievement of students who were struggling to learn this content. Research on explicit instruction also has been shown to improve the skills of students who are struggling to learn to write (Graham et al., 2012; Mason & Benedek-Wood, 2014). Explicit instruction can facilitate student learning, virtually as well as in-person, across all grade levels and in all content areas (Herburger, Holdheide, & Sacco, 2020).

Component 5.4. Candidates use flexible grouping to support the use of instruction that is adapted to meet the needs of each individual and group.

Supporting Explanation. Candidates understand that the purpose of small group instruction is to tailor teaching to meet the learning needs of each student by providing more focused, intensive instruction. Candidates reference learning goals, appropriate standards, and student learning profiles to configure groups effectively. This instruction is provided to heterogeneous and/or homogeneous groups. Group assignments are determined by factors such as knowledge of learners' backgrounds and data from formal and informal assessments, and are fluid depending on the content being addressed and student needs. Candidates hold learners accountable for both collective and individual learning and provide constructive feedback and scaffolding to support productive learning. Candidates regularly monitor each learner's progress and adjust their groupings and instruction accordingly. Candidates understand that groups are used for many purposes and take many forms to accommodate learning differences and promote in-depth academic learning.

For example, candidates may use heterogeneous groups to allow students to participate in grade level conversations around content. When this is done, a candidate must define the purpose of the group and criteria used for heterogeneous grouping. Candidates identify and use an appropriate structure for the group (e.g., cooperative learning using a strategy such as think-pair-share, numbered heads together, jigsaw), prepare students to use the structure, and ensure that students equitably participate in the groups.

An appropriate structure should support positive

interdependence within groups, and use materials and directives that promote effective, efficient, and equitable opportunities for student participation. Candidates should monitor group interactions and student learning and hold students accountable individually and collectively for learning within the group. Within heterogeneous groupings, students learn to work collaboratively and to rely on each other to successfully complete the learning task. Candidates may set up homogenous groups to support common learner interests, preferences, or skill needs. Additionally, candidates can structure homogenous groups to provide more focused intensive instruction as discussed in Standard 5.6.

Knowledge Base. Major professional education bodies agree that sound instruction is delivered in a variety of formats and groupings. Teachers should have knowledge and skill in structuring flexible formats to meet student learning needs delivered to whole classes, small groups, and individuals. InTASC standards indicate the importance of teachers as "exemplary managers of the learning environment" to support various instructional modes and groupings (CCSSO, 2011). Finally, the National Board for Professional Teaching Standards notes that students should be engaged in varied group configurations to provide positive and safe learning environments (Core Proposition 3; NBPTS, 2012a, 2012b).

High-Leverage Practice 17 (Use Flexible Grouping) emphasizes the use of both "homogenous and heterogenous groups based on explicit learning goals" (McLeskey et al., 2017, p. 24). The National Board for Professional Teaching Standards affirms that teachers must collect and use student data and learning profile information to maximize individual and collective learning opportunities (NBPTS, 2012a). For example, whole group, explicit instruction about a concept can set the stage for individual thinking and brainstorming, prior to small group collaboration and interest-based discussion. Teachers prepare students to engage meaningfully in "collaborative and cooperative groups, some of which are teacher-guided and others student-led" (NBPTS, 2012b, p. 25).

Flexible grouping can be implemented at the class or building level. Castle, Baker Deniz, and Tortora (2005) examined the impact of a literacy-focused flexible-grouping initiative in a "high-needs school" over a five-year period. The researchers distinguished flexible grouping from ability-grouping, describing

it as a way to provide individualized and high-level instruction for all students with flexible assignments and targeted support for teachers. Castle and her colleagues acknowledged a direct relationship could not be concluded but found important results for students and teachers. The percentage of students formerly performing below expectations who were able to reach expectations exceeded the district goal and the percentage of teachers using flexible grouping increased as well. Reutzel and Clark (2019) also add to the extensive evidence base in literacy instruction, which supports the use of flexible grouping.

Flexible grouping is a central feature of multitiered systems of support (MTSS) models, including response to intervention, which facilitate instruction of varying intensity based on student need (Basham et al., 2010; Gersten et al., 2008). All students receive core instruction; some students are provided supplemental support to ensure mastery; and some students receive additional individualized, intensive instruction and intervention to accelerate learning of knowledge and skills.

Component 5.5. Candidates organize and manage focused, intensive small group instruction to meet the learning needs of each individual.

Supporting Explanation. Candidates use homogeneous groups to provide focused, intensive instruction for children who have common instructional needs and configure these groups to address high priority short-term content goals and objectives. Candidates explicitly define the purpose for homogenous groups, criteria used for grouping, and the time per day that learners will participate in these groups. The size of homogeneous groups is appropriate based on the stated purpose of the group and designed to provide intensive, effective instruction that accelerates achievement. Reliable and valid assessment data that directly measure students' skills related to the content being taught is used as a primary criterion to determine student groupings. Each learner's progress in learning content is frequently monitored and instruction is adjusted accordingly. Candidates use explicit instruction, appropriate feedback, and guided practice during small group instruction, and use strategies to maximize each learner's opportunities to respond. Candidates understand that learner benefits from small group instruction include effective and efficient learning, learning to take ownership, developing self-direction, and becoming actively engaged in the learning process.

Knowledge Base. Small group instruction is emphasized in CAEP Elementary Standard 4, component f (CAEP, 2018) and InTASC Standard 3.2 (CCSSO, 2013). These standards address using small group instruction to differentiate teaching to meet the learning needs of each child by providing more focused, intensive instruction, varying the learning environment to develop a range of learner skills, and allowing students to develop self-direction and become actively engaged in the learning process. The CEC Initial Preparation Standards (e.g., Standard 2: Learning Environments; CEC, 2015) recommend the use of small groups to encourage active student participation, while CEC high-leverage practices emphasize the use of homogeneous grouping to accommodate learning differences (HLP 17), teach social skills (HLP 9), provide intensive instruction (HLP 20), and offer students with many opportunities to respond and receive immediate feedback (HLP 22) (McLeskey et al., 2017).

When well designed and implemented, homogeneous small-group instruction can accelerate the development of a variety of academic and interpersonal student outcomes (Hattie, 2009; Heward & Wood, 2015; McLeskey & Waldron, 2011). For example, extensive research has documented the effectiveness of small, homogeneous, skill-based group instruction in accelerating student learning in reading (Reutzel, Clark, & Flory, 2015), mathematics (Gersten et al., 2009), and writing (Mason, Mamlin, & Stewart, 2019). The effectiveness of these small groups is also supported by research on multi-tiered systems of support (MTSS) (Fuchs et al., 2019; Gersten et al., 2008; Gersten et al., 2009). Most evidence suggests that small groups should be highly structured and include (a) systematic goal, task, and material selection; (b) clear instructional directives; and (c) explicit strategies to maximize and equalize student response opportunities (McLeskey et al., 2017). As with all instructional practices, teachers must monitor student academic and interpersonal performance, provide positive and constructive feedback, and hold students accountable for their own and others' performance.

Finally, homogeneous small groups are an integral part of special education service delivery and are used to accelerate learning of critical academic and social

skills (McLeskey et al., 2017). This occurs because small groups provide a setting in which a range of effective practices can be delivered, including intensive instruction, explicit instruction, scaffolded supports, and feedback to guide student learning. Small groups also may be used to enhance student engagement, teach cognitive and metacognitive strategies, and teach prosocial skills (Gersten et al., 2009; Mason, Mamlin, & Stewart, 2019; McLeskey et al., 2017).

Component 5.6. Candidates plan and deliver specialized, individualized instruction that is used to meet the learning needs of each individual.

Supporting Explanation. Candidates understand that the purpose of specialized, individualized instruction is to provide more intensive and different instruction to learners individually or in small groups whose needs are not sufficiently met in whole or small groups. Learners might need more practice with a skill, further clarification of a concept, or a more enriching learning opportunity. Candidates intentionally design individualized instruction based on informal and formal assessments and the learner profile by matching instructional intensity and/or intervention to build on student's strengths and accommodate needs. Candidates employ appropriate instructional strategies (e.g., structured tutoring, modeling, evidence-based practices, data-based individualization inquiry-based learning) to meet the needs of the learner effectively and efficiently. Candidates support and scaffold instruction through explicit instruction, modeling, and guided practice to increase student success and acquisition of specific learning outcomes. In addition, candidates provide specific feedback to students during instruction, especially during guided practice to support learning and mastery. Candidates should promote the application or generalization of knowledge and skills that are mastered into other content areas and/or other educational settings by the individual students.

Knowledge Base. Since before its formal legal inception, special education as a field has sought to provide "individualized programing tailored to the nature of the child's learning needs" (Deno, 1970, p. 235). Federal law (Education for All Handicapped Children Act, 1975) subsequently guaranteed that every child is afforded a free appropriate public education (FAPE) guided and documented by an individualized education program (IEP). Even when students receiving special education services are taught in small or whole group settings, their individual needs must be considered. Further, when their needs are not met in those situations, they should receive specialized, individualized instruction to meet their needs (NBPTS, 2012a).

The importance of individualized instruction is documented in professional standards such as CAEP Standard 4 (CAEP, 2018) and InTASC Standards 2, 7, and 8 (CCSSO, 2011). Teachers are expected to use professional judgement to make "appropriate and timely provisions (e.g., pacing for individual rates of growth, task demands, communication, assessment, and response modes) for individual students with particular learning differences or needs" (CCSSO, 2011, p. 5). The American Psychological Association (2015) suggested that students be involved in individualizing their instruction, particularly pacing, setting timelines, and self-monitoring for completion.

Riccomini, Morano, and Hughes (2017) presented a nested structure to show the relationship among contemporary big ideas in special education, including high-leverage practices. The book, High Leverage Practices in Special Education (McLeskey et al., 2017), includes many specific practices related to individualizing instruction such as adapting curriculum (HLP 13), teaching cognitive and metacognitive strategies (HLP 14), providing scaffolded supports (HLP 15), and using explicit instruction (HLP 16). Most specifically, HLP 20 (providing intensive instruction) suggests that teachers "match the intensity of instruction to the intensity of the student's learning and behavioral challenges" and "frequently monitor students' progress and adjust their instruction accordingly" (McLeskey et al., 2017, p. 25).

A multi-tiered system of supports (MTSS) such as response to intervention (RtI) provides structure for increasing the intensity and individualization of instruction based on student need (Lemons et al., 2018). Fuchs, Fuchs, and Malone (2017) offer a taxonomy to focus on strength, dosage, alignment, attention to transfer, comprehensiveness, behavioral support, and individualization. The 2017 *Endrew F. v. Douglas County School District RE-1* Supreme Court decision requiring that schools provide special education services ensuring appropriate progress has increased emphasis on individualized service delivery.

Standard 6: Supporting Social, Emotional, and Behavioral Growth

Candidates create and contribute to safe, respectful, and productive learning environments for individuals with exceptionalities through the use of effective routines and procedures and use a range of preventive and responsive practices to support social, emotional, and educational well-being. They follow ethical and legal guidelines and work collaboratively with families and other professionals to conduct behavioral assessments for intervention and program development.

Component 6.1. Candidates use effective routines and procedures to create safe, caring, respectful, and productive learning environments for individuals with exceptionalities.

Supporting Explanation. Candidates structure the environment to maximize success and safety for all students. They build positive, caring relationships by taking initiative to learn students' strengths, interests, and needs and by responding to them in authentic and respectful ways. Candidates actively engage with students' families to deepen their understanding of students' diverse cultures, backgrounds, and traditions. Through their words and actions, candidates create welcoming and inclusive classroom communities. Candidates understand the importance of preventive approaches to strengthen desired performance and address challenging behavior. They arrange physical space in their classrooms to promote learning and positive peer interactions. Candidates plan and implement positive behavioral interventions and supports. They apply proactive practices within their own classes and with individual students, and may actively participate in school-wide, multi-tiered systems, such as a schoolwide positive behavior interventions and support (PBIS) framework. Candidates state clear behavioral expectations and provide examples of desired behaviors in different settings. They explicitly teach students routines and procedures for recurring activities. For example, candidates may teach routines for entering the classroom, working in cooperative groups, conducting science labs, or participating in virtual class sessions.

Explicit instruction for behavioral routines parallels that used for academic skills, as it includes clear goals, explanations, modeling, guided practice, corrective feedback, independent practice, and acknowledgements/reinforcement. Candidates collect and use data to monitor student behavior and the effectiveness of their management plans. Candidates also help students develop skills for self-monitoring their behavior and their progress toward identified goals. Candidates collaborate with teachers and other professionals, families, or caregivers in a team approach to address individual needs consistently across school, home, and community settings. They are respectful of the varied aspects of diversity and recognize how intersectionality of gender, racial, cultural, disability, and other identities may make individuals and/or groups more vulnerable to discriminatory practices, particularly with regard to student behavior and discipline. Candidates take active measures to prevent bullying, maltreatment, violence, and sexual assault, and they report any instances through appropriate channels.

Knowledge Base. This component aligns with InTASC Standard 3 (CCSSO, 2011), HLP 7 (McLeskey et al., 2017), and DEC Recommended Practice E1 (DEC, 2014) as it focuses on the creation of environments that promote positive social interactions and learning experiences. Standard 3 of the CAEP K-6 Elementary Teacher Preparation Standards (CAEP, 2018) emphasizes the importance of interpersonal relationships and social norms to motivate students and promote their social-emotional development. Additionally, DEC Recommended Practice E2 addresses universal design for learning (UDL) principles to ensure accessible environments, and Practice E3 emphasizes working with families and other adults to adapt or modify physical, social, and temporal factors to facilitate each child's participation in learning experiences (DEC, 2014).

The CEC Policy on Safe and Positive School Climate (CEC, 2008) emphasizes the need to ensure the creation of safe learning environments that contribute to all students' cognitive, academic, social-emotional, and ethical development. Positive learning environments can be created when teachers get to know students and their families and build respectful relationships (Hagiwara & Shogren, 2019; Mart, Dusenbury, & Weissberg, 2009; Turnbull et al., 2015). Caring teacher-student relationships are powerfully related to effective classroom management (Hattie, 2009). By structuring physical space, grouping configurations, time, and activities, teachers promote positive interactions and learning outcomes. They arrange their classrooms to ensure that all students, including those with sensory, physical, and other disabilities, have equitable access to instructional activities and materials (IRIS Center, 2019a; IRIS Center, 2019c; Simonsen et al., 2015).

Strong evidence supports the practices of teaching and reinforcing socially and behaviorally appropriate skills to preserve a positive classroom climate (Epstein et al., 2008). Research has consistently demonstrated the importance of clear, measurable, and positively stated behavioral expectations; well established and predictable classroom routines; explicit instruction that includes adequate modeling, practice, and feedback; and behavior specific praise to help increase, maintain, and generalize desired behaviors (Bruhn et al., 2019; Epstein et al., 2008; IRIS Center, 2019b; Simonsen et al., 2015; State, Mitchell, & Wehby, 2019). These positive and preventive strategies are considered Tier 1 supports within a schoolwide positive behavior interventions and support (PBIS) framework (Center for Adolescent Research in Schools, 2014; Positive Behavior Interventions and Support, n.d).

The intersectionality of disability with gender, racial, cultural, and other identities warrants special consideration regarding school climate and safety. The CEC Policy on Safe and Positive School Climate (CEC, 2008) emphasizes that special educators' acquisition and use of effective practices must include ways to support human and civil rights and promote social justice for the diverse student populations in today's schools. A subsequent Policy on the Prevention of and Response to Maltreatment (CEC, 2018) recommends "a consistent approach of building awareness and understanding of the maltreatment of children and youth, enhancing maltreatment recognizing and reporting mechanisms, and incorporating prevention and response strategies in everyday practice" (p. 1).

Developing and sustaining a positive and respectful environment requires collaborative relationships with families or caregivers as well as other professionals. Research supports the importance of collaboration among teachers for continued guidance and support; collaborative consultations with behavior experts as needed; and cultivation of parents and family members as active partners in teaching and reinforcing appropriate behaviors (Epstein et al., 2008).

Component 6.2. Candidates use a range of preventive and responsive practices documented as effective to support individuals' social, emotional, and educational well-being.

Supporting Explanation. Candidates recognize how antecedent circumstances and events influence student performance, and they create conditions to promote desired behaviors. They consider the students' strengths, areas of need, communication and language abilities, surroundings, and task demands as well as other triggers that could lead to potential challenges. Candidates create an environment where expectations are clear and predictable, where instructional routines and classroom procedures are used to support students and keep them actively engaged during instruction or other classroom activities. Candidates employ effective, proactive, and preventive strategies to manage challenging behaviors at the school-wide, classroom, and individual student levels. They use preventive approaches that focus on positive procedures, including prompting and cueing, positive reinforcement, nonverbal communication, and other surface management strategies such as proximity control and redirection. Candidates also recognize the impact of motivation, setting, teacher and peer interactions, and other events on student behavior. They provide frequent, positive, specific, and constructive feedback to influence student learning and behavior. Candidates consider a hierarchy of procedural alternatives when responding to challenging behavior or when teaching new social, emotional, or academic skills.

They may begin with strategies such as differential reinforcement that teach alternate or more appropriate replacement behaviors, followed by extinction where the influencing reinforcer is withheld, then consequences such as a penalty where access to preferred activities or desired items are removed, and then punishment as a last resort where students may receive an aversive consequence such as detention, extra work, repairing damage they committed, or having to overcorrect. Candidates promote generalization and maintenance of learned skills across time and settings. They teach specific self-regulation strategies, such as self-monitoring and goal setting, aimed at meeting students' academic, behavioral, or social needs. Candidates understand the influences of gender, race, culture, disability, familial, and other factors on student behavior and are conscious of biases in interventions and responses to student behavior. They are aware of issues such as

disproportionate rates of suspension or expulsion and overuse of procedures such as seclusion or restraint, and they consider these issues when using preventive and responsive practices. They conform to legal and ethical guidelines for all behavioral interventions.

Knowledge Base. This component aligns with InTASC Standards 1, 2, 3, and 9 (CCSSO, 2011), which includes skills in applying their understandings of learning development, learning differences, learning environments, and professional learning and ethical practice. In addition, this component is aligned with the high-leverage practices associated with social/emotional/behavioral practices (HLP 7, HLP 8, HLP 9, and HLP 10) in focusing on creating a positive environment, while using effective teaching and assessment practices to meet the individual social, emotional, and behavioral needs of learners, delivered in a consistent, caring, organized, respectful, and culturally responsive manner (Lewis, 2019). This component further aligns with CAEP Elementary Standard 3 that emphasizes building interpersonal relationships with students that generate motivation and promote students' social and emotional development, specifically by managing the classroom to establish and maintain social norms and behavioral expectations (3.e) and explicitly supporting motivation and engagement in learning through diverse evidence-based interventions (3.f) (CAEP, 2018).

Interventions that effectively support individuals' emotional and behavioral needs can include preventive as well as responsive practices. Preventing challenging behavior is supported by research from the Technical Assistance Center on Positive Behavior Supports (2017) and aligns with U.S. federal policy concerning suspension and expulsion (U.S. Departments of Health and Human Services and Education, 2015). Additionally, proactive measures are preferred under the Individuals with Disabilities Education Act (IDEA, 2004) and are recommended by the CEC Division for Early Childhood (DEC, 2015) and CEC Council for Children with Behavioral Disorders (CCBD, n.d.). An effective teacher creates a classroom environment with consistent classroom expectations, routines, and procedures (State, Mitchell, & Wehby, 2019); these antecedent intervention approaches can be combined with effective feedback strategies to support students' prosocial skills (Bruhn et al., 2019).

Teachers may also engage in responsive practices that emphasize fair, predictable, and ethical consequences such as reinforcement for appropriate behavior, as well as behavior reduction procedures for maladaptive or inappropriate behavior (Cooper, Heron, & Heward, 2020; IRIS Center, 2015). In some cases, there may be a need for more targeted supports or intensive behavioral interventions (National Center for Pyramid Model Innovations, n.d.; Positive Behavior Interventions and Support, n.d).

Classroom interventions and supports begin with foundational considerations that emphasize the physical setting and include the use of norms, clear expectations, procedures, and predictable routines (IRIS Center, 2015; Simonsen et al., 2015). Candidates construct and maintain a productive learning environment by adapting classroom procedures to each learner's cognitive and motivational needs. Using explicit instruction, candidates teach students appropriate behaviors, including social skills, self-regulation, problem-solving, and/or decision-making skills. Candidates teach students to set and achieve positive goals, make responsible decisions, and resolve interpersonal situations constructively. Proactive and preventative approaches are used to teach, monitor, prompt, acknowledge, and pre-correct students; however, responsive approaches may be needed as well (Simonsen et al., 2015) and may involve positive as well as occasional negative consequences.

Behavior challenges are addressed in an ethical manner, utilizing least restrictive, proactive, and preventative strategies first, followed by more intrusive consequences, as needed (IRIS Center, 2012). Educators must recognize that non-aversive procedures such as extinction and differential reinforcement can be used to decrease the occurrence of challenging behaviors (Simonsen et al., 2015) with the primary goal of preventing and improving behavioral challenges (Sugai & Horner, 2009) or teaching new, appropriate functional behaviors (Cooper, Heron, & Heward, 2020). Strategies to assist in learning and maintaining appropriate and productive behaviors may include self-monitoring (Ennis, Lane, & Oakes, 2018) and technology-based self-monitoring interventions (Bruhn & Wills, 2018).

In all cases, educators should ensure data-based individualization and decision making when planning and implementing appropriate interventions (Cooper, Heron, & Heward, 2020) at both individual and classroom levels. This is accomplished by: (a) determining the function or purpose of student behavior; (b) considering cultural, linguistic, and familial characteristics influencing behavior; and (c) collaborating with other education professionals, families, or in some cases, the students themselves (Alberto & Troutman, 2017; Gage, 2015).

Component 6.3. Candidates systematically use data from a variety of sources to identify the purpose or function served by problem behavior to plan, implement, and evaluate behavioral interventions and social skills programs, including generalization to other environments.

Supporting Explanation. Candidates use direct and indirect methods, as well as formal and informal assessment measures to determine purpose, motivation and/or function of student behavior. They may use tools such as behavioral rating scales or checklists to formally assess behavior. Candidates may use anecdotal records, interviews, or direct observation to collect other types of information on students' strengths and areas of need. Data sources might include direct observation with a clearly defined data collection method, such as frequency/event recording, rate recording, interval recording, or duration recording. Data from these multiple sources are compiled and used to identify the purpose or function served by the target behavior.

Candidates use multiple sources of data to identify or develop effective practices for class-wide or individual level interventions and to evaluate effects of behavioral interventions. Such interventions include, but are not limited to, social skills instruction, peer mediation, self-monitoring, and self-determination strategies. Candidates explicitly teach desired behaviors using modeling and scaffolding. They utilize technology as appropriate to assist in measurement, tracking, and instructional decision making related to student behavior. This technology may include, for example, web-based graphing tools or Excel software. Candidates may also collect data through the use of reinforcer surveys, via paper-and-pencil or electronic methods.

Candidates purposefully program for generalization of social, emotional, and behavioral skills to relevant environments. They follow legal and ethical guidelines when working with families, teachers, and other professionals to develop, implement, and monitor plans for generalization.

Knowledge Base. Candidates' systematic use of multiple sources of data to develop effective practices and monitor students' learning is aligned with InTASC Standard 6 (CCSSO, 2011) and Elementary Education Standard 3 (CAEP, 2018). These standards highlight candidates' use of formal and informal assessments to identify each student's unique needs to support, verify, and document progress. DEC Recommended Practices for assessment (DEC, 2014) emphasize use of a variety of methods and sources, including interviews with a student's family, to gather a wide range of information. High-Leverage Practices (HLPs) 4 and 6 focus on the use of assessment, while HLPs 7, 8, 9, and 10 focus on social, emotional, and behavioral practices with students (McLeskey, et al, 2017). To create a respectful learning environment, it is critical for teachers to adopt an instructional approach and explicitly teach and reinforce social skills across the school day. Additionally, HLPs 14, 16, 20, and 21 focus on the implementation of explicit instruction including teacher-led, peer-assisted, student-regulated, and technology-assisted practices (McLeskey, et al, 2017).

Candidates use multiple sources of data from classroom, small group, or individual assessments to identify patterns and trends and to describe progress of the whole class, smaller groups, or individual students. Once candidates identify target skills or knowledge, interventions may be planned. When these procedures are implemented with fidelity, students will increase appropriate social behavior, improve academic behavior and performance, and decrease problem behaviors (Simonsen & Myers, 2015). In order for special educators to successfully plan, implement, and evaluate interventions, they need to understand and apply an Antecedent-Behavior-Consequence (A-B-C) model (Lloyd, Wills, & Lewis, 2019). All behaviors, appropriate and inappropriate, exhibited by students serve a purpose in the student's environment.

When teachers take behavioral consequences into consideration, they can identify the purpose or function of that behavior. By looking at the antecedents, or conditions under which behaviors occur, teachers may identify how the student's environment affects the value of the consequences (Barrett et al., 2018; Lloyd, Wills, & Lewis, 2019). Candidates must consider the cultural and linguistic background of the individual when (a) identifying problem behaviors, (b) determining their purpose, function, or motivation, and (c) planning an appropriate intervention (Kozleski, Artiles, & Skrtic, 2014). Effective intervention or management plans include considerations for scope and sequence, student involvement, and ongoing evaluation, which may be developed at the individual or class-wide/group level. Interventions may involve individual or group contingencies, contracts, or token economies (Simonsen & Myers, 2015). The intervention must be monitored and evaluated for effectiveness (What Works Clearinghouse, 2016).

The ultimate goal of instruction is the development of student social, emotional, or behavioral skills that are generalized for application in other appropriate settings. To achieve this outcome, candidates must plan assessment and instructional strategies to facilitate student reflection and self-assessment to identify their successes and struggles, as well as efforts needed to reach their goals. To enhance generalization, candidates should use explicit teaching, allow sufficient practice, teach across settings, and involve other adults and peers (McIntosh & MacKay, 2018). Specific steps may increase the generalization of newly learned behaviors and social skills, including continued coaching, implementing incentive systems, and reducing competing behaviors (McIntosh & MacKay, 2008). Candidates should also develop interventions targeting students' self-regulated learning by enabling them to think about their thinking, set realistic goals, and identify motivations leading to improved performance (IRIS Center, 2008). Meta-analyses have shown that teachers are able to deliver effective social skills intervention, with no significant differences from researchers in student acquisition and maintenance of learning (Sklad et al., 2012).

Standard 7: Collaborating with Team Members

Candidates apply team processes and communication strategies to collaborate in a culturally responsive manner with families, paraprofessionals, and other professionals within the school, other educational settings, and the community to plan programs and access services for individuals with exceptionalities and their families.

Component 7.1. Candidates utilize communication, group facilitation, and problem–solving strategies in a culturally responsive manner to lead effective meetings and share expertise and knowledge to build team capacity and jointly address students' instructional and behavioral needs.

Supporting Explanation. Candidates facilitate and participate in a range of meetings with families and other professionals, such as annual planning meetings, transition meetings, and ongoing collaborative meetings essential to instructional planning, meeting the student's behavioral needs and progress monitoring. As a facilitator, they use effective strategies to develop a meeting agenda, allocate time to meet the goals of the agenda, and use effective verbal and nonverbal communication strategies to lead in ways that are culturally responsive (e.g., understanding and communicating respect for cultural values, social expectations, and home language). They develop capacity in their team members by encouraging the sharing of multiple perspectives, soliciting feedback, and responding in a supportive manner to build consensus for the identification of student learning and behavioral needs and the development, implementation, and monitoring of practices to meet students' individual needs.

Knowledge Base. The role of the special educator includes many situations where interaction with parents and professionals is critical for student success. In fact, the Individuals with Disabilities Education Act of 2004 (at §300.321) describes the team that develops the annual plan for the child as including the following members: the parents of the child; not less than one regular education teacher of the child (if the child is, or may be, participating in the regular education environment); not less than one special education teacher of the child, or where appropriate, not less than one special education provider of the child; a representative of the public agency who is qualified to provide, or supervise the provision of, specially designed instruction to meet the unique needs of children with disabilities, is knowledgeable about the general education curriculum, and is knowledgeable about the availability of resources of the public agency; an individual who can interpret the instructional implications of evaluation results; other individuals who have knowledge or special expertise regarding the child, including related services personnel as appropriate (invited at the discretion of the parent or the agency); and the child with a disability (when appropriate). Often, the special educator takes a lead role on this team.

The ability to build team competency for collaboration is also essential. InTASC Standard 10 (Leadership and Collaboration) focuses on the importance of collaboration in fostering achievement (CCSSO, 2011). Progression of skill development indicates that the candidate participates on instructional team(s) and uses advice and support from colleagues to meet the needs of all learners. The teacher participates in school-wide efforts to implement a shared vision and contributes to a supportive culture. The teacher elicits information about learners and their experiences from families and communities and uses this ongoing communication to support learner development and growth. The teacher uses technology and other forms of communication to develop collaborative relationships with learners, families, colleagues, and the local community. The National Board for Professional Teaching Standards (NBPTS) Exceptional Needs Standard IV Family Partnerships also focuses on the need to communicate with and involve families (NBPTS, 2010). In addition, NBPTS Exceptional Needs Standard IX Contribute through Collaboration cites many ways teachers can collaborate within their schools and community and emphasizes that the "accomplished teachers recognize that collaboration is a process of mutuality, and they readily seek the expertise others have and acknowledge and address others' concerns" (NBPTS, 2010, p. 69).

There is support for the skills that candidates need to participate successfully in these activities. High-Leverage Practices for Inclusive Classrooms (HLP 2, McLeskey et al., 2017) indicates that special educators need to be able to plan and conduct productive meetings. Friend and Barron (2019) elaborate on specific communication skills related to collaboration high-leverage practices, including nonverbal skills, listening, questioning, and making statements, that undergird effective collaboration and group problem-solving processes.

Verbal and nonverbal communication skills and trust for team members are key building blocks for collaboration (Hallam et al., 2015). Turnbull and colleagues (2015) stress the importance of interacting in ways that are culturally sensitive and provide suggestions to teachers to develop their cultural competence for improved communication with families and the community. Additionally, they emphasize skills of fostering empowerment within others through persistence in finding solutions by working through options. The skills of empathetic listening and respect for family and community values have also been considered essential (CCSSO, 2013). Candidates may support families by acting in ways that build on family strengths and capacities in working with their young children at risk for or with developmental delays and disabilities. For example, for an adolescent student, a candidate may jointly develop a transition plan in alignment with the family's priorities to promote the child's engagement, learning, development, and well-being (e.g., accessing natural environments and inclusive settings within the community). Together with families, candidates may identify strategies to facilitate the child's development of peer relationships, self-regulation, independence, and safety within the home, classroom, and/or community.

Component 7.2. Candidates communicate, coordinate, and collaborate with families, paraprofessionals, and other professionals within the educational setting to assess, plan, and implement effective programs and services that promote progress toward measurable outcomes for individuals with and without exceptionalities and their families.

Supporting Explanation. Candidates recognize that families, paraprofessionals, and other professionals possess diverse knowledge about, and expertise in, working with individuals with exceptionalities. Their active participation as team members is thus essential. Effective teamwork requires ongoing information sharing, collaboration, and coordination with families, paraprofessionals, and other professionals, including related service providers (e.g., physical therapists, occupational therapists, speech and language therapists, school psychologists), utilizing technology as appropriate to effectively assess and communicate assessment information in clear and understandable terms and plan for and implement effective individualized educational and transition programs and services for individuals with exceptionalities.

Candidates rely on their knowledge of human growth and development, multiple influences on development, individual differences and diversity, as well as information accessed from multiple sources such as other professionals, research, professional literature, and policies to actively share with families

and colleagues to develop individual education, transition, and behavioral plans. Candidates determine what information is most relevant and can clearly articulate that information in a variety of modalities in order to advance the collaborative process.

Candidates understand that home, community, and other linguistic and cultural experiences play a critical role in an individual's growth and development. Candidates actively seek information from and about families and take primary responsibility for maintaining respectful, ongoing, open communication to jointly identify and meet learning goals that are informed by assessment data.

Candidates understand the reciprocal relationship with general educators for effective and inclusive practices. Candidates collaboratively assume different roles based on the continuum of services required to most effectively meet the needs of individuals with exceptionalities, such as consultant, school wide problem-solving team member, co-teacher, resource teacher, lead teacher, or itinerant teacher.

Knowledge Base. InTASC Standard 10 (Leadership and Collaboration) discusses the relationship of collaboration with families and student performance (CCSSO, 2011). It cites Hughes and Kwok (2007), who reported that teacher-parent relationship quality had a significant effect on engagement and achievement of first graders. It also cites Benner and Mistry (2007), who found that if elementary teachers and parents shared high expectations for students, students were more likely to achieve at high levels.

CEC high-leverage practices (McLeskey et al., 2017) include several specific collaborative practices. One practice (HLP 1) focuses on collaboration with professionals to increase student outcomes. This practice is supported by several studies that reported on the relationship between collaboration and student outcomes. Ronfeldt and colleagues (2015) found that teachers participating more frequently and with more satisfaction in assessment teams produced higher student achievement than teachers with less frequent and less satisfactory team participation. A research synthesis of six co-teaching and inclusion studies concluded that when general and special educators work together to coordinate curriculum delivery and have needed resources, small positive effects on student academic outcomes are achieved (Solis et al., 2012). Tremblay (2013) reported that students with disabilities in co-taught classrooms made significant educational gains while students in self-contained classrooms did not, and the gap widened with time.

Another high-leverage practice (HLP 3) focuses on collaboration with families to support student learning and accessing services. Several researchers have found that application of principles of effective partnerships (e.g., communicating information using accessible and family-friendly language and media) leads to greater feelings of parent empowerment (Klein et al., 2011; Meadan et al., 2009). Research addressing collaboration with families of differing cultural backgrounds by using cultural navigators or parent or school liaisons leads to increased parent involvement and families perceiving educators as advocating for child outcomes (Balcazar et al., 2012; Hardin et al., 2009).

The DEC Recommended Practices (DEC, 2014) include five collaboration practices with the first two emphasizing that professionals from multiple disciplines and families work together as a team to plan and implement interventions. Collaboration as defined by these practices involves the "interactive relationships between adults such as family members and professionals who work together to achieve mutually agreed upon outcomes/goals" (p.15).

Component 7.3. Candidates communicate, coordinate, and collaborate with professionals and agencies within the community to identify and access services, resources, and supports to meet the identified needs of individuals with exceptionalities and their families.

Supporting Explanation. Candidates are knowledgeable about a variety of national, state/provincial, and local resources such as professional associations, technology, support groups, recreational opportunities, social and health services, and post-secondary vocational programs that support individuals with exceptionalities and their families and how these resources and supports can be accessed. Candidates understand the importance of communicating, coordinating, and collaborating on an ongoing basis with related services and other professionals and agencies within the community to remain current with what resources are available and how they can be accessed and used by individuals with exceptionalities and their families. Candidates assist as team members to develop individual education programs, transition plans, and behavioral support plans that include relevant resources and agencies. They communicate with families in a variety of ways (e.g., email, phone calls, e-messages, school/class websites, as well as parent teacher conferences, virtual meetings, home visits, annual reviews) about the use of these resources and their potential outcomes.

Knowledge Base. The special education team, including teachers, related service professionals, families and professionals, and community agencies external to the school setting, plays a key role in planning for and implementing transitions from the early childhood years through the secondary school years. The Individuals with Disabilities Education Act (IDEA, 2004) requires that postsecondary transition planning must begin before a student turns 16 and include potential employers, postsecondary education representatives, and other relevant community representatives on the planning team.

The IDEA Part C Regulations (U.S. Department of Education, 2011) specify the requirements for transition planning from Part C (infant/toddler) to Part B 619 (preschool) special education services. These requirements specify that planning is to be conducted by a team of professionals from the Part C agency and the local education agency as well as the family and requires that interagency and intra-agency agreements be developed as part of the transition process. Kemp's research (2003) suggests that the most critical factor for successful transition to an inclusive environment may be a positive working relationship between the family and service providers.

The DEC Recommended Practices (2014) expand on the importance of collaboration by stating that "practitioners in sending and receiving programs exchange information before, during, and after transition..." (p. 15). Further, these practices emphasize that the team assists each other in working with and accessing community-based services.

Kohler and colleagues (2016) state that three decades of research demonstrates that postsecondary outcomes for students with disabilities improve when educators, families, students, and community members work together in transition planning and implementation. Their research-based taxonomy for transition programming includes the role of the special educator in instruction and collaborative service delivery. Educators have consistently rated their level of involvement in transition and planning of individualized education programs (IEPs) as moderate to high; however, in essential aspects of this planning process (e.g., interagency collaboration, career development, working with families) they report not being adequately prepared (Benitez, Morningstar, & Frey, 2009). Further, secondary educators are less likely to implement evidence-based transition practices, in part, due to a lack of training (Mazzotti & Plotner, 2016).

Component 7.4. Candidates work with and mentor paraprofessionals in the paraprofessionals' role of supporting the education of individuals with exceptionalities and their families.

Supporting Explanation. Candidates understand the importance of working with paraprofessionals and the potential roles of the paraprofessional based on the needs of individual learners and the educational setting. Candidates also understand and apply with supervision the various roles that they must assume in order to work effectively with paraprofessionals. For example, they understand the importance of seeking information from paraprofessionals in order to identify specific responsibilities and skills paraprofessionals need for their roles. Candidates, at the direction of supervising teachers, may monitor, guide, or mentor paraprofessionals to ensure high fidelity of implementation for evidence-based practices and interventions. With scaffolding and collaborative support from supervising teachers, candidates may plan for and coordinate the activities of paraprofessionals in order to implement individualized plans, such as IEPs, behavioral intervention plans, and transition plans.

Knowledge Base. InTASC Standard 10 (Leadership and Collaboration) delineates how teachers must work with other school professionals to plan and jointly facilitate learning to meet the diverse needs of learners (CCSSO, 2011. CEC High-Leverage Practice 1, Collaboration, focuses on teachers' collaboration with a variety of people, including paraprofessionals (McLeskey et al., 2017). The CEC Standards for Professional Practice (2015) emphasize paraeducators in Standard 5, noting that special educators should assign only tasks for which paraeducators have been appropriately prepared; provide timely, supportive, and collegial communications and feedback to paraeducators regarding tasks and expectations; and intervene professionally when a paraeducator's behavior is illegal, unethical, or detrimental to individuals with exceptionalities.

Although paraeducator roles and titles vary widely (e.g., paraprofessionals, teacher assistants, instructional assistants, educational assistants, special needs assistants, and personal learning assistants), they are increasingly engaged in the delivery of special education services (Brown & Stanton-Chapman, 2014). The number of paraeducators serving children with disabilities ages 3-21 in 2016 was 488,247 with more paraeducators than special education teachers working in schools (U.S. Department of Education, 2018a). Giangreco and colleagues (2010) emphasize that paraprofessionals are essential to the special education team in the delivery of individualized services and increasingly in the support of instruction. Paraprofessionals serve in multiple roles in the provision of special education services, from performing clerical tasks to supporting instructional activities, behavioral interventions, or functional living skills (Causton-Theoharis, 2009; Gerlach, 2015). Appropriately credentialed special educators retain primary responsibility for designing evidenced-based instruction to address the identified needs of the students and providing explicit written plans to paraprofessionals to facilitate implementation of instruction with fidelity and collection of appropriate data that informs future instruction (Capizzi & DaFonte, 2012; Carnahan et al., 2009; Chopra et al., 2018; French & Chopra, 2006).

Special educators are often responsible for supervising and mentoring paraprofessionals; therefore, it is essential that they be prepared for this role (Fisher & Pleasants, 2012). To support special educators in mentoring paraprofessionals and to provide guidance for the preparation of paraprofessionals, CEC, in collaboration with the National Resource Center for Paraeducators, developed and validated a specialty set of knowledge and skill statements for paraeducators in special education and also another for paraeducators working with individuals with deaf-blindness (CEC, 2015). In 2015, CEC aligned the specialty set with the initial preparation standards, thus creating the Paraeducator Common Core Guidelines (PCCG).

Field Experience and Clinical Practice Standard for K-12

Special education candidates progress through a series of developmentally sequenced field and clinical experiences for the full range of ages, types and levels of abilities, and collaborative opportunities that are appropriate to the license or roles for which they are preparing. These field and clinical experiences are supervised by qualified professionals.

Supporting Explanation. Field and clinical experiences provide opportunities for candidates to apply knowledge and to practice skills in authentic culturally and linguistically diverse school and community settings. Field and clinical experience sites are developed and strengthened over time through the building of solid partnerships between special educators in the field and the university special education faculty.

Through consultation and collaboration, the placements of candidates are selected to provide developmental field experiences that support candidates' use of effective practices in varied service delivery models appropriate to the licensure areas pursued by the candidates. Field experiences are structured to ensure that candidates have experiences with individuals with exceptionalities across the age, grade, and disability ranges for which the candidate is being prepared.

Field and clinical experiences are designed to connect special education theory and research with practice by providing candidates rich, scaffolded, developmental, and graduated experiences with increasing responsibilities to develop their knowledge and skills. Thus, field experiences are aligned with coursework and occur early and throughout the EPP beginning with observation and reflection on practices and systematically progressing to implementation of practices with supervision.

Examples of these experiences include course-based field work, practice, internships, and student teaching. These experiences are coherent, extensive, and appropriately intensive for candidates to develop and demonstrate proficiencies in the professional roles for which they are preparing. Performance assessments of candidate practices articulated by the CEC standards and demonstrated in field settings are ongoing and developmentally appropriate.

In their field experiences, candidates are supervised and mentored by school- or site-based professionals who are certified or licensed in the special education areas for which the candidates are being prepared. These site-based professionals are selected for their expertise and experience in relevant K-12 special education roles, as well as their mentoring skills to scaffold and support candidates' learning. In addition, the site-based professionals effectively communicate with and engage candidates in self-reflection on the interactions and practices utilized with students, families, and other providers. Field experiences may also be supervised and evaluated by university faculty.

Section 3

Potential Performance Indicators for K-12 Standards

In the standards sets presented in Section 2, the supporting explanations elaborate on specific practices identified in the components, providing insights about what should be taught and assessed within special educator preparation programs. The following performance indicators are provided to assist programs in developing assessments and evidence that demonstrate candidate mastery of the standards. These are provided solely as examples, not as requirements. This is not an exhaustive list and use of these examples would not automatically lead to a positive SPA recognition decision.

Table 4: Performance Indicators for the Initial Practice-Based Professional Preparation Standards for Special Educators	
Components	**Potential Performance Indicators**
Standard 1: Engaging in Professional Learning and Practice within Ethical Guidelines	
1.1: Candidates practice within ethical guidelines and legal policies and procedures.	• Candidates review, compare, and contrast multiple professional codes of ethics from relevant professional organizations • Candidates identify ethical issues and how to respond to them using CEC's and other relevant codes of ethics. • Candidates adhere to national, state/provincial, and local regulations in assessing, planning and implementing instruction. • Candidates explain relevant legal guidelines to families and other professionals.

Components	Potential Performance Indicators

Table 4: Performance Indicators for the Initial Practice-Based Professional Preparation Standards for Special Educators...(continued)

Standard 1: Engaging in Professional Learning and Practice within Ethical Guidelines...(continued)

Components	Potential Performance Indicators
1.2: Candidates advocate for improved outcomes for individuals with exceptionalities and their families while addressing the unique needs of those with diverse social, cultural, and linguistic backgrounds.	• Candidates interview other professionals and family members to identify the barriers faced by students from diverse backgrounds and determine resources needed to overcome these barriers. • Candidates evaluate new assistive and augmentative technology options given student needs and plan a process to advocate for administrative support in technology implementation. • Candidates identify potential social, legal, and environmental policies that could lead to improved supports for individuals with exceptionalities from diverse backgrounds. • Candidates communicate in writing to a local, state, provincial, and/or federal representative to promote some aspect of special education services.
1.3: Candidates design and implement professional learning activities based on ongoing analysis of student learning; self-reflection; and professional standards, research, and contemporary practices.	• Candidates evaluate their own knowledge and skills based on national and state/provincial standards, and design and implement a professional development plan aligned with evidence-based practices. • Candidates evaluate student performance and use those results to inform their own professional development plan. • Candidates join local, state/provincial and/or national professional organizations and document how that membership supports student learning. • Candidates participate in professional learning communities and document how this participation enhances student learning.

Table 4: Performance Indicators for the Initial Practice-Based Professional Preparation Standards for Special Educators...(continued)	
Components	**Potential Performance Indicators**
Standard 2: Understanding and Addressing Each Individual's Developmental and Learning Needs	
2.1: Candidates apply understanding of human growth and development to create developmentally appropriate and meaningful learning experiences that address individualized strengths and needs of students with exceptionalities.	• Candidates interpret a developmental assessment to prepare an assessment summary that reports the child's strengths and needs; provide implications for intervention and instruction. • Candidates develop a student case study that comprehensively outlines the child's development across multiple domains, including their complexity and interdependence; provide recommendations for how a teacher can support the child based on their strengths and needs. • Candidates design a learning activity that includes specific strategies to modify the environment, materials, and instruction to appropriately address students' developmental needs and academic content. • Candidates plan a lesson using principles of universal design that addresses a student's IEP needs in an inclusive setting.
2.2: Candidates use their knowledge and understanding of diverse factors that influence development and learning, including differences related to families, languages, cultures, and communities, and individual differences, including exceptionalities, to plan and implement learning experiences and environments.	• Candidates develop a lesson plan that incorporates supports for children who are dual language learners and incorporates materials and/or content that is culturally responsive to students from diverse backgrounds. • Candidates interview a family to discover that family's goals for their child and describe how those goals may impact the instruction they plan for the child. • Given a case study of a student with a culturally and linguistically diverse background, candidates identify specific curriculum, programs, or strategies to help a student with a particular exceptionality meet a personalized educational goal.

Table 4: Performance Indicators for the Initial Practice-Based Professional Preparation Standards for Special Educators...(continued)	
Components	**Potential Performance Indicators**
Standard 3: Demonstrating Subject Matter Content and Specialized Curricular Knowledge	
3.1: Candidates apply their understanding of academic subject matter content of the general curriculum to inform their programmatic and instructional decisions for individuals with exceptionalities.	• Candidates develop instructional and educational plans to be implemented that align with professional and curriculum standards to increase equitable access to and participation in the general curriculum, and they differentiate challenging content to address the full range of abilities of students based upon multiple sources of assessment data. • Candidates analyze professional and curriculum standards and design appropriate, culturally responsive learning and performance accommodations and modifications for students with exceptional learning needs in academic subject matter content of the general curriculum, both individually and collaboratively with content experts and related professionals, as needed. • Candidates develop individualized accommodations and specially designed instruction as part of the individualized education program and assure each student with exceptional learning needs has the necessary instruction and support to have access to the general education curriculum as appropriate within the least restrictive environment.

Table 4: Performance Indicators for the Initial Practice-Based Professional Preparation Standards for Special Educators...(continued)	
Components	**Potential Performance Indicators**
Standard 3: Demonstrating Subject Matter Content and Specialized Curricular Knowledge...(continued)	
3.2: Candidates augment the general education curriculum to address skills and strategies that students with disabilities need to access the core curriculum and function successfully within a variety of contexts as well as the continuum of placement options to assure specially designed instruction is developed and implemented to achieve mastery of curricular standards, and individualized goals and objectives.	• Candidates modify instructional and educational plans to be implemented that align with professional and specialized curricular standards to increase equitable access to and participation in the general curriculum, and they differentiate challenging content to address the full range of abilities of students based upon multiple sources of assessment data. • Based on assessment data, candidates identify the appropriate specialized curricula and develop individualized goals and objectives aligned as appropriate with that curriculum to meet the needs of a learner. • Candidates create individual plans by recognizing barriers to accessibility and acceptance of individuals with exceptionalities and plan for ways to address those barriers through the implementation of specialized curricula. • Candidates design learning environments that adhere to universal-design principles and that facilitate active participation, self-advocacy, and independence of individuals with exceptionalities in a variety of group and individual learning activities. In addition, candidates use appropriate instructional, adaptive, and assistive technologies to meet the learning goals of students with exceptionalities using specialized curricula.

Components	Potential Performance Indicators

Components	Potential Performance Indicators
Standard 4: Using Assessment to Understand the Learner and the Learning Environment for Data-Based Decision Making	
4.1: Candidates collaboratively develop, select, administer, analyze, and interpret multiple measures of student learning, behavior, and the classroom environment to evaluate and support classroom and school-based systems of intervention for students with and without exceptionalities.	• Candidates select and administer multiple progress monitoring measures of student learning, behavior, and the classroom environment. • Candidates collaboratively engage in data-based decision making using multiple measures to evaluate and support classroom-based systems of interventions for all students. • Candidates collaboratively engage in data-based decision making using multiple measures to evaluate and support school-based systems of instruction and intervention across varying levels of support for all students.
4.2: Candidates develop, select, and administer multiple, formal and informal, culturally and linguistically appropriate measures and procedures that are valid and reliable, to contribute to eligibility determination for special education services.	• Candidates explain the rationale for using specific formal and informal assessment measures with a specific child in mind considering strengths, needs, diversity, and potential biases. • Candidates administer reliable and valid standardized assessment measures accurately and adjust items as appropriate, to address students' individual needs and diversity. • Candidates administer informal assessment tools to accurately represent a child's abilities, strengths, diversity, and needs across multiple contexts. • Candidates work collaboratively as part of a multidisciplinary team to discuss and analyze results of multiple measures to inform eligibility determination.
4.3: Candidates assess, collaboratively analyze, interpret, and communicate students' progress toward measurable outcomes, using technology as appropriate, to inform both short- and long-term planning, and make ongoing adjustments to instruction.	• Candidates engage in data-based decision making to determine if students are making adequate progress toward measurable outcomes, determine immediate instructional changes, and develop short-term goals. • Candidates administer and analyze multiple formal and informal measures (formative and summative assessments) of student performance considering cultural, linguistic, and other factors to provide input for long-term planning (e.g., Individualized Education Program development). • Candidates collaborate with educational professionals, families, and students to analyze and interpret data that informs short- and long-term planning for instruction. • Candidates use technology for test administration, accommodations, data storage, and progress monitoring as appropriate.

Table 4: Performance Indicators for the Initial Practice-Based Professional Preparation Standards for Special Educators...(continued)

Components	Potential Performance Indicators
Standard 5: Using Effective Instruction to Support Learning	
5.1: Candidates use findings from multiple assessments, including student self-assessment, that are responsive to cultural and linguistic diversity and specialized as needed, to identify what students know and are able to do. They then interpret the assessment data to appropriately plan and guide instruction to meet rigorous academic and non-academic content and goals for each individual.	• Candidates use appropriate formative and summative assessment data to plan a unit or lesson for specific individuals or groups of students. • Candidates deliver instruction based on identified learning goals derived from assessment data and responsive to students' backgrounds and needs. • Candidates implement instructional plans and collect student performance data. They then reflect upon ways instruction can be adjusted to promote continued learning progress.
5.2: Candidates use effective strategies to promote active student engagement, increase student motivation, increase opportunities to respond, and enhance self-regulation of student learning.	• Based on observation or a case study, candidates provide the rationale for selecting the appropriate practices and strategies to use with individual students based on the best-available empirical evidence as well as the wisdom and experience of the field. • Candidates develop a lesson plan that explicitly details how the principles of universal design for learning and ensuring challenging learning experiences are addressed. • Candidates select and implement effective strategies to actively engage students individually and in groups and to ensure that all students have an equitable opportunity to respond to instruction. • Candidates explicitly teach and reinforce self-regulation behaviors. • Candidates effectively use technology, including distance technologies, to enhance instruction.
5.3: Candidates use explicit, systematic instruction to teach content, strategies, and skills to make clear what a learner needs to do or think about while learning.	• Candidates plan to make explicit connections between existing and new knowledge/skills and engage students in activating their prior knowledge. • Candidates provide clear purpose statements and advance organizers for lessons. • Candidates plan and deliver clear and accurate explanations of content and demonstrations of skills within a lesson. • Candidates plan and deliver explicit, systematic instruction to teach academic and non-academic content. • Candidates scaffold instruction to enable independent learning.

Table 4: Performance Indicators for the Initial Practice-Based Professional Preparation Standards for Special Educators...(continued)	
Components	**Potential Performance Indicators**
Standard 5: Using Effective Instruction to Support Learning...(continued)	
5.4: Candidates use flexible grouping to support the use of instruction that is adapted to meet the needs of each individual and group.	• Candidates appropriately configure groups based on assessment data, learning goals, and appropriate standards, and ensure that groups are fluid based on the content being addressed and student needs. • Candidates identify and use an appropriate structure for grouping, prepare students to use the structure, and ensure that all students equitably participate. • Candidates systematically monitor student learning in groups, make adjustments to instruction and groupings as indicated, and hold students accountable individually and collectively for learning within the group.
5.5: Candidates organize and manage focused, intensive small group instruction to meet the learning needs of each individual.	• Candidates use assessment data to identify students with common instructional needs, develop instructional goals, appropriately configure groups (including number of students and time per week for instruction), and plan intensive instruction. • Candidates deliver intensive instruction to small groups using appropriate, effective instructional strategies to ensure active student engagement and sufficient opportunities to respond for each learner. • Candidates monitor the progress of each student and adjust instruction as appropriate to accelerate student learning. • When teaching small groups, candidates use strategies to support learners in taking ownership for their learning and developing self-direction.
5.6: Candidates plan and deliver specialized, individualized instruction that is used to meet the learning needs of each individual.	• Candidates use formal and informal assessment data to identify student needs and plan specialized instruction to meet those needs. • Candidates use assessment data to monitor student progress and adjust critical elements of specialized instruction to improve student learning. • Candidates use appropriate instructional strategies (e.g., explicit instruction, scaffolding, feedback) to meet student needs effectively and efficiently. • Candidates design and implement a data-based instructional (DBI) project with an individual student. • Candidates use strategies to promote and monitor the application of knowledge and skills that are mastered across content areas and educational settings.

Table 4: Performance Indicators for the Initial Practice-Based Professional Preparation Standards for Special Educators...(continued)	
Components	**Potential Performance Indicators**
Standard 6: Supporting Social, Emotional, and Behavioral Growth	
6.1: Candidates use effective routines and procedures to create safe, caring, respectful, and productive learning environments for individuals with exceptionalities.	• Candidates establish age appropriate and culturally responsive expectations, routines, and procedures within their classrooms that are positively stated and explicitly taught, practiced, and reinforced. • Candidates build mutually respectful relationships with students and engage them in creating a classroom climate that values racial, cultural, and linguistic diversity. • Candidates demonstrate the ability to establish a productive learning environment by maintaining student engagement and managing time, materials, and the physical classroom environment.
6.2: Candidates use a range of preventive and responsive practices documented as effective to support individuals' social, emotional, and educational well-being.	• Candidates develop comprehensive classroom management plans and explain the rationales for their choices of both proactive/preventive and responsive strategies to ensure positive learning environments. • Candidates deliver effective verbal or nonverbal feedback that is strategic and goal-directed, timely, contingent, genuine, meaningful, age appropriate, and at rates commensurate with the task and phase of learning (i.e., acquisition, fluency, maintenance). • Candidates reduce the potential for challenging behavior and increase student engagement by establishing, following, and reinforcing expectations of all students within the educational setting. • Candidates demonstrate use of overall classroom awareness and/or the least intrusive means to prevent or manage minor student misbehavior.

Table 4: Performance Indicators for the Initial Practice-Based Professional Preparation Standards for Special Educators...(continued)

Components	Potential Performance Indicators
Standard 6: Supporting Social, Emotional, and Behavioral Growth...(continued)	
6.3: Candidates systematically use data from a variety of sources to identify the purpose or function served by problem behavior to plan, implement, and evaluate behavioral interventions and social skills programs, including generalization to other environments.	• Candidates collect and use appropriate data to determine the purpose or function of behavior(s), then develop an intervention plan that (a) teaches the student a positive replacement behavior that will serve the same or similar function, (b) alters the environment to make the replacement behavior more efficient and effective than the problem behavior, (c) alters the environment to no longer allow the problem behavior to access the previous outcome, and (d) includes ongoing data collection to monitor progress. • Candidates determine the nature of a social skill challenge, then explicitly teach appropriate interpersonal skills, including communication, and self-management, aligning lessons with classroom and schoolwide expectations for student behavior. • Candidates develop tools for data collection, collect and analyze data, and then use the information to plan for all phases of learning from acquisition through generalization.

Table 4: Performance Indicators for the Initial Practice-Based Professional Preparation Standards for Special Educators...(continued)	
Components	**Potential Performance Indicators**
Standard 7: Collaborating with Team Members	
7.1: Candidates utilize communication, group facilitation, and problem-solving strategies in a culturally responsive manner to lead effective meetings and share expertise and knowledge to build team capacity and jointly address students' instructional and behavioral needs.	• Candidates participate in meetings with families and/or other professionals and identify the strategies that facilitated achieving the meeting's goals. • Candidates develop a meeting agenda, allocate time to meet the goals of the agenda, and conduct the meeting, demonstrating effective verbal and nonverbal communication strategies to lead in ways that are culturally responsive. • Candidates plan and deliver a presentation for their peers or colleagues on an issue or strategy identified as potentially enhancing student learning.
7.2: Candidates communicate, coordinate, and collaborate with families and other professionals within the educational setting to assess, plan, and implement effective programs and services that promote progress toward measurable outcomes for individuals with and without exceptionalities and their families.	• Candidates participate in a simulated IEP meeting and draft an IEP for a child based on a case study that includes assessment results, developmental history, and behavioral observation information. • Candidates co-plan lessons with a general education teacher, actively co-teach in an inclusive classroom, and then reflect on the student and co-teacher experience. • Candidates participate in a weekly team meeting with other professionals and paraprofessionals to review child progress for that week and plan for the next week's instruction based on IEP progress and goals.
7.3: Candidates communicate, coordinate, and collaborate with professionals and agencies within the community to identify and access services, resources, and supports to meet the identified needs of individuals with exceptionalities and their families.	• Candidates identify resources in the community for a family whose primary language is other than English. • Candidates develop with families and other professionals a transition plan for a student for postsecondary education or employment. • Candidates interview a staff person in a local community agency (e.g., health department, social services) to identify resources for families provided by that agency and develop a pamphlet for families based on that information. • Candidates participate in a local or regional interagency meeting and reflect on how those agencies are coordinating services to better meet the needs of individuals with exceptionalities and their families.

Table 4: Performance Indicators for the Initial Practice-Based Professional Preparation Standards for Special Educators...(continued)	
Components	**Potential Performance Indicators**
Standard 7: Collaborating with Team Members...(continued)	
7.4: Candidates work with and mentor paraprofessionals in the paraprofessionals' role of supporting the education of individuals with exceptionalities and their families.	• Candidates explain the importance of working with paraprofessionals and understand roles, responsibilities, and expectations of the paraprofessional related to instruction, intervention, and direct service reinforcing their own role as leader and paraprofessional as the assistant.
	• Given a list of teaching responsibilities and tasks, candidates differentiate appropriately between teacher and paraprofessional responsibilities.
	• Candidates explain the role of teachers, certified teaching assistants and paraprofessionals based upon local guidelines.
	• In school settings where appropriate, candidates develop an instructional or behavior intervention plan for a paraprofessional to implement.
	• Candidates use appropriate communication skills while interacting with paraprofessionals.

Section 4

Potential Sources of Evidence for K-12 Standards

The CEC Initial Practice-Based Professional Preparation Standards were developed so that they could be assessed using six to eight assessments consistent with requirements for SPA Program Review Option A with National Recognition. While the assessment guidelines and resources align with CAEP and SPA requirements, they may be applicable as well for program reviews conducted by state agencies or within universities/schools/departments.

Types of Assessments

Of the six to eight assessment categories required for CAEP accreditation or SPA recognition, five are defined: (1) a licensure assessment or other content-based assessment, (2) content-based assessment, (3) assessment of candidate ability to plan instruction, (4) assessment of student teaching, and (5) assessment of candidate effect on student learning. While a sixth assessment is required, the specific focus of this assessment is determined by the program's assessment system and the extent to which stronger evidence that a standard is met is needed. Initial K-12 preparation programs are strongly encouraged to submit a seventh and/or eighth assessment that they believe will further strengthen their demonstration that all standards are met. The examples provided below are neither expected nor required but are provided as possible examples.

Table 5: Potential Sources of Assessment Evidence for Candidate Performance	
Components	**Potential Sources of Assessment Evidence for Candidate Performance**
Standard 1: Engaging in Professional Learning and Practice within Ethical Guidelines	
1.1: Candidates practice within ethical guidelines and legal policies and procedures.	• Assessments of content knowledge such as course grades in content or pedagogical courses related to ethical guidelines and legal policies. • Assessments and tools used by programs to assess student teaching or internship. • Other assessments such as a project that requires candidate to review, compare, and contrast multiple professional codes of ethics from professional membership organizations related to education, special education and/or related services. • Other assessments such as a project that requires candidate to review the legal regulations that govern a current topic or issue in special education.

Table 5: Potential Sources of Assessment Evidence for Candidate Performance...(continued)	
Components	**Potential Sources of Assessment Evidence for Candidate Performance**
Standard 1: Engaging in Professional Learning and Practice within Ethical Guidelines...(continued)	
1.2: Candidates advocate for improved outcomes for individuals with exceptionalities and their families while addressing the unique needs of those with diverse social, cultural, and linguistic backgrounds.	• Assessments of planning such as lesson plans, unit plans, need assessments, and/or other planning tasks. • Assessments and tools used by programs to assess student teaching or internship. • Other assessments such a portfolio projects that require evidence of candidate's plans for and/or participation in advocacy. • Other assessments such as portfolio entries that demonstrate candidate's engagement with local, state, or national professional and advocacy groups.
1.3: Candidates design and implement professional learning activities based on ongoing analysis of student learning; self-reflection; and professional standards, research, and contemporary practices.	• Other assessments such as portfolio project entries that demonstrate candidate's self-reflections and development of professional learning activities. • Other assessments such as portfolio entries that demonstrate candidate's engagement with local, state, or national professional and advocacy groups.

Table 5: Potential Sources of Assessment Evidence for Candidate Performance...(continued)

Components	Potential Sources of Assessment Evidence for Candidate Performance
Standard 2: Understanding and Addressing Each Individual's Developmental and Learning Needs	
2.1: Candidates apply understanding of human growth and development to create developmentally appropriate and meaningful learning experiences that address individualized strengths and needs of students with exceptionalities.	• Assessments of content knowledge such as state licensure tests or professional examinations of human growth and development. • Assessments of content knowledge such as course grades in content or pedagogical courses related to learning and development. • Assessments of planning such as lesson plans, unit plans, need assessments, and/or other planning tasks. • Assessments and tools used by programs to assess student teaching or internship.
2.2: Candidates use their knowledge and understanding of diverse factors that influence development and learning including differences related to families, languages, cultures, and communities, and to individual differences, including exceptionalities, to plan and implement learning experiences and environments.	• Assessments of content knowledge such as state licensure tests or professional examinations of human growth and development. • Assessments of content knowledge such as course grades in content or pedagogical courses related to learning and development. • Assessments of planning such as lesson plans, unit plans, need assessments, and/or other planning tasks. • Assessments and tools used by programs to assess student teaching or internship.

Table 5: Potential Sources of Assessment Evidence for Candidate Performance...(continued)	
Components	**Potential Sources of Assessment Evidence for Candidate Performance**
Standard 3: Demonstrating Subject Matter Content and Specialized Curricular Knowledge	
3.1: Candidates apply their understanding of academic subject matter content of the general curriculum to inform their programmatic and instructional decisions for individuals with exceptionalities.	• Assessments of content knowledge such as state licensure tests or professional examinations of content knowledge. • Assessments of content knowledge such as course grades in content or pedagogical courses. • Assessments of planning such as lesson plans, unit plans, need assessments, and/or other planning tasks. • Assessments and tools used by programs to assess student teaching or internship.
3.2: Candidates augment the general education curriculum to address skills and strategies that students with disabilities need to access the core curriculum and function successfully within a variety of contexts and the continuum of placement options to assure specially designed instruction is developed and implemented to achieve mastery of curricular standards.	• Assessments of content knowledge such as state licensure tests or professional examinations of content knowledge. • Assessments of content knowledge such as course grades in content or pedagogical courses related to special education. • Assessments of planning such as lesson plans, unit plans, need assessments, and/or other planning tasks. • Assessments and tools used by programs to assess student teaching or internship.

Table 5: Potential Sources of Assessment Evidence for Candidate Performance...(continued)

Components	Potential Sources of Assessment Evidence for Candidate Performance
Standard 4: Using Assessment to Understand the Learner and the Learning Environment for Data-Based Decision Making	
4.1: Candidates collaboratively develop, select, administer, analyze, and interpret multiple measures of student learning, behavior, and the classroom environment to evaluate and support classroom and school-based systems of intervention for students with and without exceptionalities.	• Assessments of planning such as lesson plans, unit plans, need assessments, and/or other planning tasks. • Assessments and tools used by programs to assess student teaching or internship. • An assessment of impact on student learning such as student work samples, performance assessments such as the edTPA, teacher work samples (TWS), case studies, and classroom action research studies.
4.2: Candidates develop, select, administer, and interpret multiple, formal, and informal, culturally and linguistically appropriate measures and procedures that are valid and reliable, to contribute to eligibility determination for special education services.	• Assessments and tools used by programs to assess student teaching or internship. • An assessment of impact on student learning such as student work samples, performance assessments such as the edTPA, teacher work samples (TWS), case studies of classrooms, and classroom action research studies. • Other assessments that demonstrate candidate's ability to work collaboratively with a team to administer assessments and interpret results to contribute to eligibility determination.
4.3: Candidates assess, collaboratively analyze, interpret, and communicate students' progress toward measurable outcomes using technology as appropriate, to inform both short- and long-term planning, and make ongoing adjustments to instruction.	• Assessments of planning such as annual individualized education programs (IEPs), lesson plans, unit plans, need assessments, and/or other planning tasks. • Assessments and tools used by programs to assess student teaching or internship. • An assessment of impact on student learning such as student work samples, performance assessments such as the edTPA, teacher work samples (TWS), case studies of classrooms, and classroom action research studies.

Table 5: Potential Sources of Assessment Evidence for Candidate Performance...(continued)	
Components	**Potential Sources of Assessment Evidence for Candidate Performance**
Standard 5: Using Effective Instruction to Support Learning	
5.1: Candidates use findings from multiple assessments, including student self-assessment, that are responsive to cultural and linguistic diversity and specialized as needed, to identify what students know and are able to do. They then interpret the assessment data to appropriately plan and guide instruction to meet rigorous academic and non-academic content and goals for each individual.	• Assessments of planning such as annual individualized education programs (IEPs), lesson plans, unit plans, need assessments, and/or other planning tasks. • Assessments and tools used by programs to assess student teaching or internship. • An assessment of impact on student learning such as student work samples, performance assessments such as the edTPA, teacher work samples (TWS), case studies of classrooms, and classroom action research studies.
5.2: Candidates use effective strategies to promote active student engagement, increase student motivation, increase opportunities to respond, and enhance self-regulation of student learning.	• Assessments of planning such as lesson plans, unit plans, need assessments, and/or other planning tasks. • Assessments and tools used by programs to assess student teaching or internship. • An assessment of impact on student learning such as student work samples, performance assessments such as the edTPA, teacher work samples (TWS), case studies of classrooms, and classroom action research studies.
5.3: Candidates use explicit, systematic instruction to teach content, strategies, and skills to make clear what a learner needs to do or think about while learning.	• Assessments of planning such as lesson plans, unit plans, need assessments, and/or other planning tasks. • Assessments and tools used by programs to assess student teaching or internship. • An assessment of impact on student learning such as student work samples, performance assessments such as the edTPA, teacher work samples (TWS), case studies of classrooms, and classroom action research studies.
5.4: Candidates use flexible grouping to support the use of instruction that is adapted to meet the needs of each individual and group.	• Assessments of planning such as lesson plans, unit plans, need assessments, and/or other planning tasks. • Assessments and tools used by programs to assess student teaching or internship. • An assessment of impact on student learning such as student work samples, performance assessments such as the edTPA, teacher work samples (TWS), case studies of classrooms, and classroom action research studies.

Table 5: Potential Sources of Assessment Evidence for Candidate Performance...(continued)

Components	Potential Sources of Assessment Evidence for Candidate Performance
Standard 5: Using Effective Instruction to Support Learning...(continued)	
5.5: Candidates organize and manage focused, intensive small group instruction to meet the learning needs of each individual.	• Assessments of planning such as lesson plans, unit plans, need assessments, and/or other planning tasks. • Assessments and tools used by programs to assess student teaching or internship. • An assessment of impact on student learning such as student work samples, performance assessments such as the edTPA, teacher work samples (TWS), case studies of classrooms, and classroom action research studies.
5.6: Candidates plan and deliver specialized, individualized instruction that is used to meet the learning needs of each individual.	• Assessments of planning such as lesson plans, unit plans, need assessments, and/or other planning tasks. • Assessments and tools used by programs to assess student teaching or internship. • An assessment of impact on student learning such as student work samples, performance assessments such as the edTPA, teacher work samples (TWS), case studies of classrooms, and classroom action research studies.

Components	Potential Sources of Assessment Evidence for Candidate Performance
Table 5: Potential Sources of Assessment Evidence for Candidate Performance...(continued)	
Standard 6: Supporting Social, Emotional, and Behavioral Growth	
6.1: Candidates use effective routines and procedures to create safe, caring, respectful, and productive learning environments for individuals with exceptionalities.	• Assessments of planning such as lesson plans, unit plans, need assessments, and/or other planning tasks. • Assessments and tools used by programs to assess pre-student teaching fieldwork, student teaching or internship. • Assessments of comprehensive organization and management plans developed for hypothetical classes or candidates' clinical placements.
6.2: Candidates use a range of preventive and responsive practices documented as effective to support individuals' social, emotional, and educational well-being.	• Assessments of planning such as lesson plans, unit plans, need assessments, and/or other planning tasks. • Assessments and tools used by programs to assess pre-student teaching fieldwork, student teaching, or internship. • Assessments of candidate's plans for preventing and responding to behaviors that interfere with students' social, emotional and educational well-being developed for hypothetical classes or candidate's clinical placements.
6.3: Candidates systematically use data from a variety of sources to identify the purpose or function served by problem behavior to plan, implement, and evaluate behavioral interventions and social skills programs, including generalization to other environments.	• Assessments of planning such as lesson plans, unit plans, need assessments, and/or other planning tasks. • Assessments and tools used by programs to assess pre-student teaching fieldwork, student teaching, or internship. • Other assessments such as case studies or functional behavior assessments and behavior improvement plans (FBA-BIPs).

Table 5: Potential Sources of Assessment Evidence for Candidate Performance...(continued)

Components	Potential Sources of Assessment Evidence for Candidate Performance
Standard 7: Collaborating with Team Members	
7.1: Candidates utilize communication, group facilitation, and problem–solving strategies in a culturally responsive manner to lead effective meetings and share expertise and knowledge to build team capacity and jointly address students' instructional and behavior needs.	• Other assessment such as role plays, collaborative planning and implementation of team meeting. • Assessments and tools used by programs to assess student teaching or internship.
7.2: Candidates communicate, coordinate, and collaborate with families and other professionals within the educational setting to assess, plan, and implement effective programs and services that promote progress toward measurable outcomes for individuals with and without exceptionalities and their families.	• Assessments of collaborative planning such as annual individualized education programs (IEPs), lesson plans, unit plans, need assessments, and/or other planning tasks. • Assessments and tools used by programs to assess student teaching or internship. • Other assessments such as classroom/family communication plans, child and family case studies, role plays, and portfolio projects.
7.3: Candidates communicate, coordinate, and collaborate with professionals and agencies within the community to identify and access services, resources, and supports to meet the identified needs of individuals with exceptionalities and their families.	• Other assessments such as case studies, transition plans, collaborative development of an IEP/IFSP, planning a team meeting, collaborative development and implementation of an intervention project. • Assessments and tools used by programs to assess student teaching or internship.
7.4: Candidates work with and mentor paraprofessionals in the paraprofessionals' role of supporting the education of individuals with exceptionalities and their families.	• Assessments and tools used by programs to assess student teaching or internship. • Assessments such as case studies or collaborative development of an instructional or behavioral intervention plan for use by a paraprofessional.

Key Assessment Alignment with K-12 Standards

The matrix in Table 6 demonstrates a crosswalk between the CEC Initial K-12 Special Education Preparation Standards and the CAEP national SPA program review structure of 6 – 8 key assessments. Each "X" in the matrix shown in Table 6 represents a potential primary source of direct assessment evidence of candidate ability to meet the standard component.

Table 6: Potential Sources of Evidence: Key Assessment Alignment

	Assessment of Content (State Licensure Test)	Assessment of Content	Assessment of Planning Instruction	Assessment of Student Teaching	Assessment of Impact on Learning	Assessment #6	Assessment #7 (Optional)	Assessment #8 (Optional)
Standard 1: Engaging in Professional Learning and Practice within Ethical Guidelines								
1.1		X		X		X	X	X
1.2			X	X		X	X	X
1.3						X	X	X
Standard 2: Understanding and Addressing Each Individual's Developmental and Learning Needs								
2.1	X	X	X	X				
2.2	X	X	X	X				
Standard 3: Demonstrating Subject Matter Content and Specialized Curricular Knowledge								
3.1	X	X	X	X				
3.2	X	X	X	X				
Standard 4: Using Assessment to Understand the Learner and the Learning Environment for Data-Based Decision Making								
4.1			X	X	X			
4.2						X	X	X
4.3			X	X	X			
Standard 5: Using Effective Instruction to Support Learning								
5.1			X	X	X			
5.2			X	X	X			
5.3			X	X	X			
5.4			X	X	X			
5.5			X	X	X			
5.6			X	X	X			
Standard 6: Supporting Social, Emotional, and Behavioral Growth								
6.1			X	X		X	X	X
6.2			X	X		X	X	X
6.3				X		X	X	X
Standard 7: Collaborating with Team Members								
7.1						X	X	X
7.2			X	X		X	X	X
7.3						X	X	X
7.4						X	X	X

Section 5

Overview of the CEC Initial Practice-Based Professional Preparation Standards for Early Interventionists/Early Childhood Special Educators

Focusing on the 2020 EI/ECSE Standards, this section begins with an explanation of the need for the EI/ECSE standards. This is followed by an introduction to the standards, a description of the standards development process, and influences in the field that shaped the framing of these standards. It then highlights some of the current features, including alignment with InTASC standards.

The Need for CEC's Initial Practice-Based Professional Based Preparation Standards EI/ECSE

While CEC has long had a specialty set of knowledge and skill statements used to inform the program report and review process that articulate unique content to be addressed in the personnel preparation for special educators working in EI/ECSE, there were no personnel preparation standards specific to this age range. The national landscape of services for all young children, including those who have or are at-risk for developmental delays and disabilities, has changed dramatically during the past four decades. The passage of Public Law 99-457 in 1986 resulted in dramatic increases in the number of young children being served and in professional interest and research related to the characteristics of services that best addressed the needs of this population of children and their families. Concurrently, professional groups and organizations, policymakers, and researchers began to re-envision and study the roles, practices, and educational requirements of the EI/ECSE responsible for providing intervention and instruction to young children and their families.

As the field of early childhood continued to advance, it became clear that in addition to defining the role of the EI/ECSE, clarification of this discipline, in relation to the role of the early childhood educator (ECE), would be critical. As a result, the National Association for the Education of Young Children (NAEYC) and multiple other professional organizations, including the Council for Exceptional Children (CEC) Division for Early Childhood (DEC), developed the 2020 Professional Standards and Competencies for Early Childhood Educators. The standards and competencies defined "the core body of knowledge, values, and dispositions early childhood educators must demonstrate to effectively promote the development, learning, and well-being of all young children (NAEYC, 2020). The EI/ECSE role was identified as a specialization that requires additional standards and competencies. A set of standards unique to EI/ECSE thus builds upon the foundation of the ECE standards in which overlapping skills and knowledge are highlighted and the distinct set of skills and knowledge of the ECE and EI/ECSE are clearly articulated.

Collaborative partnerships with related services disciplines [e.g., occupational therapy (OT), physical therapy (PT), speech/language (SLP)] in the preparation of personnel to work with children birth through eight years have been advocated for more than three decades. To support efforts in cross-disciplinary personnel preparation, the Early Childhood Personnel Center (ECPC) facilitated a cross-disciplinary collaboration with DEC and related services professional associations representing OT, PT, SLP, and other early intervention providers. The purpose of this collaborative work was to develop a set of standards and resources to guide personnel preparation programs across the disciplines to integrate the unique competencies needed in working with infants, toddlers, and young children and their families into their respective preparation programs. Collaborative initiatives such as these, however, have been complicated by the fact that there were no comparable set of standards for special educator preparation for the birth through 8 age range. While DEC, as a division of CEC, has a specialty set of knowledge and skill statements that articulate unique content to be addressed in the personnel preparation for special educators working in EI/ECSE, there were no personnel preparation standards specific to this age range. Having a set of standards for the preparation of special educators that addresses the birth through 8 age range and aligns with the CEC K-12 Initial Practice-Based Preparation Standards provides a continuum of special educator personnel preparation standards for birth through age 21. Having the two sets of special educator standards provides clarity to both as to competencies that are common across the age span and clarifies those that are unique to EI/ECSE and facilitates our collaborative work across disciplines.

The body of work resulting from these movements has implications for the quality and curricula of personnel preparation programs designed to prepare highly qualified personnel, and for the consistency of preparation and licensing requirements. The potential roles for which new EI/ECSE professionals are being prepared vary widely, reflecting not only the varied settings in which services may occur but also the unique set of values and practices that have emerged from research and experience. EI/ECSE professionals must be prepared to work with children who range in age from birth through age 8, covering a period of rapid developmental change. For young children who have or are at risk for developmental delays or disabilities, EI/ECSE professionals must be able to integrate knowledge of how conditions both within children and within children's everyday home and community environments may influence their development and learning at different ages, resulting in a careful consideration of preventive, ameliorative, and functional goals and outcomes, as well as the array of intervention and instructional approaches appropriate for each age, within the context of children's natural environments. EI/ECSE professionals work closely with families who represent increasing diversity in culture, language, and socioeconomic conditions, and these professionals respect and support families as decision-makers and as essential partners in supporting their child's growth and development. EI/ECSE professionals also work in a wide variety of early childhood education programs including those in schools, homes, and community, each requiring different sets of skills, with roles as direct service providers, consultants, coaches, and service coordinators.

The diversity of potential roles for which EI/ECSE must be prepared are grounded in a core set of beliefs and practices that underlie all roles, in congruence with research, professional opinion, policy, and recommended practices. Several core themes are emphasized throughout all the proposed standards, including:

- an emphasis on families, including families as decision-makers and as partners in supporting and strengthening family capacity and promoting children's development and learning;

- recognition and respect for diversity as represented by the cultural, linguistic, and socioeconomic conditions of families, staff, and programs, and by the various developmental delays and disabilities represented in children;

- an expectation for equity for all children and families, with an emphasis on full access to, participation in, and support from programs and professionals, and for intervention and instruction that are based in and seek to enhance children's natural environments through a range of approaches, including a multifaceted use of technology;

- an expectation for individualized, developmentally, age, and functionally appropriate intervention and instruction based on sound knowledge of each child's and each family's assets, needs, and preferences for services; and

- an emphasis on partnership, collaboration and team interaction that influences the availability and quality of services for children and families, as well as team structures and processes for collaboration within programs and service systems.

Central to all our work in EI/ECSE and reflected in the core beliefs and practices noted above is inclusion. Inclusion in the early childhood years (birth through age 8) embodies the values, policies, and practices that support the right of every infant, toddler, and young child and their family to participate in a broad range of activities and contexts as full members of their communities and society. Every child should have equal access to high-quality early childhood educational opportunities. High-quality early childhood education refers to opportunities where all children are provided with individualized and appropriate supports using evidence-based interventions and practices. These early experiences for children and their families lead to a sense of belonging and membership, positive social relationships and friendships, and development and learning to meet high expectations. The defining features of inclusion that can be used to identify high quality early childhood programs and services are access, participation, and supports. EI/ECSE professionals work in partnerships with the family and the other individuals in the child and family's lives to ensure that the services experienced by children and families are consistent and integrated.

High-quality educator preparation equates to EI/ECSE professionals' expertise, which directly impacts outcomes for children and families. The CEC Initial Practice-Based Professional Preparation Standards for Early Interventionists/Early Childhood Special Educators are grounded in current evidence-based practices in EI/ECSE, which reflect current research as well as professional and family wisdom. The standards are designed to provide a foundation that will be consistent across educator preparation programs in EI/ECSE and provide guidance for state licensure aligned with research, policy, and professional opinion related to young children, families, and services.

Introduction to the Initial Practice-Based Professional Preparation Standards

CEC, in partnership with DEC and through an Early Intervention/ Early Childhood Special Education (EI/ECSE) Standards Development Task Force, established this set of Practice-Based Professional Preparation Standards for Early Interventionists/Early Childhood Special Educators (EI/ECSE) that define what EI/ECSE candidates need to know and be able to do at the completion of their initial educator preparation programs. High-quality preparation is essential to ensuring positive outcomes for young children birth through third grade who have or are at risk for

developmental delays or disabilities and their families. The EI/ECSE Standards represent the first standards to focus specifically on the preparation of early interventionists and early childhood special educators who work with young children ages birth through age 8 who have or are at risk for developmental delays and disabilities and their families, across home, classroom and community settings. These standards build on the history of EI/ECSE as an integrative but unique field of study, policy, research, and practice and emphasize the unique skills and knowledge required for specialization in working with young children and their families.

Applicability to Age or Grade Levels of Program Preparation

In the event a program prepares P-12 Educators, a program will use the following criteria to determine which set of standards are applicable:

- If the program prepares educators to teach birth through age 5 or kindergarten, use the EI/ECSE Standards.

- If the program prepares educators to teach age 3 through grade 12 (or a similar grade), use EI/ECSE Standards for the ages 3-8 (or grade 3) portion of the program and the K-12 Standards for the remaining grade levels. For this very broad age span, it is not sufficient to submit just one report, since the EI/ECSE and K-12 Standards are based upon different sets of essential practices (DEC Recommended Practices and High Leverage Practices) tailored to the specific developmental needs and service delivery models of early childhood or K-12 special education.

- If the program prepares educators to teach K-12 or K-12+, use the Initial K-12 Special Educator Standards.

The Process of Development

In 2018, DEC submitted a proposal to the CEC Board of Directors that requested approval to develop a stand-alone set of EI/ECSE standards. Data related to licensure/certification requirements for early childhood intervention/special education providers (birth to age 5) and their families was provided to support development of this set of standards. Full reports and further information may be accessed through the Early Childhood Personnel Center (ECPC) website at www.ecpcta.org/papers-publications-and-data/. The request, supported by both CEC and NAEYC, was approved by the CEC Board of Directors in May 2018 and by the SPASC in September 2018.

DEC used an application process to seek members for the Standards Development Task Force (SDTF). Members were selected to reflect various age ranges and service providers in the EI/ECSE field. Representatives from NAEYC and CEC with extensive experience in reviewing and/or auditing program submissions were also included on the Task Force. A list of the SDTF members is included in Appendix 2.

The development of the EI/ECSE Standards was a consistently collaborative, iterative, and open process (CEC, 2020). The SDTF also held two in-person listening sessions on the developing standards at the DEC Annual Conference and the CEC Teacher Education Division (TED) Conference in fall 2018. Listening sessions focused on the developing draft of standards and were held at the NAEYC 2019 Professional Learning Institute and the fall 2019 DEC and TED conferences. Approximately 400 people attended these sessions. The SDTF also hosted webinars on the new EI/ECSE standards in January 2019 and October 2019, with a combined total of more than 1,600 viewers. Each webinar discussed the background of the development process, described the current (at that time) draft of the standards, components, and supporting explanations, and offered an opportunity for public feedback through a survey. These webinars and the surveys were promoted to CEC and DEC members and nonmembers through an email newsletter, on the CEC and DEC websites, and in social media.

Feedback was also solicited from groups focused on early childhood such as NAEYC members. More than 160 responses were received for the public feedback surveys opened after these webinars.

Throughout the process, the CEC Professional Standards and Practices Committee (PSPC) and the CEC Board of Directors received updates, and both formally approved the 2020 EI/ECSE Standards in 2020. In October 2020, CAEP accepted these standards for inclusion in the Specialized Professional Association (SPA) Review Process for education program providers (EPPs) to achieve National Recognition.

Alignment with InTASC

The Model Core Teaching Standards published by the Council of Chief State School Officers (CCSSO), through its Interstate Teacher Assessment and Support Consortium (InTASC), are widely used to guide licensure and program approval efforts by state education agencies, as well as program design and improvement efforts by Education Preparation Programs (EPPs). Additionally, evidence of alignment with InTASC standards is required for CAEP Accreditation. Originally developed in 1992 and most recently updated in 2021, these InTASC standards "outline what teachers should know and be able to do to ensure every K-12 student reaches the goal of being ready to enter college or the workforce in today's world" (CCSSO, 2013, p. 3). Throughout its work, the EI/ECSE Standards Development Task Force was attentive to InTASC standards, and the following crosswalk illustrates the alignment of these two sets of standards.

Table 7: Early Interventionists/Early Childhood Special Educators Preparation Standards' Alignment with InTASC Categories

InTASC Categories	EI/ECSE Preparation Standards (primary alignment)
The Learner and Learning #1: Learner Development. The teacher understands how learners grow and develop, recognizing that patterns of learning and development vary individually within and across the cognitive, linguistic, social, emotional, and physical areas, and designs and implements developmentally appropriate and challenging learning experiences. #2: Learning Differences. The teacher uses understanding of individual differences and diverse cultures and communities to ensure inclusive learning environments that enable each learner to meet high standards. #3: Learning Environments. The teacher works with others to create environments that support individual and collaborative learning, and that encourage positive social interaction, active engagement in learning, and self-motivation.	**Standard 1: Child Development and Early Learning** Candidates understand the impact of different theories and philosophies of early learning and development on assessment, curriculum, instruction, and intervention decisions. Candidates apply knowledge of normative developmental sequences and variations, individual differences within and across the range of abilities, including developmental delays and disabilities, and other direct and indirect contextual features that support or constrain children's development and learning. These contextual factors as well as social, cultural, and linguistic diversity are considered when facilitating meaningful learning experiences and individualizing intervention and instruction across contexts.
Content #4: Content Knowledge. The teacher understands the central concepts, tools of inquiry, and structures of the discipline(s) he or she teaches and creates learning experiences that make the discipline accessible and meaningful for learners to assure mastery of the content. #5: Application of Content. The teacher understands how to connect concepts and use differing perspectives to engage learners in critical thinking, creativity, and collaborative problem solving related to authentic local and global issues.	**Standard 1: Child Development and Early Learning** Candidates understand the impact of different theories and philosophies of early learning and development on assessment, curriculum, instruction, and intervention decisions. Candidates apply knowledge of normative developmental sequences and variations, individual differences within and across the range of abilities, including developmental delays and disabilities, and other direct and indirect contextual features that support or constrain children's development and learning. These contextual factors as well as social, cultural, and linguistic diversity are considered when facilitating meaningful learning experiences and individualizing intervention and instruction across contexts.

Table 7: Early Interventionists/Early Childhood Special Educators Preparation Standards' Alignment with InTASC Categories...(continued)	
InTASC Categories	**EI/ECSE Preparation Standards (primary alignment)**
Instructional Practice	**Standard 4: Assessment Processes**
#6: Assessment. The teacher understands and uses multiple methods of assessment to engage learners in their own growth, to monitor learner progress, and to guide the teacher's and learner's decision making.	Candidates know and understand the purposes of assessment in relation to ethical and legal considerations. Candidates choose developmentally, linguistically, and culturally appropriate tools and methods that are responsive to the characteristics of the young child, family, and program. Using evidence-based practices, candidates develop or select as well as administer informal measures, and select and administer formal measures in partnership with families and other professionals. They analyze, interpret, document, and share assessment information using a strengths-based approach with families and other professionals for eligibility determination, outcome/goal development, planning instruction and intervention, monitoring progress, and reporting.
#7: Planning for Instruction. The teacher plans instruction that supports every student in meeting rigorous learning goals by drawing upon knowledge of content areas, curriculum, cross-disciplinary skills, and pedagogy, as well as knowledge of learners and the community context.	
#8: Instructional Strategies. The teacher understands and uses a variety of instructional strategies to encourage learners to develop deep understanding of content areas and their connections, and to build skills to apply knowledge in meaningful ways.	**Standard 5: Application of Curriculum Frameworks in the Planning and Facilitation of Meaningful Learning Experiences**
	Candidates collaborate with families and professionals to use an evidence-based, developmentally appropriate, and culturally responsive early childhood curriculum addressing developmental and content domains. Candidates use curriculum frameworks to create and support universally designed, high quality learning experiences in natural and inclusive environments that provide each child and family with equitable access and opportunities for learning and growth.
	Standard 6: Using Responsive and Reciprocal Interactions, Interventions, and Instruction
	Candidates plan and implement intentional, systematic, evidence-based, responsive interactions, interventions, and instruction to support all children's learning and development across all developmental and content domains in partnership with families and other professionals. Candidates facilitate equitable access and participation for all children and families within natural and inclusive environments through culturally responsive and affirming practices and relationships. Candidates use data-based decision-making to plan for, adapt, and improve interactions, interventions, and instruction to ensure fidelity of implementation.

Table 7: Early Interventionists/Early Childhood Special Educators Preparation Standards' Alignment with InTASC Categories...(continued)

InTASC Categories	EI/ECSE Preparation Standards (primary alignment)
Professional Responsibility #9: Professional Learning and Ethical Practice. The teacher engages in ongoing professional learning and uses evidence to continually evaluate his/her practice, particularly the effects of his/her choices and actions on others (learners, families, other professionals, and the community), and adapts practice to meet the needs of each learner. #10: Leadership and Collaboration. The teacher seeks appropriate leadership roles and opportunities to take responsibility for student learning, to collaborate with learners, families, colleagues, other school professionals, and community members to ensure learner growth, and to advance the profession.	**Standard 2: Partnering with Families** Candidates use their knowledge of family-centered practices and family systems theory to develop and maintain reciprocal partnerships with families. They apply family capacity-building practices as they support families to make informed decisions and advocate for their young children. They engage families in opportunities that build on their existing strengths, reflect current goals, and foster family competence and confidence to support their children's development and learning. **Standard 3: Collaboration and Teaming** Candidates apply models, skills, and processes of teaming when collaborating and communicating with families and professionals, using culturally and linguistically responsive and affirming practices. In partnership with families and other professionals, candidates develop and implement individualized plans and successful transitions that occur across the age span. Candidates use a variety of collaborative strategies while working with and supporting other adults. **Standard 7: Professionalism and Ethical Practice** Candidates identify and engage with the profession of early intervention and early childhood special education (EI/ECSE) by exhibiting skills in reflective practice, advocacy, and leadership while adhering to ethical and legal guidelines. Evidence-based and recommended practices are promoted and used by candidates.

Alignment with DEC Recommended Practices and HLPs

Upon completion of the EI/ECSE Standards, The Early Childhood Personnel Center (ECPC) worked in collaboration with the Division for Early Childhood (DEC) of the Council for Exceptional Children (CEC) to create a crosswalk of the standards with the DEC Recommended Practices (2014). The stated purpose of the crosswalk was "to assist higher education faculty and professional development providers to integrate the Standards and DEC Recommended Practices into their curricula." (ECPC, 2020, p. 2).

Each of the seven EI/ECSE standards is presented in Table 8. The left column of the table identifies components for each standard, the middle column illustrates the DEC Recommended Practices cross-referenced with the related component, and the right column cross-references the CEC High-Leverage Practices (HLPs). For example, Standard 1, Component 1.1 is cross-referenced with DEC Recommended Practices Assessment 3 (A3) and Assessment 10 (A10) and HLPs 5 and 13.

The editors of this book and CEC would like to recognize the collaboration and support of ECPC and DEC in making the information in the crosswalk available for use in program development.

Table 8: Crosswalk of the Initial Practice Based Professional Preparation Standards for Early Interventionists/Early Childhood Special Educators (2020) with the DEC Recommended Practices (2014) and High Leverage Practices (2017)		
EI-ECSE Standards	**DEC Recommended Practices***	**CEC High Leverage Practices****
Standard 1: Child Development and Early Learning: Candidates understand the impact of different theories and philosophies of early learning and development on assessment, curriculum, instruction, and intervention decisions. Candidates apply knowledge of normative developmental sequences and variations, individual differences within and across the range of abilities, including developmental delays and disabilities, and other direct and indirect contextual features that support or constrain children's development and learning. These contextual factors as well as social, cultural, and linguistic diversity are considered when facilitating meaningful learning experiences and individualizing intervention and instruction across contexts.		
1.1: Candidates demonstrate an understanding of the impact that different theories and philosophies of early learning and development have on assessment, curriculum, intervention, and instructional decisions.	A3: Practitioners use assessment materials and strategies that are appropriate for the child's age and level of development and accommodate the child's sensory, physical, communication, cultural, linguistic, social, and emotional characteristics. A10: Practitioners use assessment tools with sufficient sensitivity to detect child progress, especially for the child with significant support needs. INS4: Practitioners plan for and provide the level of support, accommodations, and adaptations needed for the child to access, participate, and learn within and across activities and routines.	HLP 5: Interpret and communicate assessment information with stakeholders to collaboratively design and implement educational programs. HLP 13: Adapt curriculum tasks and materials for specific learning goals.

*DEC RPs alignment reflect a combination of the EI/ECSE Standards Knowledge-Base document for each standard (available on the DEC of CEC website) and the cross-walk completed by ECPC (2020) available at https://ecpcta.org/wp-content/uploads/sites/2810/2020/10/Cross-Walk-of-the-Practice-Based-Professional-Preparation-Standards-EIECSE-with-DEC-RPs.pdf

**CEC HLPs alignment reflect the practices noted for each standard's components in the respective EI/ECSE Standards Knowledge-Base document.

Table 8: Crosswalk of the Initial Practice Based Professional Preparation Standards for Early Interventionists/Early Childhood Special Educators (2020) with the DEC Recommended Practices (2014) and High Leverage Practices (2017)...(Standard 1 continued)		
EI-ECSE Standards	**DEC Recommended Practices**	**CEC High Leverage Practices**
1.2: Candidates apply knowledge of normative sequences of early development, individual differences, and families' social, cultural, and linguistic diversity to support each child's development and learning across contexts.	A3: Practitioners use assessment materials and strategies that are appropriate for the child's age and level of development and accommodate the child's sensory, physical, communication, cultural, linguistic, social, and emotional characteristics. F1: Practitioners build trusting and respectful partnerships with the family through interactions that are sensitive and responsive to cultural, linguistic, and socio-economic diversity. INS2: Practitioners, with the family, identify skills to target for instruction that help a child become adaptive, competent, socially connected, and engaged and that promote learning in natural and inclusive environments. INS4: Practitioners plan for and provide the level of support, accommodations, and adaptations needed for the child to access, participate, and learn within and across activities and routines. INS11: Practitioners provide instructional support for young children with disabilities who are dual language learners to assist them in learning English and in continuing to develop skills through the use of their home language.	HLP 3: Collaborate with families to support student learning and secure needed services. HLP 4: Use multiple sources of information to develop a comprehensive understanding of a student's strengths and needs.

Table 8: Crosswalk of the Initial Practice Based Professional Preparation Standards for Early Interventionists/Early Childhood Special Educators (2020) with the DEC Recommended Practices (2014) and High Leverage Practices (2017)...(Standard 1 continued)		
EI-ECSE Standards	**DEC Recommended Practices**	**CEC High Leverage Practices**
1.3: Candidates apply knowledge of biological and environmental factors that may support or constrain children's early development and learning as they plan and implement early intervention and instruction.	A4: Practitioners conduct assessments that include all areas of development and behavior to learn about the child's strengths, needs, preferences, and interests. INT1: Practitioners, with the family, identify each child's strengths, preferences, and interests to engage the child in active learning.	HLP 7: Establish a consistent, organized, and respectful learning environment. HLP 10: Conduct functional behavioral assessments to develop individual student behavior support plans.
1.4: Candidates demonstrate an understanding of characteristics, etiologies, and individual differences within and across the range of abilities, including developmental delays and disabilities, their potential impact on children's early development and learning, and implications for assessment, curriculum, instruction, and intervention.	A3: Practitioners use assessment materials and strategies that are appropriate for the child's age and level of development and accommodate the child's sensory, physical, communication, cultural, linguistic, social, and emotional characteristics. A8: Practitioners use clinical reasoning in addition to assessment results to identify the child's current levels of functioning and to determine the child's eligibility and plan for instruction. INS4: Practitioners plan for and provide the level of support, accommodations, and adaptations needed for the child to access, participate, and learn within and across activities and routines. INS10: Practitioners implement the frequency, intensity, and duration of instruction needed to address the child's phase and pace of learning or the level of support needed by the family to achieve the child's outcomes or goals.	HLP 3: Collaborate with families to support student learning and secure needed services. HLP 4: Use multiple sources of information to develop a comprehensive understanding of a student's strengths and needs.

Table 8: Crosswalk of the Initial Practice Based Professional Preparation Standards for Early Interventionists/Early Childhood Special Educators (2020) with the DEC Recommended Practices (2014) and High Leverage Practices (2017)...(continued)		
EI-ECSE Standards	**DEC Recommended Practices**	**CEC High Leverage Practices**
Standard 2: Partnering with Families: Candidates use their knowledge of family-centered practices and family systems theory to develop and maintain reciprocal partnerships with families. They apply family capacity-building practices as they support families to make informed decisions and advocate for their young children. They engage families in opportunities that build on their existing strengths, reflect current goals, and foster family competence and confidence to support their children's development and learning.		
2.1: Candidates apply their knowledge of family-centered practices, family systems theory, and the changing needs and priorities in families' lives to develop trusting, respectful, affirming, and culturally responsive partnerships with all families that allow for the mutual exchange of knowledge and information.	F1: Practitioners build trusting and respectful partnerships with the family through interactions that are sensitive and responsive to cultural, linguistic, and socioeconomic diversity. F3: Practitioners are responsive to the family's concerns, priorities, and changing life circumstances. F5: Practitioners support family functioning, promote family confidence and competence, and strengthen family-child relationships by acting in ways that recognize and build on family strengths and capacities.	HLP 2: Organize and facilitate effective meetings with professionals and families. HLP 3: Collaborate with families to support student learning and secure needed services.

Table 8: Crosswalk of the Initial Practice Based Professional Preparation Standards for Early Interventionists/Early Childhood Special Educators (2020) with the DEC Recommended Practices (2014) and High Leverage Practices (2017)...(Standard 2 continued)		
EI-ECSE Standards	**DEC Recommended Practices**	**CEC High Leverage Practices**
2.2: Candidates communicate clear, comprehensive, objective information about resources and supports that help families to make informed decisions and advocate for access, participation, and equity in natural and inclusive environments.	F2: Practitioners provide the family with up-to-date, comprehensive and unbiased information in a way that the family can understand and use to make informed choices and decisions. F7: Practitioners work with the family to identify, access, and use formal and informal resources and supports to achieve family-identified outcomes for goals. F8: Practitioners provide the family of a young child who has or is at risk for developmental delay/disability, and who is a dual language learner, with information about the benefits of learning in multiple languages for the child's growth and development. F9: Practitioners help families know and understand their rights. F10: Practitioners inform families about leadership and advocacy skill-building opportunities and encourage those who are interested to participate.	HLP 2: Organize and facilitate effective meetings with professionals and families. HLP 3: Collaborate with families to support student learning and secure needed services.

Table 8: Crosswalk of the Initial Practice Based Professional Preparation Standards for Early Interventionists/Early Childhood Special Educators (2020) with the DEC Recommended Practices (2014) and High Leverage Practices (2017)...(Standard 2 continued)

EI-ECSE Standards	DEC Recommended Practices	CEC High Leverage Practices
2.3: Candidates engage families in identifying their strengths, priorities and concerns; support families to achieve the goals they have for their family and their young child's development and learning; and promote families' competence and confidence during assessment, individualized planning, intervention, instruction, and transition processes.	A1: Practitioners work with the family to identify family preferences for assessment processes. F3: Practitioners are responsive to the family's concerns, priorities, and changing life circumstances. F4: Practitioners and the family work together to create outcomes or goals, develop individualized plans, and implement practices that address the family's priorities and concerns and the child's strengths and needs. F5: Practitioners support family functioning, promote family confidence and competence, and strengthen family-child relationships by acting in ways that recognize and build on family strengths and capacities. F6: Practitioners engage the family in opportunities that support and strengthen parenting knowledge and skills and parenting competence and confidence in ways that are flexible, individualized, and tailored to the family's preferences. TR2: Practitioners use a variety of planned and timely strategies with the child and family before, during, and after the transition to support successful adjustment and positive outcomes for both the child and family.	HLP 2: Organize and facilitate effective meetings with professionals and families. HLP 3: Collaborate with families to support student learning and secure needed services.

Table 8: Crosswalk of the Initial Practice Based Professional Preparation Standards for Early Interventionists/Early Childhood Special Educators (2020) with the DEC Recommended Practices (2014) and High Leverage Practices (2017)...(continued)		
EI-ECSE Standards	**DEC Recommended Practices**	**CEC High Leverage Practices**
Standard 3: Collaboration and Teaming: Candidates apply models, skills, and processes of teaming when collaborating and communicating with families and professionals, using culturally and linguistically responsive and affirming practices. In partnership with families and other professionals, candidates develop and implement individualized plans and successful transitions that occur across the age span. Candidates use a variety of collaborative strategies while working with and supporting other adults.		
3.1: Candidates apply teaming models, skills, and processes, including appropriate uses of technology, when collaborating and communicating with families; professionals representing multiple disciplines, skills, expertise, and roles; and community partners and agencies.	TC1: Practitioners representing multiple disciplines and families work together as a team to plan and implement supports and services to meet the unique needs of each child and family. TC2: Practitioners and families work together as a team to systematically and regularly exchange expertise, knowledge, and information to build team capacity and jointly solve problems, plan, and implement interventions. TC3: Practitioners use communication and group facilitation strategies to enhance team functioning and interpersonal relationships with and among team members. TC4: Team members assist each other to discover and access community-based services and other informal and formal resources to meet family-identified needs. TC5: Practitioners and families may collaborate with each other to identify one practitioner from the team who serves as the primary liaison between the family and other team members based on child and family priorities and needs.	HLP 2: Organize and facilitate effective meetings with professionals and families. HLP 3: Collaborate with families to support student learning and secure needed services.

Table 8: Crosswalk of the Initial Practice Based Professional Preparation Standards for Early Interventionists/Early Childhood Special Educators (2020) with the DEC Recommended Practices (2014) and High Leverage Practices (2017)...(Standard 3 continued)		
EI-ECSE Standards	**DEC Recommended Practices**	**CEC High Leverage Practices**
3.2: Candidates use a variety of collaborative strategies when working with other adults that are evidence-based, appropriate to the task, culturally and linguistically responsive and take into consideration the environment and service delivery approach.	TC1: Practitioners representing multiple disciplines and families work together as a team to plan and implement supports and services to meet the unique needs of each child and family. TC2: Practitioners and families work together as a team to systematically and regularly exchange expertise, knowledge, and information to build team capacity and jointly solve problems, plan, and implement interventions.	HLP 2: Organize and facilitate effective meetings with professionals and families. HLP 3: Collaborate with families to support student learning and secure needed services.
3.3: Candidates partner with families and other professionals to develop individualized plans and support the various transitions that occur for the young child and their family throughout the birth through 8 age span.	TC1: Practitioners representing multiple disciplines and families work together as a team to plan and implement supports and services to meet the unique needs of each child and family. TR1: Practitioners in sending and receiving programs exchange information before, during, and after transition about practices most likely to support the child's successful adjustment and positive outcomes. TR2: Practitioners use a variety of planned and timely strategies with the child and family before, during, and after the transition to support successful adjustment and positive outcomes for both the child and family.	HLP 1: Collaborate with professionals to increase student success. HLP 2: Organize and facilitate effective meetings with professionals and families.

Table 8: Crosswalk of the Initial Practice Based Professional Preparation Standards for Early Interventionists/Early Childhood Special Educators (2020) with the DEC Recommended Practices (2014) and High Leverage Practices (2017)...(continued)		
EI-ECSE Standards	**DEC Recommended Practices**	**CEC High Leverage Practices**
Standard 4: Assessment Processes: Candidates know and understand the purposes of assessment in relation to ethical and legal considerations. Candidates choose developmentally, linguistically, and culturally appropriate tools and methods that are responsive to the characteristics of the young child, family, and program. Using evidence-based practices, candidates develop or select as well as administer informal measures, and select and administer formal measures in partnership with families and other professionals. They analyze, interpret, document, and share assessment information using a strength-based approach with families and other professionals for eligibility determination, outcome/ goal development, planning instruction and intervention, monitoring progress, and reporting.		
4.1: Candidates understand the purposes of formal and informal assessment including ethical and legal considerations, and use this information to choose developmentally, culturally and linguistically appropriate, valid, reliable tools and methods that are responsive to the characteristics of the young child, family, and program.	A3: Practitioners use assessment materials and strategies that are appropriate for the child's age and level of development and accommodate the child's sensory, physical, communication, cultural, linguistic, social, and emotional characteristics.	HLP 4: Use multiple sources of information to develop a comprehensive understanding of a student's strengths and needs.
	A4: Practitioners conduct assessments that include all areas of development and behavior to learn about the child's strengths, needs, preferences, and interests.	
	A5: Practitioners conduct assessments in the child's dominant language and in additional languages if the child is learning more than one language.	
	A6: Practitioners use a variety of methods, including observation and interviews, to gather assessment information from multiple sources, including the child's family and other significant individuals in the child's life.	
	A7: Practitioners obtain information about the child's skills in daily activities, routines, and environments such as home, center, and community.	
	A8: Practitioners use clinical reasoning in addition to assessment results to identify the child's current levels of functioning and to determine the child's eligibility and plan for instruction.	

EI-ECSE Standards	DEC Recommended Practices	CEC High Leverage Practices
4.2: Candidates develop and administer informal assessments and/or select and use valid, reliable formal assessments using evidence-based practices, including technology, in partnership with families, and other professionals.	A2: Practitioners work as a team with the family and other professionals to gather assessment information. A6: Practitioners use a variety of methods, including observation and interviews, to gather assessment information from multiple sources, including the child's family and other significant individuals in the child's life. A10: Practitioners use assessment tools with sufficient sensitivity to detect child progress, especially for the child with significant support needs.	HLP 4: Use multiple sources of information to develop a comprehensive understanding of a student's strengths and needs.
4.3: Candidates analyze, interpret, document and share assessment information using a strength-based approach with families and other professionals.	A1: Practitioners work with the family to identify family preferences for assessment processes. A10: Practitioners use assessment tools with sufficient sensitivity to detect child progress, especially for the child with significant support needs. A11: Practitioners report assessment results so that they are understandable and useful to families.	HLP 5: Interpret and communicate assessment information with stakeholders to collaboratively design and implement educational programs.
4.4: Candidates, in collaboration with families and other team members, use assessment data to determine eligibility, develop child and family-based outcomes/goals, plan for interventions and instruction, and monitor progress to determine efficacy of programming.	A3: Practitioners use assessment materials and strategies that are appropriate for the child's age and level of development and accommodate the child's sensory, physical, communication, cultural, linguistic, social, and emotional characteristics. A4: Practitioners conduct assessments that include all areas of development and behavior to learn about the child's strengths, needs, preferences, and interests. *(continued on next page)*	HLP 5: Interpret and communicate assessment information with stakeholders to collaboratively design and implement educational programs. HLP 6: Use student assessment data, analyze instructional practices, and make necessary adjustments that improve student outcomes.

EI-ECSE Standards	DEC Recommended Practices	CEC High Leverage Practices
Table 8: Crosswalk of the Initial Practice Based Professional Preparation Standards for Early Interventionists/Early Childhood Special Educators (2020) with the DEC Recommended Practices (2014) and High Leverage Practices (2017)...(Standard 4 continued)		
	A5: Practitioners conduct assessments in the child's dominant language and in additional languages if the child is learning more than one language.	
	A6: Practitioners use a variety of methods, including observation and interviews, to gather assessment information from multiple sources, including the child's family and other significant individuals in the child's life.	
	A7: Practitioners obtain information about the child's skills in daily activities, routines, and environments such as home, center, and community.	
	A8: Practitioners use clinical reasoning in addition to assessment results to identify the child's current levels of functioning and to determine the child's eligibility and plan for instruction.	
	A9: Practitioners implement systematic ongoing assessment to identify learning targets, plan activities, and monitor the child's progress to revise instruction as needed.	
	A10: Practitioners use assessment tools with sufficient sensitivity to detect child progress, especially for the child with significant support needs.	

Table 8: Crosswalk of the Initial Practice Based Professional Preparation Standards for Early Interventionists/Early Childhood Special Educators (2020) with the DEC Recommended Practices (2014) and High Leverage Practices (2017)...(continued)		
EI-ECSE Standards	**DEC Recommended Practices**	**CEC High Leverage Practices**
Standard 5: Application of Curriculum Frameworks in the Planning and Facilitation of Meaningful Learning Experience: Candidates collaborate with families and professionals to use evidenced-based, developmentally appropriate, and culturally responsive early childhood curriculum addressing developmental and content domains. Candidates use curriculum frameworks to create and support universally designed, high-quality learning experiences in natural and inclusive environments that provide each child and family with equitable access and opportunities for learning and growth.		
5.1: Candidates collaborate with families and other professionals in identifying evidence-based curriculum addressing developmental and content domains to design and facilitate meaningful and culturally responsive learning experiences that support the unique abilities and needs of all children and families.	F4: Practitioners and the family work together to create outcomes or goals, develop individualized plans, and implement practices that address the family's priorities and concerns and the child's strengths and needs. F8: Practitioners provide the family of a young child who has or is at risk for developmental delay/disability, and who is a dual language learner, with information about the benefits of learning in multiple languages for the child's growth and development.	HLP 3: Collaborate with families to support student learning and secure needed services.
5.2: Candidates use their knowledge of early childhood curriculum frameworks, developmental and academic content knowledge, and related pedagogy to plan and ensure equitable access to universally designed, developmentally appropriate, and challenging learning experiences in natural and inclusive environments.	E2: Practitioners consider Universal Design for Learning principles to create accessible environments. E3: Practitioners work with the family and other adults to modify and adapt the physical, social, and temporal environments to promote each child's access to and participation in learning experiences.	HLP 11: Identify and prioritize long- and short-term learning goals. HLP 19: Use assistive and instructional technology.

Table 8: Crosswalk of the Initial Practice Based Professional Preparation Standards for Early Interventionists/Early Childhood Special Educators (2020) with the DEC Recommended Practices (2014) and High Leverage Practices (2017)...(continued)		
EI-ECSE Standards	**DEC Recommended Practices**	**CEC High Leverage Practices**
Standard 6: Using Responsive and Reciprocal Interactions, Interventions, and Instruction: Candidates plan and implement intentional, systematic, evidence-based, responsive interactions, interventions, and instruction to support all children's learning and development across all developmental and content domains in partnership with families and other professionals. Candidates facilitate equitable access and participation for all children and families within natural and inclusive environments through culturally responsive and affirming practices and relationships. Candidates use data-based decision-making to plan for, adapt, and improve interactions, interventions, and instruction to ensure fidelity of implementation.		
6.1: Candidates, in partnership with families, identify systematic, responsive, and intentional evidence-based practices and use such practices with fidelity to support young children's learning and development across all developmental and academic content domains.	F4: Practitioners and the family work together to create outcomes or goals, develop individualized plans, and implement practices that address the family's priorities and concerns and the child's strengths and needs. INS6: Practitioners use systematic instructional strategies with fidelity to teach skills and to promote child engagement and learning. INS10: Practitioners implement the frequency, intensity, and duration of instruction needed to address the child's phase and pace of learning or the level of support needed by the family to achieve the child's outcomes or goals.	HLP 18: Use strategies to promote active student engagement. HLP 12: Systematically design instruction toward a specific learning goal. HLP 16: Use explicit instruction.

Table 8: Crosswalk of the Initial Practice Based Professional Preparation Standards for Early Interventionists/Early Childhood Special Educators (2020) with the DEC Recommended Practices (2014) and High Leverage Practices (2017)...(Standard 6 continued)		
EI-ECSE Standards	**DEC Recommended Practices**	**CEC High Leverage Practices**
6.2: Candidates engage in reciprocal partnerships with families and other professionals to facilitate responsive adult-child interactions, interventions, and instruction in support of child learning and development.	F4: Practitioners and the family work together to create outcomes or goals, develop individualized plans, and implement practices that address the family's priorities and concerns and the child's strengths and needs. INS1: Practitioners, with the family, identify each child's strengths, preferences, and interests to engage the child in active learning. INS2: Practitioners, with the family, identify skills to target for instruction that help a child become adaptive, competent, socially connected, and engaged and that promote learning in natural and inclusive environments. TC1: Practitioners representing multiple disciplines and families work together as a team to plan and implement supports and services to meet the unique needs of each child and family.	HLP 1: Collaborate with professionals to increase student success.

Table 8: Crosswalk of the Initial Practice Based Professional Preparation Standards for Early Interventionists/Early Childhood Special Educators (2020) with the DEC Recommended Practices (2014) and High Leverage Practices (2017)...(Standard 6 continued)

EI-ECSE Standards	DEC Recommended Practices	CEC High Leverage Practices
6.3: Candidates engage in ongoing planning and use flexible and embedded instructional and environmental arrangements and appropriate materials to support the use of interactions, interventions, and instruction addressing developmental and academic content domains, which are adapted to meet the needs of each and every child and their family.	E1: Practitioners provide services and supports in natural and inclusive environments during daily routines and activities to promote the child's access to and participation in learning experiences. E3: Practitioners work with the family and other adults to modify and adapt the physical, social, and temporal environments to promote each child's access to and participation in learning experiences. INS2: Practitioners, with the family, identify skills to target for instruction that help a child become adaptive, competent, socially connected, and engaged and that promote learning in natural and inclusive environments. INS5: Practitioners embed instruction within and across routines, activities, and environments to provide contextually relevant learning opportunities.	HLP 13: Adapt curriculum tasks and materials for specific learning goals. HLP 17: Use flexible grouping. HLP 21: Teach students to maintain and generalize new learning across time and settings.

Table 8: Crosswalk of the Initial Practice Based Professional Preparation Standards for Early Interventionists/Early Childhood Special Educators (2020) with the DEC Recommended Practices (2014) and High Leverage Practices (2017)...(Standard 6 continued)

EI-ECSE Standards	DEC Recommended Practices	CEC High Leverage Practices
6.4: Candidates promote young children's social and emotional competence and communication, and proactively plan and implement function-based interventions to prevent and address challenging behaviors.	A4: Practitioners conduct assessments that include all areas of development and behavior to learn about the child's strengths, needs, preferences, and interests E3: Practitioners work with the family and other adults to modify and adapt the physical, social, and temporal environments to promote each child's access to and participation in learning experiences. INT1: Practitioners promote the child's social-emotional development by observing, interpreting, and responding contingently to the range of the child's emotional expressions. INT2: Practitioners promote the child's social development by encouraging the child to initiate or sustain positive interactions with other children and adults during routines and activities through modeling, teaching, feedback, or other types of guided support. INT3: Practitioners promote the child's communication development by observing, interpreting, responding contingently, and providing natural consequences for the child's verbal and non-verbal communication and by using language to label and expand on the child's requests, needs, preferences, or interests. *(continued on next page)*	HLP 4: Use multiple sources of information to develop a comprehensive understanding of a student's strengths and needs. HLP 7: Establish a consistent, organized, and respectful learning environment. HLP 8: Provide positive and constructive feedback to guide students' learning and behavior. HLP 9: Teach social behaviors. HLP 10: Conduct functional behavioral assessments to develop individual student behavior support plans.

Table 8: Crosswalk of the Initial Practice Based Professional Preparation Standards for Early Interventionists/Early Childhood Special Educators (2020) with the DEC Recommended Practices (2014) and High Leverage Practices (2017)...(Standard 6 continued)		
EI-ECSE Standards	**DEC Recommended Practices**	**CEC High Leverage Practices**
	INS2: Practitioners, with the family, identify skills to target for instruction that help a child become adaptive, competent, socially connected, and engaged and that promote learning in natural and inclusive environments.	
	INS6: Practitioners use systematic instructional strategies with fidelity to teach skills and to promote child engagement and learning.	
	INS8: Practitioners use peer-mediated intervention to teach skills and to promote child engagement and learning.	
	INS9: Practitioners use functional assessment and related prevention, promotion, and intervention strategies across environments to prevent and address challenging behavior.	

EI-ECSE Standards	DEC Recommended Practices	CEC High Leverage Practices
6.5: Candidates identify and create multiple opportunities for young children to develop and learn play skills and engage in meaningful play experiences independently and with others across contexts.	INS7: Practitioners use explicit feedback and consequences to increase child engagement, play, and skills. INT4: Practitioners promote the child's cognitive development by observing, interpreting, and responding intentionally to the child's exploration, play, and social activity by joining in and expanding on the child's focus, actions, and intent.	HLP 7: Establish a consistent, organized, and respectful learning environment. HLP 12: Systematically design instruction toward a specific learning goal. HLP 14: Teach cognitive and metacognitive strategies to support learning and independence. HLP 15: Provide scaffolded supports.
6.6: Candidates use responsive interactions, interventions, and instruction with sufficient intensity and types of support across activities, routines, and environments to promote child learning and development and facilitate access, participation, and engagement in natural environments and inclusive settings.	INS1: Practitioners, with the family, identify each child's strengths, preferences, and interests to engage the child in active learning. INS3: Practitioners gather and use data to inform decisions about individualized instruction. INS4: Practitioners plan for and provide the level of support, accommodations, and adaptations needed for the child to access, participate, and learn within and across activities and routines. INS5: Practitioners embed instruction within and across routines, activities, and environments to provide contextually relevant learning opportunities. INS10: Practitioners implement the frequency, intensity, and duration of instruction needed to address the child's phase and pace of learning or the level of support needed by the family to achieve the child's outcomes or goals.	HLP 15: Provide scaffolded supports. HLP 20: Provide intensive instruction. HLP 22: Provide positive and constructive feedback to guide students' learning and behavior.

Table 8: Crosswalk of the Initial Practice Based Professional Preparation Standards for Early Interventionists/Early Childhood Special Educators (2020) with the DEC Recommended Practices (2014) and High Leverage Practices (2017)...(Standard 6 continued)		
EI-ECSE Standards	**DEC Recommended Practices**	**CEC High Leverage Practices**
6.7: Candidates plan for, adapt, and improve approaches to interaction, intervention, and instruction based on multiple sources of data across a range of natural environments and inclusive settings.	A2: Practitioners work as a team with the family and other professionals to gather assessment information. E4: Practitioners work with families and other adults to identify each child's needs for assistive technology to promote each child's access to and participation in learning experiences. E5: Practitioners work with the family and other adults to acquire or create appropriate assistive technology to promote each child's access to and participation in learning environments. INS3: Practitioners gather and use data to inform decisions about individualized instruction. TC1: Practitioners representing multiple disciplines and families work together as a team to plan and implement supports and services to meet the unique needs of each child and family.	HLP 3: Collaborate with families to support student learning and secure needed services. HLP 4: Use multiple sources of information to develop a comprehensive understanding of a student's strengths and needs. HLP 6: Use student assessment data, analyze instructional practices, and make necessary adjustments that improve student outcomes.

Table 8: Crosswalk of the Initial Practice Based Professional Preparation Standards for Early Interventionists/Early Childhood Special Educators (2020) with the DEC Recommended Practices (2014) and High Leverage Practices (2017)...(continued)		
EI-ECSE Standards	**DEC Recommended Practices**	**CEC High Leverage Practices**
Standard 7: Professionalism and Ethical Practice: Candidates identify and engage with the profession of early intervention and early childhood special education (EI/ECSE) by exhibiting skills in, reflective practice, advocacy, and leadership while adhering to ethical and legal guidelines. Evidence-based and recommended practices are promoted and used by candidates.		
7.1: Candidates engage with the profession of EI/ECSE by participating in local, regional, national, and/or international activities and professional organizations.	L4: Leaders belong to professional associations and engage in ongoing evidence-based professional development.	
7.2: Candidates engage in ongoing reflective practice and access evidence-based information.	L9: Leaders develop and implement an evidence-based professional development system or approach that provides practitioners a variety of supports to ensure they have the knowledge and skills needed to implement the DEC Recommended Practices.	
7.3: Candidates exhibit leadership skills in advocating for improved outcomes for young children, families, and the profession including the promotion of and use of evidenced-based practices and decision-making.	L3: Leaders develop and implement policies, structures, and practices that promote shared decision making with practitioners and families. L5: Leaders advocate for policies and resources that promote the implementation of the DEC Position Statements and Papers and the DEC Recommended Practices.	HLP 3: Collaborate with families to support student learning and secure needed services.
7.4: Candidates practice within ethical and legal policies and procedures.	L2: Leaders promote adherence to and model the DEC Code of Ethics, DEC Position Statements and Papers, and the DEC Recommended Practices. L10: Practitioners implement the frequency, intensity, and duration of instruction needed to address the child's phase and pace of learning or the level of support needed by the family to achieve the child's outcomes or goals. F9: Practitioners help families know and understand their rights.	

Key Elements of Standards Sets

The 2020 Initial Practice-Based Professional Standards for Early Interventionists/Early Childhood Special Educators (EI/ECSE) are comprised of multiple elements beyond the seven standards themselves. This includes 27 components underlying the standards, along with their supporting explanations, knowledge bases, sample performance indicators and assessments, and assessment rubrics.

Each standard outlines specific proficiencies candidates are expected to demonstrate upon completion of their initial birth-age 8 special educator preparation programs. For easy referencing, working titles are given for each of the standards but should never substitute for the more complete and substantive standards themselves. Several components accompany each standard to "unpack" important practices embedded in the standard. Components do not introduce additional practices but elaborate on those already incorporated into the overarching standard. Table 9 presents the seven standards and 27 components of the 2020 EI/ECSE Initial Standards. Note that CEC has retained a separate Field and Clinical Experience Standard described in Section 6 of this book.

Each standard represents *what* candidates are expected to do and its supporting explanation describes *how* each component of the standard looks in practice. Specific skills and desired behaviors of candidates are fleshed out more fully in the supporting explanations. The knowledge base for each component explains *why* the target proficiencies are important by referencing foundational sources within the profession. The knowledge bases note alignment with DEC Recommended Practices, HLPs, InTASC standards, and other SPA standards as appropriate. They also cite relevant laws, policies and position statements, along with research that supports the specific practices. The knowledge bases are not intended to be comprehensive reviews of literature. In many instances, the work of major national projects is cited, since centers such as ECPC (www.ecpcta.org/), The IRIS Center(www.iris.peabody.vanderbilt.edu/), Early Childhood Technical Assistance Center (ECTA) (www.ectacenter.org), and the Collaboration for Effective Educator Development, Accountability, and Reform (CEEDAR) Center (www.ceedar.education.ufl.edu), have already reviewed and synthesized major research undergirding recommended practices.

Along with the standards, additional resources are provided to guide candidate and program assessment. Examples of performance indicators (specific tasks that might be used to assess candidate proficiency) are offered for each component. Matrices are also available to show how programs can provide evidence that standards are met by citing data from six to eight typical assessment sources.

Cross-Cutting Themes

Diversity Throughout the EI/ECSE Standards

Culturally and linguistically responsive and affirming practices are not a separate standard but rather are embedded within each standard. EI/ECSE candidates should be well prepared in their professional knowledge, skills, and dispositions to teach in diverse, inclusive settings. To be well prepared, EI/ECSE candidates must understand the broader societal context and biases including those around gender, sexual orientation, ability and disability, language, national origin, indigenous heritage, religion, and other identities.

Beginning with EI/ECSE Standard 1: Child Development and Early Learning, Component 1.2 notes that EI/ECSE candidates are expected to recognize that young children may exhibit individual differences in development within a normative range, and that their own social and cultural background influences what they view as normative. Furthermore, the standard notes that they are able to identify how the family's social, cultural, and linguistic characteristics may influence, as well as support, their child's development, including the timing and order of developmental milestones.

Similarly, Standard 2: Partnering with Families Component 2.1 states that candidates form "respectful, affirming, and culturally responsive partnerships with families." To achieve this outcome, they must engage in self-reflection of their own cultures and beliefs, evaluate the impact of these on their partnerships, and use the knowledge gained to inform their interactions with families. Standard 3: Collaboration and Teaming Component 3.2 indicates the importance of using a variety of collaboration strategies and again that these need to reflect culturally and linguistically responsive practices, as the EI/ECSE candidate works with families and other adults. Standard 7: Professionalism and Ethical Practice Component

7.3 requires that EI/ECSE candidates exhibit leadership skills in advocating for improved outcomes for young children, families, and the profession. As part of this leadership and advocacy role they are expected to access evidenced-based resources to be informed of issues around implicit bias and to limit the impact of their own biases in interactions with families, children, and other professionals.

Standard 4: Assessment Processes, Standard 5: Applications of Curriculum Frameworks, and Standard 6: Using Responsive and Reciprocal Interactions, Interventions, and Instruction are all focused directly on the teaching and learning process and each directly addresses the need for EI/ECSE candidates to understand and use culturally responsive and affirming practices as they engage infants, toddlers and young children in learning and support their development. For example, in Standard 4: Assessment Processes Component 4.1, candidates are expected to make decisions regarding assessment tools and methods that include attention to those that are culturally and linguistically appropriate. Standard 5: Curriculum Framework Component 5.1 notes that as EI/ECSE candidates design and facilitate learning experiences they must reflect culturally responsive experiences that support the unique abilities and needs of each and every child and their family. Finally, Standard 6: Responsive and Reciprocal Interactions, Interventions, and Instruction states that EI/ECSE candidates are expected to facilitate equitable access and participation for all children and families by using culturally responsive and affirming practices.

In summary EI/ECSE candidates are able to partner with each child's family to create equitable, culturally responsive and affirming early learning opportunities across multiple contexts. These learning opportunities are designed such that each child experiences responsive interactions that nurture their full range of social, emotional, cognitive, physical, and linguistic abilities; and reflect and model fundamental principles of fairness and justice.

Technology Throughout the EI/ECSE Standards

Technology and interactive media are not a separate standard but rather integrated as appropriate across the standards. EI/ECSE candidates understand that technology and media when used appropriately can serve multiple roles, including as an important tool for supporting learning for young children, for supporting access, and for enhancing communication. A first step in the process of supporting the learning of children involves engaging in assessment practices to understand the current level of development of children and monitoring their ongoing development. As noted in Standard 4 (Assessment Processes) Component 4.2, the selection and use of valid assessment tools and strategies includes consideration of appropriate technology practices. As educators develop curricular content, as noted in Standard 5 (Application of Curriculum Frameworks in the Planning and Facilitation of Meaningful Learning Experiences) Component 5.2, they include consideration of how young children can learn about technology tools to explore new worlds, actively engage in fun and challenging activities, and solve problems. Standard 6 (Use Responsive and Reciprocal Interactions, Interventions, and Instruction) Component 6.6, states that EI/ECSE candidates are expected to understand how to use technology, including but not limited to assistive technology, to increase access to learning and improve learning outcomes. For example, technology can introduce the young child more directly to environments outside of their community through virtual experiences. Assistive technology can serve to remove barriers for young children with disabilities. To ensure that technology has a positive impact, EI/ECSE candidates make decisions about the use of technology and media using the best available evidence on what is best for healthy child development and how the implementation can help early learners achieve developmentally appropriate learning outcomes as expressed in Standard 1 (Child Development and Learning).

EI/ECSE candidates understand the potential for and use of technology to communicate with team members and candidates in other community agencies. For example, in Standard 3 (Collaboration and Teaming) Component 3.2, technology is a valuable tool for EI/ECSE candidates in report writing, recording, and analyzing data. Furthermore, Standard 2 (Partnering with Families) Component 2.2, EI/ECSE states that candidates understand the potential that technology has for building relationship with families. They understand how to use technology as one way to enhance communication and connections between families and educators to benefit the young child. Finally, as noted in Standard 7 (Professional and Ethical Practice) Component 7.2, EI/ECSE candidates understand the power of technology to contribute to their own professional development through immediate access on an as-needed basis to information and for more planned and systematic continuous learning opportunities. In summary, the appropriate and effective use of technology is reflected across multiple standards as EI/ECSE candidates engage in decisions about how technology can be used intentionally and appropriately to support the learning of young children, engage with families, and enhance their own professional development.

Differences from 2012 Standards

While CEC has long had a specialty set of knowledge and skill statements used to inform the program report and review process that articulate unique content to be addressed in the personnel preparation for special educators working in EI/ECSE, there were no personnel preparation standards specific to this age range. Having a set of standards for the preparation of special educators that addresses the birth through 8 age range and aligns with the K-12 Special Educator Standards provides a continuum of special educator personnel preparation standards from birth through age 21. Having the two sets of special educator standards provides clarity to both as to competencies that are common across the age span as well as clarifying those that are unique to EI/ECSE and thus facilitates collaborative work across disciplines.

Table 9: Initial Practice-Based Professional Preparation Standards for Early Interventionists/ Early Childhood Special Educators' Alignment with 2012 Standards

EI/ECSE Preparation Standard/Component	Most Comparable 2012 Standard/Component
Standard 1: Child Development and Early Learning Candidates understand the impact of different theories and philosophies of early learning and development on assessment, curriculum, instruction, and intervention decisions. Candidates apply knowledge of normative developmental sequences and variations, individual differences within and across the range of abilities, including developmental delays and disabilities, and other direct and indirect contextual features that support or constrain children's development and learning. These contextual factors as well as social, cultural, and linguistic diversity are considered when facilitating meaningful learning experiences and individualizing intervention and instruction across contexts.	Standard 1: Learner Development and Individual Learning Differences Beginning special education professionals understand how exceptionalities may interact with development and learning and use this knowledge to provide meaningful and challenging learning experiences for individuals with exceptionalities.
1.1: Candidates demonstrate an understanding of the impact that different theories and philosophies of early learning and development have on assessment, curriculum, intervention, and instruction decisions.	
1.2: Candidates apply knowledge of normative sequences of early development, individual differences, and families' social, cultural, and linguistic diversity to support each child's development and learning across contexts.	1.1: Beginning special education professionals understand how language, culture, and family background influence the learning of individuals with exceptionalities.
1.3: Candidates apply knowledge of biological and environmental factors that may support or constrain children's early development and learning as they plan and implement early intervention and instruction.	1.2: Beginning special education professionals use understanding of development and individual differences to respond to the needs of individuals with exceptionalities.
1.4: Candidates demonstrate an understanding of characteristics, etiologies, and individual differences within and across the range of abilities, including developmental delays and disabilities, their potential impact on children's early development and learning, and implications for assessment, curriculum, instruction, and intervention.	1.2: Beginning special education professionals use understanding of development and individual differences to respond to the needs of individuals with exceptionalities.

Table 9: Initial Practice-Based Professional Preparation Standards for Early Interventionists/ Early Childhood Special Educators' Alignment with 2012 Standards ...(continued)

EI/ECSE Preparation Standard/Component	Most Comparable 2012 Standard/Component
Standard 2: Partnering with Families Candidates use their knowledge of family-centered practices and family systems theory to develop and maintain reciprocal partnerships with families. They apply family capacity-building practices as they support families to make informed decisions and advocate for their young children. They engage families in opportunities that build on their existing strengths, reflect current goals, and foster family competence and confidence to support their children's development and learning.	Standard 7: Collaboration Beginning special education professionals collaborate with families, other educators, related service providers, individuals with exceptionalities, and personnel from community agencies in culturally responsive ways to address the needs of individuals with exceptionalities across a range of learning experiences.
2.1: Candidates apply their knowledge of family-centered practices, family systems theory, and the changing needs and priorities in families' lives to develop trusting, respectful, affirming, and culturally responsive partnerships with all families that allow for the mutual exchange of knowledge and information.	6.3: Beginning special education professionals understand that diversity is a part of families, cultures, and schools, and that complex human issues can interact with the delivery of special education services. 7.3: Beginning special education professionals use collaboration to promote the wellbeing of individuals with exceptionalities across a wide range of settings and collaborators.
2.2: Candidates communicate clear, comprehensive, and objective information about resources and supports that help families to make informed decisions and advocate for access, participation, and equity in natural and inclusive environments.	
2.3: Candidates engage families in identifying their strengths, priorities, and concerns; support families to achieve the goals they have for their family and their young child's development and learning; and promote families' competence and confidence during assessment, individualized planning, intervention, instruction, and transition processes.	

EI/ECSE Preparation Standard/Component	Most Comparable 2012 Standard/Component
Standard 3: Collaboration and Teaming Candidates apply models, skills, and processes of teaming when collaborating and communicating with families and professionals, using culturally and linguistically responsive and affirming practices. In partnership with families and other professionals, candidates develop and implement individualized plans and successful transitions that occur across the age span. Candidates use a variety of collaborative strategies while working with and supporting other adults.	Standard 7: Collaboration Beginning special education professionals collaborate with families, other educators, related service providers, individuals with exceptionalities, and personnel from community agencies in culturally responsive ways to address the needs of individuals with exceptionalities across a range of learning experiences.
3.1: Candidates apply teaming models, skills, and processes, including appropriate uses of technology, when collaborating and communicating with families; professionals representing multiple disciplines, skills, expertise, and roles; and community partners and agencies.	7.1: Beginning special education professionals use the theory and elements of effective collaboration.
3.2: Candidates use a variety of collaborative strategies when working with other adults that are evidence-based, appropriate to the task, culturally and linguistically responsive, and take into consideration the environment and service delivery approach.	7.1: Beginning special education professionals use the theory and elements of effective collaboration. 6.6: Beginning special education professionals provide guidance and direction to paraeducators, tutors, and volunteers.
3.3: Candidates partner with families and other professionals to develop individualized plans and support the various transitions that occur for the young child and their family throughout the birth through 8 age span.	5.5: Beginning special education professionals develop and implement a variety of education and transition plans for individuals with exceptionalities across a wide range of settings and different learning experiences in collaboration with individuals, families, and teams.

Table 9: Initial Practice-Based Professional Preparation Standards for Early Interventionists/ Early Childhood Special Educators' Alignment with 2012 Standards...(continued)

EI/ECSE Preparation Standard/Component	Most Comparable 2012 Standard/Component
Standard 4: Assessment Processes Candidates know and understand the purposes of assessment in relation to ethical and legal considerations. Candidates choose developmentally, linguistically, and culturally appropriate tools and methods that are responsive to the characteristics of the young child, family, and program. Using evidence-based practices, candidates develop or select as well as administer informal measures, and select and administer formal measures in partnership with families and other professionals. They analyze, interpret, document, and share assessment information using a strengths-based approach with families and other professionals for eligibility determination, outcome/goal development, planning instruction and intervention, monitoring progress, and reporting.	Standard 4: Assessment Beginning special education professionals use multiple methods of assessment and data sources in making educational decisions.
4.1: Candidates understand the purposes of formal and informal assessment, including ethical and legal considerations, and use this information to choose developmentally, culturally and linguistically appropriate, valid, reliable tools and methods that are responsive to the characteristics of the young child, family, and program.	4.1: Beginning special education professionals select and use technically sound formal and informal assessments that minimize bias.
4.2: Candidates develop and administer informal assessments and/or select and use valid, reliable formal assessments using evidence-based practices, including technology, in partnership with families and other professionals.	4.1: Beginning special education professionals select and use technically sound formal and informal assessments that minimize bias. 4.2: Beginning special education professionals use knowledge of measurement principles and practices to interpret assessment results and guide educational decisions for individuals with exceptionalities.
4.3: Candidates analyze, interpret, document, and share assessment information using a strengths-based approach with families and other professionals.	4.2: Beginning special education professionals use knowledge of measurement principles and practices to interpret assessment results and guide educational decisions for individuals with exceptionalities. 4.3: Beginning special education professionals, in collaboration with colleagues and families, use multiple types of assessment information in making decisions about individuals with exceptionalities.
4.4: Candidates, in collaboration with families and other team members, use assessment data to determine eligibility, develop child and family-based outcomes/goals, plan for interventions and instruction, and monitor progress to determine efficacy of programming.	4.3: Beginning special education professionals, in collaboration with colleagues and families, use multiple types of assessment information in making decisions about individuals with exceptionalities.

EI/ECSE Preparation Standard/Component	Most Comparable 2012 Standard/Component
Standard 5: Application of Curriculum Frameworks in the Planning and Facilitation of Meaningful Learning Experiences Candidates collaborate with families and professionals to use an evidence-based, developmentally appropriate, and culturally responsive early childhood curriculum addressing developmental and content domains. Candidates use curriculum frameworks to create and support universally designed, high quality learning experiences in natural and inclusive environments that provide each child and family with equitable access and opportunities for learning and growth.	Standard 2: Learning Environments Beginning special education professionals create safe, inclusive, culturally responsive learning environments so that individuals with exceptionalities become active and effective learners and develop emotional wellbeing, positive social interactions, and self-determination. Standard 3: Curricular Content Knowledge Beginning special education professionals use knowledge of general and specialized curricula to individualize learning for individuals with exceptionalities. Standard 5: Instructional Planning and Strategies Beginning special education professionals select, adapt, and use a repertoire of evidence-based instructional strategies to advance learning of individuals with exceptionalities.
5.1: Candidates collaborate with families and other professionals in identifying an evidence-based curriculum addressing developmental and content domains to design and facilitate meaningful and culturally responsive learning experiences that support the unique abilities and needs of all children and families.	2.1: Beginning special education professionals, through collaboration with general educators and other colleagues, create safe, inclusive, culturally responsive learning environments to engage individuals with exceptionalities in meaningful learning activities and social interactions.
5.2: Candidates use their knowledge of early childhood curriculum frameworks, developmental and academic content knowledge, and related pedagogy to plan and ensure equitable access to universally designed, developmentally appropriate, and challenging learning experiences in natural and inclusive environments.	3.1: Beginning special education professionals understand the central concepts, structures of the discipline, and tools of inquiry of the content areas they teach, and can organize this knowledge, integrate cross-disciplinary skills, and develop meaningful learning progressions for individuals with exceptionalities. 3.2: Beginning special education professionals understand and use general and specialized content knowledge for teaching across curricular content areas to individualize learning for individuals with exceptionalities.

Table 9: Initial Practice-Based Professional Preparation Standards for Early Interventionists/ Early Childhood Special Educators' Alignment with 2012 Standards...(continued)

Table 9: Initial Practice-Based Professional Preparation Standards for Early Interventionists/ Early Childhood Special Educators' Alignment with 2012 Standards...(continued)	
EI/ECSE Preparation Standard/Component	**Most Comparable 2012 Standard/Component**
Standard 6: Using Responsive and Reciprocal Interactions, Interventions, and Instruction Candidates plan and implement intentional, systematic, evidence-based, responsive interactions, interventions, and instruction to support all children's learning and development across all developmental and content domains in partnership with families and other professionals. Candidates facilitate equitable access and participation for all children and families within natural and inclusive environments through culturally responsive and affirming practices and relationships. Candidates use data-based decision-making to plan for, adapt, and improve interactions, interventions, and instruction to ensure fidelity of implementation.	Standard 2: Learning Environments Beginning special education professionals create safe, inclusive, culturally responsive learning environments so that individuals with exceptionalities become active and effective learners and develop emotional well-being, positive social interactions, and self-determination. Standard 4: Assessment Beginning special education professionals use multiple methods of assessment and data sources in making educational decisions. Standard 5: Instructional Planning and Strategies Beginning special education professionals select, adapt, and use a repertoire of evidence-based instructional strategies to advance learning of individuals with exceptionalities.
6.1: Candidates, in partnership with families, identify systematic, responsive, and intentional evidence-based practices and use such practices with fidelity to support young children's learning and development across all developmental and academic content domains.	2.2: Beginning special education professionals use motivational and instructional interventions to teach individuals with exceptionalities how to adapt to different environments. 5.1: Beginning special education professionals consider individual abilities, interests, learning environments, and cultural and linguistic factors in the selection, development, and adaptation of learning experiences for individuals with exceptionalities.
6.2: Candidates engage in reciprocal partnerships with families and other professionals to facilitate responsive adult-child interactions, interventions, and instruction in support of child learning and development.	2.1: Beginning special education professionals, through collaboration with general educators and other colleagues, create safe, inclusive, culturally responsive learning environments to engage individuals with exceptionalities in meaningful learning activities and social interactions.

EI/ECSE Preparation Standard/Component	Most Comparable 2012 Standard/Component
6.3: Candidates engage in ongoing planning and use flexible and embedded instructional and environmental arrangements and appropriate materials to support the use of interactions, interventions, and instruction addressing developmental and academic content domains, which are adapted to meet the needs of each and every child and their family.	5.1: Beginning special education professionals consider individual abilities, interests, learning environments, and cultural and linguistic factors in the selection, development, and adaptation of learning experiences for individuals with exceptionalities. 5.2: Beginning special education professionals use technologies to support instructional assessment, planning, and delivery for individuals with exceptionalities. 5.3: Beginning special education professionals are familiar with augmentative and alternative communication systems and a variety of assistive technologies to support the communication and learning of individuals with exceptionalities.
6.4: Candidates promote young children's social and emotional competence and communication, and proactively plan and implement function-based interventions to prevent and address challenging behaviors.	2.3: Beginning special education professionals know how to intervene safely and appropriately with individuals with exceptionalities in crisis. 5.4: Beginning special education professionals use strategies to enhance language development and communication skills of individuals with exceptionalities.
6.5: Candidates identify and create multiple opportunities for young children to develop and learn play skills and engage in meaningful play experiences independently and with others across contexts.	5.4: Beginning special education professionals use strategies to enhance language development and communication skills of individuals with exceptionalities.
6.6: Candidates use responsive interactions, interventions, and instruction with sufficient intensity and types of support across activities, routines, and environments to promote child learning and development and facilitate access, participation, and engagement in natural environments and inclusive settings.	2.2: Beginning special education professionals use motivational and instructional interventions to teach individuals with exceptionalities how to adapt to different environments. 5.6: Beginning special education professionals teach to mastery and promote generalization of learning.
6.7: Candidates plan for, adapt, and improve approaches to interactions, interventions, and instruction based on multiple sources of data across a range of natural environments and inclusive settings.	4.2: Beginning special education professionals use knowledge of measurement principles and practices to interpret assessment results and guide educational decisions for individuals with exceptionalities.

Table 9: Initial Practice-Based Professional Preparation Standards for Early Interventionists/ Early Childhood Special Educators' Alignment with 2012 Standards...(continued)	
EI/ECSE Preparation Standard/Component	**Most Comparable 2012 Standard/Component**
Standard 7: Professionalism and Ethical Practice Candidates identify and engage with the profession of early intervention and early childhood special education (EI/ECSE) by exhibiting skills in reflective practice, advocacy, and leadership while adhering to ethical and legal guidelines. Evidence-based and recommended practices are promoted and used by candidates.	Standard 6: Professional Learning and Ethical Practice Beginning special education professionals use foundational knowledge of the field and their professional ethical principles and practice standards to inform special education practice, to engage in lifelong learning, and to advance the profession.
7.1: Candidates engage with the profession of EI/ECSE by participating in local, regional, national, and/or international activities and professional organizations.	6.2: Beginning special education professionals understand how foundational knowledge and current issues influence professional practice.
7.2: Candidates engage in ongoing reflective practice and access evidence-based information to improve their own practices.	6.4: Beginning special education professionals understand the significance of lifelong learning and participate in professional activities and learning communities.
7.3: Candidates exhibit leadership skills in advocating for improved outcomes for young children, families, and the profession, including the promotion of and use of evidence-based practices and decision-making.	6.5: Beginning special education professionals advance the profession by engaging in activities such as advocacy and mentoring.
7.4: Candidates practice within ethical and legal policies and procedures.	6.1: Beginning special education professionals use professional ethical principles and professional practice standards to guide their practice.

Section 6

CEC Initial Practice-Based Professional Preparation Standards for Early Interventionists/Early Childhood Special Educators

The major portion of the section is devoted to a comprehensive presentation of the seven standard sets, complete with supporting explanations and knowledge bases for the 27 components. The Field Experience and Clinical Practice Standard for Early Interventionists/Early Childhood Special Educators is also presented. Additional resources for candidate and program assessment are also provided.

Standards and Components At-a-Glance

The following chart is a summary of the seven standards and 27 components. As explained above, careful review of the component-level supporting explanations and knowledge bases is important to understand the meaning and relevance of each standard set. These expanded elements are presented in the sections that follow.

Table 10: EI/ECSE Standards and Components	
Standards	**Components**
Standard 1: Child Development and Early Learning Candidates understand the impact of different theories and philosophies of early learning and development on assessment, curriculum, instruction, and intervention decisions. Candidates apply knowledge of normative developmental sequences and variations, individual differences within and across the range of abilities, including developmental delays and disabilities, and other direct and indirect contextual features that support or constrain children's development and learning. These contextual factors as well as social, cultural, and linguistic diversity are considered when facilitating meaningful learning experiences and individualizing intervention and instruction across contexts.	1.1: Candidates demonstrate an understanding of the impact that different theories and philosophies of early learning and development have on assessment, curriculum, intervention, and instruction decisions. 1.2: Candidates apply knowledge of normative sequences of early development, individual differences, and families' social, cultural, and linguistic characteristics to support each child's development and learning across contexts. 1.3: Candidates apply knowledge of biological and environmental factors that may support or constrain children's early development and learning as they plan and implement early intervention and instruction. 1.4: Candidates demonstrate an understanding of characteristics, etiologies, and individual differences within and across exceptionalities and developmental delays, and their potential impact on children's early development and learning.

Table 10: EI/ECSE Standards and Components...(continued)	
Standards	**Components**
Standard 2: Partnering with Families Candidates use their knowledge of family-centered practices and family systems theory to develop and maintain reciprocal partnerships with families. They apply family capacity-building practices as they support families to make informed decisions and advocate for their young children. They engage families in opportunities that build on their existing strengths, reflect current goals, and foster family competence and confidence to support their children's development and learning.	2.1: Candidates apply their knowledge of family-centered practices, family systems theory, and the changing needs and priorities in families' lives to develop trusting, respectful, affirming, and culturally responsive partnerships with all families that allow for the mutual exchange of knowledge and information. 2.2: Candidates communicate clear, comprehensive, and objective information about resources and supports that help families to make informed decisions and advocate for access, participation, and equity in natural and inclusive environments. 2.3: Candidates engage families in identifying their strengths, priorities, and concerns; support families to achieve the goals they have for their family and their young child's development and learning; and promote families' competence and confidence during assessment, individualized planning, intervention, instruction, and transition processes.
Standard 3: Collaboration and Teaming Candidates apply models, skills, and processes of teaming when collaborating and communicating with families and professionals, using culturally and linguistically responsive and affirming practices. In partnership with families and other professionals, candidates develop and implement individualized plans and successful transitions that occur across the age span. Candidates use a variety of collaborative strategies while working with and supporting other adults.	3.1: Candidates apply teaming models, skills, and processes, including appropriate uses of technology, when collaborating and communicating with families; professionals representing multiple disciplines, skills, expertise, and roles; and community partners and agencies. 3.2: Candidates use a variety of collaborative strategies when working with other adults that are evidence-based, appropriate to the task, culturally and linguistically responsive, and take into consideration the environment and service delivery approach. 3.3: Candidates partner with families and other professionals to develop individualized plans and support various transitions that occur for the young child and their family throughout the birth through 8 age span.

Table 10: EI/ECSE Standards and Components...(continued)	
Standards	**Components**
Standard 4: Assessment Processes Candidates know and understand the purposes of assessment in relation to ethical and legal considerations. Candidates choose developmentally, linguistically, and culturally appropriate tools and methods that are responsive to the characteristics of the young child, family, and program. Using evidence-based practices, candidates develop or select as well as administer informal measures, and select and administer formal measures in partnership with families and other professionals. They analyze, interpret, document, and share assessment information using a strengths-based approach with families and other professionals for eligibility determination, outcome/goal development, planning instruction and intervention, monitoring progress, and reporting.	4.1: Candidates understand the purposes of formal and informal assessment, including ethical and legal considerations, and use this information to choose developmentally, culturally and linguistically appropriate, valid, reliable tools and methods that are responsive to the characteristics of the young child, family, and program. 4.2: Candidates develop and administer informal assessments and/or select and use valid, reliable formal assessments using evidence-based practices, including technology, in partnership with families and other professionals. 4.3: Candidates analyze, interpret, document, and share assessment information using a strengths-based approach with families and other professionals. 4.4: Candidates, in collaboration with families and other team members, use assessment data to determine eligibility, develop child and family-based outcomes/goals, plan for interventions and instruction, and monitor progress to determine efficacy of programming.
Standard 5: Application of Curriculum Frameworks in the Planning of Meaningful Learning Experience Candidates collaborate with families and professionals to use an evidence-based, developmentally appropriate, and culturally responsive early childhood curriculum addressing developmental and content domains. Candidates use curriculum frameworks to create and support universally designed, high quality learning experiences in natural and inclusive environments that provide each child and family with equitable access and opportunities for learning and growth.	5.1: Candidates collaborate with families and other professionals in identifying an evidence-based curriculum addressing developmental and content domains to design and facilitate meaningful and culturally responsive learning experiences that support the unique abilities and needs of all children and families. 5.2: Candidates use their knowledge of early childhood curriculum frameworks, developmental and academic content knowledge, and related pedagogy to plan and ensure equitable access to universally designed, developmentally appropriate, and challenging learning experiences in natural and inclusive environments.

Table 10: EI/ECSE Standards and Components...(continued)

Standards	Components
Standard 6: Using Responsive and Reciprocal Interactions, Interventions, and Instruction Candidates plan and implement intentional, systematic, evidence-based, responsive interactions, interventions, and instruction to support all children's learning and development across all developmental and content domains in partnership with families and other professionals. Candidates facilitate equitable access and participation for all children and families within natural and inclusive environments through culturally responsive and affirming practices and relationships. Candidates use data-based decision-making to plan for, adapt, and improve interactions, interventions, and instruction to ensure fidelity of implementation.	6.1: Candidates, in partnership with families, identify systematic, responsive, and intentional evidence-based practices and use such practices with fidelity to support young children's learning and development across all developmental and academic content domains. 6.2: Candidates engage in reciprocal partnerships with families and other professionals to facilitate responsive adult-child interactions, interventions, and instruction in support of child learning and development. 6.3: Candidates engage in ongoing planning and use flexible and embedded instructional and environmental arrangements and appropriate materials to support the use of interactions, interventions, and instruction addressing developmental and academic content domains, which are adapted to meet the needs of each and every child and their family. 6.4: Candidates promote young children's social and emotional competence and communication, and proactively plan and implement function-based interventions to prevent and address challenging behaviors. 6.5: Candidates identify and create multiple opportunities for young children to develop and learn play skills and engage in meaningful play experiences independently and with others across contexts. 6.6: Candidates use responsive interactions, interventions, and instruction with sufficient intensity and types of support across activities, routines, and environments to promote child learning and development and facilitate access, participation, and engagement in natural environments and inclusive settings. 6.7: Candidates plan for, adapt, and improve approaches to interactions, interventions, and instruction based on multiple sources of data across a range of natural environments and inclusive settings.

Table 10: EI/ECSE Standards and Components...(continued)	
Standards	**Components**
Standard 7: Professionalism and Ethical Practice Candidates identify and engage with the profession of early intervention and early childhood special education (EI/ECSE) by exhibiting skills in reflective practice, advocacy, and leadership while adhering to ethical and legal guidelines. Evidence-based and recommended practices are promoted and used by candidates.	7.1: Candidates engage with the profession of EI/ECSE by participating in local, regional, national, and/or international activities and professional organizations. 7.2: Candidates engage in ongoing reflective practice and access evidence-based information to improve their own practices. 7.3: Candidates exhibit leadership skills in advocating for improved outcomes for young children, families, and the profession, including the promotion of and use of evidence-based practices and decision-making. 7.4: Candidates practice within ethical and legal policies and procedures.
Field Experience and Clinical Practice Standard for EI/ECSE Early Intervention/Early Childhood Special Education (EI/ECSE) candidates progress through a series of planned and developmentally sequenced field experiences for the early childhood age ranges (birth to age 3, 3 through 5 years, 5 through 8 years), range of abilities, and in the variety of collaborative and inclusive early childhood settings that are appropriate to their license and roles. Clinical experiences should take place in the same age ranges covered by the license. If the license covers all three age ranges, the program must provide clinical experiences in at least two of the three age ranges and a field experience in the third age range. These field and clinical experiences are supervised by qualified professionals.	

EI/ECSE Standards, Components, Supporting Explanations, and Knowledge Bases

Standard 1: Child Development and Early Learning

Candidates understand the impact of different theories and philosophies of early learning and development on assessment, curriculum, instruction, and intervention decisions. Candidates apply knowledge of normative developmental sequences and variations, individual differences within and across the range of abilities, including developmental delays and disabilities, and other direct and indirect contextual features that support or constrain children's development and learning. These contextual factors as well as social, cultural, and linguistic diversity are considered when facilitating meaningful learning experiences and individualizing intervention and instruction across contexts.

Component 1.1. Candidates demonstrate an understanding of the impact that different theories and philosophies of early learning and development have on assessment, curriculum, intervention, and instruction decisions.

Supporting Explanation. Candidates understand the theories and philosophies of development and learning that guide historical and current approaches to early childhood education and early childhood special education services for all children, including those at risk for and with developmental delays and disabilities, ages birth through 8. They identify the contributions and limitations of different theories and philosophies as they apply to children who vary in age, characteristics, and family backgrounds. Further, candidates critically evaluate research and practices associated with these theories and philosophies. Candidates apply these perspectives to select and implement different preventive, ameliorative, and remedial approaches for supporting the development and learning of young children at risk for or with developmental delays and disabilities.

Candidates recognize how their roles may vary in focus, emphasis, or methods across ages birth through 8 in accordance with the assumptions and practices of specific developmental and learning theories and philosophies. For example, when working with infants and toddlers, candidates may focus more on the central importance of identifying and supporting family resources and needs from a family systems perspective. Conversely, when supporting preschool and early elementary children, candidates may employ a family systems perspective to identify classroom and school resources in response to family functions, characteristics, and processes. Similarly, candidates may apply behavioral theory when designing or supporting function-based assessment and intervention in the natural environment, irrespective of age.

Throughout the birth through 8 age range, candidates demonstrate their understanding of evidence-based practices associated with various theoretical approaches as they collaborate with families and other professionals to assess child and family strengths, needs, and priorities. Additionally, they apply their understanding of various evidence-based practices as they select and implement a broad array of responsive intervention and instructional practices with each child and family.

Knowledge Base. Knowledge of early development and learning is represented in many sets of professional standards as a foundation for educational practice. InTASC Standard 1 (CCSSO, 2013) emphasizes that appropriate and challenging learning experiences should be based on an understanding of how learners grow and develop across multiple domains. Standard 1 in the CEC Preparation Standards (2015) emphasizes the importance of applying knowledge about how individual variations in abilities may interact with development and learning. Professional standards outlined by NAEYC (2011), in particular Standard 1, emphasize that knowledge of the characteristics and needs of young children from birth through 8, as well as multiple influences on early development and learning, underlie the ability to design

and provide healthy, challenging learning environments. The foundational role of knowledge of development and learning is also evident in Standard 1 of the CAEP Elementary Education Standards (2018), which states that the ability to plan and implement equitable, high-quality learning experiences and to work collaboratively with families is based on an understanding of the growth and development of children.

The CEC/DEC Initial Specialty Set for Early Childhood Special Education/Early Intervention (CEC, 2017) identifies theories of normative developmental sequences and variations of these sequences as a key component of candidate knowledge. DEC Recommended Practices (2014) Strands of Assessment and Instruction, in particular A3 and INS4, recommend that educators use their understanding of development to make appropriate accommodations and plan for appropriate supports for child participation and learning. Similarly, the CEC High-Leverage Practices (HLPs) (McLeskey et al., 2017), in the area of assessment (i.e., HLP5) and instruction (i.e., HLP13), state that educators use their knowledge of children's developmental strengths and needs to plan for and make accommodations for ensuring children's access and participation in the general curriculum.

The common theme throughout these standards is that knowledge of development and learning directly informs candidates' practices. Theories and philosophies of early development and learning reflect on how such knowledge is organized as well as on the research that leads to, tests, and expands the theories. Theories represent how societies, cultures, families, and individuals view childhood and the avenues through which they become well-functioning adults (Harkness et al., 2013). Theories guide the research predictions, hypotheses, and hypothesis testing that underlie what is known about the development of children and how optimal development is achieved through children's changing interactions with their everyday cultural and linguistic environments in their homes, communities, and schools from birth onward (Odom, 2016; Shonkoff & Richter, 2013). Developmental theory has yielded knowledge of how children develop and learn in different domains and under different conditions, including how different areas of development such as cognition and emotion are related to one another (e.g., Dunst, 2007). When young children have or are at risk for developmental delays and disabilities, theory and associated research also describe how development and learning are similar to or different from other children and how specific delays or developmental differences in one area may influence other areas of development and learning (Lewis et al., 2014; Wolff, 2016). EI/ECSE professionals take these influences into account as they plan and interpret individualized assessment, as they consider needed adaptations to learning environments, and as they design and deliver intervention and instruction.

Theories also address whether and how development and learning can be influenced through intervention and instruction. Applied researchers draw upon developmental and learning theories as they formulate and test specific interventions and instructional approaches, often with children or families with specific characteristics (Dunst, 2017). For example, a theory-base related to the role of caregiver responsiveness with young children with autism spectrum disorder (ASD) has yielded effective, research-based tools that EI/ECSE professionals are able to use as they plan and deliver intervention with young children with ASD and their families, with positive outcomes for both children and families (e.g., Siller et al., 2013).

Different theories of development and learning (e.g., developmental, behavioral, systems) underlie many historical and current models in early childhood education as well as more narrowly defined instructional interventions related to specific child outcomes (McLean et al., 2016) and areas of content knowledge. Program and practice guidelines either explicitly or implicitly represent the perspectives of different theories. Theories of development and learning, and of the programs and guidelines derived from them, have changed from a focus on child alone to a focus on child within developmental context (Sameroff, 2009; Shonkoff & Richter, 2013). All these perspectives are evident in current programs and guidelines, and thus the EI/ECSE candidate uses these perspectives to inform their practice and contexts.

A systems perspective has had a significant effect on current practices in EI/ECSE (Guralnick, 2017). For example, providing services in children's natural environments and ensuring access to the general education curriculum both reflect a view that it is important to understand and support development within the child's context. Further, from a systems perspective, families of children with disabilities are viewed as central to the provision of EI/ECSE, both as recipients of services and as a significant part of the child's developmental and learning environment. Family systems theory has yielded practice guidelines

that result in positive outcomes for both families and children (Dempsey & Dean, 2017) and is represented in recommended practices in EI/ECSE (DEC, 2014).

Theories of learning and development provide the foundation for how EI/ECSE professionals view children, families, and themselves, as well as what they do with children and their families. The EI/ECSE candidate draws from their knowledge of specific theories and from their own personal theories and philosophies about development and learning as they make decisions about assessment, intervention, and instruction, and as they collaborate with families and with other professionals (Odom, 2016). EI/ECSE candidates also apply their knowledge of a variety of developmental and learning theories to understand the history and current political context of their field, to evaluate the relevance of differing perspectives, and to reflect on their own practices.

Component 1.2. Candidates apply knowledge of normative sequences of early development, individual differences, and families' social, cultural, and linguistic characteristics to support each child's development and learning across contexts.

Supporting Explanation. Candidates articulate the sequence and milestones of normative sequences of development for each of the primary developmental domains, including cognitive, adaptive, communication, physical (gross and fine motor), play, and social-emotional. Candidates understand that abilities and skills interact with and are dependent on one another across domains. For example, candidates use their knowledge that social interaction supports young children's communication development to create opportunities for peer interactions. Candidates provide examples of how abilities and skills across developmental domains are integrated in the accomplishment of developmental growth in play, daily living, and personal characteristics such as positive approaches to learning, executive functioning, and resilience. Additionally, candidates recognize that young children may exhibit individual differences in development within a normative range, and that their own social and cultural background influences what they view as normative. Candidates consider normative ranges of development as they interpret a child observation and identify how their own expectations influence their interpretation.

Candidates identify how the family's social, cultural, and linguistic characteristics may influence and support their child's development, including the timing and order of developmental milestones. For example, a family's cultural background may influence behaviors that families view as important in daily living as well as the activities and routines that they view as supportive of their children's development and learning. Candidates apply a strengths-based perspective and seek to understand families' social, cultural, and linguistic background when determining how they can establish respectful relationships with families and collaborate with families in all aspects of assessment, intervention, and instruction.

Candidates use information about typical development, individual differences, and the influence of social, cultural, and linguistic characteristics to observe and understand young children's abilities, skills, and behaviors, and to organize and/or select appropriate environments for intervention and instruction. This includes how they interpret, assess, and support children's development, behavior, engagement, interests, and learning within natural and inclusive environments. For example, candidates use their understanding of typical development to recognize deviations that require instructional adaptations or may indicate a need for developmental screening or referral. Additionally, candidates apply this knowledge as they identify family priorities and needs, and as they plan intervention and instruction across contexts that are both developmentally and individually appropriate.

Candidates understand that early development and learning of young children are both a focus of intervention and instruction and an important context for planning and delivering intervention and instruction to all young children and families. For example, candidates consider each child's current abilities and needs as they work with families and other professionals to set priorities for child outcomes and goals that will guide the focus of intervention and instruction. At the same time, these same abilities and needs inform the candidates' planning of developmentally and individually appropriate environments, materials, accommodations, and strategies.

Knowledge Base. A variety of standards and recommended practices emphasize the importance of understanding child development for planning instruction and intervention. InTASC Standards 1 and 2 (CCSSO, 2013) require that educators apply their knowledge of how learners generally grow and develop, children's individual differences, and the role of the child's family's social, linguistic, and cultural characteristics to plan developmentally and individually appropriate educational experiences. Similarly, NAEYC Standard 1 (2011) and CAEP Elementary Standard 1 (2018) both dictate that candidates should know and understand the development of young children and use developmental knowledge to create supportive and challenging learning environments. Moreover, Standard 1 of the CAEP Elementary Standards (2018) specifically names race, religion, ethnicity, language, culture, and family configuration as potential characteristics that may influence the ways children learn best. Such information is important as educators plan and implement assessment, instruction, and intervention. IDEA specifically acknowledges that culturally and linguistically appropriate assessments should be used when determining children's special education eligibility and support needs to minimize the possibility of discrimination (IDEA, 2004). Knowledge about normative sequences of child development and learning, children's individual characteristics, and the influence of cultural and linguistic characteristics allow educators to make better decisions about what educational experiences are most likely to promote children's development and learning (Copple & Bredekamp, 2009).

Knowledge about typical child development and learning is particularly important when working with children with or at risk for developmental delays and disabilities, whose developmental characteristics may require individualized assessment, planning, instruction, and intervention as noted in CEC/DEC Specialty Set for Early Childhood Special Education/Early Intervention Sections 1 and 3 (CEC, 2017). The DEC Recommended Practices (2014) advise that intervention should build on, rather than replace, developmentally appropriate practices grounded in the principles of child development and learning. DEC Recommended Practices (2014) in the areas of Assessment (A3) and Families (F1) recommend that educators use information about children's and families' language and culture to be more responsive and effective in those areas. The CEC High-Leverage Practices (McLeskey et al., 2017) areas of collaboration and assessment, specifically HLP3 and HLP4, state that educators must work together with families using multiple sources and strategies of information to ensure that intervention planning is sensitive to the child's and family's language, culture, and experiences.

Knowledge of typical developmental sequences allows educators to make preliminary decisions about the physical environments, activities, and interactions that will best facilitate children's development (Copple & Bredekamp, 2009). Such knowledge includes understanding the ways in which different developmental domains emerge and work together as children accomplish daily activities such as play and academic learning. For example, multiple developmental domains interact to support learning and organizational processes such as motivation, executive functioning, and emotional and behavioral regulation (e.g., Liew, 2011; Ursache et al., 2012). In turn, such learning and organizational processes are positively correlated with children's later academic achievement (e.g., Guralnick, 2017; Li-Grining et al., 2010). Moreover, each developmental domain can influence the development of other domains. For example, there is evidence that early motor delays may contribute to the social and communicative behavior of young children with ASD (Bhat et al., 2011; McDonald et al., 2013). Knowledge of typical developmental sequences as well as the relationships between developmental domains allows the EI/ECSE candidate to plan and implement more effective and proactive assessment, intervention, and instruction. All children, including those with developmental delays and disabilities, benefit from high-quality early education in which the EI/ECSE professional employs developmentally appropriate practices grounded in the principles of child development (e.g., Phillips & Meloy, 2012; Weiland, 2016).

It is important to supplement knowledge of developmental sequences with an understanding that typical development varies within general normative ranges. Individual children may differ in their progression through developmental sequences (Copple & Bredekamp, 2009). A child's individual patterns of development within and across developmental domains may influence how the child learns best as well as their patterns of school readiness and academic achievement (e.g., Halle et al., 2012). These individual differences reflect the influence of biology, environmental circumstances, and early educational experiences on young children's development (Copple & Bredekamp, 2009), and do not always indicate a developmental delay or disability. Acknowledging that children may vary in their developmental sequences within normative ranges can help EI/ECSE educators

better identify when a child has a developmental delay or disability that requires special education, and when the child may simply need instruction or supports that differ from those already being offered. Instruction is more effective when EI/ECSE educators individualize instruction based on a child's particular skills in relevant developmental domain(s) (Connor et al., 2009).

Recognizing the influence of cultural and linguistic characteristics on the development of children is similarly essential when making decisions about individual supports and the presence of a developmental delay or disability, particularly when a child comes from a marginalized background (e.g., children of color, dual language learners). Understanding the influences of culture and language on child development points to the ways cultural experiences, activities, and expectations influence and interact with the timing of children's developmental milestones, and the activities and expectations that families value and support (Rogoff, 2003; Spicer, 2010). The EI/ECSE professional uses this information to more accurately assess a child's development and behavior (Banerjee & Guiberson, 2012), better collaborate with families (Rossetti et al., 2017), and plan effective, culturally responsive instruction and intervention (Aronson & Laughter, 2016; Bradshaw, 2013). Furthermore, the effects of poverty, inequities, and adverse experiences (e.g., lack of access to high quality early educational experiences, toxic stress) must be detangled by the EI/ECSE candidate from cultural, linguistic, and contextual differences (e.g., cultural expectations, immigration, bilingualism) that influence children's development in various ways (e.g., Barac et al., 2014; Hammer et al., 2014; Keels & Raver, 2009). EI/ECSE educators use a strengths-based approach to instruction and intervention that accounts for cultural and linguistic characteristics to support every child's development (Rogoff et al., 2017).

Component 1.3. Candidates apply knowledge of biological and environmental factors that may support or constrain children's early development and learning as they plan and implement early intervention and instruction.

Supporting Explanation. Candidates articulate the potential supportive and constraining influences of biological factors such as medical or genetic conditions, vision and hearing status, prematurity, health, and brain development on the development of children across developmental domains, birth through age 8. They understand the potential effects that biological factors may have on young children's interactions, relationships, approaches to learning, and ability to access supportive learning opportunities. For example, candidates identify how children's interactions with their primary caregivers and with other children may be influenced by health differences associated with prematurity. Candidates apply their understanding of how biological factors influence children's development to plan and implement assessment, intervention, and instruction.

Candidates understand that supportive or constraining characteristics in young children's environments (e.g., food resources, medical care, traumatic experiences, access to high-quality early care and education) may affect children's growth, development, and learning. They articulate how these characteristics may also have indirect effects on children through their influences on children's interactions with primary caregivers and other children as well as their access to supportive learning opportunities. Candidates apply knowledge of factors in young children's social, economic, and physical environments as they plan and implement assessment, instruction, and intervention. For example, when supporting infants and toddlers, they may identify family resources that address family food insufficiency or the mental health needs of primary caregiver(s). At the early elementary level, candidates consider children's access to environmental learning opportunities as they select and develop meaningful content curricula and learning activities.

Knowledge Base. The CEC/DEC Initial Specialty Set for Early Childhood Special Education/ Early Intervention Section 1 (CEC, 2017) states that candidates understand the biological and environmental factors that impact pre-, peri-, and postnatal development and learning. Similarly, NAEYC Standard 1 (2011) recommends that early childhood education candidates understand the multiple influences on young children's development and learning. Standard 1 of the CAEP Elementary Standards (2018) recommends that educators recognize and assess the unique learning profile and characteristics of students to understand how those differences (e.g., prior knowledge and experiences, physical and social well-being, socioeconomic status) may impact learning, motivation, and attention. Knowledge of

biological and environmental influences on development is important as educators use information about children's individual characteristics, environments, and prior experiences to shape their instruction, and as they develop and facilitate responsive environments that support children's development and learning, as outlined in InTASC Standard 1 (CCSSO, 2013). Thus, understanding how biological and environmental factors support or constrain children's development and learning is essential for effective instruction and intervention. DEC Recommended Practices (2014) INT1 and INT3 in the area of instruction recommend that educators, together with families, gather and use information about children's strengths and preferences across developmental domains to inform decisions about individualization. CEC high-leverage practices (McLeskey et al., 2017) addressing social/emotional (HLP7 and HLP10) focus the educator's attention on the impact of the child's multiple environments and note that they use this knowledge to design learning environments that support the child's growth and development.

A variety of biological factors can impact children's early development in ways that may affect both their need for intervention as well as the array of services and instructional practices they would benefit from. EI/ECSE educators who are aware of these potential effects are able to be more responsive to their emergence and the implications for assessment, intervention, and instruction. For example, prematurity or low birth weight may be associated with medical conditions that place children at risk for developmental delays or exceptionalities (DEC, 2018). Moreover, several developmental disabilities, including ASD, have been found to have a genetic heritability component (Deng et al., 2015; Lee et al., 2016). Understanding the potential biological contributors to specific aspects of children's development can help EI/ECSE candidates better support children, particularly those at risk for or with disabilities based on biological predispositions.

Children's early environments can similarly play a significant role in their development, and therefore should be considered as EI/ECSE candidates plan and implement assessment, intervention, and instruction. High-quality classroom environments that are characterized by developmentally appropriate furnishings and activities, teacher responsiveness, proactive behavior management, language supports, and opportunities for concept development have been shown to benefit children's academic engagement and support early learning and development (e.g., Aydoğan et al., 2015; Brunsek et al., 2017; Hatfield et al., 2016). Recognizing the important features of high-quality classroom environments can help the EI/ECSE candidate plan developmentally supportive classroom environments and activities. Environmental features outside of the classroom also impact children's early learning and development. For example, it is well established that parents reading to and talking with their children has a positive impact on children's language development and early literacy (Reese et al., 2010). Understanding family routines, strengths, and priorities as well as community resources can help EI/ECSE candidates effectively partner with families to ensure children have resources and experiences that support their development (Friedman et al., 2012; Guralnik, 2011; Keilty, 2019).

Research has also noted that environments with reduced developmental supports can have a constraining influence on development. For example, research has found that children from lower socioeconomic status (SES) neighborhoods have access to lower quality early education and care classrooms (e.g., Bassok & Galdo, 2015), which can negatively affect their early development (e.g., Hillemeier et al., 2013; McCoy et al., 2015). Children from low SES communities may also have reduced access to community resources that support learning, including libraries and affordable cultural activities such as museums (e.g., Gehner, 2010; Sin, 2011), and nutritious food (Walker et al., 2010). The emotional and social characteristics of families and communities may also affect children's development and learning. Early trauma associated with maltreatment and violence in the home may affect children's emotional regulation and social adjustment (Maughan & Cicchetti, 2002) as well as increase the likelihood of internalizing and externalizing challenging behaviors (Milot et al., 2010). Instruction and intervention is most effective when it is responsive to both the strengths and challenges of a child's developmental context, particularly for children experiencing significant structural inequities (e.g., Walker et al., 2011).

It is important to recognize that biological and environmental factors can interact to influence the development of children. A rich literature base examining epigenetics and the impact of the environment on brain development has illustrated how environmental features can trigger or mute genetic factors to influence children's development in ways that impact their learning. For example, both brain structure (e.g., D'Angiulli et al., 2008; Raizada et al., 2008) and neural response differences (e.g., D'Angiulli et al., 2008; Kishiyama et al., 2009) exist between children from low SES families and their higher SES peers. Such research illustrates how persistent environmental features can potentially alter the biological makeup of children in ways that affect their learning and development. Acknowledging this interaction between environment and biology can help educators better understand the pathways through which such factors affect children's development and learning, providing a foundation for their work with individual children and their families.

Component 1.4. Candidates demonstrate an understanding of characteristics, etiologies, and individual differences within and across exceptionalities and developmental delays, and their potential impact on children's early development and learning.

Supporting Explanation. Candidates describe the general characteristics of individual differences within and across the range of abilities, including developmental delays and disabilities as documented in law and policy as well as the implications of the ability ranges for intervention and instruction. They identify potential etiologies of developmental delays and disabilities, including genetic conditions, prenatal and postnatal circumstances, and early experiences. At the same time, candidates recognize that individual differences exist in how young children learn and develop such that individual children with a given delay or exceptionality may require differing types and/or intensity of intervention and instruction to facilitate their development and learning.

Candidates describe how the characteristics and etiologies of different exceptionalities may influence individual children's early development and learning, including the timing and order of developmental milestones, how children demonstrate emerging abilities and skills, and the types and intensity of developmental and instructional supports children require. Further, they recognize that the presence of a developmental delay or exceptionality is not the only determinant of the child's development or the types of intervention and instruction that they require. Candidates base decisions about interventions and supports upon an understanding of the whole child and their diverse developmental contexts, not just the developmental area(s) in which the child is showing a developmental delay or exceptionality. Such a holistic view of the child aids the candidate in selecting and developing appropriate assessments, collaborating effectively with families and other professionals, and planning and implementing appropriate intervention and instruction.

Knowledge Base. CEC Standard 1 (2015) states that educators should apply knowledge of the impacts the range of characteristics, etiologies, and abilities, including developmental delays and disabilities, may have on how children develop and learn to provide meaningful, challenging learning experiences for each child. Section 1 of the Initial Specialty Set for Early Childhood Special Education/Early Intervention (CEC, 2017) explicitly calls for knowledge of etiologies, characteristics, and classification of common disabilities in infants and young children, including the implications of those disabilities for development and learning early in life. DEC Recommended Practices (2014) in the areas of Assessment (A3) and Instruction (INS1) recommend that educators, together with the child's family, gather and use information about children's strengths, preferences, and interests to support the child's active engagement and learning. The CEC High-Leverage Practices (McLeskey et al., 2017) areas of collaboration and assessment, specifically HLP3 and HLP4, state that educators work together with families using multiple sources and strategies of information to ensure that intervention planning is sensitive to the child's strengths and needs.

Knowledge of specific exceptionalities informs determination of eligibility for special education services and provides guidance to identify specific types of services that may address strengths and needs associated with exceptionality-related characteristics and etiologies. For many young children, no clear indicators of either biological or environmental exceptionality may be apparent; instead, delay of unknown origin is used to establish eligibility for services. In the United States, for example, the presence of developmental delay(s) in one or more areas of development is used to indicate that an exceptionality may exist or may emerge, and to establish eligibility for early intervention/early childhood special education (IDEA, 2004).

Knowledge of specific exceptionalities and potential etiologies inform, but do not dictate, the identification and implementation of individualized services and instruction. The EI/ECSE candidate uses their knowledge of characteristics associated with different exceptionalities and developmental delay(s) as they plan, implement, and interpret assessments; plan and provide intervention and instruction; and identify needed child and family services (Hodapp et al., 2016). For young children whose exceptionalities are identified at birth or early in life (e.g., cerebral palsy, PKU, hearing impairment), knowledge of exceptionality characteristics and etiology also informs educators' understanding of patterns of typical and atypical development and learning that may emerge. For example, educators' knowledge of exceptionality characteristics and etiology can provide one basis for anticipating developmental and learning constraints and strengths typically associated with conditions such as visual impairment or Down syndrome (Fidler et al., 2016; Hahn, 2016). Based on this knowledge, EI/ECSE professionals, in collaboration with families and other professionals, identify goals and outcomes that respond directly to core characteristics of the child's exceptionality (Hodapp et al., 2016) and to other developmental and learning strengths and needs. For example, educators may draw upon knowledge of specific curriculum goals appropriate to children with autism spectrum disorder or visual impairment by focusing respectively on goals in the area of social interaction or mobility (Kasari et al., 2012; Lawton et al., 2014; Lewis et al., 2014; Will et al., 2014). Further, anticipating these needs can lead to an early focus on supporting development in areas that may be affected by differences in mobility or social interaction in young children with these exceptionalities. Knowledge of specific exceptionalities also enables educators to recognize patterns of development that are atypical for children with specific exceptionalities, leading to earlier identification of individual strengths as well as individual instruction and intervention needs. For children with developmental delay(s), knowledge of specific exceptionalities and the patterns of development associated with them may help identify emerging exceptionalities in areas such as academic learning or mental health. Thus, for all children, educators seek not only to remediate the primary area of delay or exceptionality, but to prevent the development of secondary delays or disabilities (Guralnick, 2017; Parker & Ivy, 2014; Will et al., 2014).

EI/ECSE candidates use their knowledge of exceptionalities and associated known or possible etiologies, along with their knowledge of typical and atypical development, to gain a comprehensive understanding of each child's unique configuration of abilities and needs. Even where exceptionalities and etiologies are known, individual children demonstrate a wide range of individual differences in the number and severity of exceptionality-related characteristics as well as their strengths and needs in other areas of development and learning (Hodapp et al., 2016). Thus EI/ECSE candidates must draw on their knowledge of exceptionalities and developmental delays, and of potential effects on development and learning, as they plan and apply adaptations to children's everyday environments and provide individualized supports that allow them to participate in a range of natural environments and benefit from the general education curriculum (Dunst et al., 2017; Sandall et al., 2016). The EI/ECSE candidate assists each child to build a larger repertoire of skills and knowledge in areas of development and learning as varied as play, language, peer interaction, and emergent literacy and math.

Interpretation of disability and developmental risk, as well as approaches to intervention and instruction, are grounded in sociocultural contexts (Harkness et al., 2013). EI/ECSE candidates use their knowledge of characteristics and etiologies of exceptionalities and developmental delays, in addition to understanding families' beliefs about their children, exceptionality, and EI/ECSE, to support all families in their central roles as supporters of their children's development (DEC, 2014; Dunst et al., 2017).

Standard 2: Partnering with Families

Candidates use their knowledge of family-centered practices and family systems theory to develop and maintain reciprocal partnerships with families. They apply family capacity-building practices as they support families to make informed decisions and advocate for their young children. They engage families in opportunities that build on their existing strengths, reflect current goals, and foster family competence and confidence to support their children's development and learning.

Component 2.1. Candidates apply their knowledge of family-centered practices, family systems theory, and the changing needs and priorities in families' lives to develop trusting, respectful, affirming, and culturally responsive partnerships with all families that allow for the mutual exchange of knowledge and information.

Supporting Explanation. Candidates understand how to apply family-centered practices to work with young children and their families. They use relational practices to foster trusting partnerships with families, including acknowledging child and family strengths as well as nurturing positive interactions by listening actively, showing empathy, and respecting family perspectives. They use participatory practices to cultivate collaboration, including soliciting families' opinions and ideas, jointly sharing information for family choice making, and meaningfully involving families in identifying and obtaining the resources they need. Candidates seek a greater understanding of families' diverse knowledge and expertise (e.g., funds of knowledge) about their children's strengths and needs. Candidates support families by acting in ways that build on family strengths and capacities in working with their young children. For example, for infants and toddlers, candidates and families jointly identify and implement individualized plans and supports around the family's priorities that promote the child's engagement, learning, development, and well-being (e.g., accessing natural environments and inclusive settings within the community). Together with families, candidates may identify strategies to facilitate the child's development.

Candidates understand family systems theory and recognize that biological, environmental, cultural, and societal factors influence families' structure, interactions, functions, and the family life cycle. They systematically gather information to develop a deeper understanding of families, their uniqueness, circumstances, and changing priorities. They consider factors such as social identities (e.g., culture, gender, sexuality, socio-economic status, marital status, and age) as well as stressors such as trauma, mental health issues, and medical conditions, as they build relationships, exchange knowledge and information, and plan for individualized supports. For example, candidates ensure that all aspects of the classroom environment, including the activities and materials, reflect the diversity of the children and families represented in the program. They modify services/supports or use technology when appropriate based on the family's/child's needs (e.g., adjusting meeting times to accommodate families' work schedules). They also understand and respect the role of each family member as it relates to their preferred engagement in planning and implementing individualized supports. Candidates engage in self-reflection of their own culture, beliefs, and experiences, and evaluate the impact it has on their partnerships with families. They use the knowledge gained through reflection to inform interactions with families and respond in sensitive and culturally affirming ways. For example, they recognize both strengths and barriers, respect home cultures and languages, and honor parenting styles and family values (e.g., candidates provide information regarding child progress in home language).

Knowledge Base. Family-centered principles are embedded among the standards of what candidates should know and be able to do in early childhood special education/early intervention. InTASC Standard 10(q) emphasizes the importance of respecting families while seeking to work collaboratively with them (CCSSO, 2013). Likewise, elements of NAEYC Standard 2 affirms the importance of developing partnerships with children's families which includes knowing family characteristics and engaging families through respectful, reciprocal relationships (NAEYC, 2011. CEC Standard 7 focuses on collaborating in a culturally responsive manner with families for the purpose of planning programs and accessing services (2012), while InTASC Standard 9(m) highlights the criticality of self-reflecting on one's own frame of reference and biases and the potential effects they have on relationships (CCSSO, 2013). Lastly, CAEP Elementary Standard 1 echoes the concepts from multiple standards that teachers work respectfully and reciprocally with families (2018).

"Almost 30 years of research and experience has demonstrated that the education of children with disabilities can be made more effective by... strengthening the role and responsibility of parents and ensuring that families of such children have meaningful opportunities to participate in the education of their children at school and at home" (IDEA, 2004). The Individuals with Disabilities Education Act (2004) protects the rights of children with disabilities and their parents; mandates that information be provided to parents; and ensures parent participation in meetings and placement decisions. Section 303.344 of IDEA outlines the requirement of family information being included in the Individualized Family Service Plan (IFSP), including an explicit statement of the family's resources, priorities, and concerns.

Recognizing the essential role of caregivers in the learning and development of their young children who have or are at risk for developmental delays or disabilities, the DEC Recommended Practices strive to offer guidance to parents and professionals who work with young children, birth through age 8 (2014). Among the seven topic areas, the family practices encompass three themes: 1) family-centered practices; 2) family capacity-building practices; and 3) family and professional collaboration. Recommended Practice F3 underscores practitioners being responsive to the family's concerns, priorities, and changing life circumstances whereas Recommended Practice F1 stresses the importance of building partnerships with families that are trusting and respectful while also sensitive to cultural, linguistic, and socio-economic diversity (2014). Furthermore, the DEC position statement on the role of special instruction in early intervention (DEC, 2014) emphasizes that IDEA (2004) Part C's early intervention services "focus on active caregiver-professional partnerships that are grounded in family-centered practices and guided by family priorities (p. 1)."

Acknowledging that working with families is essential and ultimately provides many benefits for the children, CEC high-leverage practices identify practices that support mutual sharing of knowledge and information encouraging educators to "organize and facilitate effective meetings with professionals and families (p. 18)" and to "collaborate with families to support student learning and secure needed services (p. 18)." These practices build "effective relationships and create a better understanding of students' needs" (McLeskey et al., 2017).

The Workgroup on Principles and Practices in Natural Environments (2008) key principles of early intervention includes an emphasis on families as equal partners in early intervention and that the family-professional relationship reflects mutual trust, respect, honesty, and open communication. Essential to the family-professional partnership is respect. The trust placed in professionals must be reciprocated with respect which can be provided in a variety of ways, including recognizing and abiding by the customs of families being supported and "accepting family decisions that differ from recommendations" (Hanson & Lynch, 2010, p. 167). Hedeen et al. (2013) recognize the important role and expertise of all members of teams, including parents, to develop effective plans (Individualized Family Service Plans [IFSPs] and Individualized Education Programs [IEPs]).

Dunst (2002) characterizes family-centeredness as "beliefs and practices that treat families with dignity and respect; individualized, flexible, and responsive practices; information sharing so that families can make informed decisions; family choice regarding any number of aspects of program practices and intervention options; parent-professional collaboration and partnerships as a context for family-program relations; and the provision and mobilization of resources and supports necessary for families to care for and rear their children in ways that produce optimal child, parent, and family outcomes (p. 142)." To close the gap between what professionals know about family-centered services and what they actually practice, Parette and Brotherson (2004) recommend that personnel preparation programs focus on encouraging students to adopt family-centered attitudes and support them in constructing and participating in learning communities.

Similarly, Mandell and Murray (2005) suggest that considerations for personnel preparation programs to assist in moving the field forward in its value and use of family-centered practices may include many and varied experiences with and about families, opportunities to problem-solve around obstacles experienced in the field, and instructional activities that highlight the significance of the family-professional partnership, including relationships with families whose background may be different from their own. Developing practices to be family-centered, accepting, affirming, and responsive to families of different cultures and beliefs is important. Cultivating family engagement skills in pre-service and in-service professionals leads to strengthening the family-professional partnership and improving outcomes for families who have young children with disabilities (Cosgrove et al., 2019).

Component 2.2. Candidates communicate clear, comprehensive, and objective information about resources and supports that help families to make informed decisions and advocate for access, participation, and equity in natural and inclusive environments.

Supporting Explanation. Candidates use effective communication strategies, such as attending, listening, and asking clarifying questions, to actively seek information from and about families. They articulate unbiased, comprehensive, and clear information from multiple perspectives and varied sources. Sources of information may include other professionals, policies, research, and professional literature. Candidates communicate in families' preferred modes, utilizing multiple formats, using technology when appropriate, and regularly checking for understanding (e.g., inserting intentional breaks during conversations, using interpreters) during formal and informal processes such as individualized education planning, home visits, and parent-teacher conferences. They prepare families to make informed decisions that reflect their priorities and concerns and support their young child's engagement, learning, development, and well-being. For example, they identify and connect families to resources (e.g., mental health services, health care, adult education, English language instruction, and economic support/assistance), and may help with planning transitions from one setting to another.

Candidates recognize the critical need for equitable access to supports within natural and inclusive environments for all young children and families. They use a range of strategies to support families in advocating for access and equity in natural environments and inclusive settings and share information about all available services and community resources. They reflect on their own biases in order to understand the impact they have on their communication with families. They collaboratively problem-solve and plan around the vision families have for their children and identify strategies to support families in accessing local community settings. They ensure multiple opportunities for families to be engaged in program activities and governance, including using strategies to seek family perspectives on program offerings. For example, they establish opportunities for families to connect with one another and respect families' decisions.

Knowledge Base. Family-professional partnerships are defined as interdependent relationships between practitioners and families that are built on trust, honesty, and shared responsibility (Brotherson et al., 2010). Among the essential knowledge represented in InTASC Standard 10 are the collaborative interaction skills with colleagues and families, engagement in advocacy in collaborative contexts, and continued professional learning (i.e., use of collaboration, mentorship, feedback, reflection) (CCSSO, 2013). Likewise, CEC Standard/Component 7.2 highlights the collaboration, communication, and coordination with families essential to support assessment, planning, and implementation of effective programs and services to foster progress toward child and family outcomes (2015).

Family-professional partnerships are key to realizing the intent of the law and are critical to high-quality early childhood special education/early intervention. The Individuals with Disabilities Education Act (IDEA) of 2004 mandates that information be provided to parents; ensures parent participation in meetings and placement decisions; and protects the rights of children with disabilities and their parents (IDEA, 2004).

The DEC Code of Ethics Responsive Family-Centered Practices stress that practitioners prepare families so that they can make informed decisions regarding services for their children (DEC, 2009). DEC Recommended Practice F2 highlights the importance of practitioners providing families with up-to-date and unbiased information that they can comprehend and use to make informed choices and decisions (2014). High-Leverage Practice 3 (McLeskey et al., 2017) underscores the importance of collaborating with families to ensure families are informed about their rights and special education processes as well as emphasizes the necessity of respectful, effective, communicative relationships. Addressed intermittently throughout the CEC/DEC Initial Specialty Set for Early Childhood Special Education/Early Intervention (2017), Skill ECSE.S6.6 contends that practitioners "advocate on behalf of infants and young children and their families."

In order to nurture the capacity of families, practitioners informing families about opportunities for leading and building skills for self-advocacy is

represented in DEC Recommended Practice F10 (2014), which says, "Early childhood inclusion embodies the values, policies, and practices that support the right of every infant and young child and his or her family, regardless of ability, to participate in a broad range of activities and contexts as full members of families, communities, and society. The desired results of inclusive experiences for children with and without disabilities and their families include a sense of belonging and membership, positive social relationships and friendships, and development and learning to reach their full potential. The defining features of inclusion that can be used to identify high quality early childhood programs and services are access, participation, and supports" (DEC/NAEYC, 2009, p 2).

In early childhood special education/early intervention, access, participation, and equity in natural and inclusive environments can be advocated for through the family-professional partnership. Resch et al. (2010) conclude that "caring for a child with a disability can be challenging, but many of these challenges are likely due to a lack of necessary environmental supports" (p. 149). Their study identified the most central area of concern for parents of children with disabilities as obtaining access to information and services. Pretti-Frontczak et al. (2002) and Mandell and Murray (2005) examined pre-service curricula which were designed to fully integrate the family-centered approach. The curricula aimed to strengthen students' knowledge and application of a family-centered approach, including working collaboratively with families using a variety of experiences and strategies. Creating an environment of family-centered values was supportive in students developing skills to become effective practitioners.

Component 2.3. Candidates engage families in identifying their strengths, priorities, and concerns; support families to achieve the goals they have for their family and their young child's development and learning; and promote families' competence and confidence during assessment, individualized planning, intervention, instruction, and transition processes.

Supporting Explanation. Candidates recognize family engagement as essential in supporting and strengthening family capacity and well-being to promote child development and learning and to provide high-quality, effective supports for young children and their families. They promote families as equal team members using participatory practices such as acknowledging their expertise and supporting them in identifying strengths, priorities, and concerns.

Candidates ensure multiple opportunities for active family collaboration in decision-making during assessment, planning, implementation, and transition processes. During assessment, they work in partnership with families to exchange knowledge, information, and expertise and to evaluate and synthesize information about the child's strengths and needs. They collaboratively create outcomes/goals, develop implementation plans, and identify the formal and informal supports and services necessary to achieve the outcomes/goals. They use evidence-based practices that are rooted within a culturally responsive framework to select and adapt learning strategies appropriate to each family. Candidates remain non-judgmental in their interactions and offer support aligned with identified strengths, priorities, and needs of children and families.

Candidates support families in taking actions that meet their own and their child's needs. They frequently communicate and reflect with families to evaluate, monitor, and modify services, supports, and resources. They use a range of intervention and instructional strategies to promote families' competence and confidence (e.g., video, coaching, consultation, modeling, assistive technology). They employ adult learning strategies when partnering with families across environments, activities, and programs. Candidates ensure that information and knowledge shared are understandable, immediately useful, and relevant to the family and build on prior knowledge. In preparation for and during transitions, they seek family input and provide unbiased information on a range of available supports, services, and resources (e.g., home, community, and/or school settings). They support families in evaluating transition options and making decisions to meet identified needs and priorities.

Knowledge Base. The Council of Chief State School Officers (CCSSO), the Council for Exceptional Children (CEC), the Division for Early Childhood (DEC), and the National Association for the Education of Young Children (NAEYC) recognize that family partnership and collaboration is essential in supporting and improving learning outcomes and growth for children with disabilities. InTASC Standard 10 (CCSSO, 2013) identifies the importance of

professional responsibility for leadership and collaboration as it discusses collaboration with learners, families, colleagues, other school professionals, and community members to ensure learner growth. The CEC/DEC Initial Specialty Set for Early Childhood Special Education/Early Intervention (2017) describes collaboration, in Standard 7, as critical to addressing the needs of learners when they state, that beginning educators must demonstrate the ability to collaborate with families, other educators, related service providers, individuals with exceptionalities, and personnel from community agencies in culturally responsive ways to address the needs of individuals with exceptionalities across a range of learning experiences. Standard 7 further elaborates on collaboration with families and caregivers through supporting families' choices, involving families in the development of goals and strategies, the implementation of services aligned with family resources, priorities, and concerns, and the evaluation of services as well as support throughout transitions. The specialty set also describes the role of families and the responsibility of the professional in engaging with and supporting families in the assessment process in Standard 4. Standard 6 describes the importance of respecting family choices and goals. NAEYC Standard 2 (2011) focuses on building family and community relationships as a foundation for successful early childhood education. Specifically, NAEYC highlights key elements, including knowing about and understanding diverse family and community characteristics, supporting and engaging families and communities through respectful, reciprocal relationships, and involving families and communities in young children's development and learning. NAEYC Standard 3 also highlights the importance of assessment partnerships with families to build effective learning environments (2011).

Parent participation has been a core, foundational concept since the inception of the Individuals with Disabilities Education Act (IDEA) in 1997 (Trainor, 2010b; Turnbull, 2001). The preamble of the Part C amendment states that Congress identified an "urgent and substantial need" to enhance the capacity of families to meet the special needs of their infants and toddlers (EHA Amendments of 1986, 42 U.S.C, sec. 671(a)). Furthermore, key components of the law include parental rights and safeguards that enable families to participate as full, equal team members in planning and decision-making.

The DEC Recommended Practices (2014) include a set of family practices that are considered fundamental to all other topic areas. They describe responsiveness to families' concerns, priorities, and changing life circumstances in Recommended Practice F3, while Recommended Practice F4 focuses on working together to create outcomes or goals and developing and implementing individualized plans aligned with family's priorities and goals. The professionals' role in supporting family functioning, promoting family confidence and competence, and strengthening family-child relationships is also described in Recommended Practice F5 and Recommended Practice F6. Further support for family engagement is seen in the DEC Recommended Practices definition of teaming and collaboration practices as "those that promote and sustain collaborative adult partnerships, relationships, and ongoing interactions to ensure that programs and services achieve desired child and family outcomes and goals" (2014, p. 15).

The CEC high-leverage practices (McLeskey et al., 2017) reference seven specific principles of effective partnerships, as described by Turnbull et al. (2015) and includes a focus on respecting families by treating them with dignity, honoring cultural diversity, and affirming strengths as well as a focus on equality, described as sharing power and working together with families (McLeskey et al., 2017). More specifically, HLP2 highlights collaboration with families as guidance is provided for ensuring opportunities for families to be equal partners in planning through effective team meetings. Finally, in HLP3, the importance of collaboration with families to support student learning and to secure services is identified as a key practice.

There is a strong set of knowledge and research supporting the use of practices that engage families and support them in being equal partners in assessment, planning, and intervention/instruction. Research has shown that high levels of parental involvement in early childhood and elementary education correlate with improved academic performance, more positive attitudes toward school, fewer placements in special education, lower dropout rates, and fewer suspensions (Xu, 2019). Furthermore, research has indicated when parents are involved in their children's early intervention, early childhood, and elementary and secondary school programs, better outcomes are realized (Dunst, 2002). One of the most common barriers to parent participation, as cited in the literature, includes the behaviors of special education professionals (Bezdek et al., 2010), including the use of jargon,

poor communication, and lack of support for meaningful parent participation (Wolfe & Durán, 2013). Elbaum et al. (2016) attribute many of the challenges noted above to a lack of pre-service preparation related to skills, ethics, and behaviors that are required to build partnerships with families. Mueller et al. (2019) identified major challenges experienced by graduates in the first few years, including challenges building and maintaining positive relationships with parents, scheduling meetings, obtaining support from colleagues and administrators, and experiencing low confidence leading meetings. Mueller et al. (2019) suggest inclusion of more pre-service opportunities which include real-world application, safe spaces to learn and make mistakes as well as opportunities to gain meaningful feedback in order to learn and practice strategies for fostering meaningful family-professional partnerships.

Standard 3: Collaboration and Teaming

Candidates apply models, skills, and processes of teaming when collaborating and communicating with families and professionals, using culturally and linguistically responsive and affirming practices. In partnership with families and other professionals, candidates develop and implement individualized plans and successful transitions that occur across the age span. Candidates use a variety of collaborative strategies while working with and supporting other adults.

Component 3.1. Candidates apply teaming models, skills, and processes, including appropriate uses of technology, when collaborating and communicating with families; professionals representing multiple disciplines, skills, expertise, and roles; and community partners and agencies.

Supporting Explanation. Candidates are cognizant of the roles and responsibilities of multiple disciplines (e.g., occupational and physical therapists, speech-language pathologists, orientation and mobility specialists) and family members on the team, and work and interact with them collaboratively in various team processes. Candidates apply appropriate models of interprofessional teaming such as primary service provision, transdisciplinary, interdisciplinary, multidisciplinary, and others to meet the needs of young children and their families and professionals working with them. Candidates apply teaming processes and skills in activities such as team assessment, joint goal/outcome development, and planning and implementation of services. Candidates demonstrate teaming skills and processes such as problem-solving, conflict resolution, joint decision-making, role release, group facilitation, and communication. Candidates show respect for all members of the team who represent various roles, expertise, and skill levels by being open to multiple perspectives. Team members support each other's professional growth as they learn from one another.

Candidates participate in and, in some instances, lead team meetings to support the developmental and academic content outcomes and goals of young children with developmental delays and disabilities and their families (i.e., in the United States, this would include the Individualized Family Service Plan (IFSP) and Individualized Education Program (IEP) meetings—initial, semi-annual, and annual).

Candidates are familiar with community-based services and resources and know how to access them for young children with developmental delays and disabilities and their families. These services and resources meet family-identified child and family needs. Examples of services and resources include public education agencies, private therapy, private evaluation services, private schools, early education and care, food banks, social services, and developmental pediatricians.

Candidates, when communicating with families and other team members, communicate clearly and without jargon to effectively explain children's strengths and needs. Examples include discussing a child's progress in a team meeting, during a home visit, or with an early childhood educator to support a child's inclusion in their classroom and across environments.

Candidates select and use appropriate technology platforms such as learning management and virtual communication systems as appropriate for effective teaming. Family preferences and access are considered to facilitate full participation of all team members.

Knowledge Base. The importance of collaboration and teaming is noted in InTASC Standard 10 (CCSSO, 2013). This standard emphasizes the significance of preparing candidates to collaborate with families, colleagues, and community constituents to support student learning and advance the profession.

Similarly, Standard 7 in the CEC Preparation Standards (2015) stresses the importance of candidates collaborating with families, other educators and related service personnel, individuals with disabilities, and community agencies across a range of settings and learning experiences. NAEYC Standard 2 (2012) states that candidates will involve families and communities in their children's development and learning, which requires the ability to engage in effective collaboration. CAEP Elementary Standard 5 (2018) echoes the call for candidates to work collaboratively with colleagues toward common goals that influence students' development and growth. The CEC/DEC Initial Specialty Set for Early Childhood Special Education/Early Intervention (CEC, 2017) further identified the need for candidates to understand models and strategies of consultation and collaboration as well as the ability to apply models of team processes in early childhood to collaborate with caregivers, other personnel, and agencies.

Interdisciplinary approaches to service delivery, which require expertise in teaming and collaboration, gained legislative support with the passage of the Education of the Handicapped Act of 1986 (P.L. 94-142). Subsequent legislation and the amendments to the Individuals with Disabilities Education Act (IDEA) (2004) have offered clarification and recommendations associated with teaming to enhance professional collaboration.

CEC also emphasizes the importance of collaboration in its high-leverage practices (McLeskey et al., 2017). One practice focuses on collaboration with professionals to improve student outcomes (HLP1). Another practice addresses collaboration with families to support student learning and accessing services (HLP3).

The Division for Early Childhood (DEC) Recommended Practices (DEC, 2014) address practices focused on collaboration and teaming. They are described as practices that support adult partnerships, relationships, and interactions to ensure that programs and services achieve desired outcomes and goals for families and children. These practices also emphasize that team members assist each other in accessing and partnering with community services and programs. The first two DEC Recommended Practices focus on professionals from multiple disciplines and families working as a team in the planning and implementation of interventions (TC1, TC2). The third DEC recommended practice emphasizes the importance of effective communication among team members and group processes that enhance team functioning and relationships (TC3). The fourth practice (TC4) stresses that candidates, as members of teams, should identify and use community-based informal and formal supports and resources to meet a family's self-identified needs, values, and interests. The final practice (TC5) encourages teams to select a primary liaison to support families and facilitate effective team communication.

Teaming models (such as interdisciplinary and transdisciplinary) and their characteristics and benefits are described in the literature (Woodruff & McGonigel, 1998). Shelden and Rush (2013) add to these descriptions by differentiating the primary service provider approach from the transdisciplinary approach. Also provided in the literature are insights about factors and strategies that promote teaming and collaboration to support young children and families. Team members use technology and other forms of communication to develop collaborative relationships with families, other team members, and the community (Luke, 2019; Rosetti et al., 2017). Team members must share their expertise with one another by providing information, planning jointly, engaging in modeling and reflection, and providing performance feedback. For instance, Brookman-Frazee et al. (2012) described teaming strategies used with families to improve outcomes for their children diagnosed with autism spectrum disorder. The literature indicates that team members should be knowledgeable in their area of focus; create shared goals; use data to guide intervention planning; celebrate team accomplishments; and encourage open, honest, clear, and frequent communication (Bell, 2007; Hunt et al., 2004; Mattessich & Monsey, 1992). Considerable information is available on teaming and collaborative practices that support team effectiveness (Cohen & Bailey, 1997; Mattessich & Monsey, 1992; West et al., 2004).

Content related to teaming and collaboration practices has been recognized as important to include in personnel preparation programs (Guillen & Winton, 2015; Kilgo & Bruder, 1997; Kilgo et al., 2019; Rosenkoetter & Stayton, 1997; Sexton et al., 1997; Stayton, et al., 2001). Kilgo et al. (2019) addressed the important role pre-service personnel preparation programs play in preparing personnel from multiple disciplines to learn about and implement teaming and collaboration practices.

Component 3.2. Candidates use a variety of collaborative strategies when working with other adults that are evidence-based, appropriate to the task, culturally and linguistically responsive, and take into consideration the environment and service delivery approach.

Supporting Explanation. Candidates use adult learning strategies that are appropriate to the learning preferences and existing knowledge of other adults on the team (e.g., family members, professionals, paraprofessionals) to promote and sustain collaborative partnerships. Candidates support other adults in working with young children with developmental delays and disabilities. For example, a candidate might coach a paraprofessional to implement an intervention strategy during large group time in the classroom or coach a family member in embedding strategies into mealtime routines. Candidates, as appropriate, use the role release approach to implement interventions recommended and demonstrated by another discipline as a part of their ongoing interactions with young children. For example, candidates provide proper positioning, utilize adaptive equipment, and facilitate ambulation for children with physical disabilities as recommended by physical and occupational therapists.

Candidates engage in collaborative activities such as coaching, consultation, and co-teaching with other adults, including related service personnel, general educators, paraprofessionals, family members, service coordinators, and medical professionals. Coaching could be used to support families during home visits; consultation could be used to support teachers of preschoolers in inclusive early childhood programs; and co-teaching could be used to partner with general education teachers to provide support to early elementary students (K through grade 3) in inclusive classrooms.

Candidates use a variety of strategies to increase the effectiveness of meetings with various professionals and family members, depending on the situation and environment, the needs of families and professionals, and the service delivery approach. For example, using a triadic strategy while working directly with a family member and child would be appropriate in a home or school environment, whereas using active listening and problem-solving skills would be effective in a team meeting at an office or school as well as with families.

Candidates use strategies for interacting and sharing knowledge and expertise with families and other professionals. Candidates learn from families and other professionals interacting in ways that are respectful, supportive, capacity enhancing, and culturally and linguistically responsive. Candidates access supports to increase families' understanding and engagement in collaborative activities such as using interpreters, cultural liaisons, and family support networks.

Knowledge Base. The need for candidates to know how to use a variety of collaborative strategies is noted in InTASC Standard 10 (CCSSO, 2013). Interprofessional skills such as communication, collaboration, and the use of technology are woven throughout the standards. CEC (2015) also identified the importance of collaboration in CEC Standard 7, which calls for candidates to learn to serve as a collaborative resource to colleagues and use collaboration to promote the well-being of children with exceptionalities across a wide range of settings and collaborators. Similarly, in Standard 2, NAEYC (2012) supports the need for candidates to engage in effective collaboration among families and communities to support children's learning and development. The CEC/DEC Initial Specialty Set for Early Childhood Special Education/Early Intervention (CEC, 2017) further emphasized the need for candidates to have skills in collaborating with other adults and agencies in supporting children's learning, participating as team members and using teaming strategies, and employing adult learning principles in the consultation and coaching process with other professionals and families.

In the DEC Recommended Practices (2014), multiple collaborative strategies are highlighted depending on the service delivery model and location of services. With multiple professionals working in partnership with each family, there is a need for candidates to know how to use data-based decision-making to guide interventions as indicated in TC1. TC2 highlights the importance of candidates knowing how to share information and give feedback to other team members to improve child outcomes. CEC high-leverage practices (McLeskey et al., 2017) also identify practices that focus on collaboration with professionals and families to support student learning and outcomes as well as access to services.

The literature provides support for candidates to be prepared to participate in teams with others to pool their collective expertise and exchange knowledge and competencies between team members (Cohen & Bailey, 1997; Hoegl & Gemuenden, 2001; Weiss et al., 2017; West et al., 2004). Further, there is support for the use of coaching strategies with caregivers (Friedman et al., 2012; Kaminski et al., 2008; Peterson et al., 2007) and other professionals (Fox et al., 2011; McCollum et al., 2013; Neuman & Cunningham, 2009) to improve outcomes for young children. The literature also supports the notion of candidates having knowledge of strategies associated with fostering positive relationships among team members. Studies have examined team member attributes (Bell, 2007), program attributes (Dinnebeil et al., 1999), decision-making using multiple perspectives (Hunt et al., 2004), communication and group facilitation, including team functioning (Flowers et al., 1999), and team leadership training (Hundert & Hopkins, 1992; West et al., 2003). Clearly, there is a research base to support teaming, collaboration, consultation, and co-teaching skills for early childhood special education candidates (Dinnebeil et al., 1996; Dinnebeil et al., 1999; Dinnebeil & McInerney, 2011; Friend & Cook, 2017; Olson et al., 1998).

Component 3.3. Candidates partner with families and other professionals to develop individualized plans and support various transitions that occur for the young child and their family throughout the birth through 8 age span.

Supporting Explanation. Candidates partner with families and other professionals to develop and implement individualized plans for each child. They share information about a variety of local services and a range of learning environments with family members prior to transitions to help families become informed of their options and next steps in the transition process. In collaboration with families and professionals, candidates explore and evaluate placement option(s) for young children as they transition from one environment to another. Candidates support families so that they have the information they need to be their child's own best advocate.

Candidates use a variety of planned and timely strategies to support children and families before, during, and after transitions according to their needs, priorities, and values. Candidates, partnering with families and other professionals, support transitions by helping to develop individualized transition plans to provide successful preparation, adjustment, and positive outcomes for children and families. Examples include supporting a family's observation of a new program and debriefing afterwards, holding a transition meeting where the goals of the child and family are shared between sending and receiving programs, preparing the child for transition by practicing some of the routines of the next environment before the transition, facilitating the child visiting the new program, and/or providing information to the family as they exit the current program and enter the new program.

Knowledge Base. InTASC Standard 10 (CCSSO, 2013) emphasized the need for candidates to know how to use a variety of collaborative strategies to support children and families. CEC (2015) in CEC standard 7 also identified the importance of candidates collaborating with families to address the needs of children with disabilities across a wide range of settings and collaborators as well as serve as a collaborative resource to colleagues. Further, NAEYC (2012), in Standard 2, stressed the importance of building family and community relationships through effective collaboration among families and communities to support children's learning and development. The CEC/DEC Initial Specialty Set for Early Childhood Special Education/Early Intervention (CEC, 2017) emphasized the need for candidates to have skills to assist families in transition planning and implementing practices that support transitions among settings.

Specified in the IDEA Part C regulations (U.S. Department of Education, 2011) are requirements for transition planning from Part C (birth through age 3) to Part B 619 (preschool) special education services. These regulations indicate that planning is to be conducted by a team of professionals from the Part C agency and the local education agency, in addition to the family requiring the development of interagency and intra-agency agreements in the transition process. Research suggests that the most critical factor for successful transition to natural and inclusive environments may be a positive working relationship between the family and service providers (Kemp, 2003).

The DEC Recommended Practices (2014) indicate the need for candidates to collaborate with families and professionals to foster the development of individualized plans and to facilitate transitions. TC1 calls for teams, representing practitioners from multiple disciplines and families, to plan and implement supports and services that are designed to meet each child's and family's unique needs. The DEC Recommended Practices also emphasize that the team members assist each other in working with and accessing community-based services. They also highlight the importance of collaboration during transitions (TR1, TR2) by stating that "practitioners in sending and receiving programs exchange information before, during, and after transition.... (DEC, 2014, p.16)."

Further, CEC high-leverage practices (McLeskey et al., 2017) identify practices that focus on collaboration with professionals and families to support student learning and outcomes (HLP1) and result in effective meetings (HLP2). CEC high-leverage practices also identify effective collaborative behaviors (sharing ideas, problem solving, negotiating) for professionals that focus on individualized instructional or behavioral planning to maximize student learning (HLP1) (McLeskey et al., 2017).

The literature supports the need for candidates to understand and consider the unique child, family, professional, and community factors that may affect collaboration and successful planning and implementation of intervention (Shonkoff et al., 1992). Further, the literature provides insight on factors and effective strategies that promote teaming and collaboration around supports for young children (Sloper et al., 2006).

The literature also emphasizes the importance of candidates knowing the components of transition planning and developing effective transition skills to ensure continuity of care in the lives of young children (Shonkoff & Phillips, 2000), specifically related to infant and toddler care (Kochanska et al., 2000) and young children with disabilities services (Kemp, 2003). Candidates must have communication skills (Rous et al., 2007) and planned and timed strategies to implement effective transition practices (Daly et al., 2011; Rous, & Hallam, 2012; Rous et al., 2010). The literature supports the need for candidates to collaborate with families and professionals in the development of individualized plans and the facilitation of effective transitions (Rous et al., 2007).

Standard 4: Assessment Processes

Candidates know and understand the purposes of assessment in relation to ethical and legal considerations. Candidates choose developmentally, linguistically, and culturally appropriate tools and methods that are responsive to the characteristics of the young child, family, and program. Using evidence-based practices, candidates develop or select as well as administer informal measures, and select and administer formal measures in partnership with families and other professionals. They analyze, interpret, document, and share assessment information using a strengths-based approach with families and other professionals for eligibility determination, outcome/goal development, planning instruction and intervention, monitoring progress, and reporting.

Component 4.1. Candidates understand the purposes of formal and informal assessment, including ethical and legal considerations, and use this information to choose developmentally, culturally and linguistically appropriate, valid, reliable tools and methods that are responsive to the characteristics of the young child, family, and program.

Supporting Explanation. Candidates understand the primary purposes for the assessment process, including screening, determination of eligibility, program planning, on-going instructional monitoring, child progress monitoring, and evaluation. Candidates understand that commercially developed assessment tools are developed for the specific purposes listed above. They understand that assessment tools must be used in accordance with the publisher's guidance and for its intended purposes. For example, screening tools should not be used for program evaluation and standardized formal tests should not be used for program planning.

Candidates understand how comprehensive screening methods (such as "Child Find" in the U.S.) are used systemically to identify young children who may need additional evaluation. Candidates understand that when assessing for eligibility determination, multiple tools and methods should be used by an assessment team that includes multiple professionals and the child's family.

Candidates know federal, provincial, and state regulations related to early childhood special educa-

tion assessment, birth through age 8, and understand how assessment practices may differ across services for infants and toddlers, preschoolers, and early elementary students. They understand rules for eligibility determination for early intervention and early childhood special education services.

Candidates recognize the potential for bias and plan to limit the opportunity for bias in all stages of assessment. Candidates understand that biased results can occur if standardized assessment tools are not chosen with the child in mind. For example, candidates understand that bias may occur when using a standardized tool with a norm group that does not include representation of the child being assessed, when members of the assessment team do not meet the required training and experience qualifications for the tool, when assessment items that have been translated have inaccuracies, or when items used include examples that do not align with the child's experience (e.g., in a vocabulary assessment, a photo of a diving board is used, yet the child has never been to a swimming pool). In addition, candidates understand that many standardized assessment instruments rely on children's use of either verbal or motor behaviors (e.g., pointing) to indicate their response to items when the intention is to measure another domain such as cognition, receptive language, or even social-emotional development. For example, if an item requires a child to stack a certain number of blocks for a cognitive task and the child has motor difficulties, the candidate understands that the item likely will not accurately reflect the child's cognition.

Candidates understand the unique challenges that occur when assessing infants, toddlers, and young children. For example, it is important to assess infants when they are in an alert state. Candidates gather assessment information from families through formal and informal measures and methods because they understand that families are known to be valid and reliable when providing information about their children. Because it can be difficult to gather valid and reliable assessment results with some infants and toddlers, working together with the team and guided by federal, provincial, and state regulations, the candidate understands the process and use of informed clinical opinion in determining eligibility for early intervention services.

Candidates use informal strategies such as naturalistic observation and embed assessment strategies in the curriculum and in daily routines at school and in the home to facilitate authentic assessment of infants and toddlers, preschoolers, and children in the early elementary grades (K through 3). Candidates recognize that curriculum-based measures and observation-based methods yield critical information needed for program planning and ongoing monitoring to make instructional based decisions.

Knowledge Base. Understanding the purposes of assessment and choosing tools and methods to avoid bias is noted in InTASC Standard 6 (CCSSO, 2013). Standard 4 of the CEC Preparation Standards (2012) also identifies the importance of candidates understanding the need to use multiple methods of assessment and minimizing bias. In the NAEYC Standards (2012), Standard 3 echoes the call for candidates to understand the uses of assessment and to practice responsible assessment procedures. The CEC/DEC Initial Specialty Set for Early Childhood Special Education/Early Intervention (CEC, 2017) calls for candidates to understand legal requirements for eligibility (K4.2) as well as selecting tools based on their specific purpose (S4.4), using information from multiple sources and environments (S4.6), using a variety of materials and contexts to obtain valid information given the unique challenges of assessing infants, toddlers, and young children (S4.7), and finally using culturally unbiased assessments and procedures (S4.12).

IDEA (2004) has multiple requirements related to assessment, including the use of valid and reliable assessment tools and using multiple measures. In addition, the law requires that assessment tools "are selected and administered so as not to be discriminatory on a racial or cultural basis" and "are provided and administered in the language and form most likely to yield accurate information" (PL 108-446, Part B, sec. 614 (3)(A)(i)(ii)). Furthermore, Part C of IDEA (2004) stipulates similar requirements for infants and toddlers to include "family-directed identification of the needs of each family...to assist in the development of the infant or toddler" (PL 108-446, Part C, sec. 635(a)(3)).

Moreover, the DEC Code of Ethics (2009) specifically states, "We shall use individually appropriate assessment strategies, including multiple sources of information such as observations, interviews with significant caregivers, formal and informal assessments to determine children's learning styles, strengths, and challenges" (p. 2). NAEYC (2011) also

address assessment practices in their code of ethics as follows: "I1.6 To use assessment instruments and strategies that are appropriate for the children to be assessed, that are used only for the purposes for which they were designed, and that have the potential to benefit children. I1.7 To use assessment information to understand and support children's development and learning, to support instruction, and to identify children who may need additional services" (p. 2).

These concepts are further supported through DEC Recommended Practices (2014) in the Assessment area, specifically with practices A3 through A8 in which the focus is on EI/ECSE professionals using multiple sources, adhering to appropriate assessment strategies and materials that account for developmental appropriateness, and making needed accommodations for children's sensory, physical, communication, cultural, and social-emotional characteristics. Similarly, in CEC high-leverage practices, Practice 4 in the assessment area indicates that professionals should "use multiple sources of information to develop a comprehensive understanding of a student's strengths and needs" (McLeskey et al., 2017, p. 19).

The literature also supports the notion that assessment strategies and specific measures are to be designed with specific purposes in mind (National Research Council, 2008). It is important that candidates are prepared to understand and apply assessments according to their purpose. General purposes in EI/ECSE include screening or Child Find, determining eligibility for special education services or diagnosis, program planning, monitoring child progress, and program evaluation (McLean, 2014). Given issues of under-identification of infants and toddlers with developmental delays, Dunst et al. (2011) describe evidence-based procedures to improve child find outcomes through tailoring outreach to primary referral sources that EI/ECSE professionals include in their practices with children and families.

Once young children are in the evaluation process, valid, reliable assessment can be a challenge for the EI/ECSE professional. For example, Bagnato and colleagues (2007) document that many norm-referenced tests used in early childhood special education lack adequate inclusion of children with disabilities in their norm groups. Furthermore, Benner and Grim (2013) state that assessing infants, toddlers, and young children requires that the EI/ECSE professional have a clear understanding of early development, developmental progressions, and specific skills.

For example, when assessing school-age children, it is common practice to separate children from their caregivers during the assessment process. In contrast, when EI/ECSE professionals are assessing infants, toddlers, and young children, it is recommended to have caregivers actively involved in the assessment process. In addition, as noted in Linder's (2008) Transdisciplinary Play-Based Assessment the caregiver plays a primary role in engaging the child in play such that the context supports the child's optimal display of current skill attainment. In addition, Duran et al. (2011) describe an evidence-based practice for effective evaluation of young children who are dual language learners that includes active and meaningful family participation using informal observations in natural environments that are to be implemented by EI/ECSE professionals. This fits nicely with Routines Based Interviews, a method promoted by McWilliam and colleagues (2011) as a valid method of assessment in early childhood special education. Moreover, Neisworth and Bagnato (2011) describe the use of informed opinion as a recommended assessment practice in determining eligibility in EI/ECSE when traditional testing would yield invalid results. Finally, EI/ECSE professionals using the Individual Growth and Development Indicators (IGDIs, Carta et al., 2010) for universal screening ,and progress monitoring are able to obtain far more individually reliable and valid snapshots of the child's present level of development.

Component 4.2. Candidates develop and administer informal assessments and/or select and use valid, reliable formal assessments using evidence-based practices, including technology, in partnership with families and other professionals.

Supporting Explanation. Candidates use a variety of assessment tools, including formative and summative strategies that incorporate technology. They understand the strengths, limitations, validity, and reliability of different assessment methods and tools for infants and toddlers, preschoolers, and children in the early elementary grades (K through 3). Candidates administer formal and informal assessments. Candidates understand the role of specialized assessment that may be performed by related service providers or other team members and know how to interpret results. Candidates understand how specialized assessment contributes to a holistic view of the child.

Candidates understand basic principles of psychometrics and apply these principles to critically evaluate formal and informal assessment instruments and methods. They define test reliability and validity and can identify subtypes of reliability and validity. They develop informal measures that are valid relative to the content and reliable in that they provide consistent results.

Candidates plan and use assessments that are individualized, developmentally appropriate, and culturally and linguistically appropriate for the child and family. When appropriate, cultural mediators and/or interpreters are included on the assessment team to ensure assessments are provided in ways that are responsive to the specific needs of dual language learners and their families. Candidates integrate environmental assessment processes across settings as appropriate for the child and family.

Candidates understand and use play as a context for assessment, as appropriate. Candidates participate in team-based assessments that are comprehensive, covering all domains of child development, consider relevant child medical issues, and family characteristics, including parenting skills, attitudes, and their understanding of their child's developmental strengths and challenges. Candidates apply play-based methods as appropriate alongside other informal assessments such as questioning, checking for understanding, and more formal assessments to cover academic and developmental content areas.

Knowledge Base. The need for candidates to know how to design, adapt, or select appropriate assessments is noted in Standard 6 of the InTASC standards (CCSSO, 2013). InTASC Standard 6 further indicates the importance of using technology to support assessment practices. In the CEC Preparation Standards (2012), Standard 4 also identifies the importance of selecting technically sound assessments and using knowledge of measurement principles in collaboration with colleagues and families. The NAEYC Standard 3 (2012) echoes the call for candidates to use technology in the assessment process in partnership with families and professional colleagues. The CEC/DEC Initial Specialty Set for Early Childhood Special Education/Early Intervention (CEC, 2017) calls for assessing across developmental domains, play, and temperament (S4.3) and using informal and formal assessment tools and methods (S4.5).

The IDEA (2004) has multiple requirements related to assessment, including the use of valid and reliable assessment tools to be used for the purpose for which they were developed. In addition, the law requires that "the child is assessed in all areas of suspected disability" (or delay) (PL 108-446, Part B, sec. 614 (B)). Furthermore, Part C of IDEA (2004) stipulates similar requirements for infants and toddlers to include "family-directed identification of the needs of each family…to assist in the development of the infant or toddler" (PL 108-446, Part C, sec. 635(a)(3)). This clearly supports the need for candidates to work in partnership with families and other professionals.

Moreover, the DEC Code of Ethics (2009) specifically states, "We shall use individually appropriate assessment strategies, including multiple sources of information such as observations, interviews with significant caregivers, formal and informal assessments to determine children's learning styles, strengths, and challenges" (p. 2). NAEYC (2011) also addresses assessment practices in its code of ethics as follows: "I1.6 To use assessment instruments and strategies that are appropriate for the children to be assessed, that are used only for the purposes for which they were designed, and that have the potential to benefit children. I1.7 To use assessment information to understand and support children's development and learning, to support instruction, and to identify children who may need additional services" (p. 2).

These concepts are also supported through DEC Recommended Practices (2014) in the Assessment area, specifically with practice A10 in which EI/ECSE practitioners are to "use assessment tools with sufficient sensitivity to detect child progress, especially for the child with significant support needs" (p. 8). Again, in CEC high-leverage practices, Practice 4 in the assessment area indicates that professionals compile a comprehensive learner profile by developing and using a variety of strategies, including formal and informal tools (McLeskey et al., 2017).

The literature indicates a clear need to prepare candidates to select and use the appropriate assessment tools and processes. Researchers provide ample guidance to EI/ECSE professionals in the use of valid and reliable evidence-based approaches in the assessment process. Snyder et al. (2014) outline the following four sources of evidence for EI/ECSE professionals to use to ensure score validity: content, internal structure, relationships with other variables, and the consequences of using the assessment tool. EI/ECSE personnel must be familiar with all aspects of the administration and scoring for specific assessment instruments to yield reliable results.

Duran et al. (2011) describe an evidence-based practice for effective evaluation of young children who are dual language learners by EI/ECSE professionals that includes active and meaningful family participation using linguistically responsive informal observations in natural environments. In addition, Edelman (2011) describes how EI/ECSE professionals can use technology such as digital videos to enhance authentic assessment and serve as a family friendly platform to provide information to caregivers. Finally, Benner and Grim (2013) indicate that a transdisciplinary model of assessment gives EI/ECSE professionals an opportunity to move toward an integrated model of development while tapping discipline specific expertise.

Component 4.3. Candidates analyze, interpret, document, and share assessment information using a strengths-based approach with families and other professionals.

Supporting Explanation. Candidates use a strengths-based approach in all facets of the assessment process. That is, they are able to identify the child and family strengths and build upon them. Candidates understand that the most important consideration in the assessment of a young child is the interrelationship between the child and their family. Candidates include family members and professionals in the assessment process, know the benefits of shared analysis with family members and other professionals, and, when sharing assessment results, respect confidentiality. Candidates are respectful of families and demonstrate flexibility in supporting them to participate at their level of preference.

Candidates demonstrate essential knowledge and core skills in team building and in communicating with families. They use effective communication strategies with families to ensure assessment results (e.g., eligibility determination, program planning, and progress monitoring) are conveyed in ways that facilitate families' understanding. Candidates demonstrate respect for families' knowledge, opinions, and concerns. They use communication skills during interviews and conferences with families, including active listening, furthering responses, paraphrasing, demonstrating non-judgmental attitudes, responding to affect, questioning, and summarizing to ensure that the family member's primary views have been heard accurately during the assessment process. Candidates write about, summarize, and display assessment data in a family-friendly way, without jargon. When specialized assessment results use technical terms, candidates explain those terms to family members. When asked questions about a child's assessment results by a family member or other professional, the candidate responds accurately using positive language and referring the individual to completed assessment documents.

Candidates know about the similarities and differences in approaches and assessment techniques used in early intervention, preschools, and school systems to assist with keeping families informed and to help them with transitions as children progress from program to program.

Knowledge Base. The importance of candidates' ability to analyze student data in collaboration with others is noted in Standard 6 of the InTASC Standards (CCSSO, 2013). In the CEC Preparation Standards (2012), Standard 4 also identifies the importance of interpreting assessment results in collaboration with colleagues and families. NAEYC Standard 3 (2011) echoes the call for candidates to know about assessment partnerships with families and professional colleagues. Standard 3 of the CAEP Elementary K-6 Standards (2018) calls for candidates to interpret and use assessment results to improve instruction. Finally, the CEC/DEC Initial Specialty Set for Early Childhood Special Education/Early Intervention (CEC, 2017) calls for candidates to understand the role of the family in the assessment process (K4.1), including the ability to use a strengths-based approach (S4.9) in all facets of the assessment process.

Part C of IDEA (2004) requires evaluations for infants and toddlers to include "family-directed identification of the needs of each family…to assist in the development of the infant or toddler." (PL 108-446, Part C, sec. 635(a)(3)). Moreover, the DEC Code of Ethics (2009) specifically states, "We shall use individually appropriate assessment strategies, including multiple sources of information such as observations, interviews with significant caregivers, formal and informal assessments to determine children's learning styles, strengths, and challenges" (p.2). NAEYC (2011) also addresses assessment practices in its code of ethics as follows: "I1.7 To use assessment infor-

mation to understand and support children's development and learning, to support instruction, and to identify children who may need additional services" (p. 2). These concepts are also supported through DEC Recommended Practices (2014) in the Assessment area, specifically with Practice A1 in which EI/ECSE practitioners are to "work with the family to identify family preferences (p. 8)" and Practice A11 in which they are to report assessment results so that they are understandable and useful to families. In CEC high-leverage practices, Practice 5 in the assessment area indicates that professionals interpret and involve families in the assessment process in order to collaboratively design educational programs (McLeskey et al., 2017).

Researchers in the field of EI/ECSE support the need to prepare EI/ECSE professionals to partner with families throughout the assessment process and to communicate using a strengths-based approach. Caspe and colleagues (2011) specifically state that professionals must be prepared to engage families in a strengths-based fashion to share "data about student progress and performance in an accessible, understandable, and actionable manner (p. 2)." The child's overall development is affected by the interaction of the child's family and environment (Hall et al., 2011). With this in mind, Dunst (2002) describes family-centered practices as a set of beliefs, principles, and values for supporting and strengthening the capacity of families to enhance and promote their children's development. He further indicates that research supports the notion that family-centered approaches yield better outcomes than traditional child-centered approaches.

EI/ECSE professionals must invite families to participate in the assessment process. While the family's involvement may vary based on their individual needs and preferences, the EI/ECSE professional will work together with the family to meet the family's preference throughout the process. Families' roles may include being consumers of information, informants, active team members in the assessment process, and advocates (Benner & Grim 2013).

EI/ECSE providers should tailor communication methods with families based on family preferences (Hall et al., 2011). An example of a family friendly platform to provide information to caregivers is the use of technology such as digital videos as part of an authentic assessment method (Edelman, 2011).

Component 4.4. Candidates, in collaboration with families and other team members, use assessment data to determine eligibility, develop child and family-based outcomes/goals, plan for interventions and instruction, and monitor progress to determine efficacy of programming.

Supporting Explanation. Candidates understand how formal and informal assessment data are reviewed and analyzed to determine eligibility for special education services. Candidates understand how limitations of formal and informal assessments (e.g., biases, test constructs), contextual factors (e.g., socioeconomic status, family structure, previous intervention/instruction), and child characteristics may influence accurate interpretation of assessment results. Candidates understand eligibility rules for infants, toddlers, and young children to receive early intervention or special education services. They observe and participate in team meetings, such as IEP and IFSP meetings, in which eligibility decisions are made in collaboration with families and other professionals.

Interviews, observations, and other authentic strategies (such as work samples, video recordings) are used to provide holistic, functional information on children's developmental strengths and challenges. Multiple settings (e.g., home, childcare, playground, community library) and multiple sources (e.g., family members, other caregivers) are utilized when collecting authentic assessment data. With a team that includes professionals representing multiple disciplines and families, candidates integrate formal, informal, and authentic assessment data in the development of child and family-based outcomes/goals and individualized plans. Candidates work with the team to ensure that outcomes, goals, and objectives are relevant, functional, and of high priority for the individual infant, toddler, or young child and their family.

Candidates use formative assessment (e.g., frequency, percentage, or rate data) to make data-based intervention and instructional decisions. Ongoing informal assessment (such as observations in the natural environment) is used by the candidate, together with other team members, to adapt and enhance instruction/intervention. Candidates monitor intervention/instructional effectiveness through ongoing formative child, family, and setting assessments that include formal, informal, and authentic techniques (such as

observations of routines at home, school, or other settings; interviews with family members, childcare providers, and others). Candidates use an assessment-instruction cycle to collect ongoing data in authentic contexts, interpret individual progress based on the data, and make data-based instructional decisions regarding instructional strategies or intensity of instruction.

Knowledge Base. In the CEC standards (2012), Standard 4 focuses on how assessment data is essential for educational decision-making, including developing and implementing instructional programs. Additionally, in the NAEYC standards (2012), Standard 3 focuses on using data from child-level assessment to promote positive child outcomes. In the CAEP Elementary Standards (2018), Standard 3 focuses on the use of assessment results to improve instruction and monitor learning. According to the CEC/DEC Initial Specialty Set for Early Childhood Special Education/Early Intervention (CEC, 2017), candidates must connect assessment to curriculum and progress monitoring [ECSE.K4.4], use assessment data to develop and implement individualized plans for children [ECSE.S4.8], and use assessments to monitor instructional assessment [ECSE.S4.11].

Using assessment data to plan for goals and instruction is a requirement of IDEA Parts B and C (IDEA, 2004). EI/ECSE professionals are to participate on teams, including other professionals and families, to use assessment results to plan for services and individualized programming (e.g., Individualized Family Service Plans [IFSP] and Individualized Education Plans [IEP]). For both infants and toddlers with disabilities and delays (ages birth to 3) and young children with disabilities (ages 3-8), building individualized programming (e.g., IFSP, IEP) in collaboration with families is a critical part of special education services (IDEA, 2004).

The NAEYC Developmentally Appropriate Practices Position Statement (2009) recommends that professionals use assessment results to inform the planning and implementation of instruction, to evaluate and improve programs' effectiveness [Guideline 4A], and to plan curriculum and learning experiences [Guideline 4C]. DEC Recommended Practices (2014) address guidance on how EI/ECSE professionals implement assessment to determine the child's plan for instruction [A8], identify learning targets, plan activities, and monitor child progress [A9]. CEC high-leverage practices focus on how professionals are to interpret and communicate assessments to design and implement educational programs [HLP5] as well as on professionals using child assessment data to analyze instructional practices and make adjustments to improve child outcomes [HLP6] (McLeskey et al., 2017).

Research indicates the need for EI/ECSE professionals to be prepared to collaborate with other professionals and families in the early childhood special education assessment process. Research shows that families who are more involved in the assessment process yield better child-level outcomes (Shonkoff, 2010). Research also shows that throughout this assessment and goal-building process families are a part of the team and add valuable input as to whether or not goals are socially valid for the child and their family (Bailey et al., 2012). As pertains to progress monitoring, Walker et al. (2008) found that growth and development indicators can be used effectively for both progress monitoring and intervention decision-making for young children. Otaiba and Lake (2007) found that pre-service teachers used curriculum-based assessment data to describe students' response to instruction after they were prepared to use this assessment technique with second grade students.

Standard 5: Application of Curriculum Frameworks in the Planning of Meaningful Learning Experience

Candidates collaborate with families and professionals to use an evidence-based, developmentally appropriate, and culturally responsive early childhood curriculum addressing developmental and content domains. Candidates use curriculum frameworks to create and support universally designed, high quality learning experiences in natural and inclusive environments that provide each child and family with equitable access and opportunities for learning and growth.

Component 5.1. Candidates collaborate with families and other professionals in identifying an evidence-based curriculum addressing developmental and content domains to design and facilitate meaningful and culturally responsive learning experiences that support the unique abilities and needs of all children and families.

Supporting Explanation. Candidates use the best available evidence as well as the wisdom and experience of the field to identify and evaluate early childhood curriculum. Candidates use their knowledge of curriculum content resources that address developmental (e.g., language and communication, social-emotional, cognition, play, and physical) and academic content domains (e.g., literacy, math, science, arts) as well as pedagogical knowledge as they collaborate in the identification of appropriate curricula. Candidates acknowledge that families and other professionals are integral members of the educational team, and their contributions positively influence the quality of programming for young children. Candidates recognize the importance of working with a team as they identify and implement evidence-based early childhood curriculum. Together with the team, candidates are able to assess early childhood curricula to determine the degree to which they reflect a developmentally appropriate scope and sequence across developmental and academic content domains; they are culturally responsive and align with learning expectations of the local context, including state early learning standards and community expectations. Furthermore, as a part of the team, candidates are able to engage in developing and individualizing plans for children to increase equitable access to and participation in the general early childhood curriculum as well as differentiate challenging content to address the full range of abilities.

Candidates clearly communicate developmental and educational expectations with families and children. Candidates ensure that families have opportunities to share their knowledge about their children's strengths and areas for growth, contribute to planning, and propose ideas for individualizing plans that promote their children's development and learning as they participate in the early childhood curriculum and in the varied contexts of home and community.

Candidates recognize that culture plays a central role in their collaboration with families and in children's learning. Candidates make deliberate efforts to understand the families' developmental and educational expectations for their children and children's behavior within their cultural identity. Candidates seek to understand and are open to changing their own mindset about each family's and child's strengths and needs in the context of their culture. Candidates acknowledge the families' and children's cultural background and respond to them in ways that honor and respect their cultural values. In being culturally responsive, candidates provide equitable access to learning opportunities for all families and children from all cultures and backgrounds. Candidates are proactive in embedding children's cultural references in all aspects of the learning environment (e.g., interactions, instruction, family routines, home, community outings, classroom activities and materials).

Knowledge Base. Collaboration with families and professionals is fundamental to provide optimal educational services for children. Initially, the collaborative efforts to make curriculum accessible and individualized for all children require effective communication with families and other professionals to develop a clear understanding of children's needs and development. This foundational theme is emphasized in InTASC Standard 1 (CCSSO, 2013); in CAEP Standard 1 (2018); and in NAEYC Standard 2 (2011). Another aspect of this collaboration is demonstrated by identifying and exchanging useful information and resources (InTASC Standards 2, 8, 9, and 10) and viewing families as rich sources of information (InTASC Standards 4 and 7) that can be used in planning meaningful learning opportunities for children. InTASC Standard 1 (2013) also calls for candidates, families, and other professionals to work together as a team to identify appropriate curricular modifications and effective interventions.

The DEC Recommended Practices (2014) in the Family area as well as the Teaming and Collaboration area highlight effective practices relevant to teaming and collaboration with families, which include sharing and exchanging information, planning and implementing educational programs, and facilitating communication among team members. Specifically, DEC's Recommended Practice F4 (2014) and CEC High-Leverage Practice 3 (HLP3) (McLeskey et al., 2017) call for EI/ECSE professionals to involve families and professionals in determining appropriate learning expectations, common goals, and different levels of support. In order for the curriculum to meet the needs of all children, EI/ECSE professionals need to develop a clear understanding of children's linguistic and cultural backgrounds and consider this as a valuable asset in modifying curricula and planning relevant and accessible learning activities. Being a culturally responsive EI/ECSE professional is underlined in DEC Recommended Practice F8 (2014).

Collaboration with families and professionals is the vehicle to improve the quality of EI/ECSE services and young children's outcomes. The Individuals with Disabilities Education Improvement Act (IDEA, 2004) includes a mandate that states families are essential members in the educational team and in the educational decision-making process. Further, it is critical for EI/ECSE professionals to involve families in all decisions related to curriculum because, by law, families are the legal advocates for their children in all aspects of their life, including education (Wilmshurst & Brue, 2018). As the U.S. Department of Health and Human Services and the U.S. Department of Education (2015) stipulate, failure to provide access to the general curriculum and high-quality programs is one of the barriers to fully including children in the educational system. Without appropriate access, children and their families are deprived of their fundamental right to receive equal educational opportunities. The DEC/NAYEC (2009) position paper on inclusion demonstrates the support for this notion in that accessibility of early childhood programs is defined as the removal of all barriers that prevent children from receiving equitable opportunities to fully participate in general education programs.

By definition, curriculum addresses a continuum of developmental and academic areas that are crucial for preparing children to become independent members of their society (NAEYC, 2009). Thus, curriculum application is not limited to a specific environment and setting, and it can take place in various environments and settings that promote children's learning and development. EI/ECSE professionals must strive to make the curriculum as functional as possible for children, where skills and knowledge are meaningful for children and their families, applicable in their everyday living, and supportive of the ultimate goal of helping families to raise independent individuals. To accomplish this goal, EI/ECSE professionals, as noted in the DEC Recommended Practices in the Family area (2014), need support from families and other professionals to formulate a shared vision for each child, to identify strengths and unique needs for each child, and to define appropriate contexts and levels of support needed to promote children's acquisition and generalization of knowledge and skills.

The IDEA (2014) and the DEC Recommended Practices (DEC, 2014) acknowledge the importance of collaboration with other professionals to meet the individual needs of children. There are several benefits to collaborating with professionals from related services, one of which is that EI/ECSE professionals will be more confident and successful in supporting families and their children. Further, collective efforts between EI/ECSE professionals and related service professionals save time, effort, and resources. For example, in an effective collaborative environment, families are not forced to alter their normal daily activities in order to make time for educational services at home or after school (Dettmer et al., 2013). Collaboration with professionals from different disciplines also supports the team's efforts to meet the diverse learning needs of children. Input from multiple stakeholders can be valuable in planning and implementing appropriate curricular adaptions and modifications.

EI/ECSE professionals also collaborate with families and other professionals to create culturally responsive learning opportunities as noted in the DEC position paper on cultural and linguistic diversity (DEC, 2010). EI/ECSE professionals can accomplish this by being socially and culturally conscious and acknowledging that the social context and the geographical location have an impact on families' attitude, behavior, thinking, and way of life (Villegas & Lucas, 2002). EI/ECSE professionals understand that children make meaning of new learning experiences based on their cultural references. Therefore, family involvement in planning and implementing the curriculum is vital in helping EI/ECSE professionals make adaptations to the curriculum that will meaningfully engage children in their learning environments. Villegas and Lucas (2002) propose a vision for preparing culturally responsive teachers. At the center of this vision is the implementation of culturally responsive practices. According to this vision, EI/ECSE professionals should aspire to develop a comprehensive understanding of children's culture and learn how to employ this knowledge to make the general curriculum accessible for diverse children. It is also recommended that EI/ECSE professionals be engaged in sincere conversations with families and professionals about topics that are relevant to children's culture but not addressed in the curriculum. These candid conversations will provide families and professionals with meaningful opportunities to examine the curriculum and highlight any inaccuracies, myths, imprecisions, and biased content (Ellerbrock et al., 2016). Simultaneously, it will provide families and professionals with an outlet to suggest adaptations and modifica-

tions to broaden the focus of the curriculum and make it more culturally sensitive.

Component 5.2. Candidates use their knowledge of early childhood curriculum frameworks, developmental and academic content knowledge, and related pedagogy to plan and ensure equitable access to universally designed, developmentally appropriate, and challenging learning experiences in natural and inclusive environments.

Supporting Explanation. Candidates use the best available evidence as well as the wisdom and experience of the field to identify, create, evaluate, and apply curriculum frameworks such as content or developmental curricula and state or national learning standards. Candidates apply knowledge of early childhood curriculum frameworks as a guide to make decisions about what, when, and how to promote all children's learning. Candidates understand that foundational to this decision process is creating learning experiences across developmental (e.g., language and communication, social-emotional, cognition, play, and physical) and academic (e.g., literacy, math, science, arts) domains that challenge children to achieve at a level just beyond their current mastery, while also having opportunities to practice newly acquired skills. To create such learning experiences, candidates possess a strong foundation in developmental and academic content knowledge as well as related pedagogical knowledge.

Candidates understand that young children come with a wide range of abilities, backgrounds, and family and community contexts. While this diversity brings richness to the work, ensuring all children's needs are effectively met requires that candidates engage in thoughtful, intentional planning in collaboration with families and other adults in the child's life. Candidates apply the principles of universal design for learning to ensure that learning experiences and environments are designed to allow for access and engagement to the greatest extent possible without need for adaptation. Specifically, candidates adhere to universal design for learning principles by incorporating a variety of ways for children to gain access to the curriculum content, offer multiple methods to recruit children's active engagement, and include a range of formats for children to respond and demonstrate what they know and have learned.

Whether working with infants, toddlers, preschoolers or children in the early elementary grades (K through 3), candidates plan and create universally designed, challenging learning experiences that promote access, engagement, and learning across developmental and academic content domains. In infancy, for example, this could be supporting caregivers as they engage in rich and varied forms of communication/literacy development, including singing, talking, sharing books, making funny faces, using gestures, and playing simple games such as peek-a-boo. For toddlers, this could be creating a variety of opportunities for children to engage in everyday mathematics (e.g., basic ideas about quantity, size, shape, and simple patterns). For preschoolers, for example, opportunities could be provided to conduct their own science experiments such as exploring whether a ball rolls faster down a steeper incline. In the early elementary grades, the candidate might address important social competence content such as assisting children to work with their peers in cooperative groups. Thus, as candidates engage in a variety of teacher planned activities in multiple contexts, they have the opportunity to assume different roles to accomplish tasks, solve problems, and at times settle disputes.

Knowledge Base. InTASC Standards 4 and 8 (CCSSO, 2013) highlight the importance of using Universal Design for Learning (UDL) principles in providing children with equitable access to the curriculum by using methods that match their learning. The NAEYC Standard 4 (2011) and CAEP Elementary Education Standard 4 (2018) call for using different learning approaches in order to support all children in meeting their learning outcomes. Further, InTASC Standard 4 (2013), CAEP Elementary Education Standard 2 (2018), and NAEYC Standard 5 (2011) underline the importance of candidates being knowledgeable of the different content areas and academic subjects as well as being skillful in identifying meaningful opportunities in these areas to make learning more accessible for all children.

DEC Recommended Practice E3 (2014) clearly supports the implementation of UDL principles to address making learning environments accessible for all children. CEC High-Leverage Practices 11 and 19 (McLeskey et al., 2017) explicitly note that EI/ECSE professional use the UDL principles throughout the teaching process, which includes the following: selecting, implementing, designing, and evaluating learners' outcomes in order to support equitable access to the general curriculum for each and every learner.

The call to use curriculum frameworks clearly highlights the fundamental role of EI/ECSE professionals in early childhood programs and schools. Currently, EI/ECSE professionals are expected to identify creative ways for children to access the general education curricular content; plan and implement evidence-based practices in content areas such as language, math, and science; envision how curriculum frameworks can be applied across developmental domains as well as academic subjects; and lead and be involved in making data-based instructional decisions for children throughout the age range from birth through 8 years old (CEC, 2017). EI/ECSE professionals are expected to perform all these roles while working in teams that include but are not limited to families, general education teachers, professionals from related services, and other professionals. Even though EI/ECSE professionals are not required to show expertise in all the disciplines that are included in IEP and IFSP teams, they do need to show expertise in relevant academic and content areas (e.g., math and science) in order to be able to skillfully provide EI/ECSE supports and services to children and effectively collaborate with team members (Benedict et al., 2016).

In their position statement for including children with disabilities, DEC and NAEYC (2009) addressed the need for systems that support children's participation in all learning environments and within the general education curriculum. Tiered frameworks were suggested as a meaningful addition to and not as a replacement for the curriculum (Freeman & Newcomer, 2015). Tiered frameworks provide systematic structure for adapting and individualizing content, learning activities, experiences, and opportunities for children. These frameworks support professionals in delivering proper levels of support based on children's needs and progress in the general curriculum (Hemmeter et al., 2016; Horn et al., 2016). Tiered frameworks are also important in facilitating children's engagement and learning in general education environments and in providing a structure for implementing systematic interventions across developmental domains and content areas at home and in school (Forman & Crystal, 2015). One of the common considerations among the various tiered frameworks is the need for collaborative efforts between professionals and families in identifying an appropriate tiered framework, preparing implementation plans, and collaborating in applying the framework with fidelity in all of the appropriate learning contexts to support children's learning outcomes. EI/ECSE professionals are integral members of tiered frameworks teams. As members of these teams, EI/ECSE professionals may be leading this collaborative effort for identifying meaningful opportunities and seek families' and professionals' input and feedback in planning and implementing these frameworks. Professionals also acknowledge that the success of planning and implementing these frameworks depends to a great extent on the positive collaborative relationships that exist amongst the team members (DEC, 2013).

Universal Design for Learning (UDL) is a research-based framework that provides all children, including children with disabilities, with the opportunity to not only access early childhood curriculum, but to do so in a way that meaningfully engages them in learning, thereby maximizing their full potential (Horn et al., 2016; Rose & Meyer, 2006). UDL is guided by the philosophy that there is no such thing as a one-size-fits-all approach to learning. In fact, The Center for Applied Special Technology (CAST) describes UDL as "a framework that addresses the primary barrier to fostering expert learners within instructional environments: inflexible, "one-size-fits-all" curricula. It is inflexible curricula that raise unintentional barriers to learning" (CAST, 2011, p. 4). Recent meta-analytic findings suggest UDL can and should be used effectively by EI/ECSE professionals to minimize these unintentional barriers to learning for children with a wide range of learning needs, especially children with disabilities (Al-Azawei et al., 2016; Mangiatordi & Serenelli, 2013; Rao et al., 2014). Currently, early childhood programs and schools expect EI/ECSE professionals to be proficient in inclusive education pedagogy in order to provide children with equitable access to the curriculum (Blum & Parette, 2014). EI/ECSE professionals are called to use UDL to address the diverse learning needs of not only children with disabilities, but also the needs of at-risk children who have not yet been identified for special education services (Dunst & Hamby, 2015; Horn et al., 2016). Lesson plans designed using the three guiding principles of the UDL framework can minimize learner differences, while providing children with increased opportunities to engage in appropriately challenging learning activities (Courey et al., 2012).

Standard 6: Using Responsive and Reciprocal Interactions, Interventions, and Instruction

Candidates plan and implement intentional, systematic, evidence-based, responsive interactions, interventions, and instruction to support all children's learning and development across all developmental and content domains in partnership with families and other professionals. Candidates facilitate equitable access and participation for all children and families within natural and inclusive environments through culturally responsive and affirming practices and relationships. Candidates use data-based decision-making to plan for, adapt, and improve interactions, interventions, and instruction to ensure fidelity of implementation.

Component 6.1. Candidates, in partnership with families, identify systematic, responsive, and intentional evidence-based practices and use such practices with fidelity to support young children's learning and development across all developmental and academic content domains.

Supporting Explanation. Across all age levels, candidates use effective interactions, interventions, and instructional practices that result in efficient learning of functional and socially valid skills. Effective interactions, interventions, and instructional practices are evidence-based and systematic. Candidates systematically and intentionally identify what to teach, when to teach, and how to evaluate the effects of teaching. They determine whether certain procedures are appropriate given the particular needs of the children and families with whom they are working. Further, candidates select evidence-based practices that are developmentally appropriate and are likely to have the highest expected leverage and impact on outcomes.

A considerable amount of planning is required to effectively implement systematic interactions, interventions, and instruction with fidelity. Candidates, together with other members of the team including the family, intentionally identify each child's strengths, preferences, and interests, and plan instruction to ensure the child is engaged and to maximize learning. Further, candidates plan, monitor, and intentionally use interactions, interventions, and instruction with fidelity to teach functional and socially valid skills and to promote child engagement and learning. Candidates implement the appropriate frequency, intensity, and duration of interactions, interventions, and instruction given the child's strengths, needs, and phase of learning (i.e., acquisition, fluency, generalization, and maintenance). Candidates intentionally and proactively support the child's learning and development across environments.

Knowledge Base. InTASC Standard 8 highlights the necessary skills required for candidates to be skillful in selecting evidence-based practices (CCSSO, 2013). Candidates, according to this standard, know when and how to use appropriate and varied strategies and resources to design instruction to meet the needs of learners, both individually and in groups. Both the CAEP K-6 Elementary Standard 4 (2018) and NAEYC Standard 4 (2010) emphasize that candidates must know about and use a variety of effective instructional practices that support children's learning. NAEYC Standard 4 further states that these practices be developmentally appropriate. The CEC Initial Preparation Standard 5 says that candidates "… use a repertoire of evidence-based instructional strategies to advance learning of individuals with exceptionalities" (2015, p.25). The CEC/DEC Initial Specialty Set for Early Childhood Special Education/Early Intervention (2017) requires that candidates integrate those evidence-based practices into individualized plans that align with developmental and academic content (ECSE5.S10) (CEC, 2017). Both the DEC Recommended Practices (2014) and the CEC high leverage practices (McLeskey, et al., 2017) include practices that align with the above standards. The DEC Family Recommended Practice (F4) states that EI/ECSE professionals and families collaborate to develop instructional goals, individualized plans, and implement practices that promote the child's development and learning. The DEC Instruction Recommended Practices (INS 6) (2014) calls for implementing evidence-based practices with fidelity (DEC, 2014). Additionally, CEC High Leverage Practice 18 emphasize that EI/ECSE professionals use a variety of strategies that have been shown to empirically increase student engagement and learning. Legislation also lends support for this component (McLeskey, et al., 2017). Both the Every Student Succeeds Act (2015) and IDEA (2014) emphasize the use of scientifically-based instructional practices to improve learner's academic achievement and functional performance.

CEC calls upon teacher preparation programs across the nation to use a systematic and disciplined approach to prepare candidates to identify and implement evidence-based practices in various educational settings (CEC, 2015). However, Hsiao et al., (2019) concluded that 40 percent of special education teachers who work with students with autism spectrum disorder receive little to no training relevant to evidence-based practices. Therefore, the researchers recommend that preservice preparation programs specifically address evidence-based practices in their curriculum and prepare educators to consistently implement those practices in educational settings. Reichow (2016) described a two-step process for use by EI/ECSE professionals in evaluating and selecting evidence-based practices. The first step is based on a thorough evaluation of individual studies that report positive outcomes about the target practice. The second step is to identify the amount of support that is available about the evidence. Once the evidence is evaluated, EI/ECSE professionals select the best-fit practice to address the developmental or academic need. Researchers further emphasize the importance of EI/ECSE professionals implementing practices with fidelity. Shepley and colleagues (2018) reported that EI/ECSE professionals need to be knowledgeable and skillful in collecting fidelity data to ensure that practices are delivered as planned and in a consistent manner. The systematic process for evaluating, selecting, and implementing practices with fidelity requires the educational team, including the family requires continual interaction in making decisions about effective interactions, interventions, and instruction.

Component 6.2. Candidates engage in reciprocal partnerships with families and other professionals to facilitate responsive adult-child interactions, interventions, and instruction in support of child learning and development.

Supporting Explanation. Candidates use effective collaborative behaviors (e.g., sharing ideas, active listening, questioning, problem-solving) and focus on the unique needs of adult learners as they engage in reciprocal partnerships with adults centered on positive outcomes for young children at risk for and with developmental delays and disabilities. Candidates acknowledge that each child and family is different and provide adults with relevant and immediately useful information that builds upon what they already know. Candidates use effective adult learning practices that involve active, hands-on experiences paired with real-time practice, positive reinforcement, and individualized and performance-based feedback and support.

Candidates are responsive to the individual and unique needs of each child, family, and context. Therefore, candidates consider the previous knowledge and experiences of families and other professionals (e.g., related service providers, paraprofessionals, early childhood educators) and ensure that the interactions, interventions, and instruction they identify and facilitate are built upon and around the child and family's unique set of resources, priorities, strengths, and concerns. They engage in triadic and reciprocal partnerships with other adults as they facilitate responsive adult-child interactions, model naturalistic interventions, and actively demonstrate evidence-based instructional practices that promote child learning and development. Candidates understand how adult learning strategies apply to their work in a variety of roles (e.g., transdisciplinary team member, consultant, advocate, coach) and they employ those strategies consistently, across a wide range of natural and inclusive environments.

Knowledge Base. Several sets of professional standards address the importance of supporting candidates in learning to develop partnerships with other professionals and families to create effective learning opportunities to support the diverse needs of all learners. InTASC Standard 7 (CCSSO, 2013) indicates that candidates plan and deliver effective instruction with other professionals who have specialized expertise and that they also collaborate with families in planning for instruction. InTASC Standard 10, (CCSSO, 2013) emphasizes that candidate collaborate with families and other professionals to ensure learner growth. The CAEP K-6 Elementary Standard 1 (2018), states that candidates work reciprocally with families to gain a perspective of the child's strengths and needs in order to maximize development and learning, while Standard 5, focuses on collaboration with other professionals and the student's mentors to work on goals directly related to the learner's growth and development. Likewise, NAEYC Standard 2, (2010) empha-

sizes that candidates develop reciprocal family relationships as a means to involve families in the child's development and learning. The CEC Initial Preparation Standard 7 (2015), states that candidates collaborate with families and professionals to meet the needs of students with exceptionalities. The CEC/DEC Initial Specialty Set for Early Childhood Special Education/Early Intervention (CEC, 2017) expands on the CEC standard specifying that a goal of collaboration is to support children's development and learning.

The DEC Family Recommended Practice (F4) (DEC, 2014) states that EI/ECSE professionals and families collaborate to develop instructional goals, individualized plans, and implement practices that promote the child's development and learning. DEC Recommended Practice TC1 (2014) states that EI/ECSE professionals work as a team with other professionals and families to "… plan and implement supports and services to meet the unique needs of each child and family." Further, DEC Recommended Practices INS 1 and 2 (2014) indicate that EI/ECSE professionals, with the family, identify the child's strengths, preferences, and interests and use these to jointly identify target skills for instruction. CEC High Leverage Practice 1 (McLeskey, 2017) refers to collaboration with a range of professionals as critical to support students' learning.

Legislative support for reciprocal partnerships with families and professionals is included in IDEA (2014) which mandates parent participation in the education of their children with disabilities. Further, IDEA requires multidisciplinary assessment of students to determine eligibility for services and to identify target goals and outcomes for instruction. IDEA also requires that individual plans be developed by a multidisciplinary team that includes both parents and professionals.

Effective professional teaming and collaboration and parent engagement lead to meaningful partnerships and improved student learning (Collier et al., 2015). Ongoing communication between parents and educators has been shown to be critical to predict student success (McCoach et al., 2010). Further, several effective collaboration strategies have been identified that are associated with effective partnerships and effective instruction (Ronfeldt et al., 2015). These include active listening, good communication, and ongoing coaching (Scruggs & Mastropieri, 2015).

Component 6.3. Candidates engage in ongoing planning and use flexible and embedded instructional and environmental arrangements and appropriate materials to support the use of interactions, interventions, and instruction addressing developmental and academic content domains, which are adapted to meet the needs of each and every child and their family.

Supporting Explanation. Candidates select evidence-based practices related to improvements in socially valid outcomes for young children and their families. Candidates are responsive to the individual and unique needs of each child, family, and context. They observe, interpret, and plan instruction that scaffolds the child's learning and engagement across the day; expands the child's communication, cognitive, social, and emotional repertoire; facilitates more complex play skills; and supports the child's increasing independence. They understand that although different procedures might be equally effective, one might result in more efficient learning. Thus, candidates intentionally consider efficiency of learning when planning and selecting instructional practices.

Candidates also thoroughly consider each aspect of the physical, social, and temporal environment when planning instruction to optimize outcomes and efficient learning. Each aspect influences the extent to which a young child will learn. Candidates plan for and provide the level of support and adaptations needed for the child to access, participate, and learn within and across activities, transitions, and routines. This includes engaging with families in reflecting on their competence and confidence in supporting their child's learning and development. The physical space is designed to support child independence and engagement. The social environment is designed to support ongoing social interactions, increasingly complex social play, and friendships. For example, children with stronger language and social skills might be encouraged to sit next to children who are learning language skills during mealtimes to support observational learning. The temporal environment is designed to maximize engagement and ensure children are likely to participate. For example, outdoor play time where children are active and more likely to engage in vigorous exercise might occur right before small groups when children are expected to be engaged and attentive.

Candidates establish and support environments in which diversity is honored, use flexible instructional practices that support equitable access and participation for all children, and closely monitor child progress to identify and reflect on how to remedy inequities. Candidates identify and use relevant and developmentally appropriate materials that support children's learning and development. Materials that are directly relevant to the learning goals and outcomes are used. For example, when providing early intervention in a home, materials that are already in the home and relevant to the specific interaction or routine and the child's goals are used. Likewise, classroom materials are intentionally selected based on the children's preferences, interests, strengths, and learning needs, and are systematically rotated to support engagement. In group settings, candidates capitalize on observational learning by regularly using flexible groupings (e.g., dyads, small-group instruction) and embedding instructive feedback opportunities.

Knowledge Base. InTASC Standard (CCSSO, 2013) addresses the role that candidates have in creating learning environments that support each child's "… positive social interaction, active engagement in learning, and self-motivation (p. 12)." InTASC Standard 8, Planning for Instruction, states that candidates plan instruction to meet the learning goals of each learner by creating learning experiences based on knowledge of curriculum and content areas.

Similarly, the CAEP K-6 Elementary Standards 1, 2 and 3 (CAEP, 2018) emphasize that candidates plan and implement developmentally appropriate, inclusive learning environments that facilitate access to learning experiences based on knowledge of curricular standards and content. Further, candidates create classroom contexts that allow for differentiation of instructional materials and activities and establish social norms within the classroom that support interpersonal relationships and social and emotional development. The same focus on candidates designing supportive and challenging learning environments that promote positive relationships and interactions, while planning for learning experiences based on their knowledge of developmental domains and academic disciplines, is found in NAEYC Standards 1, 4, and 5 (NAEYC, 2011).

The CEC Initial Preparation Standard 2 (CEC, 2015) also identifies candidates' role in creating safe, inclusive, and culturally responsive learning environments that support learning, emotional well-being, and positive interactions. CEC Standard 2 and CEC Standard 5 state that candidates use knowledge of general and specialized curricula and consider individual abilities and learning environments in planning for and adapting learning experiences. Moreover, the CEC/DEC Initial Specialty Set for Early Childhood Special Education/Early Intervention (CEC, 2017) includes ECSE2.S1 which states that candidates "select, develop, and evaluate … materials, equipment, and environments." In addition, ECSE3.S2 says that candidates plan developmentally appropriate curricula, instruction, and adaptations based on their knowledge of the child and developmental and academic curricula.

The DEC Environment Recommended Practices (DEC, 2014) address the importance of EI/ECSE professionals modifying and adapting the physical, social and temporal environments to promote children's access to and participation in learning experiences (E3) in natural and inclusive environments during daily routines and activities (E1). And the DEC Instruction Recommended Practices emphasize EI/ECSE professionals' role in embedding instruction within and across activities and routines (INS5) and identifying target skills to help the child become competent, socially connected and engaged (INS2) while providing the adaptations needed for each child to learn. Several of the CEC high leverage practices (McLeskey et al., 2017) lend support to this component and include: (HLP7) establish a consistent, organized, and respectful learning environment, (HLP17) use flexible grouping, (HLP13) adapt curriculum tasks and materials for specific learning goals, and (HLP21) teach students to maintain and generalize new learning across time and settings.

Examples of environmental adaptations and modifications to the physical environment that have been documented to support young children's learning include changing task directions and adjusting content amount and depth (Vaugh & Bos, 2012); providing scaffolded supports (Berk & Winsler, 1995; Rosenshine, 2012) and using visual supports or cues (Odom et al., 2010). Examples of modifications to the social environment that have been documented as effective include providing a mix of instructional groupings (Cabell et al., 2013) and peer mediated support (Strain et al., 1979). Examples of considering the temporal environment that have been shown

to be effective include use of a visual schedule to support children's engagement and ability to transition between activities (Odom et al, 2010) and the use of the "if then" or Premack principles (DePry, 2004). Given this strong empirical evidence, it is imperative that preparation programs prepare candidates to apply such evidenced-based instructional strategies and environmental arrangements.

Intentional teaching and embedded instruction, two evidenced based approaches, when used together ensure that each child has access to and actively participates in the daily activities and routines of the multiple environments of the child and family (Grisham-Brown et al., 2017). Intentional teaching involves a carefully planned balance between child-directed and teacher lead activities (Epstein, 2016). Effective intentional teachers are able to recognize to natural opportunities for children's engagement in learning and plan for and implement learning opportunities. With embedded instruction, the EI/ECSE professional creates short, intentional teaching episodes within ongoing, natural routines and activities (Horn et al., 2002; Snyder et al., 2013). Use of embedded instruction and intentional teaching leads to important developmental and learning outcomes. Therefore, it is vital that preparation programs fully prepare candidates to implement these practices.

Component 6.4. Candidates promote young children's social and emotional competence and communication, and proactively plan and implement function-based interventions to prevent and address challenging behaviors.

Supporting Explanation. Candidates partner with family members, other caregivers, and professionals to strategically promote social and emotional competence and communication to help children socially connect and engage with peers and adults across various environments. They recognize the importance of social engagement and emotional wellness for overall child growth across developmental and content area domains as well as for positive family outcomes. Throughout their work with children and families, candidates are respectful and responsive to all aspects of diversity and actively nurture reciprocal interactions and positive relationships.

Candidates plan, identify, and support proactive and preventive social environments, routines, and activities with attention to aspects such as emotional wellness, mental health, self-regulation, and prosocial behaviors. Candidates explicitly teach, reinforce, and promote social and communication skills using evidence-based interactions, interventions, and instruction with fidelity. Where applicable, candidates support young children's use of augmentative and alternative communication (AAC) and other assistive technology (AT) to support their access and engagement. They also coach other adults to employ evidence-based practices and responsive interactions across naturally occurring routines and activities. For example, in early intervention contexts, candidates enhance family and caregiver capacity to promote meaningful, positive outcomes for their children through a coaching model of service delivery. Through coaching, candidates support families and caregivers to effectively enact strategies that increase functional social engagement by helping them to embed strategies into routines and activities across natural and inclusive settings. In classroom settings, candidates coach other adults and children to embed evidence-based social communication practices into classroom routines and activities. In all settings, candidates provide specific and meaningful feedback to assist children, families, other caregivers, and professionals to engage in ongoing self-reflection and assessment.

When challenging behavior occurs, candidates conduct functional assessments to systematically identify the behavior, events that precede such behavior (antecedents), and events that can maintain such behavior (consequences). Using functional behavior assessment data, candidates identify, plan, implement, and support others to implement function-based prevention, promotion, and intervention strategies with fidelity to promote social-emotional growth for all children across a range of settings. In supporting others, candidates help in building skills that will enhance social-emotional competence, communication skills, and overall connectivity and engagement of children and families in natural and inclusive environments to make challenging behaviors ineffective and inefficient.

Where applicable, candidates utilize multi-tiered systems of support as a framework for efforts to improve social-emotional, communication, and behavior outcomes for young children and families. Such frameworks assist candidates to reduce the use of inappropriate discipline practices and promote family engagement in the intervention process. Further, candidates' application of multi-tiered systems of support

can promote the use of data for decision-making, integrate early childhood and infant mental health consultation, and foster quality, meaningful inclusion for all children and families.

Knowledge Base. InTASC Standard 1 (CCSSO, 2013), states that candidates apply understanding of learner development to promote learner growth and development across developmental domains. Further, INTASC Standard 3 focuses on candidates creating challenging and supportive environments that engage learners and support their interpersonal communication skills. InTASC Standard 8 guides candidates to utilize a wide range of instructional strategies including those that support and expand learners' communication.

The CAEP Elementary Education Standards (2018) offer additional support for the importance of social-emotional and communication and attention to behavioral needs. Standard 3 states that candidates create classroom contexts that allow for differentiation of instructional materials and activities and establish social norms within the classroom that support interpersonal relationships and social and emotional development. Under Standard 4 the importance of preparing candidates to use constructive feedback to guide children's learning, increase motivation, and increase learner engagement is addressed.

NAEYC Professional Preparation Standard 1 (2011) stresses the importance of candidates possessing a deep understanding of child development, including the social-emotional and communication domains. NAEYC Standard 4 stresses that candidates understand and use positive relationships and supportive interactions as the foundation of their work with children and families.

The CEC Personnel Preparation Standard 1 (CEC, 2015) also ensure that candidates understand learner development. CEC Standard 2 says that candidates create learning environments that allow learners to develop emotional well-being, positive social interactions, and self-determination. Further, CEC Standard 5 addresses candidates' use of augmentative and alternative communication systems and assistive technology along with general strategies to enhance language development and communication skills in children.

The CEC/DEC Initial Specialty Set for Early Childhood Special Education/Early Intervention (CEC, 2017) stresses the importance of understanding factors that affect the mental health and social-emotional development of infants and young children (K1.6). K1.9 highlights the importance of understanding the impact of language delays on other areas of development and K1.10 adds behavior. Section 2 emphasizes that candidates understand the effects of social environments on development and learning (ECSEK2.1) and structure social environments, using peer models and proximity, and responsive adults to promote interactions among peers, parents, and caregivers (ECSE2.S4). Section 3 (ECSE3.S3), specifies the importance of implementing and evaluating preventative and reductive strategies to address challenging behavior. Finally, the skill items for Section 5 highlight the importance of using individual and group guidance and problem-solving techniques to develop supportive relationship with and among children (ECSE5.S4), and the use of strategies to teach social skills and conflict resolution (ECSE5.S5).

In terms of legislation, IDEA identifies areas of eligibility which include social-emotional, communication, and behavior areas. The law also specifically states that functional behavior assessments should be conducted and behavior intervention plans should be implemented to address challenging behaviors.

The DEC Recommended Practices (DEC, 2014) also lend support for focusing on social-emotional and communication development as well as a functional approach to behavioral assessment and intervention. The recommended practices indicate that EI/ECSE professionals should assess children in all areas of development and behavior (A.4). Further, under Environments, EI/ECSE professionals are directed to work with others to modify not only physical environments, but also social and temporal environments to ensure children have access and participation in learning activities (E3). The Recommended Practices for Instruction focus on planning instruction to ensure children become adaptive, competent, socially connected, and engaged (INS2) and that systematic instructional strategies are used with fidelity to teach skills and promote child engagement and learning (INS6). The use of peer-mediated intervention is also promoted in INS8. Specific to behavior, INS9 guides EI/ECSE professionals to use functional assessment and related prevention, promotion, and intervention strategies across environments to prevent and address challenging behavior. The Interaction Recommended Practices also address the importance of this component. For example, EI/ECSE professionals are

directed to promote children's social-emotional development by observing, interpreting, and responding contingently to the range of the child's emotional expressions (INT1). Further, EI/ECSE professionals should promote the child's social development by encouraging the child to initiate or sustain positive interactions with other children and adults during routines and activities through modeling, teaching, feedback, or other types of guided support (INT2). Finally, EI/ECSE professionals are encouraged to promote children's communication development by observing, interpreting, responding contingently, and providing natural consequences for the child's verbal and nonverbal communication (INT3).

CEC high leverage practices (McLeskey et al., 2017) detail recommendations that include the use of multiple sources of information, including information related to social-emotional and communication development as well as functional behavior assessment, to develop comprehensive understandings of children's strengths and needs (HLP4). Further, an entire subset of the practices focus on social/emotional/behavioral practices. These include guidance for teachers to establish a consistent, organized, and respective learning environment (HLP7), to provide positive and constructive feedback to guide learning and behavior (HLP8), to directly teach social behaviors (HLP9), and to conduct functional behavior assessments to develop individual student behavior support plans (HLP10).

The importance of social-emotional development to school success and school readiness has been well-established. Landy (2009) labeled social-emotional competence as central to success in school and in life and stressed how vital it is that EI/ECSE professionals enter the field ready to promote children's social and emotional health. Thompson and Raikes (2007) discuss the link between social, emotional, and self-regulatory skills and later school success emphasizing that readiness is significantly influenced by relationships and social contexts.

In a policy report on the importance of young children's emotional development for their school readiness, Raver (2002) states, "Children who are emotionally well-adjusted have a significantly greater chance of early school success while children who experience serious emotional difficulty face an increased risk of early school difficulty" (p. 3). The report also includes a review of research on related intervention and reports that findings suggest, "while young children's emotional and behavioral problems are costly to their chances of school success, these problems are identifiable early, are amenable to change, and can be reduced over time" (p. 3). In a study investigating the relationships between behavioral regulation and preschoolers' literacy, vocabulary, and math skills, McClelland et al., (2007) reported that "behavioral regulation significantly and positively predicted fall and spring emergent literacy, vocabulary, and math skills on the Woodcock Johnson Tests of Achievement (all ps<.05). Moreover, growth in behavioral regulation predicted growth in emergent literacy, vocabulary, and math skills over the pre-kindergarten year (all ps<.05), after controlling for site, child gender, and other background variables" (p. 947).

It is essential that early childhood practitioners are prepared to identify, effectively address, and prevent social-emotional challenges early. As noted by Hemmeter and colleagues (2006), engaging environments that include ongoing positive adult-child interactions are necessary for children's social and emotional development and the prevention of challenging behavior. Therefore, in order to effectively promote children's social emotional competence and communication, candidates must be prepared to create, maintain, and facilitate such positive environments.

To effectively address social-emotional development and challenging behavior, the field guides practitioners to utilize multi-tiered systems of support as frameworks to provide positive behavior support (PBS) such as the Pyramid model. The Pyramid Model is a multi-tiered system of support focused on preventing challenging behavior through universal and targeted practices focused on promoting social emotional competence and teaching targeted social emotional skills (Fox et al., 2003; Fox et al., 2009). Functional behavior assessment is an important component of the Pyramid Model and leads to the creation of a behavior support plan. The effectiveness of PBS, including the use of functional behavior assessment and positive behavior support plans, is well documented for young children including those with and without disabilities and very young children (Dunlap & Fox, 2011).

Component 6.5. Candidates identify and create multiple opportunities for young children to develop and learn play skills and engage in meaningful play experiences independently and with others across contexts.

Supporting Explanation. Candidates recognize play as a critical developmental ability that contributes to the learning of young children as well as a context within which development occurs. Candidates design and support the temporal, physical, and social environment to ensure that children have sufficient periods of time to engage in child-directed, meaningful play. Candidates identify, create, and support multiple opportunities for children to engage in sustained play of increasing complexity with the needed supports for success, including promoting meaningful interactions across peers, adults, and contexts throughout the age range of birth through 8 years. They work collaboratively with families, caregivers, and other professionals to identify and enhance environments to support play and play development.

Candidates use effective practices to facilitate children's increasingly complex play with objects and others. Candidates assess, teach, and monitor children's social and object play skills and coach other adults (i.e., family members, caregivers, and other professionals) to do so. Candidates identify opportunities to focus on teaching children to engage with objects with increasing sophistication moving from sensorimotor and functional use of objects to symbolic play. Likewise, candidates identify social play goals that support children in learning to play independently, then near peers (i.e., parallel play), and eventually cooperatively with peers. Play goals should be identified with families and based on the child's current strengths, interests, and preferences. Play goals should facilitate the child's full participation and engagement in daily routines and natural environments. Effective play instruction should use evidence-based practices and focus on teaching generalized play skills across people, objects, and settings.

Candidates also recognize that developmentally appropriate play skills may increase learning opportunities for young children. Candidates use play as a context for embedding interactions, interventions, and instruction. Candidates also use play as a context to provide authentic opportunities to access additional and previously unavailable interactions with materials, peers, family members, and other individuals in the child's and family's lives.

Knowledge Base. The need for candidates to be knowledgeable about children's play are emphasized across the InTASC Standards (CCSSO, 2013). For example, developmentally appropriate instructional opportunities that promote student learning and learning environments that support individual and collaborative learning and encourage social interactions and active engagement are emphasized in InTASC Standard 1. NAEYC Professional Preparation Standard 4 (2011), emphasizes that candidates use a wide variety of developmentally appropriate approaches and instructional strategies to promote young children's development. The supporting explanation for this Standard identifies several research-based strategies that are directly related to learning and developing play skills, such as, teaching through social interactions, creating support for play, fostering oral language and communication, and setting up the indoor and outdoor environment.

The CEC/DEC Initial Specialty Set for Early Childhood Special Education/Early Intervention (CEC, 2017) emphasizes that candidates know and understand theories of typical and atypical development (ECSEK.K1) which include play development. In designing the learning environment, candidates "select, develop, and evaluate developmentally and functionally appropriate materials, equipment, and environments (ECSE2.S1)." For young children, this includes materials and environmental arrangements that facilitate play development. In planning curriculum, candidates apply research in the developmental domains, play, and temperament to learning (ECSE3.S1). And finally, candidates "facilitate child-initiated learning (ECSE5.S1) through the use of scaffolding (ECSE5.S2), and strategies that teach social skills (ECSE5.S5), a major aspect of play development.

DEC Recommended Practices (DEC, 2014) also emphasize the importance of ensuring candidates have the knowledge and skills to support children's play. The recommended practices indicate that "young children who have or are at risk for developmental delays/disabilities learn, play, and engage with adults and peers within a multitude of environments such as home, school, childcare, and the neighborhood (2014, p. 9)." DEC also emphasizes that EI/ECSE professionals use explicit feedback and consequences to increase children's play skills (see INS7, DEC, 2014, p. 12) and promote the child's development by joining in and expanding on the child's play (see INT4, DEC, 2014, p. 14). Several of the CEC high-leverage practices (HLP) (McLeskey et al., 2017) are important when promoting children's learning and development of play skills. EI/ECSE professionals must create a consistent, organized, and respectful learning environment (HLP7) to encourage young children's play. They must also design instruction focused on specific learning goals (HLP12) which for young children may be mastered effectively through play. And finally, EI/ECSE professionals provide scaffolded supports to facilitate learning (HLP15).

All children should have opportunities to learn in the context of play with their peers with and without disabilities (US DHHS & DOE, 2015), which highlights candidates should understand the importance of play. The United Nations Human Rights Office of the High Commissioner asserted that play is the right of every child because it "is essential to the cognitive, physical, social, and emotional wellbeing of children and youth" (Ginsburg et al., 2007, p. 182). Play is an early developmental milestone and provides and important context for learning other critical skills (American Academy of Pediatrics [AAP], 2007; Ginsburg et al., 2007; Lifter et al., 2011).

Research also supports the need for candidates to be knowledgeable about children's play. Play is a behavioral cusp for other important skills. For example, researchers have documented relations between play and language (Barton & Wolery, 2010; Frey & Kaiser, 2011; Lewis, 2003; Vig, 2003) and play and social skills (Freeman et al., 2015; Gulsrud et al., 2014; Kasari et al., 2012; Toth et al., 2006). Play also promotes independent participation and engagement because it provides a context for meaningful interactions with others across settings.

Many children learn to engage in increasingly complex play in quality early childhood environments (e.g., childcare, home, preschool). However, research has consistently shown that some children engage in less complex and fewer play behaviors when given the same materials in the same settings (Wilson et al., 2017). Some children will require intentional, systematic instruction to learn appropriate play skills (Barton & Wolery, 2008; Lifter, Foster-Sanda et al., 2011; Thiemann-Bourque, et al., 2012). The existing play intervention research suggests that adult modeling and prompting within a naturalistic teaching approach is effective for increasing play skills in young children (Barton & Wolery, 2008; Barton, 2015). Teaching children to play in increasingly complex ways ensures children have multiple and varied learning opportunities within playful contexts (Barton, 2015).

Component 6.6. Candidates use responsive interactions, interventions, and instruction with sufficient intensity and types of support across activities, routines, and environments to promote child learning and development and facilitate access, participation, and engagement in natural environments and inclusive settings.

Supporting Explanation. Candidates recognize that the strategic provision of a continuum of responsive interactions, interventions, and instructional strategies is the foundation for promoting developmental growth across developmental and academic content domains as well as meaningful inclusion and positive family outcomes. Candidates partner with other adults to ensure access, participation, and engagement by individualizing application of strategies to meet the needs of each child and family. They promote a wide array of activities, environments, and interactions for children to engage with adults, peers, and materials in meaningful ways. They identify and implement effective, contextually relevant, and individualized strategies, intervention, adaptations, and modifications that promote attainment of rigorous developmental and content learning standards. Further, candidates strategically identify, plan, and implement individualized interactions, interventions, and instruction across, and embedded within, environments, routines, and activities, and provide multiple modalities of engagement to ensure access and participation.

Candidates utilize comprehensive, authentic, and ecological assessment data to inform themselves of each child's strengths, preferences, needs, and interests to enhance their ability to promote active engagement in learning and participation in routines and activities. Candidates apply data-driven, responsive support of sufficient intensity across activities, routines, and environments to promote learning and development as well as meaningful inclusion by ensuring each child and family can function effectively as integral members of communities. Candidates also identify and ensure application of appropriate resources that respond to individual differences, including assistive and other forms of technology, to increase, maintain, and/or improve capabilities of young children and their families to further ensure access, participation, and engagement across settings.

In early intervention contexts, candidates promote positive and responsive parent-child and other adult-child relationships recognizing the importance of nurturing, responsive relationships to overall development. They utilize evidence-based coaching practices to assist families and other adults to employ naturalistic instruction that embeds strategies in the context of ongoing, natural activities and routines. Candidates coach and assist other adults in a child's life to employ sensitive and responsive ways to interact with the child that promotes positive peer and adult-child relationships and, in turn, positive outcomes for children and families.

Knowledge Base. Teachers are expected to use responsive interactions, interventions, and instruction with sufficient intensity across activities, routines, and environments given the evidence supporting these strategies as effective in facilitating access, participation, and inclusion of all children. InTASC standards (CCSSO, 2013), particularly Standards 1, 6, 7, and 8, promote this focus. For example, Standard 1 states that candidates should understand that each learner's particular developmental profile influences learning and use that understanding to make individualized instructional decisions. InTASC Standards 6, 7, and 8 instruct candidates to promote equitable access to rigorous learning through application of appropriate instruction and the use of multiple methods of assessment to guide the development and implementation of planning and instruction to meet the needs of all learners. The NAEYC Initial Personnel Preparation Standard 4 (2011) says that candidates know, understand, and use a wide variety of developmentally appropriate approaches and instructional strategies. Standard 5 emphasizes candidates' role in designing and implementing challenging curriculum that promotes developmental and learning outcomes for young children.

The CAEP K-6 Elementary Education Standards 1 and 4 (2018) similarly stress the importance of understanding and attending to individual children's developmental and learning needs (1.a) and guide candidates to use that understanding to plan and implement learning experiences and environments that address each individual need (1.b). Standard 4 provides further support by tasking candidates to use effective instruction to support each child's learning. Component 4.a instructs candidates to "use a variety of instructional practices that support the learning of every child" (p. 28). Component 4.g extends this guidance to task candidates to "effectively organize and manage individual instruction to provide targeted, focused, intensive instruction that improves or enhances each child's learning" (p. 32).

In the CEC Initial Preparation Standards (CEC, 2015), Standard 1 calls for candidates to use their knowledge of how exceptionalities impact development and learning to provide meaningful and challenging learning experiences for individuals. Further, CEC Standard 2 states candidates facilitate active and effective learning by creating safe, inclusive, culturally responsive learning environments. CEC Standard 3 calls for candidates to use knowledge of general and specialized curricula to individualize learning opportunities which necessitate the application of supports of sufficient intensity. CEC Standard 5 focuses on the use of a range of evidence-based instructional strategies to with sufficient intensity to advance learning.

The CEC/DEC Initial Specialty Set for Early Childhood Special Education/Early Intervention (CEC, 2017) states that candidates should develop and match learning experiences and instructional strategies to the developmental characteristics of young children (ECSE1.S2) and that those learning experiences should be embedded in daily routines and activities (ECSE2.S3). ECSE5.S6 extends this to emphasize that candidates should use a continuum of intervention strategies to facilitate access to the general education curriculum and daily routines. Several other instructional planning and strategies knowledge and skill statements expand on the candidates' implementation of a variety of responsive supports, such as, candidate scaffolded and initiated instruction

(ECSE5.S2), use of individual and group guidance and problem-solving strategies (ECSE5.S4), use of systematic instruction (ECSE5.S9), and use of adaptations as needed (ECSE5.S13).

The DEC Recommended Practices (DEC, 2014) for Instruction call for EI/ECSE professionals to "identify each child's strengths, preferences, and interests to engage the child in active learning (INS1); gather and use data to inform decisions about individualized instruction (INS3); embed instruction within and across routines, activities, and environments to provide contextually relevant learning opportunities (INS5). INS 4 specifically guides EI/ECSE professionals to "plan for and provide the level of support, accommodations, and adaptations needed for the child to access, participate, and learn within and across activities and routines and INS 10 focuses on implementation of "the frequency, intensity, and duration of instruction needed to address the child's phase and pace of learning or the level of support needed by the family to achieve the child's outcomes or goals.

The CEC high-leverage practices (McLeskey et al., 2017) also lend support and guidance to provide sufficient intensity and support for all learners. In particular, HLP 15 instructs EI/ECSE professionals to "select powerful visual, verbal, and written supports; carefully calibrate them to students' performance and understanding in relation to learning tasks; use them flexibly; evaluate their effectiveness; and gradually remove them once they are no longer needed" (p. 23). Finally, HLP 20 guides EI/ECSE professionals to "match the intensity of instruction to the intensity of the student's learning and behavioral challenges" (p. 25).

U.S. legislation provides additional guidance and justification for this component. The Individuals with Disabilities Education Act (IDEA) (2004), mandates that decisions on service delivery be based on the needs of the child and family. Additionally, IDEA (2004) includes provisions for early intervening services (EIS) designed to support students who have not been identified as needing special education but who are identified as needing additional academic and/or behavioral supports with sufficient intensity to prevent the need for special education services, if possible.

EI/ECSE professionals recognize the importance of using and promoting a continuum of strategies that are aligned with the needs of each individual child (Sandall, Schwartz, Joseph, & Gauvreau, 2019). By doing so, they can select and apply individualized strategies to ensure children receive support of sufficient intensity across environments to facilitate access, participation, and engagement in natural and inclusive environments. A wealth of research has identified a wide range of curricular modifications and adaptations when implemented with young children result in positive changes in learning and development (Odom, 2001; Odom, et al., 2012; Sandall et al., 2016; Trivette et al., 2010). Research has also indicated that individualized embedded instruction is effective in teaching a variety of skills and to support meaningful participation of children with and without disabilities (Barton & Smith, 2014; Daugherty, Grisham-Brown, & Hemmeter, 2001; Grisham-Brown et al., 2000; Horn et al., 2002; Robertson et al., 2003). An element of individualization includes examination of the particular parameters (e.g., intensity, environmental context, etc.) necessary for a strategy to be sufficient in order to ensure adequate progress, access, and participation. Indeed, effective EI/ECSE professionals identify learning opportunities and supports that are matched to each child's unique strengths and needs and work with others, including families and other professionals, to provide systematic instruction that is continually adapted based on assessment data (Sandall et al., 2019). Therefore, it is vital for preparation programs to adequately prepare initial EI/ECSE professionals to not only identify a wide range of strategies, modifications, and adaptations, but also to implement them with sufficient intensity across environments to ensure they facilitate access, participation, and engagement that promotes quality, full inclusive and rigorous, equitable learning opportunities.

The field has increasingly embraced the application of multi-tiered systems of supports (MTSS) to provide a framework of services that can help early childhood professionals align assessment data with specific teaching and intervention strategies to meet the needs of individual children (NPDCI, 2012). While this approach has been described in a variety of ways, three common components make up the framework: (a) systematic assessment of children's learning and development, (b) the use of evidence-based foundational instruction and intervention, and (c) clearly defined instructional decision-making (Buysse & Peisner-Feinberg, 2013). Effective early childhood educators recognize that such systems include quality, foundational instructional practices and supports

for all children, and the provision of specific, additional supports for individual children with diverse needs (NPDCI, 2012). In a critical analysis of tiered frameworks in early childhood, Snyder, McLaughlin, and Denney (2011) found that all the frameworks included an acknowledgement of the importance of making informed decisions about the type and level of support or intervention intensity and specificity in order to ensure children receive services of high quality marked by intentional and systematic instruction that is implemented with sufficient intensity to support learning. The application of such frameworks show potential to guide "program development, resource allocation, and decisions about the types, levels, and intensity of supports and interventions provided to all young children and their families" (Snyder et al., 2011, p. 270). Indeed, the progress monitoring in such frameworks helps inform teachers provide sufficient intensity of services (Yell et al. 2017). Lack of sufficient intensity of services has been identified as a serious issue in relation to barriers to inclusion and enactment of Free Appropriate Public Education (FAPE) (Bateman, 2011). Therefore, personnel preparation programs must ensure candidates are well prepared to operate in and implement such systems of support.

Component 6.7. Candidates plan for, adapt, and improve approaches to interactions, interventions, and instruction based on multiple sources of data across a range of natural environments and inclusive settings.

Supporting Explanation. Candidates use knowledge of evidence-based practices and multiple sources of data to systematically plan for and modify interactions, interventions, and instruction designed to promote specific child and family outcomes. They use a data-driven decision cycle (i.e., plan, implement, assess, and revise) to (a) delineate the strengths, needs, preferences, and assets of children and families, (b) develop individualized goals, (c) select and implement meaningful and effective interactions, interventions, and instruction, and (d) make necessary adaptations to goals and implementation. Candidates identify, evaluate, create, and apply formal and informal measures that are culturally and linguistically appropriate and technically sound, and ensure child and family data are collected from a range of natural and inclusive settings.

Candidates work collaboratively with the child's team, including the family, to administer, interpret, and use data from multiple, authentic assessments appropriate for the individual needs of young children and their families. Candidates collaborate with the team to continuously monitor, evaluate, and document the learning, growth, and development of children and families to ensure adequate progress toward the attainment of short-term and long-term goals. Candidates use various kinds of appropriate technology for tasks such as test administration, testing accommodations, data storage, creating digital documents and logs, charting and graphing results for ongoing assessment, and progress monitoring.

Working collaboratively with families, caregivers, and other professionals, candidates effectively utilize multiple sources of data to evaluate, revise, and improve interactions, interventions, and instruction. They regularly interpret and reflect upon progress monitoring data and make necessary adjustments and adaptations to meet the needs and build upon the strengths of the young children and families with whom they are working. Candidates systematically document all aspects of the data-driven decision cycle and consistently communicate child progress and adjustments to planned interactions, interventions, and instruction with all members of the interdisciplinary team, including the family.

Knowledge Base. InTASC Standard 6 (CCSSO, 2013), directly addresses the importance of candidates' use of multiple sources of data "to monitor learner progress and to guide the teacher's decision making." InTASC Standard 7 highlights the importance of candidates using multiple sources of data to "adjust instruction in the moment, to modify planned scaffolds and/or to provide additional support/acceleration." The same emphasis on using multiple sources of data, including systematic observations, documentation, and other effective assessment strategies in responsible ways to plan, implement and evaluate and continually improve instruction, intervention, and interaction is seen in CAEP K-6 Elementary Standard 4 (2018) and in The NAEYC Initial Personnel Preparation Standards (2011). In the CEC Initial Preparation Standards (2015), Standard 4, Assessment, states that candidates use multiple data sources and collaborate with families and other professionals to make decisions about the instructional needs of children. Further, Standard 7, Collaboration, emphasizes that

candidates collaborate with families and other professionals to meet the needs of young children across a range of learning experiences and settings.

The Individuals with Disabilities Education Act (IDEA, 2014 requires that evaluations of children with disabilities use a variety of assessment tools and strategies to determine the child's strengths and needs (IDEA regulations, 2012, 34 C.F.R. 300.304(b)). Parents, the EI/ECSE professional, and other professionals involved in the education of the child must contribute to the evaluation.

The CEC/DEC Initial Specialty Set for Early Childhood Special Education/Early Intervention (CEC, 2017) includes similar expectations for candidates. The Assessment section requires candidates to collect information from multiple sources and environments (ECSE4.S6). The Instructional Planning and Strategies section includes the expectation that candidates select intervention strategies based on information from multiple disciplines (ECSE5.S8). And finally, the Collaboration section emphasizes that candidates collaborate with families and other professionals to support children's development and learning (ECSE7.S.2). DEC Recommended Practices (DEC, 2014) expect EI/ECSE to work with families and other professionals to collect assessment data (A2). While the Environment Recommended Practices (E4 and E5) indicated that EI/ECSE professionals collaborate with families and other professionals to identify each child's needs for assistive technology and acquire or create that assistive technology. In terms of planning, the DEC Recommended Practices (DEC, 2014) state that EI/ECSE professionals along with families and professionals from multiple disciplines plan and implement supports and services for children (TC1). CEC High Leverage Practice (HLP 1) (McLeskey et al., 2017) says that EI/ECSE professional collaborate with professionals and HLP3 includes collaboration with families to support student learning. The use of multiple sources of information to identify students' strengths and needs is addressed in HLP 4.

A major goal of EI/ECSE professionals' interactions, interventions, and instruction with young children is to promote learning and development of progressively more advanced and adaptive skills (Wolery & Ledford, 2014). Collaboration has been found to positively impact child outcomes. Ronfeldt and colleagues (2015) reported that teachers participating more frequently in team activities, especially those related to assessment, produced relatively higher student achievement than teachers with less frequent team interactions. Further, when EI/ECSE professionals collaborate to set goals, children make more gains in achieving those goals, suggesting the importance of partnerships in child outcomes (Erwin et al., 2016).

Standard 7: Professionalism and Ethical Practice

Candidates identify and engage with the profession of early intervention and early childhood special education (EI/ECSE) by exhibiting skills in reflective practice, advocacy, and leadership while adhering to ethical and legal guidelines. Evidence-based and recommended practices are promoted and used by candidates.

Component 7.1. Candidates engage with the profession of EI/ECSE by participating in local, regional, national, and/or international activities and professional organizations.

Supporting Explanation. Candidates understand the nature of the profession of EI/ECSE and stay abreast of current issues as they arise (e.g., poverty, trauma, substance abuse, other issues). They apply their knowledge and skills of the profession to improve outcomes for all children and their families. Candidates engage in leadership and service opportunities that support positive outcomes for children and families. They demonstrate skilled expertise, utilize the expertise of others, and access professional resources that support positive outcomes for young children, families, and the profession.

Candidates understand the mission of professional organizations (e.g., CEC, DEC, NAEYC) and associate with them as a professional home. They engage in professional activities provided by professional organizations by accessing materials and resources (e.g., professional organization journals, webinars) to continuously improve their knowledge, expertise, and practice.

Candidates engage in continuous collaborative learning to develop skills and inform practice. They participate in learning communities in various ways (e.g., conferences, communities of practice) with other early childhood educators and professionals from other specialties, disciplines, and professions.

Candidates know and use national and state academic and personnel standards and recommended practices developed through professional organizations for planning and improving targeted services, supports, and outcomes for young children and their families.

Knowledge Base. InTASC Standard 9 (CCSSO, 2013) includes the engagement of candidates in ongoing learning opportunities to develop knowledge and skills and in meaningful and appropriate professional learning experiences aligned with one's own practices in addition to program needs. In addition, InTASC Standard 10 (CCSSO, 2013) states that candidates engage in professional learning to contribute to the knowledge and skills of others and to collaborate to advance professional practice.

The CEC Initial Preparation Standards (2015) include Professional Learning and Practice as Standard 6. Components within this standard state that professionals understand how current issues and foundational knowledge influence practice and that candidates understand the value of lifelong learning and engaging in professional activities and learning communities. Moreover, the CEC/DEC Initial Specialty Set for Early Childhood Special Education/Early Intervention (CEC, 2017) also affirms that candidates should participate in professional organizations relevant to the field of EI/ECSE (ECSE.6.S4). NAEYC Initial Personnel Preparation Standard 6 (2011) states that candidates identify and involve themselves with the field. The CAEP Elementary Education Standards Standard 5 (2018) states that candidates should engage in lifelong learning and relevant communities of practice. The DEC Recommended Practices (2014) include a strand on leadership with three practices that discuss EI/ECSE professionals expanding their professional knowledge and skills. The first recommended practice emphasizes that leaders belong to professional associations and engage in evidence-based professional development (L4).

Busby et al. (2019) note that "[p]rofessional organizations provide avenues for professional development through collaboration and networking that ultimately affect the teaching and learning process" (p. 18). The authors go on to state that EI/ECSE professionals who participate in the events of a professional organization have the opportunity to learn from and engage with leaders in the field about current research, trends, and issues in the field. Busby et al. (2019) add that professional organizations provide opportunities for EI/ECSE professionals to engage in leadership in their field and gain access to the professional knowledge base and resources through conferences, journals and other publications, and media. Exposing candidates to professional organizations as students will help them recognize the value of membership and engagement in organizations in the field.

In the Vescio et al. (2008) review of research on the engagement of teachers in collaborative professional development through processes such as professional learning communities (PLC), the authors found that the improvement in teachers' professional practices and collaboration consequently improved student learning and outcomes. Throughout the studies they reviewed, teachers identified their level of engagement and "buy in" to professional development and their own learning because it was driven by what the teachers identified as a need. Candidates will also benefit from this approach to professional development. Additionally, teachers also more readily accessed new strategies that were grounded in scholarly literature, and they became more student centered through the PLC style of professional development.

Component 7.2. Candidates engage in ongoing reflective practice and access evidence-based information to improve their own practices.

Supporting Explanation. Candidates participate in evidence-based activities and training to learn about and implement evidence-based practice and services for children and families to meet targeted outcomes. Candidates systematically reflect on their own practices and the practices of others. They reflect on their demonstration of professional personnel standards as well as the application of current research and recommended practices (e.g., DEC Recommended Practices, CEC High-Leverage Practices) in their own professional activities.

Candidates identify areas for growth within their own practices. They engage in evidence-based activities to address those areas for growth and demonstrate how their practices have improved. For example, they participate in conferences and online professional learning networks and access evidence-based resources through libraries and reputable sources. Using professional and evidence-based resources along with formative assessment data, candidates reflect on

and adjust their practices. Candidates use mentors and mentorship experiences to continually improve their own professional practice. They actively seek feedback from others such as experienced EI/ECSE providers, families, and professionals from other disciplines, and apply this input to improve their own practice.

Knowledge Base. InTASC Standard 9 (CCSSO, 2013) includes seeking resources to support analysis, reflection, and problem solving to improve practices. Standard 9 also discusses reflecting on biases and accessing resources to deepen the candidate's understanding of cultural, ethnic, gender, and learning differences in order to build relationships, create more meaningful learning experiences, and consequently improve professional practices. Standard 9 further states that candidates understand and know how to use self-assessment and problem-solving strategies to analyze and reflect on their own practices, how to use learner data to evaluate their own practices, and how to build a professional growth plan. Standard 9 goes on to state that candidates take responsibility for learner outcomes by using current policy and research as sources of analysis and reflection to improve practice. Lastly, Standard 10, Leadership and Collaboration, states that candidates should embrace the challenge of continuous improvement.

The CEC Initial Preparation Standards (2015) include Professional Learning and Practice as Standard 6. Within this standard, the significance of lifelong learning is discussed. The CEC/DEC Initial Specialty Set for Early Childhood Special Education/Early Intervention (CEC, 2017) states that candidates should use evidence-based and recommended practices in their own professional practice (ECSE.6.S5). Further, the NAEYC Initial Personnel Preparation Standards (2011) include the relationship of reflecting on one's own practice and engaging in continuous learning efforts to improve learner outcomes. Finally, the CAEP Elementary Education Standard 5 (2018) states that candidates work to continually improve practices through self-study, reflective practice, and drawing on the literature.

State, federal, and provincial policy, such as the IDEA (U.S. Department of Education, 2011), states the need for continued professional development to improve the skills and practices of educators.

The DEC Recommended Practices (2014) include one practice that outlines the need for development and implementation of evidence-based professional development in order to ensure the effective implementation of the DEC Recommended Practices (L9). Additionally, the DEC Code of Ethics (2009) states "professionals engage in ongoing and systematic reflective inquiry and self-assessment for the purpose of continuous improvement of professional performance and services to young children with disabilities and their families" (p. 1).

Ross and Bruce (2007) propose a model for educator self-assessment. The authors note that, through self-assessment, areas for growth are identified and professionals may more easily identify varieties of resources and professional development to support professional growth. Additionally, researchers (such as Brown & Weber, 2019; Jensen & Rasmussen, 2018; Powell et al., 2013) note that professional development comes in a variety of formats, including face-to-face workshops, online technologies, coaching, and reflective supervision. Jensen and Rasmussen (2016) goes on to note that the professional development of early childhood educators directly influences the positive outcomes of children.

Many authors (e.g., Davis, 2006; Freese, 2006; Garcia et al., 2006; Harland & Wondra, 2011; Welch & James, 2007) note the growing trend of reflective practice as a process for professional growth. Reflective practice allows EI/ECSE professionals to not only consider their own practices but also the practices of more seasoned and experienced professionals to continuously grow in professional practice (Arrastia et al., 2014; Ferraro, 2000; Tillema, 2000). Lastly, Schön (1983, 1987) notes that, as professionals review and reflect on their own and other pedagogical styles, they are refining their craft in order to be more effective. Reflective practice can be particularly useful in the preparation of EI/ECSE professionals as they perfect their professional practices.

Component 7.3. Candidates exhibit leadership skills in advocating for improved outcomes for young children, families, and the profession, including the promotion of and use of evidence-based practices and decision-making.

Supporting Explanation. Candidates demonstrate that they can take on leadership roles by engaging in informed advocacy for children and families and the profession. Candidates have basic knowledge of how federal/state/provincial/local policies are developed, demonstrate advocacy skills, and understand how their efforts can support systemic change and improvements in policies regarding young children at risk for and with developmental delays and disabilities and their families. They know about the central policy issues in the field, including program quality and provision of equitable access to high-quality early intervention and early childhood special education services and supports and the implications of those issues for advocacy and policy change. Candidates understand implicit bias as well as the historical and current systems of marginalization and inequities regarding young children at risk for and with developmental delays and disabilities and their families (e.g., early identification, over/under identification, suspension and expulsion, ableism, among others). Candidates access evidence-based resources to be informed of issues around implicit bias and to limit the impact of their own biases in interactions with families, children, and other professionals.

Candidates know and work within federal/state/provincial/local legislative and statutory mandates and regulations that support young children and families and the implications of this legislation for professional practice. Candidates understand how to advocate for the rights of young children and families. They recognize that program limitations and restrictions do not suppress the rights of children and families. Candidates know how to work with decision makers to minimize barriers to the rights of children and families.

They engage in and access professional organization activities and resources and/or evidence-based resources to support their own advocacy efforts as well as supporting families in their advocacy. Candidates are knowledgeable of professional organizations' policy and advocacy missions. For example, they engage in webinars, receive newsletters addressing advocacy events and initiatives, and stay abreast of current policy and advocacy issues.

Knowledge Base. InTASC Standard 7 (CCSSO, 2013) states that professionals should know about and be able to use evidence-based strategies. Additionally, Standard 10 states that professionals should help shape the mission of advocacy for learners and their success.

The CEC Initial Preparation Standards (2015) include Professional Learning and Practice as Standard 6. Components within this standard focus on candidates advancing the profession by engaging in activities such as advocacy and mentoring. Moreover, according to the CEC/DEC Initial Specialty Set for Early Childhood Special Education/Early Intervention (CEC, 2017), candidates must advocate for professional status and working conditions for those who serve infants and young children and their families (ECSE.K6.4), apply evidence-based and DEC Recommended Practices for infants and young children, including those from diverse backgrounds (ECSE.S6.5), and advocate on behalf of infants and young children and their families (ECSE.S6.6). Lastly, NAEYC Initial Personnel Preparation Standard 6 (2011) focuses on engaging in informed advocacy for young children and the early childhood profession (6e).

While providing services to children with disabilities and their families, EI/ECSE professionals must make assessment and intervention information understandable to families so that parents/guardians can be informed advocates for their children (IDEA, 2006). During service planning (e.g., Individual Education Program (IEP) and Individual Family Service Plan (IFSP) meetings), EI/ECSE professionals are asked to make decisions based on the needs of the child while keeping in mind the requirements of pertinent laws (e.g., IDEA of 2006 and others). In this way, EI/ECSE professionals must use their understanding of recommended practices and current research to advocate for appropriate items like placement, curriculum, or frequency of services for a particular child with a disability.

The DEC Recommended Practices (2014) state that EI/ECSE professionals advocate for policies and resources that promote the implementation of DEC position statements and papers as well as the DEC Recommended Practices (L5), and further develop and implement policies, structures, and practices that promote shared decision-making with practitioners and families (L3). CEC high-leverage practices (McLeskey et al., 2017) state that candidates should collaborate with families to support student learning and secure needed services through advocacy (HLP 3).

According to Hollingsworth et al. (2016), initial candidates have more of a decision-making voice in early childhood research and policy after taking an undergraduate course in policy and engaging in policy projects. Research also shows that candidates with in-

tentional advocacy assignments in higher education courses saw themselves as agents of change with increased confidence and a sense of power. Ethridge et al. (2019) reported that graduates from preparation programs that support development of these necessary skills continued to engage in advocacy efforts for their children and families.

Component 7.4. Candidates practice within ethical and legal policies and procedures.

Supporting Explanation. Candidates maintain a high level of professional competence and integrity, and exercise informed professional judgment. Candidates apply professional codes of ethics, including the DEC Code of Ethics and NAEYC Code of Ethical Conduct, in their practice with children, families, and other professionals, and are guided by the ideals and principles promoted within. They use these codes to analyze and resolve professional and ethical dilemmas related to professional practice. Further, candidates understand their responsibilities for reporting ethical and legal violations in relation to the profession as well as the safety of children and families. Candidates are familiar with relevant professional guidelines such as national, state, or local standards for content and child outcomes, recommended and high-leverage practices, and position statements about, for example, inclusion, challenging behaviors, and maltreatment of young children.

Knowledge Base. InTASC Standard 9 (CCSSO, 2013) states that candidates must advocate, model, and teach the safe, legal, and ethical use of information and technology and know the laws related to learners' rights and teachers' responsibilities. This standard also states that candidates must understand the expectations of the profession, including codes of ethics, professional standards of practice, and relevant law and policy. The CEC Initial Preparation Standards (2015) include Professional Learning and Practice (Standard 6). Within this standard, the use of professional ethical principles and professional practice standards in guiding practice is affirmed. The CEC/DEC Initial Specialty Set for Early Childhood Special Education/Early Intervention (CEC, 2017) states that candidates should understand the legal basis for services for young children (ECSE.6.S1), understand the legal, ethical, and policy issues related to services for young children and their families

(ECSE.S6.3), and "implement family services consistent with due process safeguards" (ECSE.6.S5, p.5). Standard 6 of the NAEYC Initial Personnel Preparation Standards (2011) states that candidates should know about and uphold ethical standards and other professional guidelines. Lastly, CAEP Elementary Education Standards (2018) say that candidates use pertinent ethical standards to inform their practices.

The DEC Recommended Practices (2014) include practices in the Leadership strand that address adherence to and modeling of the DEC Code of Ethics, DEC position statements and papers, and the DEC Recommended Practices (L2), and ensuring standards, laws, and regulations are followed (L10). The Family strand (F9) states that EI/ECSE professionals assist families in knowing and understanding their rights.

The DEC Code of Ethics (2009) states, "The early childhood special education professional should base his or her behaviors on ethical reasoning surrounding practice and professional issues as well as an empathic reflection regarding interactions with others. We are committed to beneficence acts for improving the quality of lives of young children with disabilities and their families" (p. 1). Additionally, the CEC Code of Ethics (2015) states that EI/ECSE professionals should maintain a high level of professional competence and integrity. Lastly, the NAEYC Code of Ethical Conduct and Commitment (2011) states that professionals have a responsibility to children, families, colleagues, and the community.

Balch et al. (2008) state, "As a professional, a teacher must promote the success of all students, partly by understanding and being responsive to the legal context of teaching (i.e., teachers' and students' rights balanced by the scales of justice). The legal context that influences teaching is invariably complex, differing in details by location. Yet, in any educational setting, a teacher's success is increasingly dependent on a sound awareness and prudent application of education law (p. 5)". The authors also note: "The quality of our education system is dependent on teacher efforts to promote the success of all students, partly by understanding and being responsive to the legal context of education. For this reason, an EI/ECSE professional's success requires a sound awareness and prudent application of education law. Pedagogy informed by law is essential because broad legal latitude is afforded the EI/ECSE professional, with many legal privileges being inferred and inherent rather than promulgated" (p. 8).

Additionally, Barrett et al. (2012) discuss the value of adhering to the law and valuing a code of conduct. While this research was conducted with school-based professionals, the implications and considerations of issues such as "boundaries" apply to the variety of early childhood learning environments as well as working with children and families. Moreover, Able, West, and Lim (2017) note that following professional codes of ethics provides a decision-making framework for evidence-based practices.

Field Experience and Clinical Practice Standard for Early Interventionists/Early Childhood Special Educators

Early Intervention/Early Childhood Special Education (EI/ECSE) candidates progress through a series of planned and developmentally sequenced field experiences for the early childhood age ranges (birth to age 3, 3 through 5 years, 5 through 8 years), range of abilities, and in the variety of collaborative and inclusive early childhood settings that are appropriate to their license and roles. Clinical experiences should take place in the same age ranges covered by the license. If the license covers all three age ranges, the program must provide clinical experiences in at least two of the three age ranges and a field experience in the third age range. These field and clinical experiences are supervised by qualified professionals.

Supporting Explanation. Field and clinical experiences provide opportunities for candidates to apply knowledge and to practice skills in culturally and linguistically diverse classrooms, home-based settings, and other community placements in partnership with families and other professionals. Field and clinical experience sites are developed and enhanced over time through collaborative partnerships among local education agencies and other community stakeholders, including families and university EI/ECSE faculty. Through collaboration and consultation, placements are selected to provide developmental field experiences that support candidates in using effective practices in a wide array of classrooms, homes, and other community settings.

Field and clinical experiences are designed to link EI/ECSE research and theory to practice and provide rich, scaffolded, developmental, and graduated experiences with increasing responsibilities for prospective early interventionists and early childhood special educators. Thus, field experiences are aligned with coursework and occur early and throughout the Educator Preparation Program beginning with observation and reflection on practices and systematically progressing to implementation of practices with supervision. Examples of these experiences include course-based field work, practica, internships, and student teaching. Field and clinical experiences are connected and sufficiently extensive and intensive that candidates are able to demonstrate through performance assessments that they have mastered the practices required for the professional roles for which they are preparing.

Field and clinical experiences are structured and varied, and ensure that candidates have experiences with infants, toddlers, and young children and their families across the age ranges and range of abilities for which they are preparing. To facilitate this, placements occur in the variety of collaborative, inclusive, and culturally and linguistically diverse early childhood programs in which infants, toddlers, and young children receive services. These include, but are not limited to, public school preschool and K-3 programs; other publicly funded programs such as Early Head Start and Head Start; community preschool and childcare programs; and the natural environments of the child and family, for example, home, park, or grocery. All candidates have some field experiences across the complete age range. For example, candidates may observe for a specific child developmental domain across the birth through age 8 age range. Or, as another example, candidates may observe and reflect on the observation in settings that go across the age ranges. Then, as field experiences focus more on application of practices, candidates complete field experiences for the age ranges included in the license and roles for which they are preparing. In addition, all candidates have some field experiences in which they observe and participate in collaborative activities with families and other professionals (e.g., home visits, parent-teacher conferences, cross disciplinary team meetings).

Clinical practice must take place in the same age ranges covered by the license. For example, if the license covers two of the three age ranges (e.g., birth to age 3 and 3 through 5 years), clinical experiences must be provided for both age ranges. If the license covers all three age ranges, the program must provide clinical experiences in at least two of the three age ranges (e.g., 3 through 5 years and 5 through 8 years) and a field experience specifically focused on the third age range (e.g., birth to age 3).

Site-based professionals are selected for their expertise and experience with infants, toddlers, and young children and for providing the services for which the candidate is preparing. They hold the certification or credential necessary to work in the EI/ECSE program. Site-based professionals demonstrate mentoring and coaching skills in supporting the learning of candidates. In addition, the site-based professionals effectively communicate with and engage the candidate in self-reflection on the interactions and practices utilized with children, families, and other providers. Although university supervisors may not be licensed or certified in the state in which they are employed, they must have substantial formal preparation in the field of EI/ECSE and have expertise and experience with infants, toddlers, and young children and services for which the candidate is preparing.

Section 7

Early Interventionist/Early Childhood Special Educator Potential Performance Indicators and Assessments

In the standards sets presented in Section 6, the supporting explanations elaborate on specific practices identified in the components, providing insights about what should be taught and assessed within special educator preparation programs. The following performance indicators are provided to assist programs in developing assessments and evidence that demonstrate candidate mastery of the standards. These are provided solely as examples, not as requirements. This is not an exhaustive list and use of these examples would not automatically lead to a positive Specialized Professional Associations (SPA) recognition decision.

Table 11: EI/ECSE Potential Performance Indicators	
Components	**Potential Performance Indicators**
Standard 1: Child Development and Early Learning	
1.1: Candidates demonstrate an understanding of the impact that different theories and philosophies of early learning and development have on assessment, curriculum, intervention, and instruction decisions.	• Candidates describe and interpret a child's learning and behavior from two different theoretical perspectives, based on observation or case study. • Candidates design a learning environment, learning activities, and instructional strategies from the perspective of a specific developmental or learning theory and justify how they represent the theory. • Candidates analyze a child or family case study from two different theoretical perspectives and determine recommended classroom practices or a family engagement plan based on the different theories; candidates compare and contrast their interpretation and recommendations based on the different theories. • Candidates interview an EI/ECSE educator about their philosophy of education; select a specific theory and analyze how practices outlined by the educator align with or differ from this theory. • Candidates compare and contrast recommendations for family engagement from two different theoretical perspectives, based on a family case study.

Components	Potential Performance Indicators

Table 11: EI/ECSE Potential Performance Indicators...(continued)

Components	Potential Performance Indicators
Standard 1: Child Development and Early Learning...(continued)	
1.2: Candidates apply knowledge of normative sequences of early development, individual differences, and families' social, cultural and linguistic diversity to support each child's development and learning across contexts.	• Candidates develop a child case study that comprehensively outlines the child's development across multiple domains, including their complexity and interdependence; provide recommendations for how a teacher can support the individual child based on their strengths and needs. • Candidates interview a family member of a child to understand the family's resources, strengths, preferences, and cultural and linguistic characteristics; use a developmental tool to facilitate a conversation about the family's perception of their child's development; write a reflection on how they can partner with the family to support the child's development. • Candidates interpret a developmental assessment to prepare an assessment summary that reports child's strengths and needs; provide implications for intervention and instruction. • Candidates develop a lesson plan that incorporates supports for children who are dual language learners and incorporates materials and/or content that is culturally responsive to students from diverse backgrounds.
1.3: Candidates apply knowledge of biological and environmental factors that may support or constrain children's early development and learning as they plan and implement early intervention and instruction.	• Candidates develop individualized plan outcomes (e.g., IFSP) for a family case study with a child receiving early intervention due to the child being born significantly premature and exhibiting early developmental delays; incorporates identified family resources, routines, strengths, preferences, and needs. • During a student teaching placement or field experience, candidates conduct a routines-based interview with a child's family to identify family resources, strengths, routines, and needs; writes a reflection for how that information would influence instruction and intervention. • Candidates develop a lesson plan and determine home-based activities that families can do to support children's development/learning in that area; home-based activity suggestions take into account the resources generally available to families in the community and are little to no cost.

Table 11: EI/ECSE Potential Performance Indicators...(continued)	
Components	**Potential Performance Indicators**
Standard 1: Child Development and Early Learning...(continued)	
1.4: Candidates demonstrate an understanding of characteristics, etiologies, and individual differences within and across the range of abilities including developmental delays and disabilities, their potential impact on children's early development and learning, and implications for assessment, curriculum, instruction, and intervention.	• During a student teaching or field experience placement, candidates develop an early elementary science lesson plan with differentiated instruction options and an embedded learning opportunity for a student in their class with an IEP; embedded instruction supports the child's meaningful participation in the activity and progress towards one of their IEP goals. • Candidates develop a plan to adapt a developmental assessment for a child with a specific disability (e.g., motor impairment, low vision); write a reflection about how the child's exceptionality changes the implementation and interpretation of the assessment to understand the child's development across domains. • Candidates develop a plan to collaborate with families to support the early literacy of a child with a specific disability (e.g., language delay); plan includes how family can effectively implement book reading activities and includes a way for families to share their observations and perspectives about their child's language and literacy development.

Table 11: EI/ECSE Potential Performance Indicators...(continued)	
Components	**Potential Performance Indicators**
Standard 2: Partnering with Families	
2.1: Candidates apply their knowledge of family-centered practices, family systems theory, and the changing needs and priorities in family's lives to develop trusting, respectful, culturally responsive and affirming partnerships with all families that allow for the mutual exchange of knowledge and information.	• Candidates role-play an interaction with a family using relational practices, such as active listening strategies, showing compassion and understanding, and respecting families' knowledge, input and perspectives. • Candidates complete self-reflection journaling of their own culture, beliefs and experiences making connections to the impact their own beliefs and experiences could have on relationship building with families. • Candidates develop a plan, outlining strategies to share information and expertise with a family in the family's home language.
2.2: Candidates communicate clear, comprehensive, objective information about resources and supports that help families to make informed decisions and advocate for access, participation, and equity in natural and inclusive environments.	• Candidates identify effective communication strategies such as attending, listening, and asking clarifying questions, that promote actively seeking information from and sharing information with families through the review of video examples. • Candidates plan and implement an early intervention visit or lesson that represents the diversity of families and children using differentiated content, materials, individual routines or activities, or community settings. • Candidates explain IDEA birth-to-age-8 systems of supports, including family and child rights, available services, and the requirement of family participation in all decisions about the child's individualized plan.
2.3: Candidates engage families in identifying their strengths, priorities and concerns; support families to achieve the goals they have for their family and their young child's development and learning; and promote families' competence and confidence during assessment, individualized planning, intervention, instruction, and transition processes.	• Candidates complete a family assessment, such as the Routines-Based Interview (RBI) or the Hawaii Early Learning Profile (HELP) Family Interview to identify the family's resources, and priorities and concerns. • Candidates synthesize assessment information gathered and collaboratively develop outcomes/goals that meet the unique needs and priorities of the child and family. • Candidates jointly design individualized plans with a family member and identify the formal and informal supports and services necessary to achieve the outcomes/goals. • Candidates use a case study to draft a comprehensive transition plan including strategies to engage the family in evaluating transition options, and identifying a range of supports, services and resources available in the home, community and/or school setting.

Table 11: EI/ECSE Potential Performance Indicators...(continued)	
Components	**Potential Performance Indicators**
Standard 3: Collaboration and Teaming	
3.1: Candidates apply teaming models, skills, and processes, including appropriate uses of technology, when collaborating and communicating with families; professionals representing multiple disciplines, skills, expertise, and roles; and community partners and agencies.	• Candidates observe a team meeting (e.g., IEP, IFSP, transition planning) in person in a school, home, or other community setting and reflect on and describe the application of models of teaming observed and discusses roles of team members represented. • Candidates use technology to team with peers/classmates/professionals/families to complete a project and analyze the effectiveness of teaming using technology. • Candidates engage with peers in a role play of or participates in a transdisciplinary team meeting to demonstrate teaming skills.
3.2: Candidates use a variety of collaborative strategies when working with other adults that are evidence-based, appropriate to the task, culturally and linguistically responsive, and take into consideration the environment and service delivery approach.	• Candidates use collaborative strategies (e.g., problem solving, joint goal development) to develop an IEP/IFSP based on a case study or of a child with whom the candidate interacts in a field placement. • Candidates collaboratively develop an agenda for a team meeting (e.g., IEP, IFSP, transition planning) with peers/classmates/professionals/families. • During field experience, candidates collaborate with mentor (cooperating teacher) and related service provider(s) to develop and implement an intervention project for a child in the learning environment of the field placement. • Candidates, working with peers/classmates, use a peer coaching model to provide feedback on instructional strategies used during an instructional or intervention activity.
3.3: Candidates partner with families and other professionals to develop individualized plans and support the various transitions that occur for the young child and their family throughout the birth-through-8 age span.	• Candidates interview family member(s) of a child with a delay or disability to learn about their experiences across different transition points in order to support effective future transitions. • Candidates engage with peers in a role play of or participate in developing a transition plan for a child with a delay or disability. • Candidates use person-centered planning approach to interview families and collaboratively determine family priorities, hopes, and dreams for their child with a delay or disability.

Table 11: EI/ECSE Potential Performance Indicators...(continued)	
Components	**Potential Performance Indicators**
Standard 4: Assessment Processes	
4.1: Candidates understand the purposes of formal and informal assessment including ethical and legal considerations, and use this information to choose developmentally, culturally and linguistically appropriate, valid, reliable tools and methods that are responsive to the characteristics of the young child, family, and program.	• Candidates observe a child in the natural environment, keep a running record, and summarize the results regarding the child's progress in achieving developmental milestones. • Candidates explain the rationale for using formal assessment measures with a specific child in mind considering culture and other factors that may cause bias. • Candidates administer assessment measures accurately and adjust items, if allowed, to address individual needs and diversity. • Candidates administer and critique standardized assessment tools appropriate for young children with delays or disabilities.
4.2: Candidates develop and administer informal assessments and/or select and use valid, reliable formal assessments using evidence-based practices, including technology, in partnership with families, and other professionals.	• Candidates complete a routines-based assessment with family members to identify the family's resources, priorities, and concerns. • Candidates research an assessment tool and analyze the psychometrics of the instrument provided in the manual. • Candidates, in a transdisciplinary model with peers, observe a child in play, collaboratively take observation notes, and analyze notes to make recommendations.
4.3: Candidates analyze, interpret, document and share assessment information using a strength-based approach with families and other professionals.	• Candidates use observation notes to develop a strengths-based, jargon-free report that summarizes assessment results for families. • Candidates meet with families to discuss assessment results and findings. • Candidates role play, with peers/classmates, a parent-teacher conference to share progress monitoring.
4.4: Candidates, in collaboration with families and other team members, use assessment data to determine eligibility, develop child and family-based outcomes/goals, plan for interventions and instruction, and monitor progress to determine efficacy of programming.	• Candidates use assessment information to develop goals/outcomes for an IEP/IFSP in collaboration with peers/classmates/professionals/families. • Candidates use assessment information to develop instructional and intervention plans in collaboration with peers/classmates/professionals/families. • Candidates, in collaboration with peers/classmates/ professionals/families, develop a plan to collect data using authentic measures during daily activities.

Table 11: EI/ECSE Potential Performance Indicators...(continued)

Components	Potential Performance Indicators
Standard 5: Application of Curriculum Frameworks in the Planning and Facilitation of Meaningful Learning Experience	
5.1: Candidates collaborate with families and other professionals in identifying evidence-based curriculum addressing developmental and content domains to design and facilitate meaningful and culturally responsive learning experiences that support the unique abilities and needs of all children and families.	• Candidates develop a plan that describes strategies to be implemented to increase equitable access to and participation in the general curriculum and differentiate challenging content to address the full range of abilities of children served based on a program case study that includes information about the perspectives of the families and all the professionals engaged in the program. • Candidates analyze an age-appropriate curriculum and describe strategies that could be used to collect information on families' developmental and educational expectations for their children to ensure their planning is culturally responsive. • Candidates develop a plan that describes strategies to be implemented to ensure that children's cultural backgrounds and experiences are embedded in all aspects of the learning environment (e.g., interactions, instruction, family routines, home, community outings, classroom activities and materials) based on a program case study that includes information on the cultural backgrounds and experiences of the children and families served by the program.
5.2: Candidates use their knowledge of early childhood curriculum frameworks, developmental and academic content knowledge, and related pedagogy to plan and ensure equitable access to universally designed, developmentally appropriate, and challenging learning experiences in natural and inclusive environments.	• Based upon an observation or case study, candidates describe how the case's decisions on what, when, and how to promote each and every child's learning aligns with the expectations of early childhood curriculum frameworks. • Candidates describe the principles of universal design for learning to ensure that learning experiences and environments are designed to allow for access and engagement to the greatest extent possible without the need for adaptation. • Candidates develop a lesson/activity plan that explicitly details how the principles of universal design for learning and ensuring challenging learning experiences are addressed.

Table 11: EI/ECSE Potential Performance Indicators...(continued)	
Components	**Potential Performance Indicators**
Standard 6: Using Responsive and Reciprocal Interactions, Interventions, and Instruction	
6.1: Candidates, in partnership with families, identify systematic, responsive, and intentional evidence-based practices and use such practices with fidelity to support young children's learning and development across all developmental and academic content domains.	• Based on observation or a case study, candidates provide the rationale for selecting the appropriate practices and strategies to use with individual children based on the best-available empirical evidence as well as the wisdom and experience of the field. • Candidates describe strategies for eliciting and using input from families pertinent to the appropriateness of evidence-based practices and the feasibility of implementing these practices within natural and inclusive environments • Candidates describe within an activity plan how they will collect and use fidelity measures to collect data about the implementation process of evidence-based practices.
6.2: Candidates engage in reciprocal partnerships with families and other professionals to facilitate responsive adult-child interactions, interventions, and instruction in support of child learning and development.	• Candidates develop a plan for engaging families and other professionals in ongoing learning that reflect theories and principles of adult learning strategies relevant to EI/ECSE. • Candidates develop a plan to support caregivers and other adults in implementing evidence-based practices assuring that they align appropriately context for the child and family. • Candidates describe a variety of strategies (e.g., feedback, modeling, active listening, questioning, problem solving, coaching) within a learning activity plan that provides adults with meaningful and relevant information that builds on what they already know.
6.3: Candidates engage in ongoing planning and use flexible and embedded instructional and environmental arrangements and appropriate materials to support the use of interactions, interventions, and instruction addressing developmental and academic content domains, which are adapted to meet the needs of each and every child and their family.	• Candidates develop a learning activity that includes specific strategies that will be used to modify the environment, materials, and instruction to appropriately address the developmental and academic content. • Candidates develop a plan for an individual child that demonstrates how instructional episodes for the child's individual learning goals will be embedded throughout the activities and routines of the day. • Candidates develop a plan, based on a child and family case study, for instructional and learning opportunities to be embedded in the natural activities and routines of the child and family's day.

Table 11: EI/ECSE Potential Performance Indicators...(continued)	
Components	**Potential Performance Indicators**
Standard 6: Using Responsive and Reciprocal Interactions, Interventions, and Instruction...(continued)	
6.4: Candidates promote young children's social and emotional competence and communication, and proactively plan and implement function-based interventions to prevent and address challenging behaviors.	• Candidates conduct an observation in a community early childhood setting paying attention to elements of the learning environment that may support or hinder children's social and emotional competence. • Candidates conduct a functional behavioral assessment of a child in a clinical placement to systematically identify the behavior, events that precede such behavior (antecedents), and events that can maintain such behavior (consequences). • Based on a case study (or actual children in a clinical placement), candidates analyze learning activities and design interventions to support individual and groups of children using multi-tiered systems of support as a framework.
6.5: Candidates identify and create multiple opportunities for young children to develop and learn play skills and engage in meaningful play experiences independently and with others across contexts.	• Candidates develop a plan to provide children with multiple opportunities to engage in sustained play within meaningful interactions across peers, adults, and contexts throughout the age range of birth to 8 years • Candidates demonstrate and apply their knowledge of instruction and play development to teach children to engage in increasingly complex play. • Candidates demonstrate and apply their knowledge of instruction to embed meaningful learning opportunities within the child's play.
6.6: Candidates use responsive interactions, interventions, and instruction with sufficient intensity and types of support across activities, routines, and environments to promote child learning and development and facilitate access, participation, and engagement in natural environments and inclusive settings.	• Candidates collect baseline and ongoing data on children's performance and use that data to analyze teaching/intervention effectiveness. • Based on a case study or actual child, candidates analyze comprehensive assessment data to identify appropriate supports for that child across a variety of learning experiences given the child's developmental, cultural, and linguistic characteristics. • Candidates view a video of their own instruction and write a reflection on their use of positive responsive interactions with children and/or families.

Table 11: EI/ECSE Potential Performance Indicators...(continued)	
Components	**Potential Performance Indicators**
Standard 6: Using Responsive and Reciprocal Interactions, Interventions, and Instruction...(continued)	
6.7: Candidates plan for, adapt and improve approaches to interactions, interventions, and instruction based on multiple sources of data across a range of natural environments and inclusive settings.	• Candidates analyze a formal progress monitoring tool describing how it adheres to expectations of technical soundness, cultural and linguistic appropriateness, and utility for collecting information across multiple settings • Candidates develop a plan based upon a program case study (e.g., early intervention program, preschool program, kindergarten) that describes how the program can monitor, evaluate, and document the learning, growth, and development of children and families to ensure adequate progress toward the attainment of short-term and long-term goals/outcomes. • Candidates develop an activity/lesson plan that includes specific plans for collecting performance data, implement the plan, and reflect upon how instruction is to be adapted to promoted continued progress on specific child and family outcomes.

Table 11: EI/ECSE Potential Performance Indicators...(continued)	
Components	**Potential Performance Indicators**
Standard 7: Professionalism and Ethical Practice	
7.1: Candidates engage with the profession of EI/ECSE by participating in local, regional, national, and/or international activities and professional organizations.	• Candidates attend a local professional meeting or event regarding early intervention/early childhood special education. • Candidates attend a local or state interagency coordinating council meeting. • Candidates volunteer for a parent advocacy/network/support group event.
7.2: Candidates engage in ongoing reflective practice and access evidence-based information to improve their own practices.	• Candidates report and reflect on professional experiences and growth during field experiences through ongoing documentation and journaling. • Candidates develop professional goals related to early intervention/early childhood special education. • Candidates identify and review websites for evidence-based resources for early interventionists/early childhood special educators.
7.3: Candidates exhibit leadership skills in advocating for improved outcomes for young children, families, and the profession including the promotion of and use of evidenced-based practices and decision-making.	• Candidates develop an article or press release on the importance of play for all young children for local news outlets. • Candidates communicate in writing or in person with a local, state, provincial, and/or federal representative to promote quality early intervention/early childhood special education. • Candidates complete a literature review on a selected evidence-based practice and presents salient facts to peers/classmates or in a professional development session such as a local or state.
7.4: Candidates practice within ethical and legal policies and procedures.	• Candidates review, compare, and contrast multiple professional codes of ethics from professional membership organizations related to education, early childhood education, special education, early intervention/early childhood special education, and/or related services such as speech- language pathology, occupational therapy, physical therapy, etc. • Candidates review the legal regulations that govern a current topic or issue in early intervention/early childhood special education issue such as suspension and expulsion, inclusion in preschool, or instruction/intervention in natural environments. • In clinical/field experience, candidates demonstrate behavior that reflects relevant codes of ethics.

Section 8

Potential Sources of Evidence for Initial Practice-Based Professional Preparation Standards for Early Interventionists/Early Childhood Special Educators

The Council for Exceptional Children (CEC) Early Intervention/Early Childhood Special Education (EI/ECSE) Initial Preparation Standards were developed so that they could be assessed using six to eight assessments consistent with requirements for Specialized Professional Associations (SPA) Program Review Option A with National Recognition. While the assessment guidelines and resources align with Council for the Accreditation of Educator Preparation (CAEP) and SPA requirements, they may be applicable as well for program reviews conducted by state agencies or within universities/schools/departments. As can be seen in the Standards/Assessment Matrix, of the six to eight assessment categories, five are defined: (1) a licensure assessment, or other content-based assessment; (2) content-based assessment; (3) assessment of candidate ability to plan instruction; (4) assessment of student teaching; and (5) assessment of candidate effect on student learning. While a sixth assessment is required, the specific focus of this assessment is determined by the program's assessment system and the extent to which stronger evidence that a standard is met is needed. EI/ECSE preparation programs are strongly encouraged to submit a seventh and/or eighth assessment that they believe will further strengthen their demonstration that all standards are met.

Types of Assessments

As stated above, The CEC EI/ECSE Initial Preparation Standards were developed so that they could be assessed using six to eight assessments consistent with requirements for SPA Program Review Option A with National Recognition. While these assessment resources align with CAEP and SPA requirements, they may be useful for program development within universities/schools/ departments and/or program review by state education agencies. The examples provided below are neither expected nor required, but are provided as possible examples.

Table 12. Potential Sources of Evidence: Types of Assessments	
Components	**Potential Sources of Assessment Evidence for Candidate Performance**
Standard 1: Child Development and Early Learning	
1.1: Candidates demonstrate an understanding of the impact that different theories and philosophies of early learning and development have on assessment, curriculum, intervention, and instruction decisions.	• Assessments of content knowledge such as state licensure tests or professional examinations of content knowledge. • Assessments of content knowledge such as course grades in content or pedagogical courses related to early learning and development. • Assessments of content knowledge such as a required capstone project (e.g., multiple days of planning or an assessment) in content or pedagogy courses related to early learning and development.
1.2: Candidates apply knowledge of normative sequences of early development, individual differences, and families' social, cultural, and linguistic diversity to support each child's development and learning across contexts.	• Assessments of content knowledge such as state licensure tests or professional examinations of content knowledge. • Assessments of content knowledge such as course grades in content or pedagogical courses related to early learning and development. • Assessments of content knowledge such as a required capstone project (e.g., multiple days of planning or an assessment) in content or pedagogy courses related to early learning and development.
1.3: Candidates apply knowledge of biological and environmental factors that may support or constrain children's early development and learning as they plan and implement early intervention and instruction.	• Assessments of content knowledge such as state licensure tests or professional examinations of content knowledge. • Assessments of content knowledge such as course grades in content or pedagogical courses related to early learning and development. • Assessments of content knowledge such as a required capstone project (e.g., multiple days of planning or an assessment) in content or pedagogy courses related to early learning and development.
1.4: Candidates demonstrate an understanding of characteristics, etiologies, and individual differences within and across the range of abilities, including developmental delays and disabilities, their potential impact on children's early development and learning, and implications for assessment, curriculum, instruction, and intervention.	• Assessments of content knowledge such as state licensure tests or professional examinations of content knowledge. • Assessments of content knowledge such as course grades in content or pedagogical courses related to early learning and development. • Assessments of content knowledge such as a required capstone project (e.g., multiple days of planning or an assessment) in content or pedagogy courses related to early learning and development.

Table 12. Potential Sources of Evidence: Types of Assessments...(continued)

Components	Potential Sources of Assessment Evidence for Candidate Performance
Standard 2: Partnering with Families	
2.1: Candidates apply their knowledge of family-centered practices, family systems theory, and the changing needs and priorities in families' lives to develop trusting, respectful, affirming, and culturally responsive partnerships with all families that allow for the mutual exchange of knowledge and information.	• Assessments and tools used by programs to assess student teaching or internship. • Other assessments such as classroom/family communication plans, child and family case studies, role plays, and portfolio projects.
2.2: Candidates communicate clear, comprehensive, and objective information about resources and supports that help families to make informed decisions and advocate for access, participation, and equity in natural and inclusive environments.	• Assessments and tools used by programs to assess student teaching or internship. • Other assessment such as child and family case studies, portfolio projects, family communication plans.
2.3: Candidates engage families in identifying their strengths, priorities, and concerns; support families to achieve the goals they have for their family and their young child's development and learning; and promote families' competence and confidence during assessment, individualized planning, intervention, instruction, and transition processes.	• Assessments and tools used by programs to assess student teaching or internship. • Other assessments such as a family assessment, development of individualized plans with a family member, case studies, and classroom-based action research studies.
Standard 3: Collaboration and Teaming	
3.1: Candidates apply teaming models, skills, and processes, including appropriate uses of technology, when collaborating and communicating with families; professionals representing multiple disciplines, skills, expertise, and roles; and community partners and agencies.	• Assessments and tools used by programs to assess student teaching or internship. • Other assessment such as role plays, collaborative planning, and implementation of team meeting.
3.2: Candidates use a variety of collaborative strategies when working with other adults that are evidence-based, appropriate to the task, culturally and linguistically responsive and take into consideration the environment and service delivery approach.	• Assessments and tools used by programs to assess student teaching or internship. • Other assessments such as case studies, collaborative development of an IEP/IFSP, planning a team meeting, collaborative development, and implementation of an intervention project.
3.3: Candidates partner with families and other professionals to develop individualized plans and support the various transitions that occur for the young child and their family throughout the birth-through-8 age span.	• Assessments and tools used by programs to assess student teaching or internship. • Other assessments such as case studies, collaborative development of an IEP/IFSP or transition plan.

Table 12. Potential Sources of Evidence: Types of Assessments...(continued)	
Components	**Potential Sources of Assessment Evidence for Candidate Performance**
Standard 4: Assessment Processes	
4.1: Candidates understand the purposes of formal and informal assessment including ethical and legal considerations, and use this information to choose developmentally, culturally and linguistically appropriate, valid, reliable tools and methods that are responsive to the characteristics of the young child, family, and program.	• Assessments of planning such as lesson plans, unit plans, need assessments, and/or other planning tasks. • Assessments and tools used by programs to assess student teaching or internship. • An assessment of impact on student learning such as student work samples, performance assessments such as the edTPA, teacher work samples (TWS), case studies of elementary classrooms, and classroom action research studies.
4.2: Candidates develop and administer informal assessments and/or select and use valid, reliable formal assessments using evidence-based practices, including technology, in partnership with families, and other professionals.	• Assessments of planning such as lesson plans, unit plans, need assessments, and/or other planning tasks. • Assessments and tools used by programs to assess student teaching or internship. • An assessment of impact on student learning such as student work samples, performance assessments such as the edTPA, teacher work samples (TWS), case studies of elementary classrooms, and classroom action research studies.
4.3: Candidates analyze, interpret, document and share assessment information using a strengths-based approach with families and other professionals.	• Assessments of planning such as lesson plans, unit plans, need assessments, and/or other planning tasks. • Assessments and tools used by programs to assess student teaching or internship. • An assessment of impact on student learning such as student work samples, performance assessments such as the edTPA, teacher work samples (TWS), case studies of elementary classrooms, and classroom action research studies.
4.4: Candidates, in collaboration with families and other team members, use assessment data to determine eligibility, develop child and family-based outcomes/goals, plan for interventions and instruction, and monitor progress to determine efficacy of programming.	• Assessments of planning such as lesson plans, unit plans, need assessments, and/or other planning tasks. • Assessments and tools used by programs to assess student teaching or internship. • An assessment of impact on student learning such as student work samples, performance assessments such as the edTPA, teacher work samples (TWS), case studies of elementary classrooms, and classroom action research studies.

Table 12. Potential Sources of Evidence: Types of Assessments...(continued)

Components	Potential Sources of Assessment Evidence for Candidate Performance
Standard 5: Application of Curriculum Frameworks in the Planning and Facilitation of Meaningful Learning Experience	
5.1: Candidates collaborate with families and other professionals in identifying an evidence-based curriculum addressing developmental and content domains to design and facilitate meaningful and culturally responsive learning experiences that support the unique abilities and needs of all children and families.	• Assessments of planning such as lesson plans, unit plans, need assessments, and/or other planning tasks. • Assessments and tools used by programs to assess student teaching or internship. • An assessment of impact on student learning such as student work samples, performance assessments such as the edTPA, teacher work samples (TWS), case studies of elementary classrooms, and classroom action research studies.
5.2: Candidates use their knowledge of early childhood curriculum frameworks, developmental and academic content knowledge, and related pedagogy to plan and ensure equitable access to universally designed, developmentally appropriate, and challenging learning experiences in natural and inclusive environments.	• Assessments of planning such as lesson plans, unit plans, need assessments, and/or other planning tasks. • Assessments and tools used by programs to assess student teaching or internship. • An assessment of impact on student learning such as student work samples, performance assessments such as the edTPA, teacher work samples (TWS), case studies of elementary classrooms, and classroom action research studies.
Standard 6: Using Responsive and Reciprocal Interactions, Interventions, and Instruction	
6.1: Candidates, in partnership with families, identify systematic, responsive, and intentional evidence-based practices and use such practices with fidelity to support young children's learning and development across all developmental and academic content domains.	• Assessments of planning such as lesson plans, unit plans, need assessments, and/or other planning tasks. • Assessments and tools used by programs to assess student teaching or internship.
6.2: Candidates engage in reciprocal partnerships with families and other professionals to facilitate responsive adult-child interactions, interventions, and instruction in support of child learning and development.	• Assessments of planning such as lesson plans, unit plans, need assessments, and/or other planning tasks. • Assessments and tools used by programs to assess student teaching or internship.

Components	Potential Sources of Assessment Evidence for Candidate Performance
Table 12. Potential Sources of Evidence: Types of Assessments...(continued)	
Standard 6: Using Responsive and Reciprocal Interactions, Interventions, and Instruction... (continued)	
6.3: Candidates engage in ongoing planning and use flexible and embedded instructional and environmental arrangements and appropriate materials to support the use of interactions, interventions, and instruction addressing developmental and academic content domains, which are adapted to meet the needs of each and every child and their family.	• Assessments of planning such as lesson plans, unit plans, need assessments, and/or other planning tasks. • Assessments and tools used by programs to assess student teaching or internship. • An assessment of impact on student learning such as student work samples, performance assessments such as the edTPA, teacher work samples (TWS), case studies of elementary classrooms, and classroom action research studies.
6.4: Candidates promote young children's social and emotional competence and communication, and proactively plan and implement function-based interventions to prevent and address challenging behaviors.	• Assessments of planning such as lesson plans, unit plans, need assessments, and/or other planning tasks. • Assessments and tools used by programs to assess student teaching or internship. • Other assessments such as case studies, functional behavior assessment, action research projects.
6.5: Candidates identify and create multiple opportunities for young children to develop and learn play skills and engage in meaningful play experiences independently and with others across contexts.	• Assessments of planning such as lesson plans, unit plans, need assessments, and/or other planning tasks. • Assessments and tools used by programs to assess student teaching or internship.
6.6: Candidates use responsive interactions, interventions, and instruction with sufficient intensity and types of support across activities, routines, and environments to promote child learning and development and facilitate access, participation, and engagement in natural environments and inclusive settings.	• Assessments of planning such as lesson plans, unit plans, need assessments, and/or other planning tasks. • Assessments and tools used by programs to assess student teaching or internship. • An assessment of impact on student learning such as student work samples, performance assessments such as the edTPA, teacher work samples (TWS), case studies of elementary classrooms, and classroom action research studies.
6.7: Candidates plan for, adapt, and improve approaches to interactions, interventions, and instruction based on multiple sources of data across a range of natural environments and inclusive settings.	• Assessments of planning such as lesson plans, unit plans, need assessments, and/or other planning tasks. • Assessments and tools used by programs to assess student teaching or internship. • An assessment of impact on student learning such as student work samples, performance assessments such as the edTPA, teacher work samples (TWS), case studies of elementary classrooms, and classroom action research studies.

Table 12. Potential Sources of Evidence: Types of Assessments...(continued)	
Components	**Potential Sources of Assessment Evidence for Candidate Performance**
Standard 7: Professionalism and Ethical Practice	
7.1: Candidates engage with the profession of EI/ECSE by participating in local, regional, national, and/or international activities and professional organizations.	• Other assessments such as portfolio entries that demonstrate candidates' engagement with local, state or national professional and advocacy groups.
7.2: Candidates engage in ongoing reflective practice and access evidence-based information to improve their own practices.	• An assessment of impact on student learning such as student work samples, performance assessments such as the edTPA, teacher work samples (TWS), case studies of elementary classrooms, and classroom action research studies. • Other assessments such as portfolio projects entries that demonstrate candidates' reflective practice.
7.3: Candidates exhibit leadership skills in advocating for improved outcomes for young children, families, and the profession including the promotion of and use of evidenced-based practices and decision-making.	• Other assessments such a portfolio projects that require evidence of candidates' plans for and/or participation in advocacy.
7.4: Candidates practice within ethical and legal policies and procedures.	• Assessments and tools used by programs to assess student teaching or internship. • An assessment of impact on student learning such as student work samples, performance assessments such as the edTPA, teacher work samples (TWS), case studies of elementary classrooms, and classroom action research studies. • Project that requires candidate to review, compare, and contrast multiple professional codes of ethics from professional membership organizations related to education, early childhood education, special education, early intervention/early childhood special education, and/or related services. • Project that requires candidates to review the legal regulations that govern a current topic or issue in early intervention/early childhood special education issue.

Key Assessment Alignment

The matrix on the next page demonstrates a crosswalk between the EI/ECSE Standards and the CAEP national SPA program review structure of 6 – 8 key assessments. Each X in the matrix represents a potential primary source of direct assessment evidence of candidate ability to meet the standard component.

Table 13: Potential Sources of Evidence: Key Assessment Alignment

	Assessment of Content (State Licensure Test)	Assessment of Content	Assessment of Planning Instruction	Assessment of Student Teaching	Assessment of Impact on Learning	Assessment #6	Assessment #7 (Optional)	Assessment #8 (Optional)
Standard 1: Child Development and Early Learning								
1.1	X	X	X	X	X			
1.2	X	X	X	X	X			
1.3	X	X	X	X	X			
1.4	X	X	X	X	X			
Standard 2: Partnering with Families								
2.1				X		X	X	X
2.2				X		X	X	X
2.3				X		X	X	X
Standard 3: Collaboration and Teaming								
3.1				X		X	X	X
3.2				X		X	X	X
3.3				X		X	X	X
Standard 4: Assessment Processes								
4.1			X	X	X			
4.2				X	X			
4.3				X				
4.4			X	X	X			
Standard 5: Application of Curriculum Frameworks in the Planning and Facilitation of Meaningful Learning Experience								
5.1			X	X	X			
5.2			X	X	X			
Standard 6: Using Responsive and Reciprocal Interactions, Interventions, and Instruction								
6.1			X	X				
6.2			X	X				
6.3			X	X	X			
6.4			X	X				
6.5			X	X				
6.6			X	X	X			
6.7			X	X	X			
Standard 7: Professionalism and Ethical Practice								
7.1						X	X	X
7.2					X	X	X	X
7.3						X	X	X
7.4				X	X			

Section 9

Initial Practice-Based Professional Preparation Standards for Gifted Education Professionals

> The Standards included in this section are the same as those included in *What Every Special Educator Must Know: Professional Ethics & Standards* (2015). These will remain in effect until updated versions are published.

For over a decade the National Association for Gifted Children (NAGC) and the Council for Exceptional Children (CEC) Association for the Gifted (TAG) Division have worked collaboratively to develop standards for the preparation of gifted education professionals at the initial and advanced levels. In 2012 NAGC and CEC revised and reordered the gifted education standards to align with new Council for the Accreditation of Educator Preparation (CAEP) guidelines for standards. These realigned standards contain all the substantive knowledge and skills relevant to effective practice in gifted education and continue to emphasize diversity (Johnsen & Clarenbach, 2016); there is no additional specialty set for gifted education. The preparation standards described here are for all programs seeking national recognition for initial and advanced gifted education preparation through the CAEP-NAGC program review process.

Note that all initial gifted education preparation programs must also demonstrate that they meet the Field Experiences and Clinical Practice Standard. The current version of this standard is included below and will be in place until revisions are published. To meet this standard, field and clinical experiences for special education teacher candidates progress through a series of developmentally sequenced field experiences for the full range of ages, types and levels of abilities, and collaborative opportunities that are appropriate to the license or roles for which they are preparing—and students are supervised by qualified professionals throughout these experiences.

Standards for the Initial Preparation of Gifted Education Professionals

Initial Preparation Standard 1: Learner Development and Individual Learning Differences

1.0	Beginning gifted education professionals understand the variations in learning and development in cognitive and affective areas between and among individuals with gifts and talents and apply this understanding to provide meaningful and challenging learning experiences for individuals with exceptionalities.

Key Elements

1.1	Beginning gifted education professionals understand how language, culture, economic status, family background, and area of disability can influence the learning of individuals with exceptionalities.
1.2	Beginning gifted education professionals use understanding of development and individual differences to respond to the needs of individuals with gifts and talents.

Supporting Explanation. Historically, gifted educators have placed the learning needs of the individual at the center of gifted education instruction. Gifted educators alter instructional practices to optimize learning for individuals with gifts and talents. Development of expertise begins with a thorough understanding of and respect for similarities and differences in all areas of human growth and development. Like all educators, beginning gifted educators first respect individuals with gifts and talents within the context of human development and Individual learning differences. Beginning gifted educators understand advanced developmental milestones of individuals with gifts and talents from early childhood through adolescence and also understand how exceptionalities can interact with development and learning and create developmentally appropriate learning environments to provide relevant, meaningful, and challenging learning experiences for individuals with gifts and talents.

Beginning gifted educators understand the variation in characteristics between and among individuals with and without gifts and talents. They know exceptionalities can interact with multiple domains of human development to influence an individual's learning in school, community, and throughout life. Moreover, they understand that the beliefs, traditions, and values across and within cultures can influence relationships among and between students, their families, and the school community. Further, experiences of individuals with exceptionalities can influence their ability to learn, interact socially, and live as fulfilled contributing members of the community. Educators of the gifted understand the phenomenon of underachievement and how it manifests itself in males and females—and they understand techniques for reversing underachievement.

Beginning gifted educators are active and resourceful in seeking to understand how the primary language, culture, family, and areas of disability interact with the gifts and talents to influence the individual's academic and social abilities, attitudes, values, interests, and career and postsecondary options. These learning differences and their interactions provide the foundation upon which beginning gifted educators differentiate instruction to provide developmentally meaningful and challenging learning for individuals with exceptionalities.

Standards for the Initial Preparation of Gifted Education Professionals...(continued)

Initial Preparation Standard 2: Learning Environments

2.0	Beginning gifted education professionals create safe, inclusive, and culturally responsive learning environments so that individuals with gifts and talents become effective learners and develop social and emotional well-being.

Key Elements

2.1	Beginning gifted education professionals create safe, inclusive, culturally responsive learning environments that engage individuals with gifts and talents in meaningful and rigorous learning activities and social interactions.
2.2	Beginning gifted education professionals use communication and motivational and instructional interventions to facilitate understanding of subject matter and to teach individuals with gifts and talents how to adapt to different environments and develop ethical leadership skills.
2.3	Beginning gifted education professionals adjust their communication to an individual's language proficiency and cultural and linguistic differences.
2.4	Beginning gifted education professionals demonstrate understanding of the multiple environments that are part of a continuum of services for individuals with gifts and talents, including the advantages and disadvantages of various settings.

Supporting Explanation. Like all educators, beginning gifted educators develop safe, inclusive, culturally responsive learning environments for all students. They also collaborate with colleagues in general education and other specialized environments that develop students' gifts and talents, engaging gifted students in meaningful learning activities that enhance independence, interdependence, and positive peer relationships.

Beginning gifted educators modify learning environments for individual needs. Knowledge regarding the interaction of an individual's language, family, culture, areas of disability, and other significant contextual factors with an individual's gifts and talents guides the beginning gifted educator in modifying learning environments and provides for the maintenance and generalization of acquired skills across environments and subjects. They adjust their communication methods to an individual's language proficiency. They value and are responsive to cultural and linguistic differences, avoiding discrimination, stereotyping, and deficit views of differences.

Beginning gifted educators structure environments to encourage self-awareness, self-regulation, self-efficacy, self-direction, personal empowerment, leadership, and self-advocacy of individuals with gifts and talents, and directly teach them how to adapt to the expectations and demands of differing environments.

Initial Preparation Standard 3: Curricular Content Knowledge	
3.0	Beginning gifted education professionals use knowledge of general and specialized curricula to advance learning for individuals with gifts and talents.
Key Elements	
3.1	Beginning gifted education professionals understand the role of central concepts, structures of the discipline, and tools of inquiry of the content areas they teach, and use their understanding to organize knowledge, integrate cross-disciplinary skills, and develop meaningful learning progressions within and across grade levels.
3.2	Beginning gifted education professionals design appropriate learning and performance modifications for individuals with gifts and talents that enhance creativity, acceleration, depth and complexity in academic subject matter and specialized domains.
3.3	Beginning gifted education professionals use assessments to select, adapt, and create materials to differentiate instructional strategies and general and specialized curricula to challenge individuals with gifts and talents.
3.4	Beginning gifted education professionals understand that individuals with gifts and talents demonstrate a wide range of advanced knowledge and performance levels and modify the general or specialized curriculum appropriately.

Supporting Explanation. The professional knowledge base in general education clearly indicates that educators' understanding of the central concepts and structure of the discipline and tools of inquiry related to the academic subject-matter content areas they teach makes a significant difference in student learning.

Within the general curricula, beginning gifted educators demonstrate in their planning and teaching a solid foundation of understanding of the theories, central concepts and principles, structures of the discipline, and tools of inquiry of the academic subject-matter content areas they teach so they are able to organize knowledge, integrate cross-disciplinary skills, develop meaningful learning progressions, and collaborate with educators in:

• Using and interpreting assessments to select, adapt, and create materials to differentiate instructional strategies and general and specialized curricula to challenge individuals with gifts and talents.

• Teaching the content of the general or specialized curriculum to individuals with gifts and talents across advanced performance levels.

• Designing appropriate learning and performance modifications for individuals with gifts and talents in academic subject matter and specialized content domains that incorporate advanced, conceptually challenging, in-depth, distinctive, and/or complex content.

• In addition, beginning gifted educators use a variety of specialized curricula to individualize meaningful and challenging learning for individuals with exceptionalities.

Standards for the Initial Preparation of Gifted Education Professionals...(continued)

Initial Preparation Standard 4: Assessment

4.0	Beginning gifted education professionals use multiple methods of assessment and data sources in making educational decisions about identification and learning.

Key Elements

4.1	Beginning gifted education professionals understand that some groups of individuals with gifts and talents have been underrepresented in gifted education programs and select and use technically sound formal and informal assessments that minimize bias.
4.2	Beginning gifted education professionals use knowledge of measurement principles and practices to differentiate assessments and interpret results to guide educational decisions for individuals with gifts and talents.
4.3	Beginning gifted education professionals collaborate with colleagues and families in using multiple types of assessment information to make identification and learning progress decisions and to minimize bias in assessment and decision-making.
4.4	Beginning gifted education professionals use assessment results to develop long- and short-range goals and objectives that take into consideration an individual's abilities and needs, the learning environment, and other factors related to diversity.
4.5	Beginning gifted education professionals engage individuals with gifts and talents in assessing the quality of their own learning and performance and in setting future goals and objectives.

Supporting Explanation. Beginning gifted educators understand measurement theory and practice for addressing issues of validity, reliability, norms, bias, and interpretation of assessment results. Bias may occur within quantitative assessments that do not have technical adequacy and from barriers within identification procedures such as low teacher expectations, exclusive definitions, and a focus on deficits rather than strengths (Ford, 1998; Ryser, 2011). Beginning gifted educators understand the appropriate use and limitations of various types of assessments and collaborate with families and other colleagues to ensure nonbiased, meaningful assessments and decision-making.

Beginning gifted educators understand the policies and ethical principles of measurement and assessment related to gifted education referral or nomination, identification, program planning, differentiated instruction, learning progress, and services for individuals with gifts and talents, including individuals with culturally, linguistically, and economically diverse backgrounds. Beginning gifted educators select and use quantitative and qualitative assessment information to support a wide variety of decisions within gifted education. They conduct formal and informal assessments of behavior, learning, achievement, and environments to differentiate the learning experiences and document the growth of individuals with gifts and talents. Moreover, they differentiate assessments to identify above level performances and to accelerate and enrich the general curriculum.

Beginning gifted educators use available technologies routinely to support their assessments and employ a variety of assessments such as performance-based assessment, portfolios, and computer simulations. Using these data, beginning gifted educators make multiple types of assessment decisions including strategic adaptations and modifications in response to an individuals' constellation of social, linguistic, and learning factors in ways to minimize bias. They also use the results of assessments to identify above-level performance, develop long-range instructional plans anchored in both general and specialized curricula, and translate these plans into carefully selected shorter-range goals and objectives to differentiate and accelerate instruction. Moreover, beginning gifted educators engage individuals with gifts and talents in assessing the quality of their own learning and performance and in providing feedback to guide them in setting future goals.

Like their general education colleagues, beginning gifted educators regularly monitor the learning progress of individuals with gifts and talents in both general and specialized content and make instructional adjustments based on these data.

Standards for the Initial Preparation of Gifted Education Professionals...(continued)	
Initial Preparation Standard 5: Instructional Planning and Strategies	
5.0	Beginning gifted education professionals select, adapt, and use a repertoire of evidence-based instructional strategies to advance the learning of individuals with gifts and talents.
Key Elements	
5.1	Beginning gifted education professionals know principles of evidence-based, differentiated, and accelerated practices and possess a repertoire of instructional strategies to enhance the critical and creative thinking, problem-solving, and performance skills of individuals with gifts and talents.
5.2	Beginning gifted education professionals apply appropriate technologies to support instructional assessment, planning, and delivery for individuals with gifts and talents.
5.3	Beginning gifted education professionals collaborate with families, professional colleagues, and other educators to select, adapt, and use evidence-based strategies that promote challenging learning opportunities in general and specialized curricula.
5.4	Beginning gifted education professionals emphasize the development, practice, and transfer of advanced knowledge and skills across environments throughout the lifespan leading to creative, productive careers in a multicultural society for individuals with gifts and talents.
5.5	Beginning gifted education professionals use instructional strategies that enhance the affective development of individuals with gifts and talents.

Supporting Explanation. In the selection, development, and adaptation of learning experiences for individuals with gifts and talents, beginning gifted educators consider an individual's abilities, interests, learning environments, and cultural and linguistic factors to achieve positive learning results in general and special curricula. Understanding these factors, curriculum models, and the implications of being recognized as gifted and talented guides the educator's development of scope and sequence plans; selection, adaptation, and creation of learning activities; pace of instruction; and use of differentiated evidence-based instructional strategies.

Beginning gifted educators possess a repertoire of evidence-based strategies to differentiate and accelerate the curriculum for individuals with gifts and talents. They select, adapt, and use these strategies to promote challenging learning opportunities in general and special curricula and to modify learning environments to enhance self-awareness, self-regulation, and self-efficacy for individuals with gifts and talents.

They enhance 21st-century student outcomes such as critical and creative thinking, problem solving, collaboration, and performance skills in specific domains and allow individuals with gifts and talents opportunities to explore, develop or research their areas of interest or talent.

Beginning gifted educators also emphasize the development, practice, and transfer of advanced knowledge and skills across environments throughout the lifespan leading to creative, productive careers in society for individuals with gifts and talents. Moreover, beginning gifted educators facilitate these actions in a collaborative context that includes individuals with gifts and talents, families, professional colleagues, and personnel from other agencies as appropriate. They are familiar with alternative and augmentative communication systems and are comfortable using technologies to support language and communication, instructional planning and differentiated instruction for individuals with exceptionalities.

Standards for the Initial Preparation of Gifted Education Professionals...(continued)	
Initial Preparation Standard 6: Professional Learning and Ethical Practice	
6.0	Beginning gifted education professionals use foundational knowledge of the field and professional ethical principles and program standards (NAGC, 2010) to inform gifted education practice, to engage in lifelong learning, and to advance the profession.
Key Elements	
6.1	Beginning gifted education professionals use professional ethical principles and specialized program standards to guide their practice.
6.2	Beginning gifted education professionals understand how foundational knowledge, perspectives, and historical and current issues influence professional practice and the education and treatment of individuals with gifts and talents both in school and society.
6.3	Beginning gifted education professionals model respect for diversity, understanding that it is an integral part of society's institutions and impacts learning of individuals with gifts and talents in the delivery of gifted education services.
6.4	Beginning gifted education professionals are aware of their own professional learning needs, understand the significance of lifelong learning, and participate in professional activities and learning communities.
6.5	Beginning gifted education professionals advance the profession by engaging in activities such as advocacy and mentoring.

Supporting Explanation. Beginning gifted educators practice in multiple roles and complex situations across wide age and developmental ranges, which requires ongoing attention to legal matters and serious consideration of professional and ethical issues. Ethical principles and program standards guide beginning gifted educators. These principles and standards provide benchmarks by which gifted educators practice and professionally evaluate each other.

Beginning gifted educators understand gifted education as an evolving and changing discipline based on philosophies, evidence-based principles and theories, policies, historical points of view that continue to influence the field of gifted education and the education of and services for individuals with gifts and talents and their families in both school and society. Beginning gifted educators understand how these factors influence professional practice, including assessment, instructional planning, services, and program evaluation.

Beginning gifted educators understand the aspects of human diversity and equity as related to academic diversity. They understand aspects of human diversity and equity regarding individuals identified as gifted and talented as well as those who have potential of being identified gifted and talented.

Beginning gifted educators are sensitive to the aspects of diversity of individuals with gifts and talents and their families, how human diversity can influence families, cultures, and schools, and how these complex issues can each interact with the delivery of gifted education services. Of special significance is the growth in the number and prevalence of ELLs and economically disadvantaged students, and the provision of effective gifted education services for these students with exceptionalities and their families. Beginning gifted educators also understand historical relationships of gifted education services related to diversity and equity and the organization of schools, school systems, and education-related agencies within the culture in which they practice.

Beginning gifted educators understand the relationships of the organization of gifted education services to the organization of schools, school systems, and education-related agencies within cultures in which they practice. They are aware of how their own and others' attitudes, behaviors, and ways of communicating can influence their practice, and use this knowledge as a foundation to inform their own personal understandings and philosophies of special education.

Beginning gifted educators engage in professional activities and participate actively in professional learning communities that benefit individuals with gifts and talents, their families, colleagues, and their own professional growth. They view themselves as lifelong learners and regularly reflect on and adjust their practice and develop and use personalized professional development plans. They plan and engage in activities that foster their professional growth and keep them current with evidence-based practices and know how to recognize their own skill limits and practice within them. They place particular emphasis on professional activities that focus on human diversity and academic diversity in all its manifestations. Moreover, educators of the gifted embrace their special role as advocates for individuals with gifts and talents. They promote and advocate for the learning and well-being of individuals with gifts and talents across multiple and varied settings through diverse learning experiences.

Standards for the Initial Preparation of Gifted Education Professionals...(continued)	
Initial Preparation Standard 7: Collaboration	
7.0	Beginning gifted education professionals collaborate with families, other educators, related service providers, individuals with gifts and talents, and personnel from community agencies in culturally responsive ways to address the needs of individuals with gifts and talents across a range of learning experiences.
Key Elements	
7.1	Beginning gifted education professionals apply elements of effective collaboration.
7.2	Beginning gifted education professionals serve as a collaborative resource with colleagues.
7.3	Beginning gifted education professionals use collaboration to promote the well-being of individuals with gifts and talents across a wide range of settings and collaborators.

Supporting Explanation. One of the significant changes in education over the past several decades is the rapid growth of collaborative educational teams to address the educational needs of students. The diversity of the students, complexity of curricular demands, growing influence of technology, and the rising targets for learner outcomes in the 21st century has created the demand for teams of educators collaborating together to ensure all students are effectively learning challenging curricula.

Beginning gifted educators embrace their role as a resource to colleagues and use the theory and elements of collaboration across a wide range of contexts and collaborators. They use culturally responsive behaviors that promote effective communication and collaboration with individuals with gifts and talents, their families, school personnel, and community members. They collaborate with their general education and other special education colleagues to create learning environments that meaningfully include individuals with gifts and talents, and that foster cultural understanding, safety and emotional well-being, positive social interactions, and active engagement. In addition, beginning gifted educators use collaboration to facilitate differentiated assessment and instructional planning to advance learning of individuals with gifts and talents across a wide range of settings and different learning experiences. They routinely collaborate with other educators in developing mentorships, internships, and vocational programming experiences to address the needs of individuals with gifts and talents.

Gifted educators have long recognized the positive significance of the active involvement of individuals with gifts and talents and their families in the education process, and gifted educators involve individuals with gifts and talents and their families collaboratively in all aspects of the education of individuals with gifts and talents.

Field Experience and Clinical Practice Standard for Initial Preparation Programs

Field experience sites are developed and enhanced over time through the building strong relationships and partnerships between special educators in field experience settings and college and university special education faculty. Through collaboration and consultation, the placement of candidates is selected to provide developmental field experiences that support candidate learning. Field experiences are supervised and mentored by school-based professionals who are certified or licensed in the special education areas for which the candidate is being prepared. In addition, field experiences are supervised and evaluated by university faculty.

Field experiences are designed to link theory to practice and provide rich, scaffolded, developmental, and graduated experiences with increasing responsibility for prospective special educators. Field experience-based activities and assignments develop candidates' knowledge and skills. Performance assessments of candidates as they interact with, instruct, guide, correct, and support students in the field experience settings are ongoing and developmentally appropriate. Field experiences are structured, varied and ensure that the candidate has experiences with individuals with a given set of specific exceptionalities across the age, grade, and severity range(s) for which the candidate is being prepared. Candidates participate in field experiences across the preparation program. Field experiences are connected and sufficiently extensive and intensive for candidates to develop and demonstrate proficiencies in the professional roles for which they are preparing.

Site-based professionals, in addition to being certified or licensed in the special education areas for which the candidate is being prepared, are selected for their expertise and experience with the individuals and services for which the candidate is preparing. Site-based professionals demonstrate mentoring skills in supporting the learning of candidates. These site-based professionals effectively communicate with and support candidates in field experiences.

Section 10

Standards for the Preparation of Advanced Gifted Education Specialists

After mastering initial standards for the preparation of teachers of the gifted, many educators in gifted education continue their professional growth toward mastery of advanced professional standards at the post-baccalaureate levels. For some this means deepening their understandings and expertise and adding new responsibilities for leadership within the classroom. Some educators in gifted education assume functions outside the classroom, moving into specializations, administering gifted education programs and services, or moving into teacher preparation and research roles.

Regardless of the specific role, educators in advanced roles share an array of functions and responsibilities in common. Reflecting this commonality, the National Association for Gifted Children, the Council for Exceptional Children, and the Association for the Gifted have approved knowledge and skills that all teachers in gifted education have mastered as a part of their preparation for advanced professional practice.

The seven Advanced Preparation Standards are described in this section.

Standards for the Preparation of Advanced Gifted Education Specialists	
Advanced Preparation Standard 1: Assessment	
1.0	Gifted education specialists use valid and reliable assessment practices to minimize bias.
Key Elements	
1.1	Gifted education specialists review, select, and interpret psychometrically sound, nonbiased, qualitative and quantitative instruments to identify individuals with gifts and talents and assess their abilities, strengths, and interests.
1.2	Gifted education specialists monitor the progress of individuals with gifts and talents in the general education and specialized curricula.

Supporting Explanation. Assessment is an essential part of the advanced roles of gifted education specialists. Underlying assessment is the knowledge of systems and theories of educational assessment, along with skills in examining the technical adequacy of instruments and the implementation of evidence-based practices in assessment. It is critical that assessments that minimize bias are used in the selection of instruments, methods, and procedures for both programs and individuals. With respect to assessment of individuals with gifts and talents, gifted education specialists in advanced roles apply their knowledge and skill to all stages and purposes of assessment, including identification of abilities, strengths, and interests and in monitoring and reporting learning progress in the general education curriculum as well as in the specialized curriculum in their gifted education placement.

Advanced Preparation Standard 2: Curricular Content Knowledge

2.0	Gifted education specialists use their knowledge of general and specialized curricula to improve programs, supports, and services at classroom, school, community, and system levels.
Key Elements	
2.1	Gifted education specialists align educational standards to provide access to challenging curriculum to meet the needs individuals with exceptionalities.
2.2	Gifted educators continuously broaden and deepen professional knowledge and expand expertise with instructional technologies, curriculum standards, effective teaching strategies, and assistive technologies to support access to and learning of challenging content.
2.3	Gifted education specialists use understanding of diversity and individual learning differences to inform the selection, development, and implementation of comprehensive curricula for individuals with exceptionalities.

Supporting Explanation. Gifted education specialists use their deep understanding of educational standards within and across domains to provide access to challenging curriculum to meet the needs of individuals with exceptionalities. Gifted education specialists continuously broaden and deepen their professional knowledge, and expand their expertise with technologies, curriculum standards, effective teaching strategies, and assistive technologies to support learning. Gifted education specialists understand how individual learning differences and diversity inform the selection, development, and implementation of comprehensive and cohesive curricula for individuals with exceptionalities.

Standards for the Preparation of Advanced Gifted Education Specialists...(continued)	
Advanced Preparation Standard 3: Programs, Services, and Outcomes	
3.0	Gifted education specialists facilitate the continuous improvement of general and gifted education programs, supports, and services at the classroom, school, and system levels for individuals with exceptionalities.
Key Elements	
3.1	Gifted education specialists design and implement evaluation activities to improve programs, supports, and services for individuals with exceptionalities.
3.2	Gifted education specialists use their understanding of cultural, social, and economic diversity and individual learner differences to inform the development and improvement of programs, supports, and services for individuals with exceptionalities.
3.3	Gifted education specialists apply knowledge of theories, evidence-based practices, relevant laws, and policies to advocate for programs, supports, and a continuum of services for individuals with exceptionalities.
3.4	Gifted education specialists design and develop systematic program and curriculum models for enhancing talent development in multiple settings.
3.5	Gifted education specialists evaluate progress toward achieving the vision, mission, and goals of programs, services, and supports for individuals with exceptionalities.

Supporting Explanation. Effective gifted educators in advanced roles design and implement research activities to evaluate the effectiveness of instructional practices and to assess progress toward the organizational vision, mission, and goals of their programs. They develop procedures for continuous improvement management systems. They use their understanding of the effects of cultural, social, and economic diversity and variations of individual development to inform their development of programs and services for individuals with exceptional learning needs. Gifted educators in advanced roles apply their knowledge of cognitive science, learning theory, and instructional technologies to improve instructional programs at the school- and system-wide levels. They provide for a continuum of services to ensure the appropriate instructional supports for individuals with exceptional learning needs. They use their deep understanding of educational standards to help all individuals with exceptional learning needs access challenging curriculum.

Advanced Preparation Standard 4: Research and Inquiry	
4.0	Gifted education specialists conduct, evaluate, and use inquiry to guide professional practice.
Key Elements	
4.1	Gifted education specialists evaluate theory, research and inquiry to identify effective practices.
4.2	Gifted education specialists use knowledge of the professional literature to improve practices with individuals with exceptionalities and their families.
4.3	Gifted education specialists evaluate and modify instructional practices in response to ongoing assessment data and engage in the design and implementation of research and inquiry.

Supporting Explanation. Research and inquiry inform the decisions of gifted educators in advanced roles in guiding professional practice. Gifted educators in advanced roles know models, theories, philosophies, and research methods that form the basis for evidence-based practices in gifted education. This knowledge includes information sources, data collection, and data analysis strategies. Gifted educators in advanced roles evaluate the appropriateness of research methodologies in relation to practices presented in the literature. They use educational research to improve instructional techniques, intervention strategies, and curricular materials. They foster an environment supportive of continuous instructional improvement and engage in the design and implementation of action research. Gifted educators in advanced roles are able to use the literature to resolve issues of professional practice and help others understand various evidence-based practices.

Standards for the Preparation of Advanced Gifted Education Specialists...(continued)

Advanced Preparation Standard 5: Leadership and Policy

5.0	Gifted education specialists provide leadership to formulate goals, set and meet high professional expectations, advocate for effective policies and evidence-based practices, and create positive and productive work environments.
Key Elements	
5.1	Gifted education specialists encourage high expectations, model respect for, and use ethical practices with all individuals with exceptionalities.
5.2	Gifted education specialists support and use linguistically and culturally responsive practices.
5.3	Gifted education specialists create and maintain collegial and productive work environments that respect and safeguard the rights of individuals with exceptionalities and their families.
5.4	Gifted education specialists advocate for policies and practices that improve programs, services, and outcomes for individuals with exceptionalities.
5.5	Gifted education specialists advocate for the allocation of appropriate resources for the preparation and professional development of all personnel who serve individuals with exceptionalities.

Supporting Explanation. Gifted educators in advanced roles promote high professional self-expectations and help others understand the needs of individuals with exceptional learning needs within the context of an organization's mission. They advocate for laws based on solid evidence-based knowledge to support high-quality education for individuals with exceptional learning needs, and for appropriate resources to ensure that all personnel involved have effective preparation. Gifted educators in advanced roles use their knowledge of organizational theory and the needs of different groups in a pluralistic society to formulate organizational goals promoting evidence-based practices and challenging expectations for individuals with exceptional learning needs. They provide leadership to create procedures that respect all individuals and permit professionals to practice ethically. They create positive and productive work environments and celebrate accomplishments with colleagues.

	Advanced Preparation Standard 6: Professional and Ethical Practice
6.0	Gifted education specialists use foundational knowledge of the field and professional ethical principles and program standards to inform gifted education practice, engage in life-long learning, advance the profession, and perform leadership responsibilities to promote the success of professional colleagues and individuals with exceptionalities.
Key Elements	
6.1	A comprehensive understanding of the history of gifted education, legal policies, ethical standards, and emerging issues informs gifted education specialist leadership.
6.2	Gifted education specialists model high professional expectations and ethical practice and create supportive environments that increase diversity at all levels of gifted and talented education.
6.3	Gifted education specialists model and promote respect for all individuals and facilitate ethical professional practice.
6.4	Gifted education specialists actively participate in professional development and learning communities to increase professional knowledge and expertise.
6.5	Gifted education specialists plan, present, and evaluate professional development focusing on effective and ethical practice at all organizational levels.
6.6	Gifted education specialists actively facilitate and participate in the preparation and induction of prospective gifted educators.
6.7	Gifted education specialists actively promote the advancement of the profession.

Supporting Explanation. Gifted education specialists in advanced roles have a comprehensive knowledge of gifted education as an evolving and changing discipline based on philosophies, evidence-based principles and theories, relevant laws and policies, diverse and historical points of view, and issues that have influenced and continue to influence gifted education and the education of and services for individuals with exceptionalities both in school and in society. They are guided by professional ethics and practice standards. In their advanced roles gifted educators have leadership responsibilities for promoting the success of individuals with exceptional learning needs, their families, and colleagues. They create supportive environments that safeguard the legal rights of students, families, and school personnel through policies and procedures that promote ethical and professional practice. Gifted educators in advanced roles continuously broaden and deepen their professional knowledge, and expand their expertise with instructional technologies, curriculum, effective teaching strategies, and assistive technologies to support access to learning. Gifted educators in advanced roles plan, present, and evaluate professional development based on models that apply adult learning theories and focus on effective practice at all organizational levels. They are actively involved in the preparation and induction of prospective gifted educators. Gifted educators in advanced roles model their own commitment to continuously improving their own professional practice by participating in professional development themselves and promote the advancement of the profession.

Standards for the Preparation of Advanced Gifted Education Specialists...(continued)

Advanced Preparation Standard 7: Collaboration

7.0	Gifted education specialists collaborate with stakeholders to improve programs, services, and outcomes for individuals with gifts and talents and their families.

Key Elements

7.1	Gifted education specialists use culturally responsive practices to enhance collaboration.
7.2	Gifted education specialists use collaborative skills to improve programs, services, and outcomes for individuals with exceptionalities.
7.3	Gifted education specialists collaborate to promote understanding, resolve conflicts, and build consensus for improving program, services, and outcomes for individuals with exceptionalities.

Supporting Explanation. Gifted educators in advanced roles have a deep understanding of the centrality and importance of consultation and collaboration to the roles within gifted education, and they use this deep understanding to improve programs, services and outcomes for individuals with exceptional learning needs. They also understand the significance of the role of collaboration and apply their skill to promote understanding, resolve conflicts, and build consensus among both internal and external stakeholders to provide services to individuals with exceptional learning needs and their families. They possess current knowledge of research on stages and models in both collaboration and consultation and ethical and legal issues related to consultation and collaboration. Moreover, gifted educators in advanced roles have a deep understanding of the possible interactions of language, diversity, culture and religion with contextual factors and how to use collaboration and consultation to enhance opportunities for individuals with exceptional learning needs.

Section 11

Standards for the Preparation of Advanced Special Education Professionals

> The Standards included in this section are the same as those included in *What Every Special Educator Must Know: Professional Ethics & Standards* (2015). These will remain in effect until updated versions are published.

CEC advanced level preparation programs are designed for candidates who are already licensed special educators and seeking training in a new role, such as an educational diagnostician or transition specialist, or in special education administration. These programs may be at the master's, specialist, or doctoral level. Programs are expected to use these standards in the development of their curriculum and key assessments, as informed by the specialty set (https://exceptionalchildren.org/standards/specialty-sets-specific-practice-areas) appropriate to each program. CEC has developed specialty sets for 12 special education advanced roles. The advanced standards are built on the assumption that candidates in these programs are trained special educators and have already demonstrated their mastery of the CEC initial preparation standards.

Standards for the Preparation of Advanced Gifted Education Specialists

Advanced Preparation Standard 1: Assessment

1.0	Special education specialists use valid and reliable assessment practices to minimize bias.
Key Elements	
1.1	Special education specialists minimize bias in assessment.
1.2	Special education specialists design and implement assessments to evaluate the effectiveness of practices and programs.

Supporting Explanation. The raison d'être for special education lies in the specialized professional knowledge and skills to individualize or personalize learning in both specialized and general curricula for individuals with exceptionalities. Since its earliest days, special education has been based on the understanding of individuals with exceptionalities and the contexts in which they live and learn in order to plan for their education. This begins with the understanding of and respect for similarities and differences in human growth and development, and it extends to designing and implementing assessments to evaluate the effectiveness of practices and programs. To ensure relevant and valid assessment information, nonbiased procedures are critical in the selection of assessment instruments, methods, and procedures for both individuals and programs. Frequently, special education specialists are a resource to school teams in selecting accommodations in assessments to minimize bias and ensure validity.

Special education specialists bring experience and engage in reflection to inform their understanding of human diversity and its influence on families, cultures, and schools, and their interaction with the delivery of education services. They use this experience to personalize instruction for individuals with exceptionalities. The identification and use of strategic accommodations and modifications depend on the understanding of specific individuals and their contexts.

With respect to assessment of individuals with exceptionalities, special education specialists apply their knowledge and skill to all stages and purposes of assessment in decision making regarding: prereferral and screening, pre-placement for special education eligibility, and monitoring and reporting learning progress in the general education curriculum and in other individualized education program goals.

Standards for the Preparation of Advanced Gifted Education Specialists...(continued)

Advanced Preparation Standard 2: Curricular Content Knowledge

2.0	Special education specialists use their knowledge of general and specialized curricula to improve programs, supports, and services at classroom, school, community, and system levels.

Key Elements

2.1	Special education specialists align educational standards to provide access to challenging curriculum to meet the needs of individuals with exceptionalities.
2.2	Special educators continuously broaden and deepen their professional knowledge and expand their expertise with instructional technologies, curriculum standards, effective teaching strategies, and assistive technologies to support access to and learning of challenging content.
2.3	Special education specialists use understanding of diversity and individual learning differences to inform the selection, development, and implementation of comprehensive curricula for individuals with exceptionalities.

Supporting Explanation. Special education specialists have a comprehensive knowledge of special education as an evolving and changing discipline based on philosophies, evidence-based principles and theories, relevant laws and policies, diverse and historical points of view, and issues that have influenced and continue to influence special education and the education of and services for individuals with exceptionalities both in school and in society. Special education specialists use their deep understanding of how to coordinate educational standards to the needs of individuals with exceptionalities to support all individuals with exceptionalities to access challenging curriculum standards.

Special education specialists work within the limits of their professional skill to facilitate access to the general education curricula and specialized supplementary curricula (e.g., academic, strategic, social-emotional, transition, independence) to individualize meaningful and challenging learning for individuals with exceptionalities. They continuously broaden and deepen their professional knowledge and expand their expertise with instructional, augmentative and assistive technologies, curriculum standards, and effective teaching strategies to support learning.

	Advanced Preparation Standard 3: Programs, Services, and Outcomes
3.0	Special education specialists facilitate the continuous improvement of general and special education programs, supports, and services at the classroom, school, and system levels for individuals with exceptionalities.
	Key Elements
3.1	Special education specialists design and implement evaluation activities to improve programs, supports, and services for individuals with exceptionalities.
3.2	Special education specialists use understanding of cultural, social, and economic diversity and individual learner differences to inform the development and improvement of programs, supports, and services for individuals with exceptionalities.
3.3	Special education specialists apply knowledge of theories, evidence-based practices, and relevant laws to advocate for programs, supports, and services for individuals with exceptionalities.
3.4	Special education specialists apply knowledge of theories, evidence-based practices, and relevant laws to advocate for programs, supports, and services for individuals with exceptionalities.
3.5	Special education specialists use instructional and assistive technologies to improve programs, supports, and services for individuals with exceptionalities.

Supporting Explanation. Special education specialists apply their knowledge of cognitive and behavioral science, learning theory, evidence-based practice, and instructional technologies to improve programs, services, and supports for individuals with exceptionalities. They continuously broaden and deepen their professional knowledge and expand their expertise with instructional, augmentative, and assistive technologies, curriculum standards, and effective teaching strategies to support access to learning.

Special education specialists use their understanding of the effects of cultural, social, and economic diversity and variations of individual development to inform their development of a continuum of programs and services to ensure the appropriate instructional supports for individuals with exceptionalities and their families. They have a sufficient facility with the breadth and scope of instructional augmentative and assistive technologies to be able to select options that will improve programs, supports, and services for individuals with exceptionalities and their families, and facilitate others' selection and use.

Standards for the Preparation of Advanced Gifted Education Specialists...(continued)	
Advanced Preparation Standard 4: Research and Inquiry	
4.0	Special education specialists conduct, evaluate, and use inquiry to guide professional practice.
Key Elements	
4.1	Special education specialists evaluate research and inquiry to identify effective practices.
4.2	Special education specialists use their knowledge of the professional literature to improve practices with individuals with exceptionalities and their families.
4.3	Special education specialists foster an environment that is supportive of continuous instructional improvement and engage in the design and implementation of research and inquiry.

Supporting Explanation. Research and inquiry inform the professional practice of special education specialists. As professionals, special education specialists view science as the principal source for information on effective practice. Special education specialists know the models, theories, philosophies, and research methods that form the basis for evidence-based practices in special education, and they use research to improve instructional techniques, intervention strategies, and curricula. Special education specialists evaluate the appropriateness of research methodologies in relation to the validation of practices and use the literature to inform professional practice.

Special education specialists foster a collegial environment supportive of continuous instructional improvement and engage in the design and implementation of research with professional colleagues. In addition, they design and implement research and evaluation activities to evaluate progress toward the organizational vision, mission, and goal, and the effectiveness of programs, services, and supports for individuals with exceptionalities.

Advanced Preparation Standard 5: Leadership and Policy

5.0	Special education specialists provide leadership to formulate goals, set and meet high professional expectations, advocate for effective policies and evidence-based practices, and create positive and productive work environments.
Key Elements	
5.1	Special education specialists model respect and ethical practice for all individuals and encourage challenging expectations for individuals with exceptionalities.
5.2	Special education specialists support and use linguistically and culturally responsive practices.
5.3	Special education specialists create and maintain collegial and productive work environments that respect and safeguard the rights of individuals with exceptionalities and their families.
5.4	Special education specialists advocate for policies and practices that improve programs, services, and outcomes for individuals with exceptionalities.
5.5	Special education specialists advocate for the allocation of appropriate resources for the preparation and professional development of all personnel who serve individuals with exceptionalities.

Supporting Explanation. Special education specialists model respect for all individuals and encourage challenging expectations for individuals with exceptionalities. Special education specialists use their knowledge of the needs of different groups in a pluralistic society to support and use linguistically and culturally responsive practices, and to promote evidence-based practices and challenging expectations for individuals with exceptionalities.

Special education specialists hold high professional self-expectations and help others more completely understand the needs of individuals with exceptionalities. They create and maintain collegial and productive work environments that respect and safeguard the rights of individuals with exceptionalities and their families. In addition, special education specialists support quality education for individuals with exceptionalities and advocate for policy based on solid scientific evidence. They also advocate for appropriate resources to ensure that all personnel involved have effective preparation. They mentor others and promote high expectations for themselves, other professionals, and individuals with exceptionalities.

Standards for the Preparation of Advanced Gifted Education Specialists...(continued)

Advanced Preparation Standard 6: Professional and Ethical Practice

6.0	Special education specialists use foundational knowledge of the field and professional ethical principles and practice standards to inform special education practice, engage in lifelong learning, advance the profession, and perform leadership responsibilities to promote the success of professional colleagues and individuals with exceptionalities.
Key Elements	
6.1	A comprehensive understanding of the history of special education, legal policies, ethical standards, and emerging issues informs special education specialist leadership.
6.2	Special education specialists model high professional expectations and ethical practice and create supportive environments that safeguard the legal rights and improve outcomes for individuals with exceptionalities and their families.
6.3	Special education specialists model and promote respect for all individuals and facilitate ethical professional practice.
6.4	Special education specialists actively participate in professional development and professional learning communities to increase professional knowledge and expertise.
6.5	Special education specialists plan, present, and evaluate professional development focusing on effective and ethical practice at all organizational levels.
6.6	Special education specialists actively facilitate and participate in the preparation and induction of prospective special educators.
6.7	Special education specialists actively promote the advancement of the profession.

Supporting Explanation. A deep understanding of the history of special education, legal policies, ethical standards, and emerging issues informs the leadership of special education specialists. They use this broad foundation to construct their own professional understanding of special education professional practice and to facilitate others' understanding of the education of and services for individuals with exceptionalities and their families, in both school and society.

Special education specialists understand how and why special education organizes its programs and services in relation to school systems and other agencies. They model and facilitate high professional expectations and ethical practice to create supportive environments that safeguard the legal rights and improve outcomes for individuals with exceptionalities and their families.

They design and deliver ongoing professional development designed to improve practice at all relevant organizational levels. Special education specialists plan, present, and evaluate professional development based on models that apply the principles of adult learning theory and focus on the use of effective practice at all organizational levels.

Special education specialists view themselves as lifelong learners and model their commitment to improving their own professional practice by continual participation in professional development. Special education specialists actively plan and engage in activities that foster their own as well as their colleagues' professional growth with evidence-based practices. In addition, they develop and use personalized professional development plans and facilitate their colleagues' development and use of personalized professional development plans.

Special education specialists recognize their responsibility to promote the advancement of the profession including facilitating and participating in the preparation and induction of prospective special educators.

Advanced Preparation Standard 7: Collaboration	
7.0	Special education specialists collaborate with stakeholders to improve programs, services, and outcomes for individuals with exceptionalities and their families.
Key Elements	
7.1	Special education specialists use culturally responsive practices to enhance collaboration.
7.2	Special education specialists use collaborative skills to improve programs, services, and outcomes for individuals with exceptionalities.
7.3	Special education specialists collaborate to promote understanding, resolve conflicts, and build consensus for improving programs, services, and outcomes for individuals with exceptionalities.

Supporting Explanation. Special education specialists have a deep understanding of the significance of collaboration with education colleagues, families, related service providers, and others from the community and use collaboration to promote understanding, resolve conflicts, and build consensus. Based on the theory and research on elements and models of effective collaboration, special education specialists use their skills to improve programs, services, and outcomes for individuals with exceptionalities. They possess current knowledge of the related ethical and legal issues and use culturally responsive practices to enhance collaboration.

References

Abedi, J. (2006). Psychometric issues in the ELL assessment and special education eligibility. *Teachers College Record, 108*(11), 2282-2303. https://dx.doi.org/10.1111/j.1467-9620.2006.00782.x

Able, H., West, T. A., & Lim, C. I. (2017). Ethical issues in early intervention: Voices from the field. *Infants & Young Children, 30*(3), 204–220.

Al-Azawei, A., Serenelli, F., & Lundqvist, K. (2016). Universal Design for Learning (UDL): A content analysis of peer reviewed journals from 2012 to 2015. *Journal of the Scholarship of Teaching and Learning, 16*(3), 39-56. https://doi.org/10.14434/josotl.v16i3.19295

Alber-Morgan, S. R., Konrad, M., Hessler, T., Helton, M. R., & Telesman, A. O. (2019). Identify and prioritize long- and short-term learning goals. In J. McLeskey, L. Maheady, B. Billingsley, M. T. Brownell, & T. J. Lewis (Eds.), *High leverage practices for inclusive classrooms* (pp. 145-156). Routledge.

Alberto, P. A., & Troutman, A. C. (2012). *Applied behavior analysis for teachers* (9th ed.). Pearson.

American Academy of Pediatrics. (2007). Position statement: Principles and guidelines for early hearing detection and intervention programs. *Pediatrics, 120*(4), 898–921. https://doi.org/10.1542/peds.2007-2333

American Psychological Association, Coalition for Psychology in Schools and Education. (2015). *Top 20 principles from psychology for preK-12 teaching and learning.* http://www.apa.org/ed/schools/cpse/top-twenty-principles.pdf

Archer, A. L., & Hughes, C. A. (2011). *Explicit instruction: Effective and efficient teaching.* The Guilford Press.

Aronson, B., & Laughter, J. (2016). The theory and practice of culturally relevant education: A synthesis of research across content areas. *Review of Educational Research, 86*(1), 163-206. doi: 10.3102/0034654315582066

Arrastia, M. C., Rawls, E. S., Brinkerhoff, E. H., & Roehrig, A. D. (2014). The nature of elementary preservice teachers' reflection during an early field experience. *Reflective Practice, 15*(4), 427-444. doi: 10.1080/14623943.2014.900018

Aydoğan, C., Farran, D. C., & Sağsöz, G. (2015). The relationship between kindergarten classroom environment and children's engagement. *European Early Childhood Education Research Journal, 23*(5), 604-618. doi: 10.1080/1350293X.2015.1104036

Bagnato, S. J., Macy, M., Salaway, J., & Lehman, C. (2007). *Research foundations for conventional tests and testing to ensure accurate and representative early intervention eligibility.* TRACE Center for Excellence in Early Childhood Assessment, Early Childhood Partnerships, Children's Hospital/University of Pittsburgh, U.S. Office of Special Education Programs, Orelena Hawks Puckett Institute.

Bailey, D. B., Raspa, M., & Fox, L. C. (2012). What is the future of family outcomes and family-centered services? *Topics in Early Childhood Special Education, 31*(4), 216-223. doi:10.1177/0271121411427077.

Baker, S., Gersten, R., & Lee, D. (2002). A synthesis of empirical research on teaching mathematics to low-achieving students. *Elementary School Journal, 103*(1), 51-73.

Baker, S., Lesaux, N., Jayanthi, M., Dimino, J., Proctor, C. P., Morris, J., Gersten, R., Haymond, K., Kieffer, M. J., Linan-Thompson, S., & Newman-Gonchar, R. (2014). *Teaching academic content and literacy to English learners in elementary and middle school (NCEE 2014-4012).* National Center for Education Evaluation and Regional Assistance (NCEE), Institute of Education Sciences, U. S. Department of Education. http://ies.ed.gov/ncee/wwc/publications_reviews.aspx

Balcazar, F. E., Taylor-Ritzler, T., Dimpfl, S., Portillo-Pena, N., Guzman, A., Schiff, R., & Murvay, M. (2012). Improving the transition outcomes of low-income minority youth with disabilities. *Exceptionality, 20*(2), 114-132. https://doi.org/10.1080/09362835.2012.670599

Balch, B. V., Memory, D. M., & Hofmeister, D. R. (2008). Teachers and the law: Application essentials, general considerations, and specific examples. *The Clearing House: A Journal of Educational Strategies, Issues and Ideas, 82*(1), 5-10.

Banerjee, R., & Guiberson, M. (2012). Evaluating young children from culturally and linguistically diverse backgrounds for special education services. *Young Exceptional Children, 15*(1), 33-45. doi: 10.1177/1096250611435368

Barac, R., Bialystok, E., Castro, D. C., & Sanchez, M. (2014). The cognitive development of young dual language learners: A critical review. *Early Childhood Research Quarterly, 29*(4), 699-714. doi: 10.1016/j.ecresq.2014.02.003

Barrett, D. E., Casey, J. E., Visser, R. D., & Headley, K. N. (2012). How do teachers make judgments about ethical and unethical behaviors? Toward the development of a code of conduct for teachers. *Teaching and Teacher Education, 28*(6), 890-898. http://dx.doi.org/10.1016/j.tate.2012.04.003

Barrett, S., Eber, L., McIntosh, K., Perales, K., & Romer, N. (2018). Teaching Social-Emotional Competencies Within a PBIS Framework. Center on Positive Behavioral Interventions and Supports (PBIS). https://www.pbis.org/Common/Cms/files/pbisresources/TeachingSocialEmotionalCompetenciesWithinAPBISFramework.pdf

Barton, E. E. (2015). Teaching generalized pretend play and related behaviors to young children with disabilities. *Exceptional Children, 81*, 489–506.

Barton, E. E., & Smith, B. J. (2014). *Fact sheet of research on preschool inclusion.* Pyramid Plus: The Colorado Center for Social Emotional Competence and Inclusion.

Barton, E. E., & Wolery, M. (2008). Teaching pretend play to children with disabilities: A review of the literature. *Topics in Early Child Education, 28*(2), 109–125. https://doi.org/10.1177/0271121408318799

Barton, E. E., & Wolery, M. (2010). Training teachers to promote pretend play in young children with disabilities. *Exceptional Children, 77*, 85-106.

Basham, J. D., Israel, M., Graden, J., Poth, R., & Winston, M. (2010). A comprehensive approach to RTI: Embedding universal design for learning and technology. *Learning Disabilities Quarterly, 33*(4), 243-255. https://doi.org/10.1177/073194871003300403

Bassok, D., & Galdo, E. (2015). Inequality in preschool quality? Community-level disparities in access to high-quality learning environments. *Early Education and Development, 27*(1), 128-144. https://doi.org/10.1080/10409289.2015.1057463

Bateman, B. D. (2011). Individual education programs for children with disabilities. In J. M. Kauffman & D. P. Hallahan (Eds.), *Handbook of special education* (pp. 91-106). Routledge.

Bell, S. T. (2007). Deep-level composition variables as predictors of team performance: A meta- analysis. *Journal of Applied Psychology, 92*(3), 595-615. https://doi.org/10.1037/0021-9010.92.3.595

Benedict, A., Holdheidt, L., Brownell, M., & Marshall Foley, A. (2016). *Learning to teach: Practice-based preparation in teacher education* (Special Issue Brief). American Institutes for Research and University of Florida. http://ceedar.education.ufl.edu/wp-content/uploads/2016/07/Learning_To_Teach.pdf

Benitez, D., Morningstar, M. E., & Frey, B. (2009). A multistate survey of special education teachers' perceptions of their transition competencies. *Career Development for Exceptional Individuals, 32*(1), 6-16. https://doi.org/10.1177/0885728808323945

Benner, A. D., & Mistry, R. S. (2007). Congruence of mother and teacher educational expectations and low-income youth's academic competence. *Journal of Educational Psychology, 99*(1), 140-153. https://doi.org/10.1037/0022-0663.99.1.140

Benner, S. M., & Grim, J. C. (2013). *Assessment of young children with special needs: A context-based approach (2nd Ed)*. Routledge.

Berk, L., & Winsler, A. (1995). *Scaffolding children's learning: Vygotsky and early childhood education (Vol. 7)*. National Association for the Education of Young Children.

Bezdek, J., Summers, J. A., & Turnbull, A. (2010). Professionals' attitudes on partnering with families of children and youth with disabilities. *Education and Training in Autism and Developmental Disabilities, 45*(3), 356-365.

Bhat, A. N., Landa, R. J., & Galloway, J. C. (2011). Current perspectives on motor functioning in infants, children, and adults with autism spectrum disorders. *Physical therapy, 91*(7), 1116-1129. doi: 10.2522/ptj.20100294

Biggs, E. E., Gilson, C. B., & Carter, E. W. (2016). Accomplishing more together: Influences to the quality of professional relationships between special educators and paraprofessionals. *Research and Practice for Persons with Severe Disabilities*, *41*(4), 256-272.

Biggs, E. E., Gilson, C. B., & Carter, E. W. (2019). "Developing that balance": Preparing and supporting special education teachers to work with paraprofessionals. *Teacher Education and Special Education, 42*(2), 117-131.

Billingsley, B.S. (2005). *Cultivating and keeping committed special education teachers: what principals and district leaders can do*. Thousand Oaks, CA: SAGE.

Bishop, A., Brownell, M. T., Klingner, J., Leko, M., & Galman, S. (2010). Differences in beginning special education teachers: The influence of personal attributes, preparation, and school environment on classroom reading practices. *Learning Disability Quarterly, 33*(2). 75-92. https://doi.org/10.1177/073194871003300202

Blanton, L., McLaughlin, V., Aceves, T., Cihak, D., Floyd, L., Landrum, T., McLeskey, J., Miller, K., Rock, M., & Stayton, V. (2017). *Shaping the future of special education: Framing CEC's Professional Preparation Standards*. Council for Exceptional Children.

Blum, C., & Parette, H. P. (2014). Universal design for learning and technology in the early childhood classroom. In K. I. Heider & M. Renck Jalongo (Eds.), *Young children and families in the information age: Applications of technology in early childhood* (pp. 165-182). Springer.

Boe, E. (2014). Teacher demand, supply, and shortage in special education. A national perspective. In P. Sindelar, E. McCray, M. Brownell, & B. Lignugaris/Kraft (Eds.), Handbook of research on special education teacher preparation (pp. 67–93). Routledge.

Boe, E. E., Cook, L. H., & Sunderland, R. J. (2008). Teacher turnover in special and general education: Exit attrition, teaching area transfer, and school migration. *Exceptional Children*, 75, 7–31.

Bradshaw, W. (2013). A framework for providing culturally responsive early intervention services. *Young Exceptional Children, 16*(1), 3-15. doi: 10.1177/1096250612451757

Brookman-Franze, L., Stahmer, A., Lewis, K., Feder, J., & Reed, S. (2012). Building a research-community collaborative to improve community care for infants and toddlers at-risk for autism spectrum disorders. *Journal of Community Psychology, 40*(6), 715-734. https://doi.org/10.1002/jcop.21501

Brotherson, M. J., Summers, J. A., Naig, L. A., Kyzar, K., Friend, A., Epley, P., Turnbull, A. P. (2010). Partnership patterns: Addressing emotional needs in early intervention. *Topics in Early Childhood Special Education, 30*(1), 32-45. https://doi.org/10.1177/0271121409360068

Brown, C. P., & Weber, N. B. (2019). Bringing being into professional development: a qualitative investigation into teachers' struggles moving beyond an epistemological framing of teaching and learning. *Early Child Development and Care, 189*(5), 763-776.

Brown, T. L., Gatmaitan, M., & Harjusola-Webb, S. M. (2014). Using performance feedback to support paraprofessionals in inclusive preschool classrooms. *Young Exceptional Children, 17*(2), 21-31. https://doi.org/10.1177/1096250613493189

Brown, T. S., & Stanton-Chapman, T. L. (2014). Experiences of paraprofessionals in U.S. preschool special education and general education classrooms. *Journal of Research in Special Educational Needs, 17*(1), 18-30. https://doi.org/10.1111/1471-3802.12095

Bruhn, A., & Wills, H. P. (2018). Emerging research and development in technology-based self-monitoring. *Advances in Learning & Behavioral Disabilities,* 30, 51-68. https://doi.org/10.1108/S0735-004X20180000030005

Bruhn, A., Freeman, J., Hirn, R., & Kern, L. (2019). Using feedback to improve student outcomes. In J. McLeskey, L. Maheady, B. Billingsley, M. T., Brownell, & T. J. Lewis (Eds.), *High leverage practices for inclusive classrooms* (pp. 95-96). Routledge.

Brunsek, A., Perlman, M., Falenchuk, O., McMullen, E., Fletcher, B., & Shah, P.S. (2017). The relationship between the Early Childhood Environment Rating Scale and its revised form and child outcomes: A systematic review and meta-analysis. *PLoS ONE, 12*(6), e0178512. https://doi.org/10.1371/journal.pone.0178512

Budin, S., Patti, A. L., & Rafferty, L. A. (2019). Teaching cognitive and metacognitive strategies to support learning and independence. In J. McLeskey, L. Maheady, B. Billingsley, M. Brownell, & T. J. Lewis (Eds.), *High leverage practices for inclusive classrooms* (pp. 181-196). Routledge.

Bullock, J. (2018). *CEC needs assessment identifies preferences in professional development. Teaching Exceptional Children,* 50(6), 396-398. https://doi.org/10.1177/0040059918776509

Busby, J., Ernst, J. V., Kelly, D. P., & DeLuca, V. W. (2019). Professional organizations. *Technology and Engineering Teacher, 78*(6), 18-20.

Buysse, V., Wesley, P. W., Snyder, P., & Winton, P. (2006). Evidence-based practice: What does it really mean for the early childhood field? *Young Exceptional Children*, 9(4), 2-10.

Buysse, V., & Peisner-Feinberg, E. S. (2013). Response to intervention: Conceptual foundations for the early childhood field. In V. Buysse & E. S. Peisner-Feinberg (Eds.), *Handbook of response to intervention in early childhood* (pp. 3-23). Paul H. Brookes Publishing.

Cabell, S. Q., DeCoster, J., LoCasale-Crouch, J., Hamre, B. K., & Pianta, R. C. (2013). Variation in the effectiveness of instructional interactions across preschool classroom settings and learning activities. *Early Childhood Research Quarterly, 28*(4), 820-830. https://doi.org/10.1016/j.ecresq.2013.07.007

Capizzi, A. M., & DaFonte, M. A. (2012). Supporting paraeducators through a collaborative classroom support plan. *Focus on Exceptional Children, 44*(6), 1-16.

Carnahan, C. R., Williamson, P., Clarke, L., & Sorensen, R. (2009). A systematic approach for supporting paraeducators in educational settings: A guide for teachers. *Teaching Exceptional Children, 41*(5), 34-43.

Carta, J. J., Greenwood, C. R., Walker, D., & Buzhardt, J. F. (2010). *Using IGDIs: Monitoring progress and improving intervention for infants and young children.* Paul H. Brookes Publishing.

Castle, S., Baker Deniz, C., & Tortora, M. (2005). Flexible grouping and student learning in a high-needs school. *Education and Urban Society, 37*(2), 139-150.

Caspe, M., Lopez, M. E., Chu, A. & Weiss, H. B. (2011, May). *Teaching the teachers: Preparing educators to engage families for student achievement. Issue Brief.* National PTA and Harvard Family Research Project. https://archive.globalfrp.org/publications-resources/publications-series/pta-and-harvard-family-research-project-issue-briefs-family-engagement-policy-and-practice/teaching-the-teachers-preparing-educators-to-engage-families-for-student-achievement

CAST. (2011). *Universal Design for Learning (UDL) guidelines version 2.2.* http://udlguidelines.cast.org

Causton-Theoharis, J. (2009). *The paraprofessional's handbook for effective support in inclusive classrooms.* Paul H. Brookes.

Cavalluzzo, L., Barrow, L., Henderson, S., Mokher, C., Geraghty, T., & Sartain, L. (2014). From large urban to small rural schools: An empirical study of National Board certification and teaching effectiveness. CNA Analysis and Solutions. https://www.cna.org/CNA_files/PDF/IRM-2015-U-010313.pdf

Center for Adolescent Research in Schools. (2014). *The CARS classroom-based interventions manual.* Center for Adolescent Research in Schools, Lehigh University. https://ed.lehigh.edu/sites/coe.lehigh.edu/files/documents/CARS%20Classroom%20Manual%202-15-1.pdf

Center for Parent Information and Resources. (2017, September). *Evaluating children for disability.* http://www.parentcenterhub.org/repository/evaluation/

Center for Research on Learning. (n.d.) *Learning strategies curriculum.* https://sim.ku.edu/learning-strategies

Center on Technology and Disability. (2018). *Assistive technology 101.* https://www.ctdinstitute.org/sites/default/files/file_attachments/CTD-AT101-V4.pdf

Chopra, R. V., & French, N. K. (2006). Teachers as executives. *Theory into Practice, 45*(3), 230-238.

Chopra, R. V., Carroll, D., & Manjack, S. (2018). Utilizing paraeducators: Issues and strategies for supporting students with disabilities in arts education. In J. B. Crockett & S. M. Malley, *Handbook of arts education and special education* (pp. 105-128). Routledge.

Chopra, R. V., & Giangreco, M. F. (2019). Effective utilization of teacher assistants in inclusive classrooms. In M. J. Schuelka, C. Johnstone, G. Thomas, & A. Artiles (Eds.), *Handbook of inclusion and diversity in education* (pp. 193-207). SAGE.

Chu, S., & Flores, S. (2011). Assessment of English language learners with learning disabilities. *Clearing House, 84*(6), 244-248. https://doi.org/10.1080/00098655.2011.590550

Clark, K. A., Allison, R., & Marable, R. (2017). *A guide for teachers/educators for collaborating with vocational rehabilitation services for youth with disabilities.* National Technical Assistance Center on Transition (NTACT), in partnership with TransCen, Inc. https://files.eric.ed.gov/fulltext/ED582404.pdf

Coburn, C., & Turner, E. (2012). The practice of data use: An introduction. *American Journal of Education, 118*(2), 99-111.

Cohen, S. G., & Bailey, D. E. (1997). What makes teams work: Group effectiveness research from the shop floor to the executive suite. *Journal of Management, 23*(3), 239-290. https://doi.org/10.1177/014920639702300303

Collier, M., Keefe, E. B., & Hirrel, L. A. (2015). Preparing special education teachers to collaborate with families. *School Community Journal, 25*(1), 117-136.

Common Core State Standards Initiative (2006). *Introduction to the Common Core Standards.* www.corestandards.org

Connor, C., Jakobsons, L., Crowe, E., & Meadows, J. (2009). Instruction, student engagement, and reading skill growth in reading first classrooms. *Elementary School Journal, 109*(3), 221-250.

Connor, C. M., Piasta, S. B., Fishman, B., Glasney, S., Schatschneider, C., Crowe, E., Underwood, P., & Morrison, F. J. (2009). Individualizing student instruction precisely: Effects of child x instruction interactions on first graders' literacy development. *Child Development, 80*(1), 77-100. https://doi.org/10.1111/j.1467-8624.2008.01247.x

Cook, B. G., & Cook, S. C. (2013). Unraveling evidence-based practices in special education. *The Journal of Special Education, 47*(2), 71-82.

Cooper, J. O., Heron, T. E., & Heward, W. L. (2020). *Applied behavior analysis* (3rd ed.). Pearson.

Copple, C., & Bredekamp, S. (Eds.) (2009). *Developmentally appropriate practice in early childhood programs serving children from birth through age 8.* National Association for the Education of Young Children.

Cosgrove, K., Gilkerson, L., Leviton, A., Mueller, M., Norris-Shortle, C., & Gouvêa, M. (2019). Building professional capacity to strengthen parent/professional relationships in early intervention: The FAN approach. *Infants & Young Children, 32*(4), 245-254.

Council for Children with Behavior Disorders. (n.d.). *About CCBD: Vision, mission, and history.* http://www.ccbd.net/about/aboutus

Council for Exceptional Children. (2000). *Bright futures for exceptional learners: An agenda to achieve quality conditions for teaching and learning.* Author.

Council for Exceptional Children. (2008). *CEC's policy on safe and positive school climate.* https://www.cec.sped.org/~/media/Files/Policy/safe%20and%20positive_FIXED.pdf

Council for Exceptional Children. (2010). *Validation study resource manual.* Arlington, VA: Author. https://www.cec.sped.org/~/media/Files/Standards/Professional%20Preparation%20Standards/Specialty%20sets/Validation%20Studies%20Resource%20Manual.pdf

Council for Exceptional Children. (2014). CEC policy manual. Arlington, VA: Author. https://www.cec.sped.org/~/media/Files/Policy/2014%20Policy%20Manual.pdf

Council for Exceptional Children. (2015). Congress passes ESSA! *Policy Insider.* http://www.policyinsider.org/2015/12/congress-passes-essa-.html

Council for Exceptional Children. (2015). *What every special educator must know: Professional ethics and standards.* Author.

Council for Exceptional Children. (2017). *Initial specialty set: Early childhood special education/early intervention.* https://www.cec.sped.org/Standards/Special-Educator-Professional-Preparation-Standards/CEC-Initial-and-Advanced-Specialty-Sets

Council for Exceptional Children. (2017). *Shaping the future of special education: Framing CEC's professional preparation standards.*

Council for Exceptional Children. (2018). *CEC's policy on the prevention of and response to maltreatment.* https://www.cec.sped.org/~/media/Files/Policy/CEC%20Professional%20Policies%20and%20Positions/FINAL%20Policy%20on%20Maltreatment%2020180925.pdf

Council for Exceptional Children. (n.d.). Common Core Standards: What special educators need to know. http://www.cec.sped.org/AM/Template.cfm?Section=CEC_Today1&TEMPLATE=/CM/ContentDisplay.cfm&CONTENTID=1526.

Council for Exceptional Children. (n.d.). Council for Exceptional Children's policy on academic subject matter content of the *general curriculum and special educators.* https://cec.sped.org/~/media/Files/Policy/CEC%20Professional%20Policies%20and%20Positions/subject%20matter.pdf

Council for the Accreditation of Educator Preparation (CAEP). (2017). *Application for approval of the 2018 standards for K-6 elementary teacher preparation programs.* Author.

Council for the Accreditation of Educator Preparation (CAEP). (2018). *K-6 elementary teacher preparation standards [initial licensure programs].*http://www.caepnet.org/standards/k-6-elementary-teacher-standards-draft

Council of Chief State School Officers (CCSSO). (1992). *Model standards for beginning teacher licensing and development: A resource for state dialog.* Author.

Council of Chief State School Officers (CCSSO). (2011). *Interstate Teacher Assessment and Support Consortium (InTASC) teaching standards: A resource for state dialogue.* Author.

Council of Chief State School Officers (CCSSO). (2011, April). *InTASC model core teaching standards: Research summaries by standard.* Author.

Council of Chief State School Officers (CCSSO). (2013). *Interstate Teacher Assessment and Support Consortium (InTASC) model core teaching standards and learning progressions for teachers 1.0: A resource for ongoing teacher development.* Author.

Council of Chief State School Officers. (CCSSO) (2013, April). *Interstate teacher assessment and support consortium InTASC model core teaching standards and learning progressions for teachers 1.0: A resource for ongoing teacher development.* Washington, DC: Author. https://ccsso.org/sites/default/files/2017-12/2013_INTASC_Learning_Progressions_for_Teachers.pdf

Crockett, J. B. (2012). Developing educational leaders for the realities of special education in the 21st century. In J. Crockett, B. Billingsley, & M. Boscardin (Eds.), *Handbook of leadership and administration for special education* (pp. 52-66). Routledge.

Courey, S. J., Tappe, P., Siker, J., & LePage, P. (2013). Improved lesson planning with universal design for learning (UDL). *Teacher Education and Special Education, 36*(1), 7-27. https://doi.org/10.1177/0888406412446178

Curda, E. H. (2018). *Students with disabilities: Additional information from education could help states provide pre-employment transition services* (Report to the Ranking Member, Committee on Health, Education, Labor, and Pensions, U.S. Senate. GAO-18-502). U.S. Government Accountability Office. https://www.gao.gov/assets/700/694378.pdf

Daley, T., Munk, T., & Carlson, E. (2011). A national study of kindergarten transition practices for children with disabilities. *Early Childhood Research Quarterly, 26*(4), 409-419. https://doi.org/10.1016/j.ecresq.2010.11.001

D'Angiulli, A., Herdman, A., Stapells, D., & Hertzman, C. (2008). Children's event-related potentials of auditory selective attention vary with their socioeconomic status. *Neuropsychology, 22*(3), 293-300.

Daugherty, S., Grisham-Brown, J., & Hemmeter, M. L. (2001). The effects of embedded skill instruction on the acquisition of target and nontarget skills in preschoolers with developmental delays. *Topics in Early Childhood Special Education, 21*(4), 213-221. https://doi.org/10.1177/027112140102100402

Davis, E. A. (2006). Characterizing productive reflection among preservice elementary teachers: Seeing what matters. *Teaching and Teacher Education, 22*(3), 281-301. doi: 10.1016/j.tate.2005.11.005

Dempsey, I., & Keen, D. (2017). Desirable outcomes associated with family-centered practices for young children with a disability. In H. Sukkar, C. J. Dunst, & J. Kirkby (Eds.), *Early childhood intervention: Working with families of young children with special needs* (pp. 59-71). Routledge.

Deng, W., Zou, X., Deng, H., Li, J., Tang, C., Wang, X., & Guo, X. (2015). The relationship among genetic heritability, environmental effects, and autism spectrum disorders: 37 pairs of ascertained twin study. *Journal of Child Neurology, 30*(13), 1794-1799. doi: 10.1177/0883073815580645

Deno, E. (1970). Special education as developmental capital. *Exceptional Children, 37*(3), 229-237.

DePry, R. L. (2005). Premack principle. In M. Hersen, J. Rosqvist, A. M. Gross, R. S. Drabman, G. Sugai, & R. Horner (Eds.). *Encyclopedia of behavior modification and cognitive behavior therapy* (pp. 966-968). Sage.

Deshler, D. D., Lenz, B. K., Bulgren, J., Schumaker, J., Davis, B., Grossen, B., & Maruquis, J. (2004). Adolescents with disabilities in high school setting: Student characteristics and setting dynamics. *Learning Disabilities: A Contemporary Journal, 2*(2), 30-48.

Dettmer, P., Knackendoffel, A., & Thurston, L. (2013). *Collaboration, consultation, and teamwork for students with special needs* (7th ed.). Pearson.

Dinnebeil, L., Hale, L., & Rule, S. (1996). A qualitative analysis of parents' and service coordinators' descriptions of variables that influence collaborative relationships. *Topics in Early Childhood Special Education, 16*(3), 322-347.

Dinnebeil, L., Hale, L., & Rule, S. (1999). Early intervention program practices that support collaboration. *Topics in Early Childhood Special Education, 19*(4), 225-235.

Dinnebeil, L., & McInerney, W. (2011). *A guide to itinerant early childhood special education services*. Paul H. Brookes Publishing.

Division for Early Childhood of the Council for Exceptional Children. (2009). *DEC code of ethics*. https://www.decdocs.org/member-code-of-ethics

Division for Early Childhood of the Council for Exceptional Children. (2010). *Responsiveness to ALL children, families, and professionals: Integrating cultural and linguistic diversity into policy and practice* [Position statement].

Division for Early Childhood of the Council for Exceptional Children, National Association for the Education of Young Children, & National Head Start Association. (2013). Frameworks for response to intervention in early childhood: Description and implications [Position Statement].

Division for Early Childhood of the Council for Exceptional Children. (2014). *DEC recommended practices in early intervention/early childhood special education 2014*. http://www.dec-sped.org/recommendedpractices

Division for Early Childhood (2015). *DEC recommended practices: Enhancing services for young children with disabilities and their families* (DEC Recommended Practices Monograph Series No. 1). Author.

Division for Early Childhood of the Council for Exceptional Children. (2015). *DEC recommended practices glossary*. http://www.dec-sped.org/recommendedpractices.

Division for Early Childhood of the Council for Exceptional Children. (2018). *Position statement on low birth weight, prematurity & early intervention*. https://www.decdocs.org/position-statement-low-birth-weight.

Division for Early Childhood /National Association for the Education for Young Children. (2009). *Early childhood inclusion: A joint position statement of the Division for Early Childhood (DEC) and the National Association for the Education of Young Children (NAEYC)*. The University of North Carolina, FPG Child Development Institute.

Douglas, S. N., Chapin, S. E., & Nolan, J. F. (2016). Special education teachers' experiences supporting and supervising paraeducators: Implications for special and general education settings. *Teacher Education and Special Education, 39*(1), 60-74.

Dunlap, G., & Fox, L. (2011). Function-based interventions for children with challenging behavior. *Journal of Early Intervention, 33*(4), 333-343. https://doi.org/10.1177/105381 5111429971

Dunst, C. J. (2002). Family-centered practices: Birth through high school. *Journal of Special Education, 36*(3), 141-149 (metanalyses). https://doi.org/10.1177%2F0022466902036 0030401

Dunst, C. J. (2007). Early intervention for infants and toddlers with developmental disabilities. In S. L. Odom, R. H. Horner, M. E. Snell, & J. Blaher (Eds.), *Handbook of developmental disabilities* (pp. 161-180). Guilford Press.

Dunst, C. J. (2017). Research foundations for evidence-informed early childhood intervention performance checklists. *Education Science, 7*(78), 1-57.

Dunst, C. J., & Hamby, D. W. (2015). Research synthesis of studies to promote parent and practitioner use of assistive technology and adaptations with young children with disabilities. In D. L. Edyburn (Ed.), *Advances in special education technology (Vol. 1): Efficacy of assistive technology interventions* (pp. 51-78). Emerald Publishing.

Dunst, C. J., Sukkar, H., & Kirkby, J. (2017). Contributions of family systems and family-centred practices for informing improvements in early childhood intervention. In H. Sukkar, C. J. Dunst, & J. Kirkby (Eds.), *Early childhood intervention: Working with families of children with special needs* (pp. 239-256). Routledge.

Dunst, C. J., Trivett, C. M., & Hill, G. (2011). Improving child find through tailored outreach to primary referral sources. In M. E. McLean & P. A. Snyder (Eds.), *Gathering information to make informed decisions: Contemporary perspectives about assessment in early intervention and early childhood special education* (Monograph 13) (pp. 1-15). *Young Exceptional Children.*

Duran, L. K., Cheatham, G. A., & Santos, R. M. (2011). Evaluating young children who are dual language learners: Gathering and interpreting multiple sources of data to make informed decisions. In M. E. McLean & P. A. Snyder (Eds.), *Gathering information to make informed decisions: Contemporary perspectives about assessment in early intervention and early childhood special education* (Monograph 13) (pp. 133-156). *Young Exceptional Children.*

Early Childhood Personnel Center at the University of Connecticut Center for Excellence in Developmental Disabilities. (2020). *Crosswalk of the initial practice-based professional preparation standards for early interventionists/early childhood special educators (2020) with the DEC recommended practices (2014).*

Education of the Handicapped Act Amendments of 1986, Pub. L. No. 99-457, 100 Stat. 1145 (1986).

Education for All Handicapped Children Act, 20 U.S.C. & 1401 note, Pub. L. No. 94–142 § 89 Stat. 773 (1975).

Edelman, L. (2011). Using digital video to enhance authentic assessment. In M. E. McLean & P. A. Snyder (Eds.), *Gathering information to make informed decisions: Contemporary perspectives about assessment in early intervention and early childhood special education* (Monograph 13) (pp. 92-110). *Young Exceptional Children.*

Edyburn, D. L. (2006). Assistive technology and mild disabilities. *Special Education Technology Practice, 8*(4), 18-28.

Elbaum, B., Blatz, E. T., & Rodriguez, R. J. (2016). Parents' experiences as predictors of state accountability measures of schools' facilitation of parent involvement. *Remedial and Special Education, 37*(1), 15-27. https://doi.org/10.1177%2F0741932515581494

Ellerbrock, C. R., Cruz, B. C., Vásquez, A., & Howes, E. V. (2016). Preparing culturally responsive teachers: Effective practices in teacher education. *Action in Teacher Education, 38*(3), 226-239.

Endrew F. v. Douglas County School District RE-1, 137 S.Ct. 988 (2017).

Ennis, R. P., Lane, K. L., and Oakes, W. P. (2018). Empowering teachers with low-intensity strategies to support instruction: Self-monitoring in an elementary resource classroom. *Preventing School Failure: Alternative Education for Children and Youth, 62*(3), 176–189. https://doi.org/10.1080/1045988X.2017.1408055

Epstein, A. S. (2016). *The intentional teacher (Revised Edition): Choosing the best strategies for young children's learning.* NAEYC.

Epstein, M., Atkins, M., Cullinan, D., Kutash, K., and Weaver, R. (2008). *Reducing behavior problems in the elementary school classroom: A practice guide* (NCEE #2008-012). National Center for Education Evaluation and Regional Assistance, Institute of Education Sciences, U.S. Department of Education. https://ies.ed.gov/ncee/wwc/PracticeGuide/4

Erwin, E., Maude, S. P., Palmer, S. B., Summers, J. A., Brotherson, M. J., Haines, S. J., Stroup-Rentier, V., Zheng, Y., and Peck, N. F. (2016). Fostering the foundations of self-determination in early childhood: A process for enhancing child outcomes across home and school. *Early Childhood Education Journal, 44*(4), 325-333. https://doi.org/10.1007/s10643-015-0710-9

Esparza-Brown, J., & Doolittle, J. (2008). A cultural, linguistic, and ecological framework for response to intervention with English language learners. *Teaching Exceptional Children, 40*(5), 66-72.

Esparza-Brown, J., & Sanford, A. (2011). *RTI for English language learners: Appropriately using screening and progress monitoring tools to improve instructional outcomes.* National Center on Response to Intervention. rti4success.org/sites/default/files/rtiforells.pdf

Ethridge, E. A., Lake, V. E., & Beisly, A. H. (2019). "If not me, then who?": An integrated model of advocacy for early childhood teacher education. In M. Khosrow-Pour (Ed.), *Early childhood development: Concepts, methodologies, tools, and applications* (pp. 1264-1285). IGI Global.

Every Student Succeeds Act of 2015, Pub. L. No. 114-95, 114 Stat. 1177 (2015-2016).

Feng, L. & Sass, T. (2013). What makes special education teachers special? Teacher training and achievement of students with disabilities. Economics of Education Review, 36, 122-134.

Ferraro, J. M. (2000). *Reflective practice and professional development (Report No. ED449120 2000-10-00). ERIC Digest.* https://files.eric.ed.gov/fulltext/ED449120.pdf

Fiedler, C. R., & Van Haren, B. (2009). A comparison of special education administrators' and teachers' knowledge and application of ethics and professional standards. *The Journal of Special Education, 43*(3), 160-173. https://doi.org/10.1177/0022466908319395

Fidler, D. J., Daunhauer, L. A., Will, B., Gerlachl-McDonald, B., & Schworer, E. (2016). The central role of etiology in science and practice in intellectual disability. *International Review of Research in Developmental Disabilities, 50*, 33-68.

Fisher, M., & Pleasants, S. L. (2012). Roles, responsibilities, and concerns of paraeducators: Findings from a statewide survey. *Remedial and Special Education, 33*(5), 287-297.

Flowers, N., Mertens, S., & Mulhall, P. (1999). The impact of teaming: Five research-based outcomes. *Middle School Journal, 31*(1), 57-60.

Ford, D. Y. (1998). The underrepresentation of minority student in gifted education: Problems and promises in recruitment and retention. *The Journal of Special Education, 32,* 4–14.

Forman, S. G., & Crystal, C. D. (2015). Systems consultation for multitiered systems of supports (MTSS): Implementation issues. *Journal of Educational and Psychological Consultation, 25*(2-3), 276-285.

Fox, L., Carta, J., Strain, P., Dunlap, G., & Hemmeter, M. L. (2009). *Response to intervention and the pyramid model.* University of South Florida, Technical Assistance Center on Social Emotional Intervention for Young Children.

Fox, L., Dunlap, G., Hemmeter, M. L., Joseph, G., & Strain, P. (2003). The Teaching Pyramid: A model for supporting social competence and preventing challenging behavior in young children. *Young Children, 58*(4), 48-53.

Fox, L., Hemmeter, M. L., Snyder, P., Binder, D., & Clarke, S. (2011). Coaching early childhood special educators to implement a comprehensive model for promoting young children's social competence. *Topics in Early Childhood Special Education, 31*(3), 178-192. https://doi.org/10.1177%2F0271121411404440

Francis, D., Rivera, M., Lesaux, N., Kieffer, M., & Rivera, H. (2006). *Practical guidelines for the education of English language learners: Research-based recommendations for instruction and academic interventions* (Under cooperative agreement grant S283B050034 for U.S. Department of Education). RMC Research Corporation, Center on Instruction.

Freeman, R., Miller, D., & Newcomer, L. (2015). Integration of academic and behavioral MTSS at the district level using implementation science. *Learning Disabilities: A Contemporary Journal, 13*(1), 59-72.

Freeman, S., Gulsrud, A., & Kasari, C. (2015). Brief report: Linking early joint attention and play to later reports of friendships for children with ASD. *Journal of Autism and Developmental Disorders, 45,* 2259-2266. https://doi.org/10.1007/s10803-015-2369-x

Freese, A. R. (2006). Reframing one's teaching: Discovering our teacher selves through reflection and inquiry. *Teaching and Teacher Education, 22*(1), 100-119. doi: 10.1016/j.tate.2005.07.003

Frey, J. R., & Kaiser, A. P. (2011). The use of play expansions to increase the diversity and complexity of object play in children with disabilities. *Topics in Early Childhood Special Education, 31*(2), 99-111. doi:10.1177/0271121410378758

Friedman, M., Woods, J., & Salisbury, C. (2012). Caregiver coaching strategies for early intervention providers: Moving toward operational definitions. *Infants & Young Children, 25*(1), 62-82. doi: 10.1097/IYC.0b013e31823d8f12

Friend, M., & Barron, T. (2019). Collaborating with colleagues to increase student success. In J. McLeskey, L. Maheady, B. Billingsley, M. Brownell, & T. J. Lewis (Eds.), *High leverage practices for inclusive classrooms* (pp. 3-14). Routledge.

Friend, M., & Cook, L. (2017). *Interactions: Collaboration skills for school professionals* (8th ed.). Pearson.

Fuchs, D., Fuchs, L. S., & Compton, D. L. (2012). Smart RTI: A next-generation approach to multilevel prevention. *Exceptional Children, 78*(3), 263-279.

Fuchs, D., Patton, S., Fuchs, L. (2019). Combining reading comprehension instruction with cognitive training to provide intensive intervention to at-risk students. In P. Pullen & M. Kennedy (Eds.). *Handbook of response to intervention and multi-tiered systems of support* (pp. 198-217). Taylor & Francis.

Fuchs, L. S., & Fuchs, D. (1986). Effects of systematic formative evaluation: A meta-analysis. *Exceptional Children, 53*(3), 199-208.

Fuchs, L. S., Fuchs, D., & Malone, A. S. (2017). The taxonomy of intervention intensity. *Teaching Exceptional Children, 50*(1), 35-43.

Fuchs, L. S., Fuchs, D., Prentice, K., Burch, M., Hamlett, C. L., Owen, R., & Schroeter, K. (2003). Enhancing third-grade students' mathematical problem solving with self-regulated learning strategies. *Journal of Educational Psychology, 95*(2), 306-315.

Gage, N. A. (2015). *Evidence-based practices for classroom and behavior management: Tier 2 and Tier 3 strategies* (Document No. IC-15). University of Florida, Collaboration for Effective Educator, Development, Accountability, and Reform Center. https://ceedar.education.ufl.edu/wp-content/uploads/2015/11/Behavior-Management-tier-two-and-three-strategies.pdf

Gallagher, C., & Worth, P. (2008). *Formative assessment policies, programs, and practices in the Southwest Region* (Issues & Answers Report, REL 2008–No. 041). U.S. Department of Education, Institute of Education Sciences.

Garcia, M., Sanchez, V., & Escudero, I. (2006). Learning through reflection in mathematics teacher education. *Educational Studies in Mathematics, 64*(1), 1-17. doi: 10.1007/s10649-006-9021-9

García, S. B., & Ortiz, A. A. (2008). A framework for culturally and linguistically responsive design of Response to Intervention models. *Multiple Voices for Ethnically Diverse Exceptional Learners, 11*(1), 24-41.

García, S. B., & Ortiz, A. A. (2013). Intersectionality as a framework for transformative research in special education. *Multiple Voices for Ethnically Diverse Exceptional Learners, 13*(2), 32-47.

Gehner, J. (2010). Libraries, low-income people, and social exclusion. *Public Library Quarterly, 29*(1), 39-47.

Gerlach, K. (2015). *Let's team up: A checklist for teachers, paraeducators, and principals.* National Professional Resources.

Gersten, R., Beckmann, S., Clarke, B., Foegen, A., Marsh, L., Star, J. R., & Witzel, B. (2009). *Assisting students struggling with mathematics: Response to Intervention (RtI) for elementary and middle schools* (NCEE 2009-4060). National Center for Education Evaluation and Regional Assistance, Institute of Education Sciences, U.S. Department of Education.

Gersten, R., Chard, D., Jayanthi, M., Baker, S., Morphy, P., & Flojo, J. (2009b). Mathematics instruction for students with learning disabilities: A meta-analysis of instructional components. *Review of Educational Research, 79*(3), 1202-1242.

Gersten, R., Compton, D., Connor, C. M., Dimino, J., Santoro, L., Linan-Thompson, S., and Tilly, W. D. (2008). *Assisting students struggling with reading: Response to Intervention and multi-tier intervention for reading in the primary grades. A practice guide* (NCEE 2009-4045). National Center for Education Evaluation and Regional Assistance, Institute of Education Sciences, U.S. Department of Education.

Gersten, R., Compton, D., Dimino, J., Santoro, L., Linan-Thompson, S., & Tilly, D. (2009a). *Assisting students struggling with reading: Response to intervention (RtI) for elementary and middle schools* (NCEE 2009-4060). Institute for Education Sciences, U.S. Department of Education.

Gersten, R., Keating, T., Yovanoff, P., & Harniss, M. K. (2001). Working in special education: Factors that enhance special educators' intent to stay. *Exceptional Children, 67*, 535–567.

Gersten, R., Schiller, E. P., & Vaughn, S. (Eds.) (2000). *Contemporary special education research: Synthesis of the knowledge base on critical instructional issues.* Lawrence Erlbaum.

Giangreco, M. F. (2013). Teacher assistant supports in inclusive schools: Research, practices, and alternatives. *Australasian Journal of Special Education, 37*(2), 93-106. doi: 10.1017/jse.2013.1.

Giangreco, M. F., Edelman, S. W., Broer, S. M., & Doyle, M. B. (2001). Paraprofessional support of students with disabilities: Literature from the past decade. *Exceptional Children, 68*(1), 45-63.

Giangreco, M. F., Suter, J. C., & Doyle, M. B. (2010). Paraprofessionals in inclusive schools: A review of recent research. *Journal of Educational and Psychological Consultation, 20*(1), 41-57.

Ginsburg, K. R., the Committee on Communications, & the Committee on Psychosocial Aspects of Child and Family Health. (2007). The importance of play in promoting healthy child development and maintaining strong parent–child bonds. *Pediatrics, 119*(1), 182-191. https://doi.org/10.1542/peds.2006-2697

Gohl, E. M., Gohl, D., & Wolf, M. A. (2009). Assessments and technology: A powerful combination for improving teaching and learning. In L. M. Pinkus (Ed.), *Meaningful measurement: The role of assessments in improving high school education in the twenty-first century* (pp. 183-197). Alliance for Excellent Education.

Goldenberg, C., Rueda, R., & August, D. (2006). Social and cultural influences on the literacy attainment of language-minority children and youth. In D. August & T. Shanahan (Eds.), *Developing literacy in second-language learners: Report of the National Literacy Panel on Language-Minority Children and Youth* (pp. 269-318). Lawrence Erlbaum.

Graham, S., Bollinger, A., Booth Olson, C., D'Aoust, C., MacArthur, C., McCutchen, D., & Olinghouse, N. (2012). *Teaching elementary school students to be effective writers: A practice guide* (NCEE 2012- 4058). National Center for Education Evaluation and Regional Assistance, Institute of Education Sciences, U.S. Department of Education. https://ies.ed.gov/ncee/wwc/Docs/PracticeGuide/writing_pg_062612.pdf

Graham, S., & Harris, K. R. (2000). The role of self-regulation and transcription skills in writing and writing development. *Educational Psychologist, 35*(1), 3-12.

Graham, S., McKeown, D., Kiuhara, S., & Harris, K. R. (2012). "Meta-analysis of writing instruction for students in elementary grades": Correction to Graham et al. (2012). *Journal of Educational Psychology, 104*(4), 896. https://doi.org/10.1037/a0029939

Grigorenko, E. L., Compton, D. L., Fuchs, L. S., Wagner, R. K., Willcutt, E. G., & Fletcher, J. M. (2020). Understanding, educating, and supporting children with specific learning disabilities: 50 years of science and practice. *American Psychologist, 75*(1), 37-51. https://doi.org/10.1037/amp0000452

Grisham-Brown, J., Hemmeter, M. L., & Pretti-Frontczak, K. (2017). *Blended practices for teaching young children in inclusive settings* (2nd Ed.). Paul H. Brookes Publishing.

Grisham-Brown, J., Schuster, J. W., Hemmeter, M. L., & Collins, B. C. (2000). Using an embedding strategy to teach preschoolers with significant disabilities. *Journal of Behavioral Education, 10(2-3)*, 139-162. https://doi.org/10.1023/A:1016688130297

Guillen, C., & Winton, P. (2015). Teaming and collaboration: Thinking about how as well as what. In Division for Early Childhood (Ed.), *DEC Recommended Practices: Enhancing services for young children with disabilities and their families* (DEC Recommended Practices Monograph Series No. 1) (pp. 99-108). Division for Early Childhood.

Gulsrud, A., Hellemann, G., Freeman, S., & Kasari, C. (2014). Two to ten years: developmental trajectories of joint attention in children with ASD who received targeted social communication interventions. *Autism Research, 7*(2), 207-215. https://doi.org/10.1002/aur.1360

Guralnick, M. J. (2011). Why early intervention works: A systems perspective. *Infants and young children, 24*(1), 6-28. doi: 10.1097/IYC.0b013e3182002cfe

Guralnick, M. J. (2017). Early intervention for young children with developmental delays: Contributions of the developmental systems approach. In H. Sukkar, C. J. Dunst, & J. Kirkby (Eds.), *Early childhood intervention: Working with families of young children with special needs* (pp. 17-34). Routledge.

Hagiwara, M., & Shogren, K.A. (2019). Collaborate with families to support student learning and secure needed services. In J. McLeskey, L. Maheady, B. Billingsley, M. T. Brownell, & T. Lewis, *High leverage practices for inclusive education* (pp. 34-47). Routledge.

Hahn, L. J. (2016). Joint attention and early social developmental cascades in neurogenetic disorders. *International Review of Research in Developmental Disabilities, 51*, 123-152. doi: 10.1016/bs.irrdd.2016.08.002

Hall, A. H., Rutland, J. H., & Grisham-Brown, J. (2011). Family involvement in the assessment process. In J. Grisham-Brown & K. Pretti-Frontczak (Eds.), *Assessing young children in inclusive settings: The blended practice approach (pp.37-60)*. Paul H. Brookes Publishing.

Hallam, P. R., Smith, H. R., Hite, J. M., Hite, S. J., & Wilcox, B. R. (2015). Trust and collaboration in PLC teams: Teacher relationships, principal support, and collaborative benefits. *NASSP Bulletin, 99*(3), 193-216. doi: 10.1177/0192636515602330

Halle, T. G., Hair, E. C., Wandner, L. D., & Chien, N. C. (2012). Profiles of school readiness among four-year-old Head Start children. *Early Childhood Research Quarterly, 27*(4), 613-626. doi: 10.1016/j.ecresq.2012.04.001

Hammer, C. S., Hoff, E., Uchikoshi, Y., Gillanders, C., Castro, D. C., & Sandilos, L. E. (2014). The language and literacy development of young dual language learners: A critical review. *Early Childhood Research Quarterly, 29*(4), 715-733. doi: 10.1016/j.ecresq.2014.05.008

Hamilton, L., Halverson, R., Jackson, S., Mandinach, E., Supovitz, J., & Wayman, J. (2009). *Using student achievement data to support instructional decision making* (NCEE 2009-4067). National Center for Education Evaluation and Regional Assistance, Institute of Education Sciences, U.S. Department of Education. http://ies.ed.gov/ncee/wwc/Docs/PracticeGuide/dddm_pg_092909.pdf

Hanhimäki, E., & Tirri, K. (2009). Education for ethically sensitive teaching in critical incidents at school. *Journal of Education for Teaching, 35*(2), 107-121, doi: 10.1080/02607470902770880

Hanson, M. J., & Lynch, E. W. (2010). Working with families from diverse backgrounds. In R. A. McWilliam (Ed.), *Working with families of young children with special needs* (p. 167). Guilford Press.

Hardin, B. J., Mereoiu, M., Hung, H. F., & Roach-Scott, M. (2009). Investigating parent and professional perspectives concerning special education services for preschool Latino children. *Early Childhood Education Journal, 37*, 93-102.

Harkness, S., Super, C. M., Mavridis, C. J., Barry, O., & Zeitlin, M. (2013). Culture and early childhood development: Implications for policy and programs. In P. R. Britto, P. L. Engle, & C. M. Super (Eds.), *Handbook of early childhood development research and its impact on global policy* (pp. 142-160). Oxford University.

Harland, D. J., & Wondra, J. D. (2011). Preservice teachers' reflection on clinical experiences. *Journal of Digital Learning in Teacher Education, 27*(4), 128-133. doi: 10.1080/21532974.2011.10784669

Hartmann, E. S. (2016). Understanding the everyday practice of individualized education program team members. *Journal of Educational & Psychological Consultation, 26*(1), 1-24. doi:10.1080/10474412.2015.1042975

Hatfield, B. E., Burchinal, M. R., Pianta, R. C., & Sideris, J. (2016). Thresholds in the association between quality of teacher-child interactions and preschool children's school readiness skills. *Early Childhood Research Quarterly, 36*, 561-571. doi: 10.1016/j.ecresq.2015.09.005 0885-2006

Hattie, J. (2009). *Visible learning: A synthesis of over 800 meta-analyses relating to achievement.* Routledge.

Hattie, J. (2012). *Visible learning for teachers.* Routledge.

Hattie, J., & Timperley, H. (2007). *The power of feedback. Review of Educational Research, 77*(1), 81-112.

Hedeen, T., Peter, M., Moses, P., & Engiles, A. (2013). *Individualized Education Program (IEP)/Individualized Family Service Plan (IFSP) facilitation: Practical insights and programmatic considerations.* Center for Appropriate Dispute Resolution in Special Education (CADRE).

Hemmeter, M. L., Ostrosky, M., & Fox, L. (2006). Social and emotional foundations for early learning: A conceptual model for intervention. *School Psychology Review, 35*(4), 583-601.

Hemmeter, M. L., Snyder, P. A., Fox, L., & Algina, J. (2016). Evaluating the implementation of the Pyramid Model for promoting social-emotional competence in early childhood classrooms. *Topics in Early Childhood Special Education, 36*(3), 133-146.

Herburger, D., Holdheide, L., & Sacco, D. (2020). *Removing barriers to effective distance learning by applying the High-Leverage Practices: Tips and tools.* CEEDAR Center and National Center for Systemic Improvement. https://ceedar.education.ufl.edu/wp-content/uploads/2020/10/CEEDER-Leveraging-508.pdf

Heward, W. L., & Wood, C. L. (2015, April). *Improving educational outcomes in America: Can a low tech, generic teaching practice make a difference?* https://storage.outreach.psu.edu/autism/80.%20Handout%205.pdf

Hightower, A. M., Delgado, R. C., Lloyd, S. C., Wittenstein, R., Sellers, K., & Swanson, C. B. (2011, December). *Improving student learning by supporting quality teaching: Key issues, effective strategies.* Editorial Projects in Education.

Hillemeier, M. M., Morgan, P. L., Farkas, G., Maczuga, S. A. (2013). Quality disparities in childcare for at-risk children: Comparing Head Start and non-Head Start settings. *Maternal and Child Health Journal, 17*(1), 180-188.

Hodapp, R. M., Fidler, D. J., & Depta, E. (2016). Blurring boundaries, continuing change: The next 50 years of research in intellectual and developmental disabilities. *International Review of Research in Developmental Disabilities, 50*, 1-31.

Hoegl, M., & Gemuenden, H. (2001). Teamwork quality and the success of innovative projects: A theoretical concept and empirical evidence. *Organization Science, 12*(4), 435-449.

Hollingsworth, H. L., Knight-McKenna, M., & Bryan, R. (2016). Policy and advocacy concepts and processes: innovative content in early childhood teacher education. *Early Child Development and Care, 186*(10), 1664-1674.

Horn, E., & Banerjee, R. (2009). Understanding curriculum modifications and embedded learning opportunities in the context of supporting all children's success. *Language, Speech, and Hearing in Schools, 40*(4), 406-415. https://doi.org/10.1044/0161-1461(2009/08-0026)

Horn, E., Lieber, J., Sandall, S., Schwartz, I. & Li, S. (2002;). Supporting young children's IEP goals in inclusive setting through embedded learning opportunities. *Topics in Early Childhood Special Education, 20*, 208-223.

Horn, E., Kang, J., Classen, A., Butera, G., Palmer, S., Lieber, J., Friesen, A., & Mihai, A. (2016). Role of universal design for learning and differentiation in inclusive preschools. In L. Meyer & T. Catalino (Eds), *DEC recommended practices: Environment* (DEC Recommended Practices Monograph Series No. 2) (pp. 51-66). Division of Early Childhood.

Horn, E., Lieber, J., Sandall, S., Schwartz, I., & Li, S. (2002). Supporting young children's IEP goals in inclusive setting through embedded learning opportunities. *Topics in Early Childhood Special Education, 20*(4), 208-223. https://doi.org/10.1177%2F027112140002000402

Horn, E., Palmer, S., Butera, G., & Lieber, J. (2016). *Six steps to inclusive preschool curriculum: A UDL-based framework for children's school success*. Paul H. Brookes Publishing.

Horton, P. B., McConney, A. A., Gallo, M., Woods, A. L., Senn, G. J., & Hamelin, D. (1993). An investigation of the effectiveness of concept mapping as an instructional tool. *Science Education, 77*(1), 95-111.

Hsiao, Y.-J., & Sorensen Petersen, S. (2019). Evidence-based practices provided in teacher education and in-service training programs for special education teachers of students with autism spectrum disorders. *Teacher Education and Special Education, 42*(3), 193-208. https://doi.org/10.1177/0888406418758464

Hughes, C., Riccomini, P., & Morris, J. (2018). Use explicit instruction. In J. McLeskey, L. Maheady, B. Billingsley, M. T. Brownell, & T. Lewis, *High leverage practices for inclusive education* (pp. 215-236). Routledge. doi: 10.4324/9781315176093-20

Hughes, J., & Kwok, O.-m. (2007). Influence of student-teacher and parent-teacher relationships on lower achieving readers' engagement and achievement in the primary grades. *Journal of Educational Psychology, 99*(1), 39-51. https://doi.org/10.1037/0022-0663.99.1.39

Hundert, J., & Hopkins, B. (1992). Training supervisors in a collaborative team approach to promote peer interaction of children with disabilities in integrated preschools. *Journal of Applied Behavior Analysis, 25*(2), 385-400. https://dx.doi.org/10.1901%2Fjaba.1992.25-385

Hunt, P., Soto, G., Maier, J., Liboiron, N., & Bae, S. (2004). Collaborative teaming to support preschoolers with severe disabilities who are placed in general education early childhood programs. *Topics in Early Childhood Special Education, 24*(3), 123-142. https://doi.org/10.1177/02711214040240030101

Husu, J., & Tirri, K. (2001). Teachers' ethical choices in sociomoral settings. *Journal of Moral Education, 30*(4), 361-375. doi: 10.1080/03057240120094850.

Imazeki, J. & Goe, L. (2009). The distribution of highly qualified, experienced teachers: challenges and opportunities. TQ Research & Policy Brief. National Comprehensive Center for Teacher Quality. http://www.gtlcenter.org/sites/default/files/docs/August2009Brief.pdf

Individuals with Disabilities Education Act (IDEA) of 2004, 20 U.S.C. 1400 et seq. (2004).

Individuals with Disabilities Education Act, 20 U.S.C. ss 1400 et seq. (2006 & Supp. V. 2011).

Individuals with Disabilities Education Act Regulations, 34 C.F.R. s 300. (2012).

Individuals with Disabilities Education Improvement Act. (2014).

The IRIS Center. (2008). *SOS: Helping students become independent learners*. https://iris.peabody.vanderbilt.edu/module/sr/

The IRIS Center. (2012). *Classroom management (part 2): Developing your own comprehensive behavior management plan*. https://iris.peabody.vanderbilt.edu/module/beh2/

The IRIS Center. (2015). *Intensive intervention (part 1): Using data-based individualization to intensify instruction*. https://iris.peabody.vanderbilt.edu/module/dbi1/

The IRIS Center. (2016). *School counselors: Facilitating transitions for students with disabilities from high school to post-school settings*. https://iris.peabody.vanderbilt.edu/module/cou2/

The IRIS Center. (2019). *Instructional accommodations: Making the learning environment accessible for students with visual disabilities*. https://iris.peabody.vanderbilt.edu/module/v02-successsight/#content

The IRIS Center. (2019a). *Accommodations to the physical environment: Setting up a classroom for students with visual disabilities*. https://iris.peabody.vanderbilt.edu/module/v01-clearview/

The IRIS Center. (2019b). *Classroom management (part 1): Learning the components of a comprehensive behavior management plan*. https://iris.peabody.vanderbilt.edu/module/beh1/cresource/#content

The IRIS Center. (2019c). *Early childhood environments: Designing effective classrooms*. https://iris.peabody.vanderbilt.edu/module/env/

Israel, M., Ribuffo, C., & Smith, S. (2014). *Universal Design for Learning: Recommendations for teacher preparation and professional development* (Document No. IC-7). University of Florida, Collaboration for Effective Educator, Development, Accountability, and Reform Center. https://ceedar.education.ufl.edu/wp-content/uploads/2014/08/IC-7_FINAL_08-27-14.pdf

Jensen, P., & Rasmussen, A. W. (2019). Professional development and its impact on children in early childhood education and care: A meta-analysis based on European studies. *Scandinavian Journal of Educational Research, 63*(6), 935-950. https://doi.org/10.1080/00313831.2018.146 6359

Johnsen, S., & Clarenbach, J. (2016). Using the National Gifted Education Standards for Pre-K Grade 12 Professional Development. Sourcebooks.

Johnsen, S. K., VanTassel-Baska, J., Robinson, A., Cotabish, A., Dailey, D., Jolly, J., Clarenbach, J., & Adams. C. (2015). Using the national gifted education standards for teacher preparation programs. National Association for Gifted Children.

Jung, P.-G., McMaster, K. L., Kunkel, A. K., Shin, J., & Stecker, P. M. (2018). Effects of data-based individualization for students with intensive learning needs: A meta-analysis. *Learning Disabilities Research & Practice, 33*(3), 144–155. doi: 10.1111/1drp.12172

Kalyanpur, M., & Harry, B. (2012). *Cultural reciprocity in special education: Building family professional relationships*. Brookes.

Kamil, M. L., Borman, G. D., Dole, J., Kral, C. C., Salinger, T., & Torgesen, J. (2008). *Improving adolescent literacy: Effective classroom and intervention practices*. National Center for Education Evaluation and Regional Assistance, Institute of Education Sciences, U.S. Department of Education.

Kaminski, J., Valle, L., Filene, J., & Boyle, C. (2008). A meta-analytic review of components associated with parent training program effectiveness. *Journal of Abnormal Psychology, 36*(4), 567-589. https://doi.org/10.1007/s10802-007-9201-9

Kasari, C., Gulsrud, A., Feeman, S., Paparella, T., & Hellemann, G. (2012). Longitudinal follow-up of children with autism receiving targeted interventions on joint attention and play. *Journal of the American Academy of Child & Adolescent Psychiatry, 51*(5), 487-495.

Kearns, D., Pollack, M. S., & Whaley, V. M. (2019). Provide intensive instruction. In J. McLeskey, L. Maheady, B. Billingsley, M. T. Brownell, & T. J. Lewis (Eds.), *High leverage practices for inclusive classrooms* (pp. 279-301). Routledge.

Keels, M., & Raver, C. C. (2009). Early learning experiences and outcomes for children of U.S. immigrant families: Introduction to the special issue. *Early Childhood Research Quarterly, 24*(4), 363-366. doi: 10.1016/j.ecresq.2009.09.002

Keilty, B. (2019). Assessing the home environment to promote infant-toddler learning within everyday family routines. *Young Exceptional Children.* doi: 10.1177/1096250619864076

Kemp, C. (2003). Investigating the transition of young children with intellectual disabilities to mainstream classes: An Australian perspective. *International Journal of Disability, Development and Education, 50*(4), 403-433. https://doi.org/10.1080/1034912032000155194

Kilgo, J., & Bruder, M. B. (1997). Creating new visions in IHEs: Interdisciplinary approaches to personnel prevention. In P. Winton, J. McCollum, & C. Catlett (Eds), *Interdisciplinary personnel preparation.* Paul H. Brookes Publishing.

Kilgo, J. L., Vogtle, L., Aldridge, J., & Ronilo, W. (2019). The power of teams: Time to move forward in interprofessional personnel preparation. In Division for Early Childhood (Ed.), *Teaming and collaboration: Building and sustaining partnerships* (DEC Recommended Practices Monograph Series No. 6) (pp. 135-143). Division for Early Childhood.

Kim, A. H., Vaughn, S., Wanzek, J., & Wei, S. (2004). Graphic organizers and their effects on the reading comprehension of students with LD: A synthesis of research. *Journal of Learning Disabilities, 37*(2), 105-118.

Kishiyama, M. M., Boyce, W. T., Jimenez, A. M., Perry, L. M., & Knight, R. T. (2009). Socioeconomic disparities affect prefrontal function in children. *Journal of Cognitive Neuroscience, 21*(6), 1106-1115.

Klein, S., Wynn, K., Ray, L., Demeriez, L., LaBerge, P., Pei, J., & Pierre, C. S. (2011). Information sharing during diagnostic assessments: What is relevant for parents? *Physical & Occupational Therapy in Pediatrics, 31*(2), 120-132.

Kochanska, G., Murray, K. T., & Harlan, E. T. (2000). Effortful control in early childhood: Continuity and change, antecedents, and implications for social development. *Developmental Psychology, 36*(2), 220-232. https://doi.org/10.1037/0012-1649.36.2.220

Kohler, P. D. (1996). *Taxonomy for transition programming.* University of Illinois.

Kohler, P. D., Gothberg, J. E., Fowler, C., & Coyle, J. (2016). *Taxonomy for transition programming 2.0: A model for planning, organizing, and evaluating transition education, services, and programs.* Western Michigan University. https://www.transitionta.org/system/files/resourcetrees/Taxonomy_for_Transition_Programming_v2.pdf?file=1&type=node&id=1727&force=

Kozleski, E. B., Artiles, A. J., & Skrtic, T. M. (2014). What is high quality instruction for English Language Learners in inclusive schools?. In J. McLeskey, N. L. Waldron, F. Spooner, & B. Algozzine (Eds.), *Handbook of effective inclusive schools: Research and practice.* Routledge.

Kozleski, E. B., & Waitoller, F. R. (2010). Teacher learning for inclusive education: Understanding teaching as a cultural and political practice. *International Journal of Inclusive Education, 14*(7), 655-666. https://doi.org/10.1080/13603111003778379

Kumashiro, K. (2012). Bad teacher! How blaming teachers distorts the bigger picture. Teachers College Press.

Landmark, L. J., Ju, S., & Zhang, D. (2010). Substantiated best practices in transition: Fifteen plus years later. *Career Development for Exceptional Individuals, 33*(3), 165-176. https://doi.org/10.1177/0885728810376410

Landy, S. (2009). *Pathways to competence: Encouraging healthy social and emotional development in young children* (2nd ed.). Paul H. Brookes Publishing.

Lane, K., Oakes, W., & Menzies, H. (2019). Comprehensive, integrated, three-tiered (Ci3T) models of prevention: The role of systematic screening to inform instruction. In P. Pullen & M. Kennedy (Eds.), *Handbook of response to intervention and multi-tiered systems of support* (pp. 63-76). Routledge.

Lawton, K., Hannigan, S., & Ellawadi, A. B. (2014). Moving beyond the status quo: Using evidence-based practice to improve autism core deficits in the preschool classroom. *International Review of Research in Developmental Disabilities, 47*, 99-150.

Lee, N., Maiman, M., & Godfrey, M. (2016). What can neuropsychology teach us about intellectual disability?: Searching for commonalities in the memory and executive function profiles associated with Down, Williams, and Fragile X syndromes. *International Review of Research in Developmental Disabilities, 51*, 1-40. doi: 10.1016/bs.irrdd.2016.07.002

Lee, S.H., Soukup, J. H., Little, T. D., & Wehmeyer, M. L. (2009). Student and teacher variables contributing to access to the general education curriculum for students with intellectual and developmental disabilities. *The Journal of Special Education, 43*(1). 29-44. https://doi.org/10.1177/0022466907313449

Lee, S.H., Wehmeyer, M. L., Soukup, J. H., & Palmer, S. B. (2010). Impact of curriculum modifications on access to the general education curriculum for students with disabilities. *Exceptional Children, 76*(2), 213-233. https://doi.org/10.1177/001440291007600205

Leko, M. M., Brownell, M. T., Sindelar, P. T., & Kiely, M. T. (2015). Envisioning the future of special education personnel preparation in a standards-based era. *Exceptional Children, 82*(1), 25-43. https://doi.org/10.1177/0014402915598782

Lembke, E., Smith, R. A., Thomas, C. N., McMaster, K. L., & Mason, E. N. (2019). Using student assessment data, analyzing instructional practices, and making necessary adjustments that improve student outcomes. In J. McLeskey, L. Maheady, B. Billingsley, M. T. Brownell, T. J. Lewis (Eds.), *High leverage practices for inclusive classrooms* (pp. 80-93). Routledge.

Lemons, C. J., Vaughn, S., Wexler, J., Kearns, D. M., & Sinclair, A. C. (2018). Envisioning an improved continuum of special education services for students with disabilities: Considering intervention intensity. *Learning Disabilities Research & Practice, 33*(3), 131-143.

Lewis, M. (2014). Toward the development of the science of developmental psychopathology. In M. Lewis & K. D. Rudolph (Eds.), *Handbook of developmental psychopathology* (3rd ed.) (pp. 3-22). Springer.

Lewis, S., Savaiano, M. E., Blankenship, K., & Greeley-Bennett, C. (2014). Three areas of the expanded core curriculum for students with visual impairment: Research priorities for independent living skills, self-determination, and social interaction skills. *International Review of Research in Developmental Disabilities, 46*, 207-252.

Lewis, T. J. (2019). Social/emotional/behavioral high leverage practices. In J. McLeskey, L. Maheady, B. Billingsley, M. T., Brownell, & T. J. Lewis (Eds.), *High leverage practices for inclusive classrooms* (pp. 95-96). Routledge.

Lewis, V. (2003). Play and language in children with autism. *Autism, 7*(4), 391–399. https://doi.org/10.1177%2F1362361303007004005

Liew, J. (2011). Effortful control, executive functions, and education: Bringing self-regulatory and social-emotional competencies to the table. *Child development perspectives, 6*(2), 105-111. doi: 10.1111/j.1750-8606.2011.00196.x

Lifter, K., Foster-Sanda, S., Arzamarski, C. A., Briesch, J., & McClure, E. (2011). Overview of play: Its uses and importance in early intervention/early childhood special education. *Infants & Young Children, 24*(3), 225-245.

Lifter, K., Mason, E. J., & Barton, E. E. (2011). Children's play: Where we have been and where we could go. *Journal of Early Intervention, 33*(4), 281-297.

Li-Grining, C. P., Votruba-Drzal, E., Maldonado-Carreño, C., & Haas, K. (2010). Children's early approaches to learning and academic trajectories through fifth grade. *Developmental Psychology, 46*(5), 1062-1077. http://dx.doi.org/10.1037/a0020066

Linder, T. (2008). *Transdisciplinary play-based assessment* (2nd ed.). Paul H. Brookes Publishing.

Linn, D., & Hemmer, L. (2011). English language learner disproportionality in special education: Implications for the scholar-practitioner. *Journal of Educational Research and Practice, 1*(1), 70-80. doi: 10.5590/JERAP.2011.01.1.06

Little, M. E., & Slanda, D. D. (2017). Collaborating with general education colleagues. In K. Mitchem, K. Kossar, & J. Goeke (Eds.), *Re-designing high incidence teacher preparation: Challenges and solutions.* Wiley-Blackwell.

Lloyd, B. P., Wills, H. P., & Lewis, T. J. (2018). Conducting functional behavior assessments to develop individualized behavior support plans. In J. McLeskey, L. Maheady, B. Billingsley, M. T., Brownell, & T. J. Lewis (Eds.), *High leverage practices for inclusive classrooms* (pp. 131-141. Routledge.

Loughran, J. (2005). Researching teaching about teaching: Self-study of teacher education practices. *Studying Teacher Education, 1*(1), 5-16. https://doi.org/10.1080/17425960500039777

Luke, S. E. (2019). Using technology to support teaming with families that are culturally and linguistically diverse. In Division for Early Childhood (Ed.), *Teaming and collaboration: Building and sustaining partnerships* (DEC Recommended Practices Monograph Series No. 6) (pp. 13-23). Division for Early Childhood.

MacDonald, M., Lord, C., & Ulrich, D. (2013). The relationship of motor skills and adaptive behavior skills in young children with autism spectrum disorders. *Research in Autism Spectrum Disorders, 7*(11), 1383-1390. doi: 10.1016/j.rasd.2013.07.020

Mandell, C. J., & Murray, M. M. (2005). Innovative family-centered practices in personnel preparation. *Teacher Education and Special Education, 28*(1), 74-77.

Mandinach, E. B., & Gummer, E. S. (2013). Defining data literacy: A report on a convening of experts. *Journal of Educational Research and Policy Studies, 13*(2), 6-28.

Mangiatordi, A., & Serenelli, F. (2013). Universal design for learning: A meta-analytic review of 80 abstracts from peer reviewed journals. *Research on Education and Media, 5*(1), 109-118.

Marchand-Martella, N. E., Slocum, T. A., & Martella, R. C. (Eds.) (2004). *Introduction to direct instruction*. Pearson Education.

Mart, A., Dusenbury, L., & Weissberg, R. P. (2011). Social, emotional, and academic learning: Complementary goals for school-family partnerships. In S. Redding, M. Murphy, & P. Sheley (Eds.), *Handbook on family and community engagement* (pp. 37-44). Information Age Publishing.

Mason, L., & Benedek-Wood, E. (2014). Effective writing instruction in inclusive schools. In J. McLeskey, N. Waldron, F. Spooner, & B. Algozzine (Eds.), *Handbook of effective inclusive schools: Research and practice* (pp. 247-260). Routledge.

Mason, L., Mamlin, N., & Stewart, K. (2019). Evidence-based writing interventions: Three tiers of instruction for elementary students. In P. Pullen & M. Kennedy (Eds.), *Handbook of response to intervention and multi-tiered systems of support* (pp. 218-232). Taylor & Francis.

Mathematics Advisory Panel. (2008). *Foundations for success: The final report of the National Mathematics Advisory Panel.* U.S. Department of Education. https://www2.ed.gov/about/bdscomm/list/mathpanel/report/final-report.pdf

Mattessich, P., & Monsey, B. (1992). *Collaboration: What makes it work.* Amherst H. Wilder Foundation.

Matthews, M. S., & Shaunessy, E. (2008). Culturally, linguistically, and economically diverse gifted students. In F. A. Karnes & K. R. Stephens (Eds.), *Achieving excellence: Educating the gifted and talented* (pp. 99–115). Pearson.

Maughan, A., & Cicchetti, C. (2002). Impact of child maltreatment and interadult violence on children's emotion regulation abilities and socioemotional adjustment. *Child Development, 73*(5), 1525-1542.

Mazzotti, V. L., & Plotner, A. J. (2016). Implementing secondary transition evidence-based practices: A multi-state survey of transition service providers. *Career Development and Transition for Exceptional Individuals, 39*(1), 12-22. https://doi.org/10.1177%2F216514 3414544360

McClelland, M. M., Cameron, C. E., McDonald Connor, C., Farris, C. L., Jewkes, A. M., &Morrison, F. J. (2007). Links between behavior regulation and preschoolers' literacy, vocabulary, and math skills. *Developmental Psychology, 43*(4), 947-959. https://doi.org/10.1037/0012-1649.43.4.947

McCoach, D. B., Goldstein, J., Behuniak, P., Reis, S. M., Black, A. C., Sullivan, E. E., & Rambo, K. (2010). Examining the unexpected: Outlier analysis of factors affecting student achievement. *Journal of Advanced Academics, 21*(3), 426-468.

McCollum, J., Hemmeter, M., & Hsieh, W. (2013). Coaching teachers for emergent literacy instruction using performance-based feedback. *Topics in Early Childhood Special Education, 33*(1), 28-37. https://doi.org/10.1177%2F0271121411431003

McCoy, D. C., Connors, M. C., Morris, P. A., Yoshikawa, H., & Friedman-Krauss, A. H. (2015). Neighborhood economic disadvantage and children's cognitive and social-emotional development: Exploring Head Start classroom quality as a mediating mechanism. *Early Child Research Quarterly, 32*(3), 150-159.

McFarland, J., Hussar, B., de Brey, C., Snyder, T., Wang, X., Wilkinson-Flicker, S., Gebrekristos, S., Zhang, J., Rathbun, A., Barmer, A., Bullock Mann, F., and Hinz, S. (2017). *The condition of education 2017* (NCES 2017144). National Center for Education Statistics. https://nces.ed.gov/pubsearch/pubsinfo.asp?pubid=2017144

McIntosh, K., & MacKay, L. D. (2008). Enhancing generalization of social skills: Making social skills curricula effective after the lesson. *Beyond Behavior, 18*(1), 18-25.

McLean, M. (2014). Assessment and its importance in early intervention/early childhood special education. In M. E. McLean, M. L. Hemmeter, & P. Snyder (Eds.), *Essential elements for assessing infants and preschoolers with special needs* (pp. 2-36). Pearson.

McLean, M., Sandall, S. R., & Smith, B. J. (2016). A history of early childhood special education. In B. Reichow, B. A. Boyd, E. E. Barton, & S. L. Odom (Eds.). *Handbook of early childhood special education* (pp. 3-20). Springer.

McLeskey, J., Barringer, M-D., Billingsley, B., Brownell, M., Jackson, D., Kennedy, M., Lewis, T., Maheady, L., Rodriquez, J., Scheeler, M. C., Winn, J., & Ziegler, D. (2017). *High-leverage practices in special education.* Council for Exceptional Children & CEEDAR Center.

McLeskey, J., Maheady, L., Billingsley, B., Brownell, M. T., & Lewis, T. J. (Eds.) (2019). *High leverage practices for inclusive classrooms.* Routledge.

McLeskey, J., & Waldron, N. (2011). Educational programs for elementary students with learning disabilities: Can they be both effective and inclusive? *Learning Disabilities Research & Practice, 26*(1), 48-57.

McWilliam, R. A., Casey, A. M., Ashley, D., Fielder, J., Rowley, P., DeJong, K., M.,

Meadan, H., Ostrosky, M. M., Zaghlawan, H. Y., & Yu, S. Y. (2009). Promoting the social and communicative behavior of young children with autism spectrum disorders: A review of parent-implemented intervention studies. *Topics in Early Childhood Special Education, 29*(2), 90-104.

Mellin, A., & Winton, P. (2003). Interdisciplinary collaboration among higher education early intervention faculty members. *Journal of Early Intervention, 25*(3), 173-188. https://doi.org/10.1177/105381510302500303

Mickel, J., Stricklin, S. B., & Votava, K. (2011). Assessment of family-identified needs through the routines-based interview. In M. E. McLean & P. A. Snyder (Eds.), *Gathering information to make informed decisions: Contemporary perspectives about assessment in early intervention and early childhood special education* (Monograph 13) (pp. 43-63). Young Exceptional Children.

Milot, T., Éthier, L. S., St-Laurent, D., & Provost, M. A. (2010). The role of trauma symptoms in the development of behavioral problems in maltreated preschoolers. *Child Abuse & Neglect, 34*(4), 225-234. doi: 10.1016/j.chiabu.2009.07.006

Montague, M. (2008). Self-regulation strategies to improve mathematical problem solving for students with learning disabilities. *Learning Disability Quarterly, 31*(1), 37-44. https://doi.org/10.2307%2F30035524

Mueller, T. G., Massafra, A., Robinson, J., & Peterson, L. (2019). Simulated individualized education program meetings: Valuable pedagogy within a preservice special educator program. *Teacher Education and Special Education, 42*(3), 209-226. https://doi.org/10.1177%2F0888406418788920

Mukeredzi, T. G. (2015). Creating space for pre-service teacher professional development during practicum: A teacher educator's self-study. *Australian Journal of Teacher Education, 40*(2), 125-145.

National Association for Gifted Children. (2010). Pre-K–Grade 12 gifted education programming standards. Washington, DC: Author. http://www.nagc.org/sites/default/files/standards/K-12%20programming%20standards.pdf

National Association for Gifted Children - Council for Exceptional Children. (2013). *Teacher Preparation Standards in Gifted and Talented Education.* National Association for Gifted Children. https://www.nagc.org/sites/default/files/standards/NAGC-%20CEC%20CAEP%20standards%20(2013%20final).pdf

National Association for the Education of Young Children. (2009). *Developmentally appropriate practice in early childhood programs serving children from birth through age 8.* NAEYC.

National Association for the Education of Young Children. (2009). *Where we stand on curriculum, assessment, and program evaluation: NAEYC and NAECS/SDE.* NAEYC. http://www.naeyc.org/positionstatements

National Association for the Education of Young Children. (2011). *2010 NAEYC standards for initial and advanced early childhood professional preparation programs.* NAEYC.

National Association for the Education for Young Children (2011). NAEYC code of ethical conduct and statement of commitment. NAEYC. https://www.naeyc.org/sites/default/files/globally-shared/downloads/PDFs/resources/position-statements/Ethics%20Position%20Statement2011_09202013update.pdf

National Association of School Psychologists. (2010). *Standards for the credentialing of school psychologists.* Author.

National Board for Professional Teaching Standards. (2010). *Exceptional needs standards for teachers of students ages birth-21+* (2nd ed.). Author. http://www.nbpts.org/wp-content/uploads/ECYA-ENS.pdf

National Board for Professional Teaching Standards. (2012a). *Early childhood generalist standards, 3rd edition: For teachers of students ages 3-8.* Author.

National Board for Professional Teaching Standards. (2012b). *Middle childhood generalist standards, 3rd edition: For teachers of students ages 7-12.* Author.

National Board for Professional Teaching Standards. (2013). Early childhood through young adulthood exceptional needs specialist. http://www.nbpts.org/sites/default/files/documents/certificates/Aaag/ECYA_ENS_AssessAtaGlance_05.14.13_Final.pdf

National Center for Pyramid Model Innovations. (n.d.). *The Pyramid Model for promoting social emotional competence in infants and young children.* https://challengingbehavior.cbcs.usf.edu/docs/pyramid_model_fact_sheet.pdf

National Center on Intensive Intervention. (2013). *Data-based individualization: A framework for intensive intervention.* Office of Special Education, U.S. Department of Education. http://www.intensiveintervention.org/resource/data-based-individualization-framework-intensive-intervention

National Center on Response to Intervention. (June 2010). *What is Response to Intervention (RTI).* National Center on Response to Intervention, Office of Special Education Programs, U.S. Department of Education. https://files.eric.ed.gov/fulltext/ED526859.pdf

National Council for Accreditation of Teacher Education. (2010). NCATE glossary. http://www.ncate.org/Standards/UnitStandards/Glossary/tabid/477/Default.aspxNational Professional Development Center on Inclusion (NPDCI). (2012). *Response to intervention (RTI) in early childhood: Building consensus on the defining features.* University of North Carolina, Frank Porter Graham Child Development Institute. https://npdci.fpg.unc.edu/sites/npdci.fpg.unc.edu/files/resources/NPDCI-RTI-Concept-Paper-FINAL-2-2012.pdf

National Research Council. (2001). *Knowing what students know: The science and design of educational assessment.* The National Academies Press. https://doi.org/10.17226/10019

National Research Council. (2008). *Early childhood assessment: Why, what, and how.* The National Academies Press.

Neisworth, J. T., & Bagnato, S. J. (2011). Using your good judgement: Informed opinion for early intervention. In M. E. McLean & P. A. Snyder (Eds.), *Gathering information to make informed decisions: Contemporary perspectives about assessment in early intervention and early childhood special education* (Monograph 13) (pp. 79-91). *Young Exceptional Children.*

Nesbit, J. C., & Adesope, O. O. (2006). Learning with concepts and knowledge maps: A meta-analysis. *Review of Educational Research, 76*(3), 413-448.

Neuman, S., & Cunningham, L. (2009). The impact of professional development and coaching on early language and literacy instructional practices. *American Educational Research Journal, 46*(2), 532-566. https://doi.org/10.3102%2F0002831208328088

Newman, L., Wagner, M., Knokey, A.-M., Marder, C., Nagle, K., Shaver, D., & Wei, X., (with Cameto, R., Contreras, E., Ferguson, K., Greene, S., & Schwarting, M.) (2011). *The post high school outcomes of young adults with disabilities up to 8 years after high school: A report from the National Longitudinal Transition Study-2 (NLTS2)* (NCSER 2011-3005). SRI International.

Odom, J., Murphy, C. L., & Olson, P. (1998). Building effective, successful teams: An interactive teaming model for inservice education. *Journal of Early Intervention, 21*(4), 339-349.

Odom, S. L. (2016). The role of theory in early childhood special education and early intervention. In B. Reichow, B. A. Boyd, E. E. Barton, & S. L. Odom (Eds.). *Handbook of early childhood special education* (pp. 21-36). Springer.

Odom, S. L., Buysse, V., & Soukakou, E. (2012). Inclusion for young children with disabilities: A quarter century of research perspectives. *Journal of Early Intervention, 33*(4), 344-356. https://doi.org/10.1177%2F1053815111430094

Odom, S. L., Collet-Klingenberg, L., Rogers, S., & Hatton, D. (2010). Evidence-based practices in interventions for children and youth with autism spectrum disorders. *Preventing School Failure: Alternative Education for Children and Youth, 54*(4), 275-282, doi: 10.1080/10459881003785506

Ortiz, A. A., & Robertson, P. (2018). Preparing teachers to serve English learners with language and/or literacy-related difficulties and disabilities. *Teacher Education and Special Education, 4*(3), 176-187.

OSEP Technical Assistance Center on Positive Behavioral Interventions and Supports. (2017). *Positive Behavioral Interventions & Supports* [Website]. www.pbis.org

Otaiba, S. A., & Lake, V. E. (2007). Preparing special educators to teach reading and use curriculum-based assessments. *Reading and Writing, 20*(6), 591-617.

Panadero, E., Kirschner, P. A., Järvelä, S., Malmberg, J., & Järvenoja, H. (2015). How individual self-regulation affects group regulation and performance: A shared regulation intervention. *Small Group Research, 46*(4), 431-454.

Parette, H., & Brotherson, M. (2004). Family-centered and culturally responsive assistive technology decision making. *Infants and Young Children, 17*(4), 355-367.

Parker, A. T., & Ivy, S. E. (2014). Communication development of children with visual impairment and deaf blindness: A synthesis of intervention research. *International Review of Research in Developmental Disabilities, 46*, 101-143. https://doi.org/10.1016/B978-0-12-420039-5.00006-X

Peters, S., & Reid, D. K. (2009). Resistance and discursive practice: Promoting advocacy in teacher undergraduate and graduate programmes. *Teaching and Teacher Education. 25*(4), 551-558. https://doi.org/10.1016/j.tate.2009.02.006

Peterson, C., Luze, G., Eshbaugh, E., Jeon, J., & Kantz, K. (2007). Enhancing parent-child interactions through home visiting: Promising practice or unfulfilled promise? *Journal of Early Intervention, 29*(2), 119-140. https://doi.org/10.1177%2F105381510702900205

Phillips, D. A., & Meloy, M. E. (2012). High-quality school-based pre-k can boost early learning for children with special needs. *Exceptional Children, 78*(4), 471-490. doi: 10.1177/001440291207800405

Polly, D., McGee, J., Wang, C., Martin, C., Lambert, R., & Pugalee, D. K. (2015). Linking professional development, teacher outcomes, and student achievement: The case of a learner-centered mathematics program for elementary school teachers. *International Journal of Educational Research, 72*(1), 26-37. http://dx.doi.org/10.1016/j.ijer.2015.04.002

Powell, D. R., Diamond, K. E., & Cockburn, M. K. (2013). Promising approaches to professional development for early childhood educators. In O. N. Saracho & B. Spodek (Eds.), *Handbook of research on the education of young children* (3rd ed.) (pp. 385-392). Routledge.

President's Commission on Excellence in Special Education. (2002). *A new era: Revitalizing special education for children and their families.* Office of Special Education and Rehabilitative Services, U.S. Department of Education. https://eric.ed.gov/?id=ED473830

Pretti-Frontczak, K., Giallourakis, A., Janas, D., & Hayes, A. (2002). Using a family-centered preservice curriculum to prepare early intervention and early childhood special education personnel. *Teacher Education and Special Education, 25*(3), 291-297. https://doi.org/10.1177/088840640202500308

Raizada, R. D., Richards, T. L., Meltzoff, A., & Kuhl, P. K. (2008). Socioeconomic status predicts hemispheric specialization of the left inferior frontal gyrus in young children. *Neuroimage, 40*(3), 1392-1401.

Rao, K., Ok, M. W., & Bryant, B. R. (2014). A review of research on universal design education-al models. *Remedial and Special Education, 35*(3), 153-166. doi: 10.1177/0741932513518980

Rappolt-Schlictman, G., Boucher, A., and Evans, M. (2018). From deficit remediation to capacity building: Learning to enable rather than disable students with dyslexia. *Speech and Hearing Services in Schools, 49*(4), 864-874.

Raver, C. C. (2002). Emotions matter: Making the case for the role of young children's emotional development for early school readiness. *Social Policy Report, 16*(3), 1-20. https://doi.org/10.1002/j.2379-3988.2002.tb00041.x

Reese, E., Sparks, A., & Leyva, D. (2010). A review of parent interventions for preschool children's language and emergent literacy. *Journal of Early Childhood Literacy, 10*(1), 97-117. doi: 10.1177/1468798409356987

Reichow, B. (2016). Evidence-based practice in the context of early childhood special education. In B. Reichow, B. Boyd, E. Barton, & S. Odom (Eds.), *Handbook of early childhood special education* (pp. 107-121). Cham, Switzerland: Springer.

Reichow, B. (2016). Evidence-based practice in the context of early childhood special education. In B. Reichow, B. Boyd, E. Barton, & S. Odom (Eds.), *Handbook of early childhood special education* (pp. 107-121). Springer.

Resch, J., Mireles, G., Benz, M., Grenwelge, C., Peterson, R., & Zhang, D. (2010). Giving parents a voice: A qualitative study of the challenges experienced by parents of children with disabilities. *Rehabilitation Psychology, 55*(2), 139-50. doi: 10.1037/a0019473

Reutzel, D. R., Clark, S. K., & Flory, M. (2015). Organizing effective literacy instruction: Differentiating instruction to meet the needs of all literacy learners. In L. M. Morrow, L. B. Gambrell, & M. Pressley (Eds.), *Best practices for literacy instruction* (5th ed.) (pp. 365-389). Guilford Press.

Reutzel, R., & Clark, S. (2019). Organizing effective literacy instruction: Differentiating instruction to meet student needs. In L. Morrow & L. Gambrell (Eds.), *Best practices in literacy instruction* (6th ed.) (pp. 359-385). Guilford.

Riccomini, P. J., Morano, S., & Hughes, C. A. (2017). Big ideas in special education: Specially designed instruction, high-leverage practices, explicit instruction, and intensive instruction. *Teaching Exceptional Children, 50*(1), 20-27.

Richards-Tutor, C., Aceves, T., & Reese, L. (2016). *Evidence-based practices for English language learners* (Document No. IC-18). University of Florida, Collaboration for Effective Educator, Development, Accountability, and Reform Center. https://ceedar.education.ufl.edu/wp-content/uploads/2016/11/EBP-for-english-learners.pdf

Robertson, J., Green, K., Alper, S., Schloss, P. J., & Kohler, F. (2003). Using a peer-mediated intervention to facilitate children's participation in inclusive childcare activities. *Education & Treatment of Children, 26*, 182-197.

Rogers, K. B. (2002). Effects of acceleration on gifted learners. In M. Neihart, S. M. Reis, N. M. Robinson, & S. M. Moon (Eds.), *The social and emotional development of gifted children: What do we know?* (pp. 3–12). Prufrock.

Rogoff, B. (2003). *The cultural nature of human development*. Oxford University Press.

Rogoff, B., Coppens, A. D., Alcalá, L., Aceves-Azuara, I., Ruvalcaba, O., López, A., & Dayton, A. (2017). Noticing learners' strengths through cultural research. *Perspectives on Psychological Science, 12*(5), 876-888. https://doi.org/10.1177/1745691617718355

Ronfeldt, M., Farmer, S., McQueen, K., & Grissom, J. (2015). Teacher collaboration in instructional teams and student achievement. *American Educational Research Journal, 52*(3), 475–514.

Roorda, D. L., Koomen, H. M. Y., Spilt, J. L., & Oort, F. J. (2011). The influence of affective teacher-student relationships on students' school engagement and achievement: A meta-analytic approach. *Review of Educational Research, 81*(4), 493-529.

Rose, D. H., & Meyer, A. (Eds.). (2006). *A practical reader in universal design for learning*. Harvard Education Press.

Rosenkoetter, S., & Stayton, V. D. (1997). Designing and implementing innovative, interdisciplinary practica. In P. J. Winton, J. A. McCollum, & C. Catlett (Eds.), *Reforming personnel preparation in early intervention: Issues, models, and practical strategies* (pp. 453–474). Paul H. Brookes Publishing.

Rosenshine, B. (2012). Principles of instruction: Research-based strategies that all teachers should know. *American Educator, 36*(1), 12-19.

Ross, J. A., & Bruce, C. D. (2007). Teacher self-assessment: A mechanism for facilitating professional growth. *Teaching and Teacher Education, 23*(2), 146-159.

Rossetti, Z., Redash, A., Sauer, J. S., Bui, O., Wen, Y., & Regensburger, D. (2018). Access, accountability, and advocacy: Culturally and linguistically diverse families' participation in IEP meetings. *Exceptionality.* Advance online publication. doi:10.1080/09362835.2018.1480948

Rossetti, Z., Sauer, J. S., Bui, O., & Ou, S. (2017). Developing collaborative partnerships with culturally and linguistically diverse families during the IEP process. *Teaching Exceptional Children, 49*(5), 328-338. doi: 10.1177/0040059916680103

Rous, B., & Hallam, R. (2012). Transition services for children with disabilities: Research, policy and practice. 25th Anniversary Volume. *Topics in Early Childhood Special Education, 31*(4), 232-240.

Rous, B., Hallam, R., McCormick, K., & Cox, M. (2010). Practices that support the transition to public preschool programs: Results from a national survey. *Early Childhood Research Quarterly, 25*(1), 17-32.

Rous, B., Myers, C., & Stricklin, S. (2007). Strategies for supporting transitions for young children with special needs. *Journal of Early Intervention, 30*(1), 1-18.

Ryser, G. R. (2011). Fairness in testing and nonbiased assessment. In S. K. Johnsen (Ed.), Identifying gifted students: A practical guide (2nd ed., pp. 63–74). Prufrock.

Sameroff, A. (2009). The transactional model. In A. Sameroff (Ed.), *The transactional model of development: How children and contexts shape each other* (pp. 3-21). American Psychological Association.

Sandall, S., Schwartz, I., Joseph, G. E., Gauvreau, A. N., Lieber, J. A., Horn, E., & Odom, S. (2019). *Building blocks for teaching preschoolers with special needs* (3rd Ed.) Paul H. Brookes Publishing.

Sandall, S. R., Schwartz, I. S., & Gauvreau, A. (2016). Using modifications and accommodations to enhance learning of young children with disabilities: Little changes that yield big impacts. In B. Reichow, B. A. Boyd, E. E. Barton, & S. L. Odom (Eds.), *Handbook of early childhood special education* (pp. 349-361). Springer.

Schön, D. (1983). *The reflective practitioner: How professionals think in action.* Basic Books.

Schön, D. (1987). *Educating the reflective practitioner: Toward a new design for teaching and learning in the professions.* Jossey-Bass Inc.

Schunk, D. H., & Zimmerman, B. J. (2007). Influencing children's self-efficacy and self-regulation of reading and writing through modeling. *Reading & Writing Quarterly, 23*(1), 7-25.

Scruggs, T. E., Mastropieri, M. A., & McDuffie, K. A. (2007). Co-teaching in inclusive classrooms: A metasynthesis of qualitative research. *Exceptional Children, 73*(4), 392-416. https://doi.org/10.1177%2F001440290707300401

Scruggs, T. E., & Mastropieri, M. A. (2017). Making inclusion work with co-teaching. *Teaching Exceptional Children, 49*(4), 284-293.

Seo, S., Brownell, M. T., Bishop, A. G., & Dingle, M. (2008). Beginning special education teachers' classroom reading instruction: Practices that engage elementary students with learning disabilities. *Exceptional Children, 75*(1), 97-122.

Sexton, J. D., Snyder, P., Lobman, M., Kimbrough, P., & Matthews, K. (1997). A team-based model to improve early intervention programs: Linking preservice and inservice. In P. J. Winton, J. McCollum, & C. Catlett (Eds.), *Interdisciplinary personnel preparation*. Paul H. Brookes Publishing.

Shelden, M., & Rush, D. (2013). *The early intervention teaming handbook: The primary service provider approach*. Paul H. Brookes Publishing.

Shepley, C., Lane, J. D., Grisham-Brown, J., Spriggs, A. D., & Winstead, O. (2018). Effects of a training package to increase teachers' fidelity of naturalistic instructional procedures in inclusive preschool classrooms. *Teacher Education and Special Education, 41*(4), 321-339.

Shonkoff, J. P. (2010). Building a new biodevelopmental framework to guide the future of early childhood policy. *Child Development, 81*(1), 357-367. https://doi.org/10.1111/j.1467-8624.2009.01399.x

Shonkoff, J. P., Hauser-Cram, P., Krauss, M., & Upshur, C. (1992). Development of infants with disabilities and their families: Implications for theory and service delivery [Special issue]. *Monographs of the Society for Research and Child Development, 57*(6) 1-153.

Shonkoff, J. P., & Phillips, D. (Eds.) (2000). *From neurons to neighborhoods: The science of early childhood development*. The National Academies Press.

Shonkoff, J. P., & Richter, L. (2013). The powerful reach of early childhood development. In P. R. Britto, P. L. Engle, & C. M. Super (Eds.), *Handbook of early childhood development research and its impact on global policy* (pp. 24-34). Oxford University.

Siller, M., Hutman, T., & Sigman, M. (2013). A parent-mediated intervention to increase responsive parental behaviors and child communication in children with ASD: A randomized clinical trial. *Journal of Autism & Developmental Disorders, 43*(3), 540-55.

Simonsen, B., Freeman, J., Godman, S., Mitchell, B., Swain-Bradway, J., Flannery, B., Sugai, G., George, H., & Nad Putman, B. (2016). *Supporting and responding to behavior: Evidence-based classroom strategies for teachers*. Center on Positive Behavioral Interventions and Supports. https://www.pbis.org/common/cms/files/pbisresources/Supporting%20and%20Responding%20to%20Behavior.pdf

Simonsen, B., & Myers, D. (2015). *Classwide positive behavior interventions and supports: A guide to proactive classroom management*. The Guilford Press.

Sin, S. J. (2011). Neighborhood disparities in access to information resources: Measuring and mapping U.S. public libraries' funding and service landscapes. *Library & Information Science Research, 33*(1), 41-53.

Sklad, M., Diekstra, R., De Ritter, M., & Ben, J. (2012). Effectiveness of school-based universal social, emotional, and behavioral programs: Do they enhance students' development in the area of skill, behavior, and adjustment? *Psychology in the Schools, 49*(9), 892-908.

Slanda, D. D., & Little, M. E. (2018). Exceptional education is special. In G. E. Hall, L. F. Quinn & D. M. Gollnick (Eds.), *The Wiley handbook of teaching and learning*. John Wiley & Sons. https://doi.org/10.1002/9781118955901.ch11

Sloper, P., Greco, V., Beecham, J., & Webb, R. (2006). Key worker services for disabled children: What characteristics of services lead to better outcomes for children and families? *Child: Care, Health & Development, 32*(2), 147-157. https://doi.org/10.1111/j.1365-2214.2006.00592.x

Snyder, P., Hemmeter, M. L., McLean, M., Sandall, S., & McLaughlin, T. (2013). Embedded instruction to support early learning in response to intervention frameworks. In V. Buysse, E. S. Peisner-Feinber, & H. P. Ginsburg (Eds.), *Handbook of response to intervention in early childhood* (pp. 283-298). Paul H. Brookes Publishing.

Snyder, P. A., McLaughlin, T., & Denney, M. K. (2011). Program focus in early intervention. In J. M. Kauffman, D. P. Hallahan, & M. Conroy (Eds.), *Handbook of special education* (Section XII: Early identification and intervention in exceptionality) (pp. 716-730). Routledge.

Snyder, P., McLean, M., & Bailey, D. B. (2014). Types and technical characteristics of assessment instruments. In M. E. McLean, M. L. Hemmeter, & P. Snyder (Eds.), *Essential elements for assessing infants and preschoolers with special needs* (pp. 38-85). Pearson.

Sobeck, E. E., Douglas, S. N., Chopra, R., & Morano, S. (in press). Paraeducator supervision in pre-service teacher preparation programs: Results of a national survey. *Psychology in the Schools*. https://doi.org/10.1002/pits.22383

Sobeck, E. E., Robertson, R., & Smith, J. (2020). The effects of didactic instruction and performance feedback on paraeducator implementation of behavior support strategies in inclusive settings. *Journal of Special Education, 53*(4), 245-255.

Solis, M., Vaughn, S., Swanson, E., & McCulley, L. (2012). Collaborative models of instruction: The empirical foundations of inclusion and co-teaching. *Psychology in the Schools, 49*(5), 498-510.

Spicer, P. (2010). Cultural influences on parenting. *Zero to Three, 30*(4), 28-32.

Spires, H. A., Lee, J. K., Turner, K. A., & Johnson, J. (2008). Having our say: Middle grade student perspectives on school, technologies, and academic engagement. *Journal of Research on Technology in Education, 40*(4), 497-515.

Squires, J. (2015). Assessment: Guiding principles for accurate and efficient decision making. In Division for Early Childhood, *DEC recommended practices: Enhancing services for young children with disabilities and their families* (pp. 37-52). Division for Early Childhood.

State, T. M., Mitchell, B. S., & Wehby, J. (2019). Consistent, organized, respectful learning environment. In J. McLeskey, L. Maheady, B. Billingsley, M. T., Brownell, & T. J. Lewis (Eds.), *High leverage practices for inclusive classrooms* (pp. 97-106). Routledge.

Stayton, V., Whittaker, S., Jones, E., & Kersting, F. (2001). Interdisciplinary model for the preparation of related services and early intervention personnel. *Teacher Education and Special Education, 24*, 395-401.

Stecker, P. M., Fuchs, L. S., & Fuchs, D. (2005). Using curriculum-based measurement to improve student achievement: Review of research. *Psychology in the Schools, 42*(8), 795-819. https://doi.org/10.1002/pits.20113

Strain, P. S., Kerr, M. M., & Ragland, E. U. (1979). Effects of peer-mediated social initiations and prompting/reinforcement procedures on the social behavior of autistic children. *Journal of Autism and Developmental Disorders, 9*(1), 41-54. https://doi.org/10.1007/BF01531291

Sugai, G., & Horner, R. H. (2009). Defining and describing schoolwide positive behavior support. In W. Sailor, G. Dunlop, G. Sugai, & R. Horner (Eds.), *Issues in clinical child psychology. Handbook of positive behavior support* (pp. 307-326). Springer Publishing Co. https://doi.org/10.1007/978-0-387-09632-2_13

Swanson, L., & Hoskyn, M. (2001). Instructing adolescents with learning disabilities: A component and composite analysis. *Learning Disabilities Research and Practice, 16*(2), 109-119.

Thiemann-Bourque, K. S., Brady, N. C., & Fleming, K. K. (2012). Symbolic play of preschoolers with severe communication impairments with autism and other developmental delays: More similarities than differences. *Journal of Autism and Developmental Disorders, 42*(5), 863-873. doi: 10.1007/s10803-011-1317-7

Thompson, R. A., & Raikes, H. A. (2007). The social and emotional foundations of school readiness. In D. F. Perry, R. K. Kaufmann, & J. Knitzer (Eds.), *Social and emotional health in early childhood: Building bridges between services and systems* (p. 13-35). Paul H. Brookes Publishing.

Tillema, H. H. (2000). Belief change towards self-directed learning in student teachers: Immersion in practice or reflection on action. *Teaching and Teacher Education, 16*(6), 575-591. doi: 10.1016/S0742-051X(00)00016-0

Tomlinson, C. A., & Hockett, J. A. (2008). Instructional strategies and programming models for gifted learners. In F. A. Karnes & K. R. Stephens (Eds.), *Achieving excellence: Educating the gifted and talented* (pp. 154–169). Pearson.

Toth, K., Munson, J., Meltzoff, A., & Dawson, G. (2006). Early predictors of communication development in young children with autism spectrum disorder: Joint attention, imitation, and toy play. *Journal of Autism Developmental Disorders, 36*(8), 993-1005. https://doi.org/10.1007/s10803-006-0137-7

Tremblay, P. (2013). Comparative outcomes of two instructional models for students with learning disabilities: Inclusion with co-teaching and solo-taught special education. *Journal of Research in Special Educational Needs, 13*(4), 251-258.

Trivette, C. M., Dunst, C. J., Hamby, D. W., & O'Herin, C. E. (2010). *Effects of different types of adaptations on the behavior of young children with disabilities.* Research Brief, 4(1). Tots-n-Tech Institute. http://ctdinstitute.org/sites/default/files/file_attachments/TnT-RB-V4.1-2010-Effects-of-adaptations-on-behavior.pdf

Turnbull, A. P., Turnbull, H. R., Erwin, E. D, Soodak, L. C., & Shogren, K. A. (2015). *Families, professionals, and exceptionality: Positive outcomes through partnership and trust* (7th ed.) Merrill Prentice Hall.

Uitto, D. J., Chopra, R. V., & Stivers, J. (2018). Position paper on training for paraeducators in special education. Teacher Education Division of the Council for Exceptional Children. https://tedcec.org/wp-content/uploads/2018/09/Final-Para-PD-Paper_03-10-2017.pdf

U.S. Department of Education. (2005). *Twenty-fifth annual report to Congress on the implementation of the Individuals with Disabilities Education Act.* Author.

U.S. Department of Education. (2011). *Part C of the Individuals with Disabilities Education Act final regulations.* Office of Special Education and Rehabilitative Services, Office of Special Education Programs, U.S. Department of Education. https://sites.ed.gov/idea/files/original_Final_Regulations-_Part_C-DOC-ALL.pdf

U.S. Department of Education. (2011, September 28). Early intervention program for infants and toddlers with disabilities (34 CFR, Part 303). *Federal Register, 76*(188). 60140-60283. https://www.govinfo.gov/content/pkg/FR-2011-09-28/pdf/2011-22783.pdf

U.S. Department of Education. (2015). *Teacher shortage areas nationwide listing 1990–1991 through 2015–2016.* Author.

U.S. Department of Education. (2016). *Racial and ethnic disparities in special education. Office of Special Education and Rehabilitative Services.* http://www2.ed.gov/programs/osepidea/618-data/LEA-racial-ethnic-disparities-tables/disproportionality-analysis-by-state-analysis-category.pdf

U.S. Department of Education. (2017). *A transition guide to postsecondary education and employment for students and youth with disabilities.* Office of Special Education and Rehabilitative Services, U.S. Department of Education. https://www2.ed.gov/about/offices/list/osers/transition/products/postsecondary-transition-guide-may-2017.pdf

U.S. Department of Education. (2018a). *40th annual report to Congress on the implementation of the Individuals with Disabilities Education Act, 2018* https://www2.ed.gov/about/reports/annual/osep/2018/parts-b-c/40th-arc-for-idea.pdf

U.S. Department of Education. (2018b). *EDFacts submission system: FS112 -Special education paraprofessionals file specifications.* https://www2.ed.gov/about/inits/ed/edfacts/sy-18-19-nonxml.html

U.S. Department of Education. (n.d.). *Assessment.* Office of Educational Technology, U.S. Department of Education. https://tech.ed.gov/netp/assessment/

U.S. Department of Health and Human Services and U.S. Department of Education. (2014). *Policy statement on expulsion and suspension policies in early childhood settings.* https://www2.ed.gov/policy/gen/guid/school-discipline/policy-statement-ece-expulsions-suspensions.pdf

U.S. Department of Health and Human Services & U.S. Department of Education. (2015). *Policy statement on inclusion of children with disabilities in early childhood programs.* https://www2.ed.gov/policy/speced/guid/earlylearning/joint-statement-full-text.pdf

Ursache, A., Blair, C., & Raver, C. C. (2012). The promotion of self-regulation as a means of enhancing school readiness and early achievement in children at risk for school failure. *Child Development Perspectives, 6*(2), 122-128. doi: 10.1111/j.1750-8606.2011.00209.x

Vandervoort, L. G., Amrein-Beardsley, A., and Berliner, D. C. (2004). National Board Certified teachers and their students' achievement. *Education Policy Analysis Archives, 12*(46). https://doi.org/10.14507/epaa.v12n46.2004

Vasquez, O. V., & Caraballo, J. N. (1993, August). *Meta-analysis of the effectiveness of concept mapping as a learning strategy in science education.* Paper presented at the Third International Seminar on the Misconceptions and Educational Strategies in Science and Mathematics Education.

Vaughn, S., & Bos, C. S. (2012). *Strategies for teaching students with learning and behavior problems (8th ed.).* Pearson.

Vaughn, S., Gersten, R., & Chard, D. J. (2000). The underlying message in LD intervention research: Findings from research syntheses. *Exceptional Children, 67*(1), 99-114.

Vescio, V., Ross, D., & Adams, A. (2008). A review of research on the impact of professional learning communities on teaching practice and student learning. *Teaching and Teacher Education, 24*(1), 80-91.

Vig, S. (2007). Young children's object play: A window on development. *Journal of Developmental and Physical Disabilities, 19*, 201-215. doi: 10.1007/s10882-007-9048-6

Villegas, A. M., & Lucas, T. (2002). Preparing culturally responsive teachers: Rethinking the curriculum. *Journal of teacher education, 53*(1), 20-32.

Waldron, N., Parker, J., & McLeskey, J. (2014). How are data systems used in inclusive schools? In J. McLeskey, N. Waldron, F. Spooner, & B. Algozzine (Eds.), *Handbook of effective inclusive schools: Research and practice* (pp. 155-166). Routledge.

Walker, D., Carta, J. J., Greenwood, C. R., & Buzhardt, J. F. (2008). The use of individual growth and developmental indicators for progress monitoring and intervention decision making in early education. *Exceptionality, 16*(1), 33-47. doi:10.1080/09362830701796784

Walker, R. E., Keane, C. R., & Burke, J. G. (2010). Disparities and access to healthy food in the United States: A review of food deserts literature. *Health & Place, 16*(5), 876-884.

Walker, S. P., Wachs, T. D., Grantham-McGregor, S., Black, M. M., Nelson, C. A., Huffman, S. L., Baker-Henningham, H., Chang, S. M., Hamadani, J. D., Lozoff, B., Gardner, J. M., Rahman, A., & Richter, L. (2011). Inequality in early childhood: Risk and protective factors for early child development. *The Lancet, 378*(9799), 1325-1338. doi:10.1016/S0140-6736(11)60555-2

Weaver, A. D., & Ouye, J. C. (2015). A practical and research-based guide for improving IEP team meetings. *NASP Communiqué, 44*(3), 1.

Weiland, C. (2016). Impacts of the Boston prekindergarten program on the school readiness of young children with special needs. *Developmental Psychology, 52*(11), 1763-1776. doi: 10.1037/dev0000168

Weiss, M., Pellegrino, A., & Brigham, F. (2017). Practicing collaboration in teacher preparation: Effects of learning by doing together. *Teacher Education and Special Education, 40*(1), 65-76. https://doi.org/10.1177%2F0888406416655457

Welch, M., & James, R. C. (2007). An investigation on the impact of guided reflection technique in service-learning courses to prepare special educators. *Teacher Education and Special Education, 30*(4), 276-285. doi: 10.1177/088840640703000407

West, M., Borrill, C., Dawson, J., Brodbeck, F., Shapiro, D., & Haward, B. (2003). Leadership clarity and team innovation in health care. *The Leadership Quarterly, 14*(4), 393-410. https://doi.org/10.1016/S1048-9843(03)00044-4

West, M., Brodbeck, F., & Richter, A. (2004). Does the 'romance of teams' exist? The effectiveness of teams in experimental and field settings. *Journal of Occupational and Organizational Psychology, 77*(4), 467-473. https://doi.org/10.1348/0963179042596450

What Works Clearinghouse. (2009, September). *Using student achievement data to support instructional decision making* (NCEE 2009-4067). Institute of Education Sciences, U.S. Department of Education. http://ies.ed.gov/ncee/wwc/Docs/PracticeGuide/dddm_pg_092909.pdf

What Works Clearinghouse. (2016, December). *Functional behavioral assessment-based interventions*. What Works Clearinghouse Intervention Report, Institute of Education Sciences. https://ies.ed.gov/ncee/wwc/Docs/InterventionReports/wwc_fba_011017.pdf

Whitby, P. J. S., Marx, T., McIntire, J., & Wienke, W. (2013). Advocating for students with disabilities at the school level: Tips for special educators. *TEACHING Exceptional Children, 45*(5), 32-39. https://doi.org/10.1177/004005991304500504

Will, E., Fidler, D., & Daunhauer, L. A. (2014). Executive function and planning in early development in Down syndrome. *International Review of Research in Developmental Disabilities, 47*, 77-98.

Wilmshurst, L., & Brue, A. W. (2018). *The complete guide to special education: Expert advice on evaluations, IEPs, and helping kids succeed*. Routledge.

Wilson, K. P., Carter, M. W., Wiener, H. L., DeRamus, M. L., Bulluck, J. C., Watson, L. R., Crais, C. R., & Baranek, G. T. (2017). Object play in infants with autism spectrum disorder: A longitudinal retrospective video analysis. *Autism & Developmental Language Impairments*. https://doi.org/10.1177/2396941517713186

Wolery, M., & Ledford, J. (2014). Monitoring intervention and children's progress. In M. Mclean, M. L. Hemmeter, & P. Snyder (Eds.), *Essential elements for assessing infants and preschoolers with special needs* (pp. 383-400). Pearson.

Wolfe, K., & Durán, L. K. (2013). Culturally and linguistically diverse parents' perceptions of the IEP Process: A review of current research. *Multiple Voices for Ethnically Diverse Exceptional Learners, 13*(2), 4-18.

Wolff, J. (2016). Accounting for the developing brain. In B. Reichow, B. A. Boyd, E. E. Barton, & S. L. Odom (Eds.), *Handbook of early childhood special education* (pp. 565-578). Springer.

Workgroup on Principles and Practices in Natural Environments, OSEP TA Community of Practice: Part C Settings. (2008, February). Agreed upon practices for providing early intervention services in natural environments. http://www.ectacenter.org/~pdfs/topics/families/AgreedUponPractices_FinalDraft2_01_08.pd

Woodruff, G., & McGonigel, M. (1988). Early intervention team approaches: The transdisciplinary model. In J. B. Jordan, J. J. Gallagher, P. L. Hutinger, & M. B. Karnes (Eds.), *Early childhood special education: Birth to three* (pp. 163-181). Council for Exceptional Children.

Xu, Y. (2019). Partnering with families of young children with disabilities in inclusive settings. In L. Lo & Y. Xu (Eds.), *Family, school, and community partnerships for students with disabilities. Advancing inclusive and special education in the Asia-Pacific* (pp. 3-15). Springer.

Yates, P., Chopra, R. V., Douglas, S., Walker, V., Schulze, R., Sobeck, E., & Morano, S. (2019). *Preparing teachers for effective paraeducator supervision.* Council for Exceptional Children, Teacher Education Division (Issue 3). https://tedcec.org/wp-content/uploads/2019/11/TED-Brief-3-Para-Supervision-Revised-Final-PDF.pdf

Yates, P. A., Chopra, R. V., Sobeck, E. E., Douglas, S. N., Morano, S., Walker, V. L., & Schulze, R. (2020, in press). Working with paraeducators: Tools and strategies for planning, performance feedback, and evaluation. *Intervention in School and Clinic.* https://doi.org/10.1177/1053451220910740

Yell, M. L., Katsiyannis, A., & Bradley, M. R. (2017). The Individuals with Disabilities Education Act: The evolution of special education law. In J. M. Kauffman, D. P. Hallahan, & P. Cullen (Eds.), *Handbook of special education* (2nd ed.) (pp. 55-70). Taylor & Francis.

Zeitlin, V. M., & Curcic, S. (2014). Parental voices on Individualized Education Programs: 'Oh, IEP meeting tomorrow? Rum tonight!' *Disability & Society, 29*(3), 373-387. https://doi.org/10.1080/09687599.2013.776493

Zhang, D., Katsiyannis, A., Ju, S., & Roberts, E. (2014). Minority representation in special education: 5-year trends. *Journal of Child and Family Studies, 23*(1), 118-127. http://dx.doi.org/10.1007/s10826-012-9698-6

Appendices

Appendix 1		
CEC Initial K-12 Special Education Practice-Based Professional Preparation		
Standards Development Workgroup (SDWG) Members		
Name	Organization	City, State
Dee Berlinghoff, Ph.D. (Co-chair)	Mount St. Mary College (CEC Reviewer)	Newburgh, New York; Charlotte, North Carolina
Virginia McLaughlin, Ed.D. (Co-chair)	William & Mary	Williamsburg, Virginia
Tisa Aceves, Ph.D.	Loyola Marymount University (CEC Board Member)	Los Angeles, California
Rachelle Bruno, Ph.D.	Northern Kentucky University (CEC Auditor)	Cincinnati, Ohio
Shannon Budin, Ph.D.	SUNY Buffalo State	Buffalo, New York
Ginevra Courtade, Ph.D.	University of Louisville	Louisville, Kentucky
Theresa Garfield, Ph.D.	Texas A&M University—San Antonio (CEC PSPC Chair, 2020-2022)	San Antonio, Texas
John Johnston, Ph.D.	University of Memphis (SPASC Member, External Member)	Memphis, Tennessee; Asheville, North Carolina
Mary Little, Ph.D.	University of Central Florida	Orlando, Florida
Erica McCray, Ph.D.	University of Florida; CEEDAR Center	Gainesville, Florida
James McLeskey, Ph.D.	University of Florida; CEEDAR Center (CEC PSPC Chair, 2014-2019)	Gainesville, Florida
Kevin Rubenstein, Ed.D.	Elmhurst Community Unit School District 205	Elmhurst, Illinois
Vicki Stayton, Ph.D.	Early Childhood Personnel Center, University of CT Health Center	Farmington, Connecticut; Bowling Green, Kentucky

The SDWG acknowledges the significant contributions of Margaret Crutchfield who served as a consultant to the project.

Appendix 2

Early Interventionists/Early Childhood Special Education Standards Development Task Force (SDTF) Members

Name	Organization	City, State
Eva Horn, Ph.D. (Chair)	University of Kansas	Lawrence, Kansas
Erin Barton, Ph.D.	Vanderbilt University	Nashville, Tennessee
Susan Connor, Ph.D.	University of Illinois, Early Intervention Training Program	Champaign, Illinois
Natalie Danner, Ph.D.	University of Nebraska at Kearney	Kearney, Nebraska
Lorraine DeJong, Ph.D.	Furman University (NAEYC Auditor)	Greenville, South Carolina
Christy Hooser, Ph.D.	Eastern Illinois University (CEC Auditor)	Charleston, Illinois
Jennifer Kilgo, Ph.D.	University of Alabama	Birmingham, Alabama
Hailey Love, Ph.D.	University of Nevada Las Vegas	Las Vegas, Nevada
Jeanette McCollum, Ph.D.	University of Illinois Urbana-Champaign	Champaign, Illinois
Ann Mickelson, Ph.D.	University of North Carolina-Charlotte	Charlotte, North Carolina
Megan Purcell, Ph.D.	Purdue University	West Lafayette, Indiana
Cynthia Vail, Ph.D.	University of Georgia	Athens, Georgia
Serena Wheeler, Ph.D.	University of Louisville for Kentucky Early Intervention System	Louisville, Kentucky
Hasan Zaghlawan, Ph.D.	University of Northern Colorado	Greeley, Colorado

The Standards Development Task Force recognizes Sandra Robbins, Ph.D., who is no longer with us. Her work as part of this group and her dedication to high-quality preparation of early interventionists and early childhood special educators have made this work possible.

Appendix 3

Glossary Of Terms and Related Resources

For consistency in use of terminology across key CEC documents that support these standards, this glossary draws heavily from glossaries accompanying High-Leverage Practices (2017) and DEC Recommended Practices (2015).

TERM	DEFINITION	REFERENCE/RESOURCE
Accommodation	An adaptation or change to educational environments and practices designed to help students overcome the challenges presented by their disabilities and to allow them to access the same instructional opportunities as students without disabilities. An accommodation does not change the expectations for learning or reduce the requirements of the task.	The Iris Center (2016a)
Assistive/adaptive technology	Any item, piece of equipment, or product system, whether acquired commercially off the shelf, modified, or customized, that is used to increase, maintain, or improve the functional capabilities of a child with a disability.	IDEA, 20 U.S.C. § 1401(1)
Collaboration	A style for direct interaction between at least two coequal parties voluntarily engaged in shared decision making as they work toward a common goal. In educational settings this typically includes planning, implementing, or evaluating a specific aspect of an educational program for a student or group of students.	Friend & Cook (2017, p. 5); The IRIS Center (2007, p.3)
Comprehensive learner profile	Provides information about a students' academic, social and emotional, functional and motivation strengths and needs as a means of establishing how a student learns best. Includes information about a student's interests, culture, and language. Teachers use the comprehensive learner profile to craft a robust individualized educational plan.	Inclusive Education Planning Tool (2011); National Joint Committee on Learning Disabilities (2010)
Corrective feedback	Constructive comments provided as soon as possible following the implementation of an activity in order to help an individual learner improve his or her performance.	Archer & Hughes (2011)

Glossary Of Terms and Related Resources

TERM	DEFINITION	REFERENCE/RESOURCE
Co-teaching	The partnering of a general education teacher and a special education teacher or another specialist for the purpose of jointly delivering instruction to a diverse group of students, including those with disabilities or other special needs, in a general education setting and in a way that flexibly and deliberately meets their learning needs.	Friend, Hurley-Chamberlain, & Shamberger (2010, p. 11)
Culturally relevant/responsive practices	Instruction that incorporates the diverse cultures of the students in order to provide content relative to students' experiences. Such approaches involve consciously creating social interactions to help individuals meet the criteria of academic success, cultural competence, and critical consciousness and include creating individual-centered learning environments that affirm cultural identities; foster positive learning outcomes; develop children's abilities to connect across lines of difference; elevate historically marginalized voices; empower children as agents of social change; and contribute to individual child engagement, learning, growth, and achievement through the cultivation of critical thinking. These approaches challenge norms (e.g., expectations regarding language, behavior, social interactions) in order to be responsive to marginalized children and families and work towards greater equity.	Aronson & Laughter (2016) CEC Division for Early Childhood (2020); Ladson-Billings (2014)
Curriculum-based assessment (CBA)	A method of evaluating student performance by directly and frequently collecting data on their academic progress.	The IRIS Center (2016a)
Curriculum-based measurement (CBM)	A type of progress monitoring conducted on a regular basis to assess student performance throughout an entire year's curriculum; teachers can use CBM to evaluate student progress and the effectiveness of their instructional methods.	The IRIS Center (2016a)

Appendix 3...(continued)

Glossary Of Terms and Related Resources

TERM	DEFINITION	REFERENCE/RESOURCE
Data-based individualization	Gradually individualizing and intensifying interventions through the systematic use of assessment data, validated interventions, and research-based adaptation strategies.	National Center on Intensive Intervention (2013)
DEC Recommended Practices (RPs)	A set of practices based on the best available empirical evidence as well as the wisdom and experience of the field that were developed to guide EI/ECSE professionals and families about the most effective ways to improve learning outcomes and promote the development of young children, birth through 5 years of age, who have or at risk for developmental delays or disabilities.	CEC Division for Early Childhood (2015)
Developmental domains	Specific areas of human growth and development such as cognition, social-emotional, motor/physical, communication, play, and adaptive behavior.	U.S. Department of Education (n.d.)
Developmentally appropriate	An approach to intervention and instruction whereby an early childhood professional bases decisions about children's developmental and learning goals and experiences on (a) knowledge of child development and learning in order to determine experiences likely to promote positive outcomes, (b) knowledge of each child's individual abilities and characteristics to adapt and be responsive for each child, and (c) knowledge of children's social, linguistic, and cultural contexts to ensure that learning experiences are relevant and respectful for each child and family.	National Association for the Education of Young Children (2019)
Differential reinforcement	Providing positive consequences (reinforcers) contingent upon a given behavior for the child and not for other behaviors or delivering a reinforcer for a behavior in one situation but not in other situations.	CEC Division of Early Childhood (2015b)

Glossary Of Terms and Related Resources

TERM	DEFINITION	REFERENCE/RESOURCE
Differentiated instruction	An approach whereby teachers adjust their curriculum and instruction to maximize the learning of all students (e.g., typical learners, English language learners, struggling students; students with learning disabilities, gifted and talented students); not a single strategy but rather a framework that teachers can use to implement a variety of evidence-based strategies.	The IRIS Center (2010, Page 1)
Eligibility	If a child is found to be a "child with a disability," as defined by IDEA, he or she is eligible for special education and related services. Within 30 calendar days after a child is determined eligible, the IEP team must meet to write an IEP for the child.	U.S. Department of Education (2006)
Evidence-based practice	Educational practice or strategy that has empirical evidence to support its efficacy.	Council for Exceptional Children (2014)
Exceptionalities	Include individuals with sensory, physical, emotional, social, cognitive differences, developmental delays, and gifts and talents; individuals whose needs differ so as to require personalized special education services in addition to or in tandem with educational services available through general education programs and other human service delivery systems.	Council for Exceptional Children (2015, p.3)
Explicit instruction	Instructional approach in which teachers clearly identify the expectations for learning, highlight important details of the concept or skill, offer precise instruction, and connect new learning to earlier lessons and materials.	Archer & Hughes (2011)
Extinction	In behavioral interventions, refers to the *withholding* of something that is *pleasant* in order to *eliminate* the likelihood that a behavior will occur in the future.	The IRIS Center, (2016a)

Appendix 3...(continued)

Glossary Of Terms and Related Resources

TERM	DEFINITION	REFERENCE/RESOURCE
Family	Defined as two or more people who regard themselves as family and who carry out the functions that families typically perform. This means that people who are not related by birth, marriage, or adoption and who do not reside together may be a family unit if they regard each other as family and if they jointly carry out the functions that are typically assumed by families.	Turnbull et al (2015)
Feedback	Information about one's performance that could come from a person (e.g., parent, teacher, peer, self) or the environment (e.g., book, toy).	Hattie & Timperley (2007).
Fidelity of implementation	The degree to which an intervention is implemented accurately, following the guidelines or restrictions of its developers.	The IRIS Center (2016a)
Flexible grouping	A fluid or dynamic method of grouping students. Rather than being set, group membership changes to meet the different needs of the students.	Cox (n.d.)
Formative assessment	A form of formal or informal evaluation used to plan instruction in a recursive way, providing regular assessment of student progress which enables teachers to diagnose skill, ability, and knowledge gaps; measure progress; and evaluate instruction.	Center on Response to Intervention (2014)
Functional behavioral assessment (FBA)	Collection of data to investigate the environmental variables maintaining and/or contributing to a challenging behavior. A functional assessment includes systematically identifying the challenging behavior, events that precede such behavior (antecedents), and events that maintain such behavior (consequences) with results used to plan and work with others to implement individual behavior support plans.	Behavioradvisor.com (n.d.); Dunlap & Fox (2011); The IRIS Center (2021b)
Generalization	The transfer of learned information from particular instances to other environments, people, times, and events.	The IRIS Center (2016a)

Glossary Of Terms and Related Resources

TERM	DEFINITION	REFERENCE/RESOURCE
Guided practice	A method of practice that involves working with students on activities that focus on a previously modeled or taught skill.	The IRIS Center (2016a)
High Leverage Practices (HLPs) in Special Education	The essence of effective practice in special education. HLPs focus directly on instructional practice, occur with high frequency in teaching, are research-based and known to foster student engagement and learning, are broadly applicable in any content area or teaching approach, and are so important that skillfully executing them is fundamental to effective teaching.	McLeskey et al (2017, p.10); McLeskey et al (2019)
Heterogeneous grouping	Placing students of varying abilities (i.e., lower achieving, typically achieving, higher achieving) together in a small instructional group.	Lewis (2016a)
Homogeneous grouping	Placing students of similar abilities/ skills together into groups to provide more intensive instruction to students who are working at a similar level and who can benefit from instruction that is designed for their specific learning needs.	Lewis (2016b)
Inclusive environments	Settings where the values, policies, and practices support the right of every child and his or her family, regardless of ability, to participate in a broad range of activities and contexts as full members of families, communities, and society.	CEC Division of Early Childhood/NAEYC. (2009).
Individual behavior support/ intervention plan (BIP)	A set of strategies designed to address the function of a student's behavior as a means through which to alter it; requires a functional behavioral assessment and an associated plan that describes individually determined procedures for both prevention and intervention.	The IRIS Center (2016a); (2021b)

Appendix 3...(continued)

Glossary Of Terms and Related Resources

TERM	DEFINITION	REFERENCE/RESOURCE
Individual family services plan (IFSP)	A plan collaboratively developed with the family of children with developmental delays or disabilities ages birth to 3 and early intervention providers that focuses on the family's prioritized outcomes for their child and family and details the early intervention services to be provided, including when, where, and how often. The IFSP is based on an in-depth assessment of the child's needs and includes information on the child's level of development in all areas, outcomes for the child and family, and services the child and family will receive.	Youngren (2013); PACER Center (2011)
Individualized education program (IEP)	A written statement for the child with a disability that is developed, reviewed, and revised in a meeting in accordance with federal law and regulations. The IEP must include a statement of the child's present levels of academic achievement and functional performance, a statement of measurable annual academic and functional goals to meet the child's needs, and services that will be provided to enable the child to make progress in the general education curriculum.	U.S. Department of Education (2006)
Individualized instruction	A set of practices that are evidence-based, intentional, systematic, and support development and learning for all young children across developmental and content domains. Instruction includes the intentional structuring of children's environments and learning experiences as well as methods used to teach a curriculum. Instruction is used across natural environments and inclusive settings in collaboration with families and other professionals.	CEC Division of Early Childhood (2016b)
Instructional scaffolding	A process through which a teacher adds supports for students to enhance learning and aid in the mastery of tasks. The teacher does this by systematically building on students' experiences and knowledge as they are learning new skills.	The IRIS Center (2005, Page 1)

Glossary Of Terms and Related Resources

TERM	DEFINITION	REFERENCE/RESOURCE
Instructional technology	Any device or instrument that exists in a classroom and teachers use for the purpose of day-to-day instruction; such devices, when assigned to an individual student through an IEP, are known as assistive technology.	The IRIS Center (2016a)
Intensive intervention	Additional instruction designed to support and reinforce classroom skills characterized by increased intensity and individualization based on data.	The IRIS Center (2015, Page 1)
Intersectionality	Examines how the numerous biological, social, and cultural categories such as gender, race, class, ability, and other aspects of identity interrelate on multiple and simultaneous dimensions.	Boveda & Aronson (2019)
Learning strategies	Instructional methods employed to help students to read, comprehend, and study better by helping them to strategically organize and collect information.	The IRIS Center (2008); (2016a)
Maintenance	A term used to describe the extent to which a student's behavior is self-sustaining over time.	The IRIS Center (2016a)
Metacognition	The processes used to plan, monitor, and assess one's understanding and performance.	Chick (2017)
Modification	Any of a number of services or supports that allow a student to access the general education curriculum but in a way that fundamentally alters the content or curricular expectations in question.	The IRIS Center (2016a)
Multitiered system of support (MTSS)	A prevention framework that organizes resources to address an individual student's academic and/or behavioral needs within intervention tiers that vary in intensity and represents a continuum of supports from less intense to more intense.	Center on Response to Intervention (2014)

Appendix 3...(continued)

Glossary Of Terms and Related Resources

TERM	DEFINITION	REFERENCE/RESOURCE
Paraprofessional	An individual who assists with supervision in providing special education and related services to students with exceptionalities. They are appropriately trained and supervised in accordance with state law, regulation, or written policy.	IDEA, 20 U.S.C. 1412(a)(14)(b); Giangreco, Suter, & Doyle (2010)
Peer mediated interventions	A collection of procedures, all of which involve using peers to promote the behavior of a child with disabilities, including modeling specific behaviors, tutoring, initiating social interactions to the child with disabilities, and responding to social initiations by the child with disabilities.	CEC Division for Early Childhood (2015b)
Progress monitoring	Used to assess a student's performance and improvement in response to instruction/ intervention. Allows teachers to evaluate the effectiveness of interventions and adjust instruction to meet students' needs. Progress monitoring can be implemented with individual students or groups of students (e.g., whole class).	Center on Response to Intervention (2014); The IRIS Center (2004a, Page 1)
Positive Behavior Interventions and Supports (PBIS)	An evidence-based three-tiered framework to improve and integrate all of the data, systems, and practices affecting student outcomes every day.	Center on Positive Behavioral Interventions & Supports (PBIS) (n.d.)
Positive Reinforcement	A means by which teachers can *increase* the probability that a behavior will occur in the future.	The IRIS Center (2021c)
Reflective practice	The process by which educators examine their own assumptions, values, beliefs, and professional practices and consider actions to be taken to continuously improve their own practice and/or reconstruct their assumptions, values, and/or beliefs.	McFarland et al (2009); Sellars (2017)
Scaffolding	See instructional scaffolding above.	

Glossary Of Terms and Related Resources

TERM	DEFINITION	REFERENCE/RESOURCE
Self-monitoring	A strategy that teaches students to self-assess their behavior and record the results. Though it does not create new skills or knowledge, self-monitoring does increase or decrease the frequency, intensity, or duration of existing behavior.	The IRIS Center (2021c, p. 4)
Self-regulation	A person's ability to regulate his or her own behavior.	The IRIS Center (2016a)
Special education process	The activities that occur from the time a child is referred for evaluation through being identified with a disability and provided with special education services via an IEP. These activities include request for an evaluation, a multidisciplinary evaluation, eligibility determination, and the development of the IEP. Families of students who are being evaluated must be informed of all activities and have opportunities to participate in meetings and decisions about their child.	Center for Parent Information and Resources (2014); PACER Center (2006)
Specially designed instruction	Specially designed instruction means adapting, as appropriate to the needs of an eligible child, the content, methodology, or delivery of instruction— (a) To address the unique needs of the child that result from the child's disability; and (b) To ensure access of the child to the general curriculum, so that the child can meet the educational standards within the jurisdiction of the public agency that apply to all children.	IDEA regulations, 34 C.F.R. § 300.39
Student engagement	The amount of time children spend involved with the environment (with adults, peers, or materials) in a way that is appropriate for the children's age, abilities, and surroundings.	CEC Division of Early Childhood (2015b)
Summative assessment	An evaluation administered to measure student learning outcomes, typically at the end of a unit or chapter. Often used to evaluate whether a student has mastered the content or skill.	The IRIS Center (2016a)

Appendix 3...(continued)

Glossary Of Terms and Related Resources

TERM	DEFINITION	REFERENCE/RESOURCE
Surface Management Strategies	Simple, nonintrusive ways to respond to minor disruptive behavior without interrupting classroom instruction.	The IRIS Center (2021a)
Transition services	Instruction, related services, and community experiences designed to support the student with a disability in developing academic and functional skills suited to the student's postschool goals.	IDEA regulations, 34 C.F.R. § 300.43(a)
	Per federal regulations, this is a results-oriented process that considers including postsecondary education, vocational education, integrated employment (including supported employment), continuing and adult education, adult services, independent living, or community participation, appropriate for the individual student's needs and taking into consideration the child's strengths, preferences, and interests.	
	Also refers to the events, activities and processes associated with key transitions during the early childhood years. These are the transition from hospital to home, the transition into early intervention (Part C) programs, the transition out of early intervention, the transition into Part B/619, and the transition to kindergarten or school age programs.	CEC Division of Early Childhood (2015b)
Universal design for learning (UDL)	A framework to improve and optimize teaching and learning for all people based on scientific insights into how humans learn. UDL guides the design of instructional goals, assessments, methods, and materials that can be customized and adjusted to meet individual needs.	CAST (n.d.); The IRIS Center (2016b)

Glossary References

Alper, S., & Raharinirina, S. (2006). Assistive technology for individuals with disabilities: A review and synthesis of the literature. *Journal of Special Education Technology, 21*(2), 47-64. https://doi.org/10.1177/016264340602100204

Archer, A. L., & Hughes, C. A. (2011). *Explicit instruction: Effective and efficient teaching.* Guilford.

Aronson, B., & Laughter, J. (2016). The theory and practice of culturally relevant education: A synthesis of research across content areas. *Review of Educational Research, 86*(1), 163-205. doi:10.3102/0034654315582066

Behavioradvisor.com. (n.d.) *Functional behavior assessment (FBA).* http://www.behavioradvisor.com/FBA.html

Boveda, M., & Aronson, B.A. (2019). Special education preservice teachers, intersectional diversity, and the privileging of emerging professional identities. *Remedial and Special Education, 40*(4), 248-260. https://doi.org/10.1177/0741932519838621

CAST. (n.d.). *About Universal Design for Learning.* https://www.cast.org/impact/universal-design-for-learning-udl

Center for Parent Information and Resources. (2014, May). *Evaluating children for disability.* Author. http://www.parentcenterhub.org/repository/evaluation/

Center on Positive Behavioral Interventions & Supports (PBIS). (n.d.). https://www.pbis.org/pbis/getting-started

Center on Response to Intervention. (2014, March). *Response to intervention glossary of terms.* American Institutes for Research and National Center on Intensive Intervention. http://www. rti4success.org/sites/default/files/CenterOnRTIGlossary.pdf

Chick, N. (2017). *CFT teaching guide: Metacognition.* Vanderbilt University Center for Teaching. https://cft.vanderbilt.edu/guides-sub-pages/metacognition/

Council for Exceptional Children. (2014). *Standards for evidence-based practices in special education.* Author. https://cecpioneers.exceptionalchildren.org/sites/default/files/2021-04/EBP_FINAL.pdf

Council for Exceptional Children. (2015). *What every special educator must know: Professional ethics and standards* (7th ed.) CEC.

Cox, J. (n.d.) *Flexible grouping as a differentiated instruction strategy.* http://www.teachhub.com/flexiblegroupingdifferentiatedinstruction strategy

Division for Early Childhood. (2015a). *DEC recommended practices: Enhancing services for young children and their families* (DEC Recommended Practices Monograph Series No. 1). Author. https://www.dec-sped.org/dec-recommended-practices

Division for Early Childhood. (2015b). *DEC recommended practices interactive glossary.* Division for Early Childhood. https://divisionearlychildhood.egnyte.com/dl/HuhkP0kIhl/?

Division for Early Childhood. (2020). *EI/ECSE Standards: Glossary* . https://d4ab05f7-6074-4ec9-998a232c5d918236.filesusr.com/ugd/95f212_bcd2ad0edb264d71890379cc7a07706b.pdf?index=true

Division for Early Childhood, & The National Association for the Education of Young Children. (2009). *Early childhood inclusion: A joint position statemen of the Division for Early Childhood (DEC) and the National Association for the Education of Young Children (NAEYC).* https://divisionearlychildhood.egnyte.com//dl/gzlWswGVOg

Dunlap, G., & Fox, L. (2011). Function-based interventions for children with challenging behavior. *Journal of Early Intervention, 33*(4), 333-343. https://doi.org/10.1177/105381 5111429971

Friend, M., & Cook, L. (2017). *Interactions: Collaboration skills for school professionals* (8th ed.). Upper Saddle River, NJ: Pearson.

Friend, M., Cook, L., Hurley-Chamberlain, D., & Shamberger, C. (2010). Co- teaching: An illustration of the complexity of collaboration in special education. *Journal of Educational and Psychological Consultation, 20*(1), 9–27. doi:10.1080/10474410903535380

Giangreco, M. F., Suter, J. C., & Doyle, M. B. (2010). Paraprofessionals in inclusive schools: A review of recent research. *Journal of Educational and Psychological Consultation, 20*(1), 41–57. doi:10.1080/10474410903535356

Hattie, J., & Timperley, H. (2007). The power of feedback. *Review of Educational Research, 77*(1), 81- 112. doi10.3102/003465430298487

IDEA regulations, 34 C.F.R. § 300 (2012).

Inclusive Education Planning Tool (IEPT). (2011). *What is a learner profile?* (Action on Inclusion). Alberta, Canada: Parkland School Division. https://sites.google.com/a/fmcsd.ab.ca/inclusive-education-planning-tool- iept/learnerprofiles

Individuals With Disabilities Education Act, 20 U.S.C. §§ 1400 *et seq*. (2006 & Supp. V. 2011)

The IRIS Center. (2005). *Providing instructional supports: Facilitating mastery of new skills* [Training module]. Peabody College, Vanderbilt University. http://iris.peabody.vanderbilt.edu/module/cnm/

The IRIS Center. (2007). *Serving students with visual impairments: The importance of collaboration* [Training module]. Peabody College, Vanderbilt University. http://iris.peabody.vanderbilt.edu/module/v03- focusplay/

The IRIS Center. (2008). *SRSD: Using learning strategies to enhance student learning* [Training module]. Peabody College, Vanderbilt University. http://iris.peabody.vanderbilt.edu/module/srs/

The IRIS Center. (2010). *Differentiated instruction: Maximizing the learning of all students* [Training module]. Peabody College, Vanderbilt University. http://iris.peabody.vanderbilt. edu/module/di/

The IRIS Center. (2015). *Intensive Intervention (Part 1): Using Data-Based Individualization To Intensify Instruction* [Training module]. Peabody College, Vanderbilt University. http:// iris.peabody. vanderbilt.edu/module/dbi1/

The IRIS Center. (2016a). *Glossary.* Peabody College, Vanderbilt University. http://iris.pea-body.vanderbilt.edu/glossary/

The IRIS Center. (2016b). *Universal design for learning: Creating a learning environment that challenges and engages all students* [Training module]. Peabody College, Vanderbilt University. http:// iris.peabody.vanderbilt.edu/module/udl/

The IRIS Center. (2021a). *Classroom behavior management (part 1).* [Training module]. Peabody College, Vanderbilt University. https://iris.peabody.vanderbilt.edu/module/beh1/cresource/q2/p07/#content

The IRIS Center. (2021b). Functional behavioral assessment: Identifying the reasons for problem behavior and developing a behavior plan. [Training Module]. Peabody College, Vanderbilt University.https://iris.peabody.vanderbilt.edu/module/fba/#content

The IRIS Center (2021c). *SOS: Helping students become independent learners.*[Training Module]. Peabody College, Vanderbilt University. https://iris.peabody.vanderbilt.edu/module/sr/cinit/#content

Ladson-Billings, G. (2014). Culturally relevant pedagogy 2.0: aka the remix. Harvard Educational Review, 84(1), 74-84.

Lewis, B. (2016a, September). *Heterogeneous groups.*http:// k6educators.about.com/od/educationglossary/g/gheterogeneous.htm

Lewis, B. (2016b, September). *Homogeneous groups.* http:// k6educators.about.com/od/educationglossary/g/ghomogeneous.htm

Love, . R., & Horn, E. (2019). Definition, context, quality: Current issues in research examining high-quality inclusive education. *Topics in Early Childhood Special Education.* https://doi.org/10.1177/0271121419846342

McFarland, L., Saunders, R., & Allen, S. (2009). Reflective practice and self-evaluation in learning positive guidance: Experiences of early childhood practicum students. *Early Childhood Education Journal, 36*(6), 505-511. DOI:10.1007/s10643-009-0315-2

McLeskey, J., Barringer, M-D., Billingsley, B., Brownell, M., Jackson, D., Kennedy, M., Lewis, T., Maheady, L., Rodriguez, J., Scheeler, M. C., Winn, J., & Ziegler, D. (2017, January). *High-leverage practices in special education.* Arlington, VA: Council for Exceptional Children & CEEDAR Center.

McLeskey, J., Billingsley, B., Brownell, M.T., Maheady, L., & Lewis, T. J. (2019). What are high-leverage practices for special education teachers and why are they important? *Remedial and Special Education, 40*(6), 331-337. https://doi.org/10.1177/0741932518773477